A Special Issue of
*Language and Cognitive Processes*

# Conceptual Representation

Edited by

## Helen Moss

*University of Cambridge, UK*

and

## James Hampton

*City University, UK*

Psychology Press
Taylor & Francis Group

Published in 2003 by Psychology Press Ltd
27 Church Road, Hove, East Sussex, BN3 2FA
www.psypress.co.uk

Simultaneously published in the USA and Canada
by Taylor & Francis Inc.
325 Chestnut Street, Suite 800, Philadelphia, PA 19106

Psychology Press is part of the Taylor & Francis Group
© 2003 by Psychology Press Ltd

*British Library Cataloguing in Publication Data*
A catalogue record for this book is available from the British Library

ISBN 1-84169-958-6 (hbk)
ISSN 0169-0965

Cover design by Jim Wilkie
Typeset in the UK by Mendip Communications Ltd., Frome, Somerset
Printed in the UK by Henry Ling Ltd., Dorchester
Bound in the UK by TJ International, Padstow

# Contents*

_____

*This book is also a special issue of the journal *Language and Cognitive Processes*, and forms issue 5 & 6 of Volume 18 (2003). The page numbers are taken from the journal and so begin with p. 505.

LANGUAGE AND COGNITIVE PROCESSES, 2003, *18* (5/6), 505–512

# Concepts and meaning: Introduction to the special issue on conceptual representation

James A. Hampton
*City University, London, UK*

Helen E. Moss
*University of Cambridge, UK*

Conceptual representation is arguably the most important cognitive function in humans. It stands at the centre of the information processing flow, with input from perceptual modules of differing kinds, and is centrally involved in memory, speech, planning, decision-making, actions, inductive inferences and much more besides.

It is therefore unsurprising that it is also a domain of interest to the full range of cognitive sciences—linguistics via lexical semantics, psychology through the use of concepts in thought and categorisation and children's acquisition of concepts and word meanings, AI through the development of systems for knowledge representation, neuroscience through the recent development of interest in dissociations between knowledge domains and the role of perceptual and motor areas in concept representation, and finally philosophy which originally began the whole process of trying to find the basic building blocks of thought and knowledge. In this collection, we set our authors the task of attempting to draw together current thinking in their own field, and to lay out their views on the importance of their particular approach to concept representation. The result has been a series of papers that by and large have been broader and possibly more speculative than would normally appear in a top peer-reviewed journal

Requests for reprints should be addressed to Professor J.A. Hampton, Psychology Department, City University, Northampton Square, London, EC1V 0HB, or Dr Helen Moss, Department of Experimental Psychology, University of Cambridge, Downing Street, Cambridge, CB2 3EB, UK.

http://www.tandf.co.uk/journals/pp/01690965.html    DOI: 10.1080/01690960344000161

such as *Language and Cognitive Processes*. We believe that our authors have responded with considerable courage to our call to consider a bigger picture, and we are delighted with the resulting articles.

In this introductory piece we aim to set the scene for the papers that appear later. It is necessarily a rather artificial task to take our eight papers and to cast them into a single framework. However, we were struck by the number of common issues and links that we found.

A major theme that emerges from the papers in this collection is the issue of the relation of thought to language—or concepts to meanings. Wisniewski, Lamb, and Middleton (this issue) present a review of a large number of studies investigating what initially appears to be a purely linguistic phenomenon—the distinction in many languages between count nouns such as *bicycle* and mass nouns such as *spinach*. The former can be counted (two bicycles), whereas the latter are modified by quantifiers suggesting they are undifferentiated masses (a lot of spinach). It has been argued that the distinction is largely a matter of convention, varying from language to language in an unpredictable way. For example, in English, *rain* is a mass noun but *shower* a count noun, *rice* a mass noun but *lentil* a count noun. In reviewing their evidence, Wisniewski et al. reveal some of the many subtle cognitive dimensions underlying the syntactic distinction. There are, to be sure, some specifically linguistic effects, often dependent on historical change. However, they show in a series of experiments that, for example, people typically interact with the referents of mass (e.g., furniture) as opposed to count (e.g., vehicle) superordinate nouns in different ways, and that they consider object parts to be more important properties of count superordinates than of mass superordinates. Consequently Wisniewski et al. suggest that people conceptualise the two forms of superordinate concepts in different ways.

The syntactic forms of a language, then, can be shown to bear strong relations to conceptual distinctions in thought. The reverse conclusion is proposed by Levy (this issue) in his review of Wittgenstein's Private Language Argument (PLA), and its implications for the philosophy and psychology of concepts. In an argument that is reminiscent of both functionalism and social constructionism, the PLA purports to show that the determination of the content of a person's internal representation of a concept is itself dependent on a publicly shared language. Levy presents different possible views of how we might have concepts that enable us to *think the same thoughts* as others—something which seems a desirable property for any theory of concepts. He describes Peacocke's theory of concept possession in which the individuation of concepts is achieved by determining the set of predispositions and abilities that a person must show in order for them to be deemed to possess the concept (Peacocke, 1992). To possess the concept of *bicycle* is to be able to do a number of things—for example, recognise one, know what it is for, how it works. Levy then provides an account of Fodor's theory of concepts as atomic symbols representing external properties (Fodor, 1988, 2000). He argues that both of these influential theories of concepts fail fully to account for the problems raised in Wittgenstein's PLA. He concludes by tentatively endorsing Dummett's Priority thesis that the "order of explanation" must take language first and concepts second. It follows that it will not be possible to provide an account of, say, concept acquisition, without first providing an account of language acquisition (Dummett, 1991). It is only through study of the usage of terms in a public language that we can have an independent way of fixing the contents of people's concepts.

The way in which concepts and word meanings are acquired is the key question in the paper by Diesendruck (this issue). He reviews a range of literature on the way in which children learn to label, categorise and reason about the world. From his review, he draws the conclusion that there may be strong domain differences in the way that one might apply a principle like the Language Priority thesis. He finds that whereas artefact kinds such as tools, furniture and vehicles are highly susceptible to linguistic and cultural factors in learning, natural kinds like animals are relatively immune to such effects. Diesendruck notes that this evidence is consistent with a modular account of domain-specific learning, in which a naïve essentialism is applied very early on to the acquisition of categories of animals. Children understand very quickly that animal kinds are based on deep causal principles and not on superficial appearance. Interestingly, the categorisation of people appears to fall somewhere between animals and artefacts in the scale of essentialist thinking.

The issue of differences in representation and processing across conceptual domains is clearly one that arises in a number of the contributions to this issue (see for example the cognitive neuropsychological papers described later). Sloman and Malt (this issue) provide a challenging paper in which they argue that artefacts should not be considered as "kinds" in the way that natural kinds are. They consider (among other positions) arguments for the categorisation of artefact kinds being based on a belief in a common essence—such as the function that the object was intended to have when it was created. They claim that the only non-circular way to test such a notion is in relation to the linguistically determined name categories—the classes of objects that get called by the same name. But the cross-linguistic diversity and the context-dependent nature of naming is not consistent with any direct or stable relation between classes defined by intended function and those defined by naming data. They draw the conclusion that artefacts do not come grouped into stable kinds. Their paper therefore sits well alongside Levy's in the sense that both raise important issues about the relation between concepts and language. Levy questions the feasibility of determining conceptual content in the absence of a prior analysis of language use, whereas Sloman and Malt argue that, in the case of artefacts, different tasks (of which naming is one) will lead to different ways of creating conceptual groupings.

Keil's (this issue) paper is concerned with an important aspect of conceptual thinking—the role of causal notions in the contents of our concepts. It has become a commonplace criticism of the simple similarity-based views of concept structure proposed by prototype or exemplar theories that our concepts play a crucial role in our theoretical understanding and explanation of the world and how it works. This "theory theory" was introduced in a seminal paper by Murphy and Medin (1985), and has had a particularly strong following among developmentalists. Demonstrations of causal theory effects in young children have ironically sometimes given the impression that young children have far more sophisticated concepts than do adults. Keil starts to unravel this puzzle, and to flesh out the often vague proposals of the theory theory. He presents a set of experiments introducing the Illusion of Explanatory Depth (IOED), in which he shows that people confidently believe they know how things work, but when challenged are forced to acknowledge that their understanding is superficial and even incoherent. Our concepts cannot therefore be like the concepts in scientific theories in which the definition and role of the concepts is clearly specified in axiomatic fashion. Keil suggests that what remains of the theory theory notion is that we have deep knowledge of a higher but coarser level of causal information. For example, children quite quickly develop an understanding of what dimensions of a domain are likely to prove important for classification. They learn, for example, that colour is important in differentiating plants, but not in differentiating cars. They also develop a sophisticated understanding of the way in which human knowledge is divided up into domains of expertise. Knowing whom to ask if you have a desire to know more about a concept is a key part of the representation of the conceptual domain itself. Once again, domains of knowledge are a central theme here, as different dimensions and different forms of expertise are relevant in each domain.

Several of the papers in this collection address the issue of the relationship between conceptual representations and sensory-motor systems. Concepts allow us to access knowledge about the physical attributes of objects in the world, including colour, shape, motion, sound and texture as well as the actions we associate with them. Nevertheless, there is a traditional view in the fields of cognitive psychology and neuropsychology, that conceptual representations are different in kind from those computed within the perceptual input systems and motor output systems that feed into and out of them; that concepts are amodal symbolic representations, abstracted from their modality-specific perceptual bases. This position is challenged by Barsalou (this issue) who develops the thesis that there is a common representational format for conceptual and sensory-motor processing, as part of his *situated simulation account.* He argues that situated simulation is dynamic, context-dependent and goal-driven. Barsalou marshals an impressive array of data from behavioural experiments, lesion studies and functional neuro-imaging studies in support of his claim that perceptual simulations represent concepts. Barsalou and colleagues have also conducted several studies using property generation and verification paradigms, which suggest a ubiquitous role for perceptual variables (such as property shape and size) in conceptual processing. In one study, for example, they found that subjects were slower to verify the properties of objects that would normally be occluded from view (e.g., the roots of a lawn), but that this was not the case if the concept was presented in a linguistic context that revealed those properties (e.g., *rolled-up lawn*).

Barsalou also interprets evidence from functional neuro-imaging studies of conceptual processing within the situated simulation framework. Many studies have found that areas of the brain adjacent to specific sensory-motor systems are differentially activated as a function of the conceptual category or type of property being processed; for example, visual areas are relatively more activated when people process objects for which the visual modality is important (e.g., animals), while certain motor areas are activated when people process motor-related objects such as tools. As Barsalou points out, the areas activated are not necessarily the primary sensory-motor areas that are involved in perception and action themselves, but rather adjacent areas, which leaves open a number of interpretations. Some studies have also interpreted domain effects in terms of the nature of conceptual processing required rather than the sensory-motor contents of the representations *per se* (e.g., Tyler & Moss, 2001).

Studies of neuropsychological patients with impairments to the conceptual system provide further insights into the format and organisation of conceptual knowledge and its relation to sensory-motor systems. Barsalou suggests an integrative framework that reconciles apparently conflicting hypotheses about category and modality specific conceptual deficits. Essentially he suggests a series of convergence zones (cf. Damasio & Damasio, 1994) which integrate increasingly widely distributed modality-specific representations located within the sensory-motor systems of the brain. The importance of neuropsychological data in theoretical development of these issues is reflected in the final two papers in this volume; Rogers, Hodges, Lambon Ralph, and Patterson (this issue) and Saffran, Coslett, Martin, and Boronat (this issue). These two papers also address the issue of the relation between conceptual knowledge and sensory systems, and echo many of the points raised by Barsalou. First, Saffran et al. put forward a view that has become quite widely accepted in the neuropsychological literature; that conceptual knowledge is distributed across a network of modality-specific attribute systems determined by the mode of input of acquisition. For example, there are held to be visual, auditory, verbal and kinaesthetic systems. This proposal has several elements in common with Barsalou's account, although it is framed within a more traditional semantic memory system, in which the attribute systems *may* be seen as amodal redescriptions of sensory-motor properties. Nevertheless, different parts of the conceptual representation are claimed to be preferentially accessed by different input modalities, and crucially the attribute systems are held to be localised in different regions of the brain and so may be selectively impaired by brain damage.

In support of their theoretical claims Saffran et al. present data from a patient, BA who has a progressive disorder of conceptual knowledge, with a significantly greater difficulty accessing conceptual information from words than from pictures. The interpretation of BA's deficit highlights one way that Saffran et al.'s position diverges from that of Barsalou. Saffran et al. propose that BA's impairment on semantic tasks with words is attributable to selective damage to a propositional/encyclopaedic attribute sub-system; words are held to initially access this type of conceptual knowledge (since they were the mode of input responsible for its acquisition), whereas pictures primarily access the visual store. Barsalou's situated simulation account does not incorporate the idea that verbal inputs preferentially access a propositional semantic system, since words are claimed to involve sensory-motor simulations in just the same way as pictures. Indeed, there would be no separate propositional sub-system.

The nature of the conceptual/perceptual interface is also the central issue addressed by Rogers et al. (this issue). In a similar vein to Barsalou, Rogers et al. distinguish between two broad views of the conceptual/perceptual relationship. One is a multi-modal distributed network, in which conceptual representations emerge from the associations among the representations that subserve perception, recognition and action across different modalities. This is contrasted with the "traditional" view, in which there is a central conceptual system, separate to "pre-semantic" modality-specific input systems, such as structural descriptions for object recognition, or lexical representations in the language system. In their exposition, Rogers et al. refer to the former approach as a *process-based* account of conceptual information—semantic memory serves the function of associating sets of modality specific representations, while the latter account is described as a *content-based* approach, in that semantic memory is defined as having content or meaning, while non-semantic representations such as structural descriptions (i.e., stored representations of object shapes) do not. The content-based view of the conceptual system has been supported by reports of neuropsychological patients with apparent dissociations between impaired semantic memory and intact structural descriptions, as revealed in tasks such as object decision—where patients are asked to distinguish between line drawings of real versus chimeric objects or creatures. This has been interpreted as evidence for the functional (and perhaps neural) separation of conceptual and perceptual representations. Rogers et al. present data from a set of novel object decision tasks, challenging this apparent dissociation. When materials are appropriately controlled for object typicality, patients with semantic deficits do show problems in object decision; they tend to accept as real those chimeric objects which have features typical of members of the category, and reject real objects with atypical features (e.g., they may reject a drawing of a camel as being a non-object, because it has an atypical feature—a hump—but accept a chimeric picture of a camel with its hump removed, since this produces a more typical animal shape).

Thus there is considerable common ground across this group of three papers concerning the interface between conceptual and sensory-motor systems. All three challenge the view that there is a single static system of amodal conceptual representations. All three propose the distribution of conceptual knowledge across multiple sets of modality-specific attributes, which may be neurally as well as functionally distinct. And all three seem to share the assumption that concepts emerge from the interactive activation or simultaneous simulation of multiple modalities of information, perhaps implemented in terms of cross-modal convergence zones. As reviewed in each of these papers, many sources of psychological, neuropsychological and neuro-imaging data are consistent with these general claims.

However, there remain critical differences between the approaches taken in the three papers. For example, although Saffran et al. and Rogers et al. both claim that conceptual knowledge is distributed over multiple modality-specific attributes, rather than residing in a central amodal semantic system, they differ in the nature of the proposed relation between structural and semantic systems. Saffran et al.'s framework suggests a number of semantic subsystems, each storing semantic properties relevant to a specific modality (visual semantics, tactile semantics, etc.), with a separate level of pre-semantic perceptual systems corresponding to each modality (e.g., structural descriptions for visual objects). For Rogers et al., there is no such distinction between a semantic and structural level of representation; rather there is a unitary semantic system—better described as a process or function than a level of representation—which consists of the associations among the modality-specific structural or perceptual representations. Moreover, the Saffran et al. framework is consistent with the view that the sensory-motor properties within each semantic subsystem are represented as amodal symbolic redescriptions, distinct from the modality-specific representational format of the input/output systems to which they are linked. In this respect it is very different to Barsalou's situated simulation model.

In summary, the eight papers in this issue address many central issues in the study of conceptual representations. We hope that the juxtaposition of these papers in the current issue—tackling related questions but from very different perspectives—will prompt debate as to whether it is the similarities or the differences among the approaches that are the more significant.

# REFERENCES

Barsalou, L.W. (this issue). Situated simulation in the human conceptual system. *Language and Cognitive Processes, 18*, 513–562.

Damasio, A.R., & Damasio, H. (1994). Cortical systems for retrieval of concrete knowledge: The convergence zone framework. In C. Koch & J.L. Davis (Eds.), *Large-scale neuronal theories of the brain* (pp. 6174). Cambridge, MA: MIT Press.

Diesendruck, G. (this issue). Categories for names or names for categories? The interplay between domain-specific conceptual structure and language. *Language and Cognitive Processes, 18*, 759–787.

Dummett, M. (1991). *Frege and other philosophers.* Oxford: Oxford University Press.

Fodor, J. (1988). *Concepts: Where cognitive science went wrong.* Oxford: Clarendon Press.

Fodor, J. (2000). Doing without what's within: Fiona Cowie's critique of nativism. *Mind, 110*, 99–148.

Keil, F.C. (this issue). Categorisation, causation and the limits of understanding. *Language and Cognitive Processes, 18*, 663–692.

Levy, D.K. (this issue). Concepts, language and privacy: An argument "vaguely Viennese in provenance". *Language and Cognitive Processes, 18*, 693–723.

Murphy, G.L., & Medin, D.L. (1985). The role of theories in conceptual coherence. *Psychological Review, 92*, 289–316.

Peacocke, C. (1992). *A study of concepts.* Cambridge, MA: MIT Press.

Rogers, T.T., Hodges, J.R., Lambon Ralph, M.A., & Patterson, K. (this issue). Object recognition under semantic impairment: The effects of conceptual regularities on perceptual decisions. *Language and Cognitive Processes, 18*, 625–662.

Saffran, E.M., Branch Coslett, H., Martin, N., & Boronat, C.B. (this issue). Access to knowledge from pictures but not words in a patient with progressive fluent aphasia. *Language and Cognitive Processes, 18*, 725–757.

Sloman, S.A., & Malt, B.C. (this issue). Artifacts are not ascribed essences, nor are they treated as belongings to kinds. *Language and Cognitive Processes, 18*, 563–582.

Tyler, L.K., & Moss, H.E. (2001). Towards a distributed account of conceptual knowledge. *Trends in Cognitive Sciences, 5*, 244–252.

Wisniewski, E.J., Lamb, C.A., & Middleton, E.L. (this issue). On the conceptual basis for the count and mass noun distinction. *Language and Cognitive Processes, 18*, 583–624.

LANGUAGE AND COGNITIVE PROCESSES, 2003, *18* (5/6), 513–562

# Situated simulation in the human conceptual system

## Lawrence W. Barsalou

*Emory University, Atlanta, GA, USA*

Four theories of the human conceptual system—semantic memory, exemplar models, feed-forward connectionist nets, and situated simulation theory—are characterised and contrasted on five dimensions: (1) architecture (modular vs. non-modular), (2) representation (amodal vs. modal), (3) abstraction (decontextualised vs. situated), (4) stability (stable vs. dynamical), and (5) organisation (taxonomic vs. action–environment interface). Empirical evidence is then reviewed for the situated simulation theory, and the following conclusions are reached. Because the conceptual system shares mechanisms with perception and action, it is non-modular. As a result, conceptual representations are multi-modal simulations distributed across modality-specific systems. A given simulation for a concept is situated, preparing an agent for situated action with a particular instance, in a particular setting. Because a concept delivers diverse simulations that prepare agents for action in many different situations, it is dynamical. Because the conceptual system's primary purpose is to support situated action, it becomes organised around the action–environment interface.

After briefly reviewing current theories of the conceptual system, this article explores the proposal that situated simulations lie at the heart of it. The emphasis will be on empirical evidence for this view. For theoretical development, see Barsalou (1999), Barsalou (in press), and Simmons and Barsalou (2003b).

Generally speaking, a conceptual system contains knowledge about the world. A fundamental property of this knowledge is its categorical nature. A conceptual system is *not* a collection of holistic images of the sort that a

Requests for reprints should be addressed to Lawrence W. Barsalou, Department of Psychology, Emory University, Atlanta, GA 30322, USA. E-mail: barsalou@emory.edu. http://userwww.service.emory.edu/~barsalou/.

I am grateful to James Hampton for the opportunity to write this paper. I am also grateful to James Hampton, Helen Moss, Art Glenberg, and three anonymous reviewers for helpful comments on an earlier draft. This work was supported by National Science Foundation Grants SBR-9421326, SBR-9796200, SBR-9905024, and BCS-0212134 to Lawrence W. Barsalou.

http://www.tandf.co.uk/journals/pp/01690965.html    DOI: 10.1080/01690960344000026

camera, video recorder, or audio recorder captures. Instead a conceptual system is a collection of category knowledge, where each represented category corresponds to a *component* of experience—not to an entire holistic experience.

Whenever selective attention focuses consistently on some component (or components) of experience, knowledge of a category develops (cf. Schyns, Goldstone, & Thibaut, 1998). Each time a component is attended to, the information extracted becomes integrated with past information about the same component in memory. When attention focuses on a blue patch of colour, for example, the information extracted is stored with previous memories of *blue*, thereby producing categorical knowledge for this component.[1] Over time, myriad components accumulate memories in a similar manner, including objects, events, locations, times, introspective states, relations, roles, properties, and so forth.

Certainly the learning that produces categorical knowledge occurs within a biologically constrained architecture and thus is biased towards learning some categories more easily than others. Furthermore some preliminary category representations are likely to be in place before learning begins. The relative contributions of learning and biology do not receive further discussion here, although their interaction is central to the development of conceptual systems.

Categorical knowledge for components of experience plays fundamental roles in the cognitive system, providing representational support for all cognitive processes. Consider online processing. As people interact with the environment and attempt to achieve goals, the conceptual system contributes in three ways. First, it supports perception, predicting the entities and events likely to be perceived in a scene, thereby speeding their processing (e.g., Biederman, 1981; Palmer, 1975). The conceptual system also helps construct perceptions through figure-ground segregation, anticipation, filling in, and other sorts of perceptual inferences (e.g., Peterson & Gibson, 1994; Reed & Vinson, 1996; Samuel, 1997; Shiffrar & Freyd, 1990, 1993). Second, the conceptual system supports categorisation. As entities and events are perceived, the conceptual system assigns them to categories. Third, once something has been assigned to a category, category knowledge provides rich inferences constituting expertise about the world. Rather than starting from scratch when interacting with something, agents benefit from knowledge of previous category members.

Besides being central to online processing of the environment, the conceptual system is central to offline processing in memory, language, and

---

[1] Italics will be used to indicate concepts, and quotes will be used to indicate linguistic forms (words, sentences). Thus, *SKY* indicates a concept, and "sky" indicates the corresponding word. Within concepts, uppercase words will represent categories, whereas lowercase words will represent properties of categories (e.g., *SKY* vs. *blue*).

thought. In each of these tasks, processing a non-present situation is often of primary importance, with perception of the current environment being suppressed to facilitate processing the imagined situation (Glenberg, Schroeder, & Robertson, 1998). In memory, a past situation is reconstructed. In language, a past or future situation is represented, or even an impossible one. In thought, a past, future, or counter-factual situation is analysed to support decision making, problem solving, planning, and causal reasoning. In all three types of offline processing, the conceptual system plays central roles. In memory, the conceptual system provides elaboration at encoding, organisational structure in storage, and reconstructive inference at retrieval. In language, the conceptual system contributes to the meanings of words, phrases, sentences, and texts, and to the inferences that go beyond them. In thought, the conceptual system provides representations of the objects and events that occupy reasoning.

Finally the conceptual system plays a third central role in cognition. Besides supporting online and offline processing, it supports the productive construction of novel concepts (e.g., Hampton, 1997; Rips, 1995; Wisniewski, 1997). The conceptual system is not limited to representing entities and events that an agent has experienced in the world. Because the conceptual system establishes categorical knowledge about components of experience, it can combine these components in novel ways to represent things never encountered. Thus an agent can combine categorical knowledge for *striped* and *WATERFALL* to represent the novel category, *STRIPED WATERFALL*. Because of this ability, the conceptual system can categorise novel entities during online processing (e.g., a striped waterfall), and it can represent these novel entities offline in language and thought. This powerful process allows humans to imagine non-present situations, thereby increasing their fitness in the evolutionary landscape (cf. Donald, 1991, 1993).

## THEORIES OF THE CONCEPTUAL SYSTEM

Theorists have proposed many accounts of the conceptual system. This section first sketches three types of theory that have dominated research for the last 30 years: semantic memory, exemplar models, and feedforward connectionist nets. In reviewing these theories, only their most standard forms are presented. For each theory, a wide variety of models exists, and an even wider variety is possible. Presenting the standard forms of these theories serves simply to illustrate the diversity of the theories possible. When relevant, important variants to standard forms are noted. Following these first three approaches, a fourth and relatively novel approach is presented: situated simulation theory.

To characterise and contrast these four approaches, they will be positioned on five dimensions that structure the space of possible theories. Certainly other dimensions are potentially relevant, but these particular five capture important differences between the four types of theory considered here. These dimensions are also useful in organising the literature review that follows. As Table 1 illustrates, these five dimensions are architecture, representation, abstraction, stability, and organisation. Their definitions will become clear as the four theoretical approaches are presented.

## Semantic memory

Semantic memory is the classic theory of the conceptual system, arising from a proposed distinction between semantic and episodic memory (Tulving, 1972). Semantic memory models still dominate much theoretical thinking about the human conceptual system. Specific examples include the network models of Collins and Quillian (1969), Collins and Loftus (1975), and Glass and Holyoak (1975). As Hollan (1975) notes, prototype and other feature set models (e.g., Reed, 1972; Rosch & Mervis, 1975) are roughly equivalent to their network counterparts, together forming a more general class of semantic memory models. For an extensive review of semantic memory models, see Smith (1978).

As Table 1 illustrates for architecture, semantic memory is widely viewed as modular, that is, as an autonomous system, separate from the episodic memory system and also from sensory-motor systems. Semantic memory does not share representation and processing mechanisms with these other modules, but is instead a relatively independent module with distinct characteristics.

TABLE 1
Four theories of the human conceptual system and their properties

| Dimension | Semantic memory | Exemplar models | Feed-forward nets | Situated simulation theory |
|---|---|---|---|---|
| Architecture | Modular | Modular | Modular | Non-Modular |
| Representation | Amodal | Amodal | Amodal | Modal |
| Abstraction | Decontextualised | Situated | Situated | Situated |
| Stability | Stable | Stable | Dynamical | Dynamical |
| Organisation | Taxonomic | (Taxonomic) | (Taxonomic) | Action–Environment Interface |

*Note.* The most standard form of each theory is characterised in this table. As the text illustrates, many variants exist for each theory. For organisation, "taxonomic" in parentheses indicates that taxonomic structure is implicit in these theories, not explicit.

One of these distinct characteristics is its representational format. As Table 1 illustrates, representations in semantic memory are widely viewed as amodal. Most basically, they are not the same as representations in sensory-motor systems. Instead they are *redescriptions* of sensory-motor representations into some new representation language that does not have sensory-motor qualities. Rather than being modality-specific, these representations are amodal, namely, arbitrary symbols that stand for sensory-motor representations and for the environmental entities they represent.

Representations in semantic memory are further viewed as relatively decontextualised, as the dimension for abstraction in Table 1 illustrates. In the typical theory, the representation of a category is a prototype or definition that distills relatively invariant properties from exemplars. Lost in the distillation are idiosyncratic properties of exemplars and background situations. Thus the representation of *chair* might be a decontextualised prototype that includes *seat, back,* and *legs,* with idiosyncratic properties and background situations filtered out. Although functional properties may be extracted and stored, they again are decontextualised invariants, not detailed information about specific situations. The resulting representation has the flavour of a detached encyclopedia description in a database of categorical knowledge that describes the world.

Along with being decontextualised, semantic memory representations are typically viewed as relatively stable. For a given category, different people share roughly the same representation, and the same person uses the same representation on different occasions.

Finally, semantic memory is widely viewed as organised taxonomically. Increasingly specific categories are nested in more general ones, with central sets of categories arising at the superordinate, basic, and subordinate levels of taxonomic hierarchies. Similarity plays a central role in establishing the inclusion relations that underlie these hierarchies, with similar categories at one level being nested in the same category at the next higher level. Background theories constrain the similarity computations that produce individual categories and clusters of categories (e.g., Murphy & Medin, 1985).

## Exemplar models

Beginning with Medin and Schaffer's (1978) context model, exemplar models have provided a strong competitor to semantic memory models. Many important variants of the basic exemplar model have been developed, including Nosofsky (1984), Estes (1986), Heit (1998), and Lamberts (1998).

Architecturally, exemplar models are generally modular in that exemplar knowledge is assumed to reside in memory stores outside sensory-motor systems. Those exemplar models, though, that view exemplar representations as implicit memories can be construed as non-modular, given that they use sensory-motor systems for storing exemplar memories (e.g., Brooks, 1978; Jacoby & Brooks, 1984). According to these latter models, exemplars are perceptual memories of encoded events, and can therefore be construed as residing in sensory-motor systems. Because the dominant exemplar models tend not to view exemplar memories this way, at least explicitly, they are coded as modular in Table 1.

To the extent that exemplar memories are stored outside sensory-motor systems, their representations are amodal, differing from sensory-motor representations. Similar to semantic memory models, redescriptions in an amodal language represent the content of exemplar memories, standing in for the sensory-motor properties experienced for them originally. Typically in these models, symbols represent the values of an exemplar on relevant sensory-motor dimensions. Again, though, exemplar models that view exemplars as implicit memories can be construed as having modal representations, where the representation of an exemplar is a reenactment of the sensory-motor state encoded for it (e.g., Roediger & McDermott, 1993).

Where exemplar models differ most from semantic memory models is on the dimension of abstraction. Whereas semantic memory models distill properties across exemplars and store them as abstractions, exemplar models simply store exemplar memories, which can include much situational detail. Because exemplar models store situation-specific knowledge of category members, rather than abstracting across them, these models are coded as situated for the abstraction dimension in Table 1.

On the dimension of stability, exemplar models, like semantic memory models, are relatively stable. Most exemplar models assume that all exemplar memories for a category are accessed every time the category is processed. Although an exemplar set can be very large, its constant application across different occasions is relatively stable, with all exemplars being applied. Exemplar models that sample small subsets of exemplars, on the other hand, are dynamic (e.g., Barsalou, Huttenlocher, & Lamberts, 1998; Nosofsky & Palmeri, 1997). Because such models are relatively rare, exemplar models have been coded as stable in Table 1.

Exemplar models typically do not address the dimension of organisation in Table 1. Nevertheless, exemplar models can be viewed as implicitly producing taxonomic organisation via the similarity mechanisms that control exemplar retrieval. Specifically, when a new exemplar is presented to an exemplar model, clusters of similar exemplars tend to become most active. When a new dog is presented, *DOG* exemplars tend to become the most active, and also *MAMMAL* and *ANIMAL* exemplars to lesser extents. In general, an exemplar memory becomes increasingly active as it shares properties with the new exemplar. The clusters that result from these activation gradients can be viewed as implementing implicit taxonomic organisation, where the implicit nature of this organization is indicated in Table 1 by parentheses around "taxonomic". It is important to add, however, that theorists have not yet developed accounts of how exemplar models utilise this implicit structure to perform taxonomic reasoning (Hampton, 1998).

## Feed-forward connectionist nets

Feed-forward nets constitute a relatively recent but increasingly influential theory of the conceptual system. For general accounts of these nets, see Rumelhart, Hinton, and Williams (1986) and Bechtel and Abrahamsen (2002). For specific applications of the feed-forward architecture to representing conceptual knowledge, see Hinton (1989), Kruschke (1992), and Rumelhart and Todd (1993). A variety of other connectionist formalisms have also been used to model the conceptual system, which are not covered here (e.g., Farah & McClelland, 1991; Gluck & Bower, 1988; McClelland & Rumelhart, 1985; Shanks, 1991). Of primary interest here are the properties of feed-forward nets as an account of conceptual knowledge.

Architecturally, feed-forward nets maintain a modular conceptual system. Whereas the input layer of a feed-forward net is typically interpreted as a perceptual system, its hidden layer is typically viewed as a conceptual system. Thus one "module" of units underlies perception, whereas a second underlies conception, thereby maintaining a modular distinction between the two. Complex interactions do indeed arise between these two systems, such that they are not modular in the sense of being impenetrable (cf. Fodor, 1983; Pylyshyn, 1984). Nevertheless different representational systems underlie perception and cognition, thereby maintaining modularity. As will be seen shortly, it is possible to formulate a conceptual system in which the same neural units represent information in both perception and conception. It is also worth noting that other connectionist architectures operate this way as well. Thus modularity only applies to connectionist nets of the feed-forward variety, along with others that have separate pools of units for perception and conception.

Because of this modular architecture, the internal representations in feed-forward nets are amodal. Prior to learning, connections between the input and hidden layers are set initially to small random values, making learning possible. As a result, a somewhat arbitrary mapping develops between the input and hidden layers, with conceptual representations being redescriptions of the perceptual representations. With each new set of weights, a different mapping develops.[2] The arbitrariness that results is much in the spirit of semantic memory representations. In both cases, conceptual representations on the hidden units differ from perceptual representations on the input units. Clearly details of the representations differ, with connectionist representations being statistical, and semantic memory representations being symbolic. Nevertheless both are amodal redescriptions of perceptual input at a more general level of analysis.

On the dimension of organisation, feed-forward nets implicitly organise categories around taxonomic similarity, as in exemplar models. To the extent that different exemplars share similar properties, the same hidden units represent them. As a result, taxonomic clusters develop attractors in the net's weight space to represent them implicitly (e.g., Rumelhart & Todd, 1993). On presenting a new exemplar to a net, attractors for the closest taxonomic clusters—at multiple levels—are most likely to become active.

Where feed-forward nets depart from semantic memory models is on abstraction and stability. Rather than establishing decontextualised representations of categories, feed-forward nets store situated representations in two senses. First, these nets store much idiosyncratic information about exemplars (as in exemplar models), rather than discarding it during the abstraction of category invariants. Although invariants may be abstracted, much idiosyncratic information is maintained that plays central roles in processing. Second, feed-forward nets store background information about the settings in which exemplars occur. Rather than extracting focal knowledge of a particular chair from a living room scene, much correlated information about the scene is stored as well (e.g., Rumelhart, Smolensky, McClelland, & Hinton, 1986). As a result, activating an exemplar typically retrieves setting information, and vice versa.

On the dimension of stability, the conceptual representations in feed-forward nets are highly dynamical. Rather than representing a category with a stable representation, as in semantic memory and exemplar models, a connectionist net represents a category with a space of representations. Essentially a category's representation is an attractor within the possible activation states of the hidden units, with an infinite number of states around the attractor providing possible representations. On a given occasion, the representation activated is a function of the network's current state, input, and learning history. Thus a concept is a dynamical

---

[2] Important invariants exist across the different mappings. Nevertheless many mappings are possible, with each being a redescription of the input. As we will see, it is possible to conceive of conceptual representations that are not redescriptions.

system that produces a family of representational states, depending on current conditions.

## The situated simulation theory

The view of the conceptual system advanced here differs from semantic memory on all five dimensions in Table 1. First, the situated simulation theory is non-modular. Rather than having separate systems for sensory-motor and conceptual processing, a common representational system underlies both. As described shortly, conceptual processing uses reenactments of sensory-motor states—simulations—to represent categories. Although perception and conception are similar, they are not identical, given that bottom-up mechanisms dominate the activation of sensory-motor systems during perception, whereas top-down mechanisms are more important during conception. Furthermore the representations activated in conception are *partial* reenactments of sensory-motor states, and may often exhibit bias and reconstructive error. Nevertheless perception and conception are far from being modular autonomous systems.

As a result of this non-modular architecture, conceptual representations are modal, not amodal. The same types of representations underlie perception and conception. When the conceptual system represents an object's visual properties, it uses representations in the visual system; when it represents the actions performed on an object, it uses motor representations. The claim is not that modal reenactments constitute the sole form of conceptual representation. As described later, hidden unit representations, like those in feed-forward nets, may also play a role. The claim is simply that modal reenactments are an important and widely utilised form of representation.

Turning to abstraction and stability, the situated simulation view assumes that conceptual representations are contextualised and dynamical. A concept is not a single abstracted representation for a category, but is instead a skill for constructing idiosyncratic representations tailored to the current needs of situated action. As described in more detail later, a concept is a simulator that constructs an infinite set of specific simulations (Barsalou, 1999). Thus the simulator for *CAR* can construct many simulations of different cars, from different perspectives, used for different purposes. In principle, a simulator can produce an infinite number of simulations, varying dynamically with the agent's current goal and situation.

More than the focal category is represented in a given simulation. As discussed later, additional information about background settings, goal-directed actions, and introspective states are also typically included in these simulations, making them highly contextualised. Furthermore, because a simulator tailors simulations to current situations, a wide variety of simulations represents the category across different situations, not just one. The result is a conceptual system that is highly contextualised and dynamical, much like feed-forward nets, but with modal representations instead of amodal ones.

Finally, the situated simulation view proposes that the conceptual system is organised around situated action, not around taxonomies. As described later, a fundamental problem in situated action is mapping action effectively into the world, and an intriguing possibility is that the conceptual system develops to facilitate this mapping. In particular, ad hoc and goal-derived categories develop to bind roles in action with instantiations in the environment. As systems of these mappings develop, the conceptual system becomes organised around the action–environment interface. Classic taxonomies play a secondary role in organising sub-domains of knowledge to support this interface.

## EVIDENCE FOR
## THE SITUATED SIMULATION THEORY

The remainder of this article reviews evidence that situated simulation underlies the conceptual system. The review will be organised around the five dimensions in Table 1. Because the dimensions of architecture and representation are tightly coupled, evidence showing that conceptual representations are non-modular and modal will be reviewed together in the next section. In the third section (abstraction), findings will show that conceptual representations are contextualised to support situated action. In the fourth section (stability), findings will show that the simulations serving situated action arise from dynamical systems. In the fifth section (organisation), findings will suggest that the conceptual system becomes organised around the action–environment interface.

### Evidence for a modal non-modular conceptual system

On the dimensions of architecture and representation, the issues are, first, whether the conceptual system is separate from sensory-motor systems, and second, whether it uses modal vs. amodal representations. At this point it is useful to define the construct of a sensory-motor state. First, such states can be defined as patterns of neural activation in a sensory-motor system. On seeing a chair, for example, its representation in the visual system is a pattern of neural activation along the ventral and dorsal streams. This way of thinking about sensory-motor states is well established and widely accepted (e.g., Palmer, 1999; Zeki, 1993). Second, these states can be viewed as conscious mental experiences. Clearly, though, what becomes conscious is a relatively small subset of the unconscious processing taking place neurally. Furthermore various theoretical issues arise in discussing conscious experience that are tangential to those of interest here. For these two reasons, the remainder of this article focuses on the neural representation of sensory-motor states. The subsets of these states that achieve consciousness will be of secondary interest, although this is certainly an important issue.

Viewing sensory-motor states as active patterns in modality-specific neural systems provides a means of distinguishing modular amodal views from non-modular modal views. According to modular amodal views, a conceptual representation is not a neural pattern in a sensory-motor system—the neural pattern that represents an entity during its perception is not active during its conceptualisation. Instead neural activation in some other brain system represents the object conceptually. Furthermore the neural representation in conception takes a different form than the one in perception, with the same form representing conceptual properties across different modalities.

In contrast, non-modular modal views make a very different claim. When a category is represented conceptually, the neural systems that processed it during perception and action become active in much the same way as if a category member were present (again, though, not identically). On conceptualising *CAR*, for example, the visual system might become partially active as if a car were present. Similarly the auditory system might reenact states associated with hearing a car, the motor system might reenact states associated with driving a car, and the limbic system might reenact emotional states associated with enjoying the experience of driving (again all at the neural level).

Thus a fairly large and significant difference exists between how the modular amodal and the non-modular modal views represent concepts. As a result, it would seem that much research in the literature would have addressed which is correct. Surprisingly little research has. Instead widespread acceptance of modular amodal views reflects theoretical considerations. As Barsalou (1999) conjectured, the rise of modular amodal systems reflected the development of logic, statistics, and computer science in the early twentieth century, and the later incorporation of these developments into the cognitive revolution. Because amodal representation languages have considerable expressive power, because they can be formalised, and because they can be implemented in technology, they captured the imagination of the field, took over theoretical thinking, and became widely practised.

Clearly, however, a strong empirical case should exist for such an assumption, even if it is useful theoretically. The next three sub-sections review findings that question it. In the first, much research indicates that sensory-motor representations are widespread throughout cognition, and therefore should be likely in the conceptual system as well. The second sub-section reviews recent behavioural tests designed explicitly to assess whether categories are represented in modality-specific systems. The third sub-section reviews recent evidence from cognitive neuroscience that bears on this issue.

*Behavioural evidence for sensory-motor representations throughout cognition.*   In studying diverse forms of cognitive processing, researchers have obtained widespread evidence for sensory-motor representations. In some cases, demonstrating such representations was a goal. In most cases, though, researchers were addressing other hypotheses but nevertheless reported findings that can be interpreted post hoc as indicating the presence of sensory-motor representations. Indeed some of these researchers might not agree with this post hoc interpretation of their findings! For this reason, direct a priori tests of this issue are critical, and the results of such tests will be reported in the next two sub-sections, after reviewing more general evidence here.

In perception, filling-in and anticipatory inferences suggest that sensory-motor representations from the conceptual system enter fluently into perceptual processing. In the phoneme restoration effect, hearers simulate the experience of a phoneme—absent in the speech signal—using sensory-motor knowledge about the word that contains it, and also about the speaker's voice (e.g., Warren, 1970). Recently Samuel (1997) reported that these simulations activate early sensory systems, implicating sensory representations in these linguistic inferences. Similarly, in representational momentum, viewers simulate the visual trajectory of an object beyond the trajectory displayed physically (e.g., Freyd, 1987), implicating visual knowledge in these inferences. Knowledge about whether a particular type of object moves quickly or slowly affects simulated trajectories, suggesting that object representations contain perceptual representations of motion (e.g., Reed & Vinson, 1996). Visual inferences from knowledge about the body similarly influence perceived bodily motion, overriding the minimal transformation law of apparent motion (e.g., Shiffrar & Freyd, 1990, 1993; Stevens, Fonlupt, Shiffrar, & Decety, 2000). Perceivers fill in the blind spot with perceptual representations that underlie conceptual knowledge about object shape (Ramachandran, 1992, 1993). Perceptual representations of objects also drive figure-ground segregation towards representations of known objects (e.g., Peterson & Gibson, 1994). In all these cases, sensory-motor representations in conceptual knowledge appear to fuse with incoming sensory information to construct perceptions (Hochberg, 1998).

Sensory-motor representations have been widely implicated in working memory, particularly in mental imagery. Considerable amounts of behavioural work indicate that mental imagery results from activating sensory-motor representations (e.g., Finke, 1989; Kosslyn, 1980; Shepard & Cooper, 1982), as does much neural work (e.g., Farah, 2000; Kosslyn, 1994). Sensory-motor representations are not only central in visual imagery, they are also central in motor imagery (e.g., Grezes & Decety, 2001; Jeannerod, 1995, 1997; Deschaumes-Molinaro, Dittmar, & Vernet-Maury, 1992; Parsons, 1987a,b) and in auditory imagery (e.g., Zatorre, Halpern, Perry, Meyer, & Evans, 1996).

Sensory-motor representations are widely implicated in long-term memory. In the literature on mnemonic strategies, imagery and concreteness effects implicate such representations (e.g., Paivio, 1986). In the boundary extension effect, images of scenes appear responsible for extending a picture's memory beyond its boundary (e.g., Intraub, Gottesman, & Bills, 1998). In verbal overshadowing, images activated via words appear responsible for distortions of studied pictures and other sensory-motor experiences (e.g., Schooler, Fiori, & Brandimonte, 1997). In haptic priming, images of motor movements prime memory (e.g., Klatzky, Pelligrino, McCloskey, & Dougherty, 1989). In implicit memory, perceptual processing is essential for establishing robust implicit learning (e.g., Jacoby, 1983), and also explains the narrow transfer gradients around it (e.g., Jacoby & Hayman, 1987). Furthermore, imagining a stimulus produces about 60% of the priming produced by actually perceiving it, consistent with the presence of perceptual representations (e.g., Roediger & McDermott, 1993). Finally, neural work has localized both implicit and explicit memory in sensory-motor systems (e.g., Buckner, Petersen, Ojemann, Miezin, Squire, & Raichle, 1995; Nyberg, Habib, McIntosh, & Tulving, 2000; Wheeler, Petersen, & Buckner, 2000). Glenberg (1997) reviews further findings that implicate sensory-motor representations in memory.

Considerable evidence also exists for sensory-motor representations in language. In numerous experiments, Bower and Morrow (1990) found that mental models of text meaning have spatial qualities (also see Glenberg, Meyer, & Lindem, 1987). Much earlier work on comprehension inferences similarly suggested the presence of spatial representations (e.g., Bransford & Johnson, 1973). Other research has shown that readers take spatial perspectives on scenes described in texts (e.g., Black, Turner, & Bower, 1979; Spivey, Tyler, Richardson, & Young, 2000). Intraub and Hoffman (1992) showed that readers confuse pictures with texts, suggesting that they imaged the texts' meanings. Gernsbacher, Varner, and Faust (1990) found that comprehension ability for pictured events correlated highly with comprehension ability for texts, suggesting that sensory-motor representations underlie both. Potter, Kroll, Yachzel, Carpenter, and Sherman (1986) showed that replacing words with pictures did not disrupt sentence processing, suggesting that the pictures were integrated effortlessly into a sensory-motor representation of the sentence's meaning (also see Glaser, 1992). Gibbs (1994) reviews findings suggesting that sensory-motor representations are central to the processing of metaphor (also see Lakoff & Johnson, 1980).

Finally, sensory-motor representations have been implicated in various forms of thought. In decision making, Kahneman and Tversky (1982) suggested that people use a simulation heuristic to evaluate possible choices. In reasoning, Johnson-Laird (1983) and Fauconnier (1985, 1997) argued that mental models underlie reasoning, where mental models can be viewed as sensory-motor representations. In causal reasoning, Ahn and Bailenson (1996) argued that imagining causal mechanisms is central to causal reasoning, where these imagined mechanisms could be implemented as simulations. Philosophers of science frequently note that scientific and mathematical discoveries arise from imagery (e.g., Barwise & Etchemendy, 1990, 1991; Hadamard, 1949; Nersessian, 1999). Similarly, researchers have argued that children and adults use mental models in basic arithmetic reasoning (e.g., Huttenlocher, Jordon, & Levine, 1994).

Together all of these findings implicate sensory-motor representations across the spectrum of cognitive processes, from perception to abstract thought. It thus seems quite likely that such representations would also occur in the conceptual system. Clearly, however, one must be cautious about post hoc interpretations of previous work, and applying them to the representation of concepts. Direct a priori assessments of sensory-motor representations in conceptual processing are obviously much more desirable. The next two sub-sections review such work.

*Direct behavioural assessments of modal vs. amodal representations*
For the past 10 years, my students and I have been designing experiments to assess whether perceptual simulations represent concepts (see Barsalou, Solomon, & Wu, 1999, for an early review). We have focused on two tasks that are widely believed to access conceptual knowledge: property generation and property verification. In property generation, a participant hears the word for a category (e.g., "chair"), and then verbally generates characteristic properties of the underlying concept out loud (e.g., "seat, legs, back, you sit on it"). In property verification, a participant reads the word for a category on a computer (e.g., "chair"), and then verifies whether a subsequently presented property is true or false of the category (e.g., "seat" vs. "faucet"). Whereas property generation is an active, production-oriented task extended over time, property verification is a more passive, recognition-oriented task under time pressure.

Nearly all accounts of these tasks have assumed that participants access amodal representations to perform them (e.g., Collins & Quillian, 1969; Conrad, 1972; Kosslyn, 1976; Rosch & Mervis, 1975; Smith, 1978). When producing or verifying properties, participants consult semantic networks, feature lists, frames, etc. to produce the required information. In contrast, we hypothesized that participants simulate a category member to represent a category, and then consult the simulation to produce the requested information. In property generation, participants scan across the simulation, and produce words for properties in its sub-regions. In property verification, participants evaluate whether the test property can be found in a sub-region of the simulation.

*Instructional equivalence.*    To assess these theoretical possibilities, we evaluated two types of evidence: instructional equivalence and perceptual work. To assess instructional equivalence, the performance of neutral participants was compared with the performance of imagery participants. Neutral participants received the standard task instructions used through-out the literature. For property generation, they were asked to generate properties characteristic of each object concept. For property verification, they were asked to verify whether or not each property was true of the object. Imagery participants were explicitly asked to use imagery. For property generation, they were asked to image each object and then describe the image. For property verification, they were asked to image the object and only respond true once they found the property in the image. Much previous work in the imagery literature demonstrates that participants instructed to use imagery do so, and our experiments independently demonstrate this as well.

Of primary interest for instructional equivalence is how the performance of the neutral and imagery participants compares. According to amodal views, these two groups should perform differently. Whereas neutral participants should use amodal representations, imagery participants should use sensory-motor representations (or at least pretend to use them because of task demands). As a result, significant differences should occur between the two groups.

Various amodal views make this prediction. On Pylyshyn's (1981) tacit knowledge view, subjects only have amodal knowledge, but know how to deploy it so that they appear to be using imagery. If this account is correct, then imagery instructions should induce the tacit knowledge that produces imagery-like performance, but the neutral instructions should not—neutral participants should spontaneously employ amodal representations in a non-imagery-like manner. As a result, the two groups should perform differently.

Similarly, views that postulate modal representations alongside amodal ones also tend to predict differences in performance. In Kosslyn's (1980) original theory, imagery primarily arises when task demands induce participants to construct it in working memory. When participants can use amodal representations, they tend to fall back on them, because these representations can be deployed more rapidly and easily. As a result, imagery and neutral performance should differ. Kosslyn (1976) offers empirical evidence for this prediction.

In contrast, the simulation view predicts that neutral and imagery participants should generally perform similarly. Neutral participants should spontaneously run the same sorts of simulations as imagery participants. Because they do not have amodal representations, they simulate categories to represent them, even when not asked explicitly to do so. As a result, neutral and imagery participants produce the same basic patterns of performance.[3]

Findings from Wu and Barsalou (2003) support the simulation account. In Wu and Barsalou, the properties generated were coded into 37 property types, with the frequency of each type computed once for the neutral condition and once for the imagery condition. The 37 average frequencies for the neutral participants were then correlated with those for the imagery participants. Across three experiments, the correlations were .99, .81, and .96, after correcting for unreliability of the mean frequencies. This high agreement suggests that the neutral and imagery participants accessed the same sorts of representations as they produced properties, not different ones.

One potential concern is that the critical result is a null effect. Thus it is important to show that instructional manipulations can change property distributions. For this reason, a third instructional condition was included in which participants generated associated words for each category name. When the frequency distributions for this condition were compared to the neutral and imagery conditions, the correlations were substantially lower. Clearly an instructional manipulation can change the distribution of properties. Of interest is that the imagery instructions did not change the distribution relative to the neutral condition.[4]

---

[3] An important caveat is that neutral participants will readily use word associations—instead of simulations—to perform conceptual tasks, when task conditions allow this superficial form of processing. In several papers described shortly, this superficial processing was observed (Kan et. al., 2003; Solomon & Barsalou, 2003; Wu & Barsalou, 2003; for a review, see Glaser, 1992). Most importantly, however, when task conditions block superficial responding based on word associations, the conceptual processing enforced appears to consist of simulations, as findings in each paper indicate.

[4] One difference that did occur was the imagery participants produced more properties than neutral participants, consistent with the conclusion that imagery instructions induce participants to construct more detailed simulations than those constructed spontaneously by neutral participants. Again, though, the distributions of properties were virtually identical between the two groups, suggesting that both constructed the same type of representation.

One might worry that participants use simulation in property generation because the task is production oriented, and because they have unlimited time to use all of their resources to represent categories. Perhaps such simulations would not occur in a recognition-oriented task under time pressure (cf. Kosslyn, 1976, 1980). For this reason, we also assessed the presence of simulations in property verification (Solomon & Barsalou, 2003).

To assess instructional equivalence, the average verification time and error rate were first computed for each critical concept-property pair (e.g., *CHAIR-seat*). The data across 100 or more pairs in a given experiment were then regressed onto a large set of potential predictors, namely, various factors that we thought might predict RTs and errors. These predictors fell into three general groups: linguistic, perceptual, and expectancy. The linguistic predictors included the associative strength between the concept and property words in both directions, the word frequency of the properties, and their length. The perceptual predictors included the size and position of the properties, whether they were occluded, whether they would be handled during situated action, and so forth. The expectancy predictors assessed the polysemy of the property words (i.e., the typical property word takes many different senses across objects; consider *leg, handle, button,* etc.).

Of primary interest was that the regression equations for the neutral and imagery conditions were qualitatively the same—indeed in some analyses, they were quantitatively identical. The same pattern of predictors explained performance in both conditions. Generally speaking, perceptual variables were most important for both, followed by the expectancy variables, and then the linguistic variables. This finding in two experiments suggests that imagery and neutral participants used similar representations to perform the task. Neutral participants appeared to be using simulations, similar to imagery participants.[5]

Thus the instructional equivalence found in property generation was not an artifact of the task being production oriented and having no time pressure (i.e., property listing). In a recognition-oriented task under time pressure (i.e., property verification), a similar result occurred. Again, the prediction of a null effect is tempered by the fact that in other conditions not described here, qualitatively different regression equations explained

---

[5] One difference that did occur was the imagery participants verified properties more slowly than neutral participants, consistent with the conclusion drawn for property generation that imagery instructions induce participants to construct more detailed simulations than those constructed spontaneously by neutral participants. Again, though, the regression equations were virtually identical between the two groups, suggesting that both constructed the same type of representation.

performance. Different strategies for performing the task are possible, yet imagery instructions did not change performance relative to the neutral condition.

*Perceptual effort.* To further assess the presence of simulations in conceptual processing, we and other researchers have manipulated perceptual variables, such as occlusion, size, shape, orientation, and modality, analogous to previous work in mental imagery. If participants are constructing perceptual simulations to represent categories, then perceptual variables should affect task performance. In contrast, if participants are using amodal representations, it is much less obvious that such variables should have effects. Indeed no amodal theory has ever predicted that variables like size, orientation, and occlusion should affect conceptual processing.

Wu and Barsalou (2003) manipulated occlusion by having half the participants generate properties for noun concepts (e.g., *LAWN*), and the other half generate properties for the same nouns preceded by revealing modifiers (e.g., *ROLLED-UP LAWN*). In perception, occluded properties do not receive much attention because they are hidden behind an object's surface. Thus we predicted that if people simulate *LAWN* to generate its properties, they should rarely produce its occluded properties, such as *dirt* and *roots*. In contrast, when people perceive a rolled-up lawn, its normally occluded properties become visible and more salient. Thus we predicted that when people produce properties for *ROLLED-UP LAWN*, previously occluded properties would become salient in simulations and be produced more often. Amodal theories of conceptual combination do not readily make this prediction, given that they are relatively compositional in nature (e.g., Smith, Osherson, Rips, & Keane, 1988). Unless additional post hoc assumptions are added that produce interactions between nouns and modifiers, the properties for *LAWN* are not obviously changed by *ROLLED UP* in these theories (e.g., the accessibility of *dirt* and *roots* does not vary).

As predicted, the number of internal properties was higher when revealing modifiers were present than when they were not. Internal properties were also produced earlier in the protocols and in larger clusters. This effect occurred not only for familiar noun combinations, such as *HALF WATERMELON*, but also for novel ones, such as *GLASS CAR*. Furthermore, the increase in occluded properties was not the result of rules for properties stored with the modifiers, given that a particular modifier did not always increase occluded properties (e.g., *ROLLED-UP SNAKE*). Occluded properties only increased when the modifiers referred to entities whose internal parts become unoccluded in the process of conceptual combination (e.g., *ROLLED-UP LAWN*). Together this pattern of results is consistent with the prediction that when a simulation reveals occluded properties, they are produced more often, relative to when they are occluded in a simulation.

Turning to property verification, Solomon and Barsalou (2003) found that perceptual variables predicted performance for neutral participants better than did linguistic and expectancy variables. In particular, property size was the most important of the perceptual variables (as measured by per cent unique variance explained). As a property became larger, it took longer to verify, presumably because a larger region of a simulation had to be processed. Notably property size was the most central predictor of performance in a conceptual task with linguistic materials and no imagery instructions, after removing variance explained by all other variables.

Solomon and Barsalou (2001) similarly found that property shape was a critical factor in property verification. When participants verified a property on one trial, it facilitated verifying the same property later, but only if the detailed shape was similar. Thus verifying *mane* for *PONY* was facilitated by previously verifying *mane* for *HORSE* but not by verifying *mane* for *LION*. This effect was not the result of the greater overall similarity between *HORSE* and *PONY* than between *HORSE* and *LION*. When the similarity of a property between all three concepts was high, facilitation was the same. For example, verifying *belly* for *PONY* was facilitated as much by verifying *belly* for *LION* as by verifying *belly* for *HORSE*. Thus perceptual similarity of the property was the critical factor, not conceptual similarity.

Zwaan, Stanfield, and Yaxley (2002) similarly reported that property shape affects conceptual processing, but during language comprehension. Participants read a short vignette about an object that implied one of several possible shapes. Whereas some participants read about a flying bird, others read about a sitting bird (i.e., the implied shape of the bird differed between the two vignettes). After reading the vignette, participants named a visually presented object (shown in isolation, not in a scene). When a bird was shown, sometimes it was flying, and other times sitting. As the simulation view predicts, participants named objects faster when their shapes matched the implied shapes in the vignettes than when they did not. As participants read the vignettes, they simulated objects in the implied shapes.

Stanfield and Zwaan (2001) similarly showed that orientation affects conceptual processing during language comprehension. Participants read vignettes that implied objects in particular orientations. Whereas some participants read about pounding a nail into the wall, others read about pounding a nail into the floor. Immediately thereafter, participants saw an isolated object and had to indicate whether it had been mentioned in the vignette. Sometimes the orientation of an object matched its implied orientation in the text, and sometimes it did not (e.g., a horizontal nail vs. a vertical one). Verification was fastest when the orientations matched.

Two other recent findings further support simulations in language comprehension (Glenberg & Robertson, 2000; Kaschak & Glenberg, 2000). When participants read about a novel object performing a function, their comprehension of it was effortless, as long as the object's affordances produced the function. For example, when a character in a story needed a pillow, participants understood immediately that a sweater filled with leaves would work, but that a sweater filled with water would not. Similarly, in the context of hitting things with a baseball bat, "crutching an apple" to someone made perfect sense, even though it was a novel construction. According to these researchers, people understand such constructions by simulating the corresponding events and assessing the functional affordances in these simulations, much as they would assess them in actual perception. When affordances produce the critical function, comprehension occurs. Most importantly, it is difficult and cumbersome for amodal representation languages to compute these affordances. The fact that they arise so naturally in simulations further supports the presence of simulations in comprehension.

Finally, Pecher, Zeelenberg, and Barsalou (2003) have shown modality-switching effects in conceptual processing. Previous work in perception shows that detecting a signal on a modality suffers when the previous signal was on a different modality than on the same one (e.g., Spence, Nicholls, & Driver, 2000). For example, verifying the presence of a light flash is faster when the previous signal was a light flash than when it was an auditory tone. Pecher et al. demonstrated a similar phenomenon in property verification using linguistic materials and no imagery instructions. When participants verified a conceptual property on one modality, processing was faster when the previous property came from the same modality as opposed to a different one. For example, verifying *loud* for *BLENDER* was faster when *rustling* was verified for *LEAVES* on the previous trial than when *tart* was verified for *CRANBERRIES*. Scaling of the materials found that properties drawn from the same modality were no more associated than the properties from different modalities. Furthermore, when highly associated properties were verified on contiguous trials, they were verified no faster than unassociated properties. Thus switching between modalities was responsible for the obtained effects, not associative strength.

*Evidence from cognitive neuroscience.*    As the previous two sections illustrate, a strong behavioural case is developing for simulations in the conceptual system. A strong neural case is developing as well in the lesion and neuroimaging literatures. In these latter areas, researchers have explored the hypotheses that categories are represented in sensory-motor areas of the brain, and have reported much evidence for it.

In the lesion literature, researchers have reported that a lesion in a particular sensory-motor system increases the likelihood of losing categories that rely on that system for processing exemplars online. For example, damage to visual areas increases the chances of losing *LIVING THINGS,* because visual processing is often the dominant modality when interacting with these entities (e.g., Damasio & Damasio, 1994; Gainotti, Silveri, Daniele, & Giustolisi, 1995; Humphreys & Forde, 2001; McRae & Cree, 2002; Warrington & Shallice, 1984). Conversely, damage to motor areas increases the chances of losing *MANIPULABLE ARTIFACTS* such as *TOOLS*, because motor processing is often the dominant modality (e.g., Damasio & Damasio, 1994; Gainotti et al., 1995; Humphreys & Forde, 2001; McRae & Cree, 2002; Warrington & McCarthy, 1987). Similarly, damage to colour processing areas produces deficits in colour knowledge (e.g., DeRenzi & Spinnler, 1967; Damasio & Damasio, 1994), and damage to spatial processing areas produces deficits in location knowledge (e.g., Levine, Warach, & Farah, 1985).

Controversy currently surrounds these findings, with some theorists stressing the importance of other factors besides damage to sensory-motor systems. For example, Caramazza and Shelton (1998) propose that localized brain areas represent specific categories that are evolutionarily important, such as *ANIMALS*. Tyler, Moss, Durrant-Peatfield, and Levy (2000) propose that the statistical distribution of property information determines the localization of categories and their vulnerability to lesion-based deficits.

Simmons and Barsalou (2003b) argue that all these views are correct and propose a theory that integrates them. Following Damasio (1989), Simmons and Barsalou propose that two levels of representation underlie conceptual knowledge. At one level, reenactments of sensory-motor states are central to representing categories. At a second level, statistical representations in association areas—much like those on the hidden layers of feed-forward nets—conjoin sensory-motor states into coherent representations. Simmons and Barsalou argue that these conjunctive hidden units cluster spatially by similarity. For example, the hidden units that organise sensory-motor features for *ANIMALS* cluster spatially together, whereas the hidden units that organise sensory-motor features for *ARTIFACTS* cluster spatially elsewhere (in a more distributed manner, due to lower within-category similarity). Such organisation implements the localised category representations important for Caramazza and Shelton, and also the statistical structure important for Tyler et al. Nevertheless the reenactment of sensory-motor states is also central. A primary function of statistical representations in association areas is to reactivate sensory-motor states in feature maps so that information relevant to the current task can be extracted from these simulations.

Most importantly, lesions at various levels of this system can produce the diverse forms of deficits found throughout the lesion literature. Whereas lesions in association areas can produce deficits for individual categories, lesions in feature maps can produce deficits across multiple categories that rely on them (e.g., McRae & Cree, 2002). Depending on which mechanism of the simulation process is lesioned, different deficits result.

The neuroimaging literature offers further support for simulations in conceptual processing. Consistent with the lesion literature, different sensory-motor areas become active for different types of categories. When people process categories for which the visual modality is important (e.g., *ANIMALS*), visual areas become active (e.g., Martin, Ungerleider, & Haxby, 2000; Martin, Wiggs, Ungerleider, & Haxby, 1996; Perani, Schnur, Tettamanti, Gorno-Tempini, Cappa, & Fazio, 1999; Pulvermüller, 1999; Spitzer et al., 1998). Conversely, when people process categories for which the motor modality is important (e.g., *TOOLS*), motor areas become active (e.g., Martin, Haxby, Lalonde, Wiggs, & Ungerleider, 1995; Martin et al., 2000; Martin et al., 1996; Perani et al., 1999; Pulvermüller, 1999; Spitzer et al., 1998). Similarly, when people process colour, colour areas become active (e.g., Chao & Martin, 1999; Rösler, Heil, & Hennighausen, 1995; Martin et al., 1995; Martin et al., 2000). Finally, when people process locations, spatial systems become active (e.g., Rösler et al., 1995). All these results are consistent with the conclusion that people simulate categories in sensory-motor systems.

Notably, however, the sensory-motor areas identified by fMRI studies of conceptual processing are typically not identical to the primary sensory-motor areas active in actual perception and action. Instead, the two sets of areas are usually immediately adjacent within the same modality-specific system (e.g., both in the visual system). An important issue for future work is to provide greater insight into the specific roles that these two sets of areas play. For example, the areas active in conceptual processing could be feature maps common to both conception and sensory-motor processing, whereas the areas active only in sensory-motor processing are used exclusively in bottom-up processing and execution. Alternatively, the areas active in conceptual processing could be the association areas described earlier that conjoin sensory-motor features (Damasio, 1989; Simmons & Barsalou, 2003b). Still another possibility is that these areas implement classic amodal symbols. Much further work of many types is necessary to resolve this issue. Single-cell recording studies may be particularly informative, especially on the question of whether associative neurons reactivate feature map neurons to produce simulations.

Finally, neural support has accumulated for three lines of the behavioural work described earlier. Kan et al. (2003) repeated Solomon and Barsalou's (2003) property verification study in an fMRI scanner (only using neutral subjects), and found activation in the fusiform gyrus, a visual area important in high-level object processing and imagery. Notably, when conditions of the experiment allowed participants to use word association instead of imagery, the fusiform was no longer active, indicating its role only when simulations were predicted to represent categories. Whereas superficial conceptual processing can effectively utilize word representations, deeper conceptual processing appears to trigger—and perhaps require—simulations (also see Solomon & Barsalou, 2003; Wu & Barsalou, 2003).

Simmons, Pecher, Hamann, Zeelenberg, and Barsalou (2003) repeated the Pecher et al. (2003) modality-switching study in an fMRI scanner. In this particular version of the experiment, participants verified properties in blocks organised into six modalities: vision, audition, movement, touch, smell, and taste. For each modality, a profile of sensory-motor modalities became active, which corresponded to the profile of modalities that people reported experiencing subjectively for the respective concept-property pairs. Thus, processing these pairs engaged multi-modal sensory-motor processing.

Finally Zwaan, Stanfield, Yaxley, and Scheffers (2001) measured ERPs in further studies on object shape. When an object's shape in a text and a picture mismatched, ERPs occurred that indicate visual mismatches, further implicating visual representations in language processing.

*Theoretical issues.* If one is convinced by the empirical case for simulation in the conceptual system, a problem arises. For decades, theorists have argued that perceptual representations do not have sufficient expressive power to represent conceptual knowledge (e.g., Pylyshyn, 1973). Even if empirical evidence exists for simulations, it remains to be shown how they could implement a fully functional conceptual system.

Barsalou (1999) offers an existence proof that a fully functional conceptual system could rest on sensory-motor simulations. In principle, such a system can distinguish types from tokens, produce categorical inferences, generate novel concepts productively in conceptual combination, represent the propositional hierarchies that underlie text comprehension, and represent abstract concepts. Clearly a computational implementation of such a theory must be developed, and considerable empirical evidence must be gathered for its specific mechanisms. In principle, though, it appears feasible, at least, that sensory-motor mechanisms could help implement the human conceptual system.

Furthermore the following empirical conclusions appear warranted at this time. The conceptual system appears neither fully modular nor fully amodal. To the contrary, it is non-modular in sharing many important mechanisms with perception and action. Additionally it traffics heavily in the modal representations that arise in sensory-motor systems.

## Evidence for situated simulations

Two metaphors capture the opposing positions on the issue of abstraction (i.e., Dimension 3 in Table 1). At one extreme, the conceptual system is a *detached database*. As categories are encountered in the world, their invariant properties are extracted and stored in descriptions, much like an encyclopaedia. The result is a database of generalised categorical knowledge that is relatively detached from the goals of specific agents. At the other extreme, the conceptual system is an *agent-dependent instruction manual*. According to this metaphor, knowledge of a category is not a general description of its members. Instead a concept is a skill that delivers highly specialised packages of inferences to guide an agent's interactions with specific category members in particular situations. Across different situations, different packages tailor inferences to different goals and situational constraints. According to this view, the information stored for a category is organised into situation-specific units, not into a general description.

A package of situation-specific inferences will be referred to as a *situated conceptualisation*. Across different situations, a concept generates different conceptualisations, each designed to optimise one particular type of situated action with the respective category. A given situated conceptualisation contains four types of information:

(1) contextually-relevant properties of the focal category;
(2) information about the background setting;
(3) likely actions that the agent could take to achieve an associated goal;
(4) likely introspective states that the agent might have while interacting with the category, such as evaluations, emotions, cognitive operations, etc.[6]

Following the previous section, it will be assumed that these four types of inferences are delivered via neural simulations in the respective

---

[6] An unaddressed issue is whether contextual information about settings, actions, and mental states resides within concepts proper or is associated to them externally. Alternatively no clear demarcation may exist between them, with one shading into the other. Resolution of this issue is not critical to the thesis here, which is simply that packages of correlated inferences are delivered to support situated action, regardless of where they originate.

modality-specific areas. Specifically, contextually relevant object properties are simulated in the ventral stream, settings are simulated in parietal areas, actions are simulated in the motor system, and introspective states are simulated in areas that process emotion and reasoning. Together, simulations of these four inference types produce the experience of *being there conceptually* (Barsalou, 2002). When it becomes necessary to process a category, its concept delivers a situated conceptualisation that creates a multi-modal representation of what it would be like to process the category in that situation.[7]

The next four sub-sections review evidence that the conceptual system delivers situated conceptualisations, with each sub-section providing evidence for one type of situated inference: contextualised category representations, background settings, actions, and introspective states.

*Evidence for contextualised category representations.*    Much research across multiple literatures demonstrates that concepts do not produce the same representation over and over again across situations. Instead a concept produces one of many possible representations that is tailored to the current context.

Barsalou (1982) provides a typical example of this finding. Participants read a sentence and then verified whether a subsequent property was true or false of the underlined subject noun. Between participants, the predicate of the sentence varied to manipulate the situation, as between:

> The *basketball* was used when the boat sank.
> The *basketball* was well worn from much use.

As this example illustrates, the predicate in each sentence situates *BASKETBALL* in a different context. Immediately after reading one of these sentences, participants verified whether *floats* was true of *BASKETBALL*. When *floats* was relevant to the sinking situation in the first sentence, participants verified it faster than when it was irrelevant to the normal use situation in the second sentence. As participants read about the boat sinking, the concept for *BASKETBALL* produced relevant inferences—it did not produce the same representation in both contexts.

---

[7] The phrase "being there conceptually" could be taken to mean that agents experience these contexts of action consciously. The sense of "being there conceptually" intended here is that neural systems ready themselves for perceptions and actions likely to be present while processing a category in the current situation. Clearly these neural systems may produce conscious states as they prepare themselves for situated action. Again, though, much more neural processing takes place than consciousness reveals, and the focus continues to be on the neural processing that underlies consciousness.

Many additional studies have reported similar results (for a review, see Yeh & Barsalou, 2003). In online studies of sentence processing, for example, context effects on lexical access are legion (e.g., Kellas, Paul, Martin, & Simpson, 1991; Tabossi, 1988). Similarly in memory research, context effects on word encoding are widespread (e.g., Greenspan, 1986; Tulving & Thomson, 1973). In category learning, background knowledge about a situation constrains the properties of objects salient in them (e.g., Murphy, 2000).

*Evidence for setting inferences.*   When the conceptual system represents a category, it does not represent the category in isolation. Instead it typically situates the category in a background setting. Again much work supports this conclusion, as reviewed in Yeh and Barsalou (2003).

Consider an experiment by Vallée-Tourangeau, Anthony, and Austin (1998). Participants performed the instance generation task, namely, they received a category (e.g., *FRUIT*) and produced instances of it (e.g., *APPLE, KIWI, PEAR*). Virtually all accounts of this task assume that participants generate instances from conceptual taxonomies. For *FRUIT*, participants might first produce instances from *CITRUS FRUIT*, then from *TROPICAL FRUIT*, then from *WINTER FRUIT*, and so on. In contrast, Vallée-Tourangeau et al. (1998) conjectured that participants situate the category in a background setting, scan across the setting, and report the instances present. To produce *FRUIT*, for example, participants might imagine being in the produce section of their grocery store and report the instances found while scanning through it.

To assess this possibility, Vallée-Tourangeau et al. (1998) first had participants produce the instances of common taxonomic categories (e.g., *FRUIT*) and also of ad hoc categories (e.g., *THINGS PEOPLE TAKE TO A WEDDING*). After producing instances for all the categories, participants were asked how they produced instances for each category, indicating one of three possible strategies. First, if the instances came to mind automatically, participants indicated the *unmediated strategy*. Second, if the instances were retrieved in clusters from a taxonomy, participants indicated the *semantic strategy*. Third, if the instances were retrieved from a situation, participants indicated the *experiential strategy*.

As Vallée-Tourangeau et al. predicted, searching situations was the dominant strategy for producing instances. Participants used the experiential strategy 54% of the time, followed by the semantic strategy (29%) and the unmediated strategy (17%). Surprisingly this pattern was the same for taxonomic and ad hoc categories. Because ad hoc categories arise in goal-directed events, it is not surprising that they would be associated with situations. Surprisingly, though, taxonomic categories were equally situated. Walker and Kintsch (1985) and Bucks (1998) report similar findings.

The Wu and Barsalou (2003) experiments described earlier further demonstrate that categories are situated in background settings. Participants were explicitly asked to produce characteristics true of the target objects (e.g., *WATERMELON*). Nothing in the instructions requested or even implied the relevance of background settings. As Figure 1 shows, however, participants produced setting information regularly. Across four experiments, the percentage of setting information ranged from 19% to 35%, averaging 25%. As participants simulated the target objects, they implicitly situated them in background settings, leading to the inadvertent production of many setting properties (e.g., *park, picnic table*, etc. for *WATERMELON*).

Much evidence further demonstrates a tight coupling between object representations and situations (as reviewed in Yeh & Barsalou, 2003). For example, work on visual object processing shows that objects are strongly linked to background scenes (e.g., Biederman, 1981; Bar & Ullman, 1996; Intraub, Gottesman, & Bills, 1998; Mandler & Parker, 1976; Mandler & Stein, 1974; Murphy & Wisniewski, 1989). When an isolated object is perceived, a background scene is typically inferred immediately.

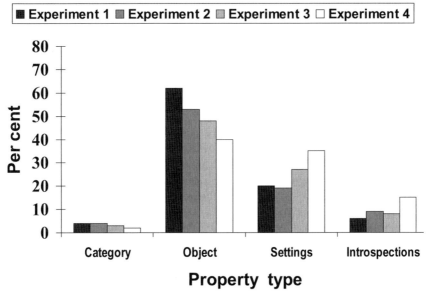

**Figure 1.** Proportion of property types across the four experiments in Wu and Barsalou (2003). Properties of the target objects were explicitly requested in the instructions to participants (Object). However, participants also produced related taxonomic categories (Category), along with information about the background settings (Settings) and agents' introspective states (Introspections).

*Evidence for action inferences.*    Thus far we have seen that conceptual representations contain contextually relevant properties, and that they are situated in background settings. As the results in this next sub-section show, the conceptual system places agents squarely in these settings, producing inferences about the actions they could take on situated objects.

Consider an fMRI experiment by Chao and Martin (2000). As participants viewed pictures in the scanner, their task was to name them implicitly. Four types of pictures were presented: manipulable objects (e.g., *HAMMER* ), dwellings, animals, and human faces. All participants were right-handed and lay motionless in the scanner. Nevertheless a circuit involving the motor system became active while participants perceived the manipulable objects. Notably this circuit did not become active for the other pictures. Furthermore it was only active in the left hemisphere, namely, the side that controls right-handed movements—again the participants were right handed. This finding suggests that on seeing a manipulable object, such as a hammer, the conceptual system generated appropriate motor inferences for handling it with the right hand. Even though the target task was visual categorisation, and even though participants were required to lie still in the scanner, their motor systems nevertheless implicitly generated movements for interacting with the manipulable objects. Presumably such inferences prepare agents for situated action.

Consider a similar finding from Adolphs, Damasio, Tranel, Cooper, and Damasio (2000). Again participants' task solely involved visual processing, but this time the visual categorisation of facial expressions. On each trial, participants saw a face and had to indicate whether the expression was happy, sad, angry, etc., with the correct response being defined as the dominant emotion categorisation across a large group of judges. Of interest to Adolphs et al. were the brain areas that produce these categorisations. To assess this, they sampled from a registry of patients having lesions in different brain areas. If an area is important for categorising visual expressions of emotion, then lesions in the area should produce task deficits. The critical finding was that large deficits were found for patients with lesions in somatosensory cortex. Why would somatosensory lesions produce deficits on a visual task? Adolphs et al. argue that simulating facial expressions on one's own face is central to visually recognising expressions on other faces. When somatosensory cortex is damaged, such simulations become difficult, and facial categorisation suffers.

Work in social cognition supports this conclusion. Wallbott (1991) videotaped participants' faces as they visually categorised emotional expressions on other faces. Interestingly, participants regularly simulated the emotional expressions that they were categorising on their own faces.

More importantly, when a participant correctly simulated the expression being categorised, their accuracy increased. Similarly Niedenthal, Brauer, Halberstadt, and Innes-Ker (2001) found that preventing participants from simulating expressions decreased their ability to categorise facial expressions on others, relative to participants free to move their faces. Together all these findings illustrate that the motor and somatosensory systems become involved in the visual processing of faces.

Such simulations can be viewed as motor inferences produced by the conceptual system to support situated action. In many settings, if another person is experiencing an emotion, it is often useful for the perceiver to enter the same state. Thus, if another person is angry about something, it may be supportive to be angry as well. Social contagion similarly supports being jointly happy or jointly sad about a shared event. In these cases, once the concept for a particular emotion becomes active, appropriate motor and somatosensory states for entering into it follow.

Other recent studies further support the importance of action inferences in high-level cognition. Smith, Thelen, Titzer, & McLin (1999) concluded that the motor system plays a central role in the A-not-B error (i.e., misremembering that an object is hidden at an earlier location rather than at its current one). Rather than being a purely cognitive phenomenon reflecting factors such as object permanence, this error results from the close coupling of the cognitive and motor systems. Perseverative reaches by the motor system to old locations interfere with spatial memory, when these actions are inconsistent with an object's current location.

Glenberg and Kaschak (2002) similarly show that comprehending a sentence about a motor movement can interfere with the act of responding. For example, when participants used a *forward* hand movement to indicate that sentences are coherent and not anomalous, they responded faster when the judged sentence described a forward movement than a backward one (e.g., "Close the drawer" vs. "Open the drawer"). Glenberg (1997) discusses other such findings.

Finally, when participants perform motor actions while generating properties, the actions change conceptual simulations in predictable ways. In Barbey and Barsalou (2003), participants believed that the experiment addressed the ability to perform factory operations while communicating with a supervisor. Following Wu and Barsalou's (2003) occlusion effect, Barbey and Barsalou (2003) had participants occasionally perform an action that would open up an object and reveal its internal properties (e.g., the motion of opening a drawer while producing properties for *DRESSER*). As predicted, participants produced more internal properties (e.g., *socks* and *sweater* for *DRESSER*) when they performed revealing actions (e.g., opening a drawer) than when they performed non-revealing actions (e.g., turning a wheel chair's wheels). Only a few participants had an inkling of the hypothesis (never a complete understanding), and the effect was no stronger for these participants than for the others. Furthermore, a control group was generally unable to label the actions correctly, and the probability of labelling actions correctly was unrelated to the production of action-related properties. Thus revealing actions appeared to produce object simulations that prepared participants for situated action. Simmons and Barsalou (2003a) similarly show that motor actions affect visual categorisation. When an action is consistent with a visual object, the object is categorised faster than when the action is inconsistent (e.g., categorising a *FAUCET* while performing the motion of turning a faucet vs. turning a dial).

Together all these results suggest a close coupling between the motor and conceptual systems. On the one hand, when people conceptualise a category, they infer relevant actions that they could take on it. On the other, when people perform an action, it influences the construction of conceptual representations. Barsalou, Niedenthal, Barbey, and Ruppert (in press) review many additional findings in social psychology that point to the same conclusion.

*Evidence for introspective state inferences.*    Not only do people infer possible actions that they could take on categories in background settings, they further infer introspective states likely to arise during these interactions. Again consider the Wu and Barsalou (2003) data in Figure 1. As we saw earlier, participants produced many properties about background settings when the explicit instruction was to produce proper-ties of target objects. Of interest here is the fact that participants also produced many properties about the likely introspective states of agents during situated action. These included evaluations of whether objects are good, bad, effective, etc. They also included emotional reactions to objects, such as happiness, along with other cognitive states and operations relevant to interacting with them (e.g., comparing an object to alternatives). On the average, 10% of the properties produced were about introspective states, ranging from 6% to 15% across experiments. As participants simulated the target objects, they situated them in background settings that included themselves as agents. Because these simulations of "being there" included introspective states, properties of these states entered the protocols.

Perspective effects in various tasks further implicate introspective states in conceptual simulations. Spivey et al. (2000) had participants listen to a vignette while wearing an eye-tracking helmet (which they believed was turned off at the time). Different participants heard different vignettes, where the critical variable was the implied perspective for viewing a scene. Some participants, for example, heard about the top of a skyscraper, whereas others heard about the bottom of a canyon. As participants listened to their story, they tended to adopt the relevant perspective motorically. Participants hearing about the skyscraper top were most likely to look up, whereas participants hearing about the canyon bottom were most likely to look down. Participants adopted the relevant perspective on the situation, acting as if they were "there". Other findings similarly show that the cognitive system produces the perspective of "being there" while comprehending language and retrieving information from memory (e.g., Anderson & Pichert, 1978; Black et al., 1979; Spivey & Geng, 2001).

Further work demonstrates the role of perspective in conceptual processing. Barsalou, Barbey, & Hase (2003) videotaped participants as they produced properties for object concepts. Occasionally the object was something that would typically be above a person (e.g., *BIRD*) or on the ground (e.g., *WORM*). When participants produced properties for objects above them, their eyes, face, and hands were more likely to drift up than for objects below them, and vice versa. These findings suggest that participants simulated "being there" with the objects as they produced their properties.

Finally Borghi and Barsalou (2003) found that participants typically generate properties from perspectives relevant to situated action. Thus participants tended to produce properties that would be experienced up close to an object and from its front, as if interacting with it.

*"Being there" conceptually.*    Results reviewed in the previous four sub-sections support the conclusion that the conceptual system is not a detached database of encyclopaedic knowledge. Instead the conceptual system is more like an agent-dependent instruction manual, tailoring conceptual representations to the current needs of situated action. Furthermore these situated conceptualisations take the form of simulations that create the experience of "being there" with category members. These simulations include contextually relevant properties of the focal category, background information about the setting, inferences about likely actions, and inferences about likely introspective states. Together these packages of simulated inferences prepare agents for situated action.

## Evidence for dynamical simulations

Rosch (1975) assessed the stability of typicality gradients and reported stabilities over .90. On the basis of such findings, many researchers concluded that stable prototypes represent concepts in semantic memory (i.e., Dimension 4 in Table 1). Different people share the same prototype, and the same individual uses the same prototype on different occasions.

We have just seen, however, that the conceptual system tailors conceptualisations to specific situations. Thus it would appear that stable representations do not underlie concepts. Instead a concept produces many different conceptualisations, depending on current goals and constraints. How do we reconcile these findings with empirical reports of stability?

The measures that Rosch reported assessed the stability of *mean* typicality judgements. What she showed is that stable typicality judgements can be obtained when enough participants contribute to average ratings (i.e., the central limit theorem). To assess agreement between *individual* participants, other measures of stability are required. Barsalou (1987, 1989, 1993) reported such measures, and they tell a very different story. For typicality judgements, the average correlation between pairs of participants averaged around .40 across studies. Different participants appeared to use very different prototypes for judging typicality. Furthermore, the same participant appeared to use different prototypes on different occasions. When the same participant judged typicality again 2 weeks later, the average correlation with their earlier judgements was around .80, suggesting a modest change in how they represented the categories.

One possibility is that variability in typicality judgements simply reflects noise. An unpublished study, however, obtained .94 agreement between participants and .98 agreement within participants when the task was to rank the same exemplars by physical weight instead of by typicality. Thus the ranking task is highly sensitive and relatively noise free when weight is judged. In typicality judgements, though, much larger variability results from different participants retrieving different information to represent a category. Additional findings also ruled out the interpretations that atypical exemplars, stochastic sampling, and knowledge differences underlie this variability (Barsalou, 1993).

Other tasks besides typicality judgement show similar variability in how people conceptualise categories. McCloskey and Glucksberg (1978) had participants assign basic level categories to superordinates in two sessions separated by a month. Roughly 25% of the basic level categories changed superordinate membership across the two sessions for natural kinds as well as for artifacts, indicating considerable variability in the criteria used to assign membership. Similarly Barsalou (1989) reported considerable variability in property generation. On average, two participants only produced 44% of the same properties for a given category. Across a 2-week delay, the same participant only produced 66% of the same properties in the two sessions. Together with the typicality and membership data, these findings suggest that stable representations do not underlie concepts.

Instead Barsalou (1987, 1989, 1993) concluded that a concept is a dynamical system, which produces a wide variety of representational states, depending on current conditions. Smith and Samuelson (1997) reached a similar conclusion after reviewing similar findings from the conceptual development literature. In long-term memory, a tremendous amount of stored information underlies a concept. On a given occasion, only a small subset of this information is retrieved, namely, the information that is currently most accessible.

Three factors dynamically determine the most accessible subset of a concept's content on a given occasion: frequency, recency, and context. As information is processed frequently for a category, it becomes better established in memory, and more accessible across contexts. If one person regularly experiences large dogs, whereas another regularly experiences small ones, *large* and *small* will become relatively more accessible for each individual, respectively. Similarly information processed recently for a category becomes temporarily elevated in accessibility, such that its inclusion in concepts increases during a brief temporal window. If a person was recently licked by a dog, *licks* becomes temporarily elevated for a limited time, and is more likely to be included in representations of *DOG*. Finally the current context affects the accessibility of conceptual information. As shown earlier, *floats* becomes more accessible for *BASKETBALL* in the context of needing a life preserver than in other contexts (Barsalou, 1982). Presumably, associations from the current context prime related properties in the knowledge for a concept, increasing their accessibility temporarily.

As these examples illustrate, frequency, recency, and context together determine the category information most accessible for a particular conceptualiser in a particular context. From individual to individual, and from context to context, the information most accessible for a category fluctuates dynamically, producing conceptualisations that vary considerably.

*Viewing conceptual variability from the perspective of situated action.* The earlier theme of situated action is consistent with the results on conceptual variability. According to the situated action view, a concept is not a general description used over and over again across situations. Instead a concept is an ability or skill to construct specific representations that support different courses of situated action. Because a concept produces a wide variety of situated conceptualisations, substantial variability in its representation arises. Because different information about a category is needed in different situations, different conceptualisations are constructed.

Finally we saw earlier that a concept produces experiences of "being there" with a category. For this reason, Barsalou (1999) proposed that a concept is a *simulator*. Rather than being a detached database of category information, a simulator produces a wide variety of simulations that create the experience of "being there" in different contexts of situated action. Thus the simulator for *CHAIR* produces simulations of interacting with a living room chair, an office chair, a theatre chair, a jet chair, a ski-lift chair, and so forth. To create the experience of "being there" in each of these situations, the simulator produces situation-relevant information about the relevant chair, along with situation-relevant information about the setting, actions, and introspective states. As a person's expertise with a category develops, the ability to simulate the relevant contexts of situated action grows. The result is a dynamical system that supports skilled interaction with the category across contexts.

## Evidence for organisation around the action–environment interface

The three previous sections have focused on the internal structure of individual concepts, addressing their representational format, situatedness, and dynamical character. This final section addresses the broader organisation of the conceptual system (i.e., Dimension 5 in Table 1). Two metaphors capture the opposing positions on this dimension. At one extreme, people are intuitive taxonomists. Their goal is to discover the categorical structure of the world, develop taxonomic systems that represent this structure, and establish background theories that frame these taxonomies. At the other extreme, people are goal achievers who organise knowledge to support situated action. On this view, the primary organisation of the conceptual system supports executing actions effectively in the environment, with taxonomic hierarchies constituting a secondary-level of organisation that supports this activity.

*Ad hoc and goal-derived categories.*    The presence of categories that arise specifically to achieve goals intimates the importance of goal achievement in organising the conceptual system. In particular, ad hoc categories, such as *THINGS TO PACK IN A SUITCASE*, are derived in the course of achieving specific goals (e.g., taking a trip). Over time, some of these categories become well established in memory, as when a frequent traveller packs the same things repeatedly in a suitcase (e.g., Barsalou & Ross, 1986). Barsalou (1983, 1985, 1991) refers to this general class of categories as *goal-derived categories*, and to novel ones constructed online as *ad hoc categories* (see Ross & Murphy, 1999, for related work).

Various properties of these categories indicate that they originate in situated action. Barsalou and Borghi (in prep.) collected protocols of participants talking about goal-directed events and found that for every action mentioned, there was a 75% chance of a goal-derived category being mentioned along with it. Thus these categories are ubiquitous in everyday cognitive processing of events. At a given moment in time, one is likely to find them operative.

Barsalou (1983) demonstrated that ad hoc categories only become salient in the context of pursuing the goals they serve. For example, people have trouble seeing the category that *CHAIR, WASTEBASKET, BOX*, and *ROCK* form. When a story character has the problem of holding a door open on a hot windy day, however, the category *THINGS TO HOLD A DOOR OPEN* comes to mind immediately. Such context effects suggest that ad hoc categories are closely coupled with reasoning about goals.

Barsalou (1985) reports that goal-derived categories are organised internally to optimise goal achievement. When the typicality gradients of these categories are assessed, ideals associated with goal-achievement underlie them. The members of a goal-derived category do not become more typical as they approach its prototypical (average) properties. Instead they become more typical as they approach ideal values. Thus members of *THINGS TO PACK IN A SUITCASE* do not become more typical as they approach average size and weight for the category; instead they become more typical as they approach ideally small size and ideally light weight.

The association of ideals with goal-derived categories further indicates their close coupling with goals. When achieving a goal, it is usually necessary to instantiate relevant goal-derived categories to implement a plan (Barsalou, 1991). When taking a trip, for example, it is necessary to instantiate *THINGS TO PACK IN A SUITCASE*. The association of ideals with these categories helps maximise goal achievement. By comparing possible instantiations to a category's ideals, an agent can find instantiations that will be optimally effective. For example, comparing *THINGS TO PACK IN A SUITCASE* with *ideally small and light* helps identify those instantiations that contribute to optimal travel.[8]

Notably taxonomic categories are also associated with ideals, further showing that even these categories serve situated action. For example, the ideal of *sweetness* is associated with *FRUIT*, whereas the ideal of *nutritiousness* is associated with *VEGETABLES* (Barsalou, 1985). By

---

[8] Although ideals are useful for optimising instantiations in planning, they aren't sufficient for determining category membership. Other properties must typically be considered as well.

selecting instantiations close to these ideals while eating, goals related to taste and diet are optimised. Additional research similarly demonstrates the centrality of ideals across a wide variety of conceptual domains (e.g., Borkenau, 1990; Chaplin, John, & Goldberg, 1988; Lehrer, 1992; Loken & Ward, 1990; Lynch, Coley, & Medin, 2000).

In summary, goal-derived categories arise during the process of achieving goals. They are mentioned frequently during goal-related events, they typically become salient during goal pursuit, and their internal representations optimise goals.

*The role of goal-derived categories in the cognitive system.* One might think that goal-derived categories are merely a quaint curiosity of the conceptual system. Although interesting, they are relatively peripheral, with taxonomic categories constituting the core. Thus the question arises: What role do goal-derived categories play in the conceptual system?

To answer this question, it is instructive to consider standard models of problem solving and planning (e.g., Newell & Simon, 1972). Perhaps by examining these models, the role of goal-derived categories in them can be ascertained. According to standard models of problem solving and planning, goal achievement has the following basic phases:

(1) An agent selects a goal to pursue.
(2) The agent selects a sequence of actions to achieve the goal.
(3) The agent executes the action sequence in the environment.
(4) The agent evaluates the outcome of the action sequence. If the outcome is satisfactory, goal pursuit ends; if it is not, the agent iterates through Steps 1, 2, and 3 until the goal is achieved or abandoned.

Where might goal-derived categories arise in this sequence? One possibility is in Step 3 during the execution of action sequences in the environment. To implement an action sequence, it is necessary to solve the *interface problem,* that is, the problem of integrating action with the environment effectively (see *meshing* in Glenberg, 1997, for a similar construct). Consider shopping for groceries. To buy groceries successfully, it is necessary to interface the shopping sequence with the environment. The instantiation of roles in event sequences is central to this process (Barsalou, 1991). Roles in grocery shopping include *STORES THAT SELL GROCERIES, TRANSPORTATION TO THE STORE, PAYMENTS THE STORE ACCEPTS,* and *STORE HOURS.* To successfully achieve grocery shopping, it is necessary to map each of these roles into environmental instantiations appropriately (e.g., a particular store, transportation, payment, hours). When one of these roles is not instantiated successfully, the goal may fail.

For highly routinised action sequences in familiar environments, the interface problem is not salient. Because mappings from roles to the environment have become well-established in memory, people integrate action with the environment effortlessly (e.g., in weekly grocery shopping). The interface problem becomes salient when knowledge of these mappings is absent, as while grocery shopping in a country very different from one's own. Under such conditions, the importance of mappings between roles in action and entities in the environment becomes apparent.

Based on the above analysis of the interface problem, Barsalou (1991) concluded that goal-derived categories constitute the mappings between roles in event sequences and instantiations in the environment. Furthermore, establishing these mappings is essential to achieving the four basic phases of problem solving and planning just described. In the absence of successful mappings, problem solving and planning fail. Goal-derived categories appear to be a fundamental component of goal-directed behaviour.

Figure 2 illustrates this account within the framework of situated simulation theory (see Barsalou, 1999, for further discussion). Imagine having the goal of changing a burned-out light bulb on the ceiling. Panel B of Figure 2 illustrates the scene that the agent might see. Panel A represents the agent's simulated attempt to change the light bulb. After simulating a failed reach to the bulb while standing on the floor, the agent concludes that it is beyond reach. Thus the agent simulates something to stand on and tries again. Notably at this point, the agent may not simulate a particular thing to stand on, but only the idea of standing on a large sturdy object that resides in a schematic space-time region of the simulation. As Barsalou (1999) illustrates, simulations can contain schematic components that partially represent entities, not just detailed representations of them. One can imagine standing on a large sturdy object without knowing exactly what it is—one simply knows that it can be stepped onto safely and extend one's reach significantly.

Once the agent has simulated standing on something to reach the bulb, the environment is searched for possible instantiations of the schematic region. As the mapping between Panels A and B illustrates, several objects in the scene might seem likely to work, based on running them as instantiations in the simulation (i.e., the stool, chair, and table). Once this mapping from the schematic role to the environment has been established, it creates an ad hoc category, namely, *THINGS THAT COULD BE STOOD ON TO CHANGE THE LIGHTBULB*.

Broadly speaking, the account just provided could underlie ad hoc and goal-derived categories in general. By and large, these categories can be viewed as mapping a space-time region in a simulated action sequence to a set of possible instantiations in the environment. Panel C of Figure 2

A

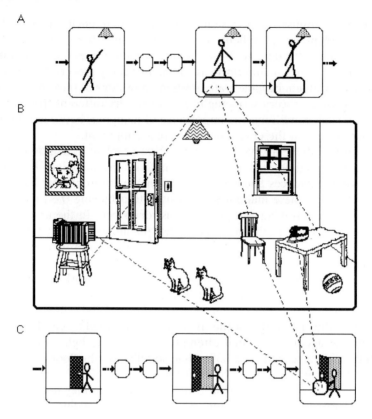

B

C

**Figure 2.** Accounting for the ad hoc categories of *THINGS THAT COULD BE STOOD ON TO CHANGE A LIGHTBULB* (A) and *THINGS THAT COULD BE USED TO HOLD A DOOR OPEN* (C), which construe common entities in the same scene differently (B). From Barsalou (1999), with permission from Cambridge University Press.

illustrates another example, namely, *THINGS THAT COULD BE USED TO HOLD THE DOOR OPEN.*

Furthermore, many of these mappings are so conventionalized that simple lexemes name them (Barsalou, 1991). For *BUY*, the lexemes "seller", "buyer", "merchandise", and "payment" name roles in the verb's meaning for *AGENT, PATIENT, THEME*, and *INSTRUMENT*, respectively. Each of these roles can be viewed as a space-time region in a simulation that maps into possible instantiations in the environment. Lexemes similarly name mappings for many other common verbs, projecting from their associated roles to goal-derived categories (e.g., *FOOD* and *UTENSIL* for *EAT*).

To the extent that this account is correct, it suggests that the action-environment interface is central to the conceptual system. Most notably, it suggests that an important class of categories arises at this interface. Categories do not simply arise from discovering structure in the environment, as is typically assumed for common taxonomic categories. Instead a central class of categories arises from binding space-time regions in simulated action sequences with instantiations in the environment. Without this sort of conceptual structure, people could not achieve goals effectively.

*Organisation around the action–environment interface.* If important categories originate at the action–environment interface, it suggests a larger organisation of the conceptual system (Barsalou, 1991). Rather than being organized around taxonomic categories, the conceptual system may be organised around this interface, with taxonomic categories playing a supporting role. On this view, the three most basic domains of the conceptual system represent *action*, the *environment*, and the *mapping* between them. Each of these domains is addressed briefly in turn.

The domain of action represents conceptual knowledge about how to achieve goals. Included in this domain is knowledge about particular goals, the action sequences used to achieve them, and the roles within these action sequences. Classic theories of scripts and frames provide preliminary accounts of what this knowledge might look like (e.g., Schank & Abelson, 1977).

The domain of the environment contains two important kinds of information. First, it contains knowledge of specific settings that an agent knows, such as homes, work environments, neighbourhood environments, and so forth. A given person has a *world model* that represents the settings he or she has experienced. Surprisingly little work has addressed such knowledge, with most related work addressing either route finding in cognitive maps or generic concepts for settings (e.g., Tversky & Hemenway, 1983). Much more work seems necessary to explore how people represent the *specific* physical settings that they experience regularly in their respective worlds (cf. Minsky, 1977).

Second, conceptual knowledge of the environment contains classic taxonomies. To represent specific settings in one's environment, it is useful to have knowledge about the particular kinds of things encountered in them. As one enters a new office, for example, knowledge of *CHAIRS* and *TABLES* is retrieved to recognise and interact with new category members, and to establish representations of them in knowledge for the specific setting. In a sense, common taxonomies are like palettes in object-oriented drawing programs: They provide a tool for creating tokens of known categories in the representation of new settings. On this account, taxonomic categories play a secondary role in supporting the action–environment interface.

Finally, the third knowledge domain is the system of mappings between the first two. As agents increasingly solve the interface problem, they establish goal-derived categories that link roles in action sequences with instantiations in the environment. The result is a much more complicated system of relations than shown in Figure 2. In Figure 2, direct mappings link roles directly to instantiations. In actuality, deep hierarchies of mappings appear to mediate action and the environment. In Barsalou (1991), participants often described subcategories of mappings between a role and its instantiations (also see Barsalou & Borghi, in prep.). Consider *PAYMENTS*. This role in *BUY* does not map directly into the concrete forms of payment available to an agent. Instead it first maps into subcategories such as *CASH, CHECKS, CREDIT CARDS, LOANS,* etc. In turn, each of these may map into more specific subcategories, such as *CREDIT CARDS* breaking down into *CREDIT CARDS WITH AVAILABLE BALANCE* and *CREDIT CARDS WITH LOW INTEREST RATES*. Eventually this taxonomy maps into particular instances in the environment. As expertise with achieving an action sequence develops, extensive systems of mappings like these grow to support it, thereby constituting a third basic domain of the conceptual system.

## CONCLUSIONS

Three general conclusions follow from the work reviewed here. First, the conceptual system develops to serve situated action. At the broad level of organisation, an important class of categories arises to streamline the action–environment interface. During goal pursuit, goal-derived categories provide mappings from roles in action sequences to instantiations in the environment. At the level of individual categories, simulators produce situated conceptualisations that support goal achievement. Each conceptualisation is a package of inferences that specifies contextually relevant properties of the focal category, information about a likely background setting, possible actions that an agent could take, and likely introspective states that might arise. Together these inferences produce the experience of "being there" with a category member, preparing an agent for situated action in a particular context.

Second, these situated conceptualisations are delivered via multimodal simulations. Whereas inferences about objects are delivered via sensory systems, inferences about actions are delivered via motor and somatosensory systems. Similarly inferences about introspective states are delivered via limbic and frontal areas that process emotion and thought. Rather than arising in a modular and amodal conceptual system, these representations arise as simulations or partial reenactments in modality-specific brain areas. As a result, each type of inference is represented in a different representation language native to its modality—a single representation language does not redescribe them all amodally.

Third, a concept is a dynamical system. A given simulator can construct an indefinitely large number of specific simulations to represent the respective category. Rather than a concept being a fixed representation, it is a skill for tailoring representations to the constraints of situated action. Because the same category can take different forms, be encountered in a variety of settings, and serve many goals, a fixed representation would not be optimal. No single representation could possibly serve all of these different situations well. A much better solution arises from having a simulator tailor conceptualisations to particular situations.

Clearly many open questions remain. Empirically the literature reviewed earlier is certainly not the final say on the matter. Nevertheless, these findings are sufficiently compelling to indicate that the situated simulation view should be entertained seriously. Theoretically a host of issues arises in explaining how situated simulations achieve important conceptual functions, such as productivity, propositions, and abstract concepts. Although Barsalou (1999) and Barsalou (in press) present preliminary solutions, further development is clearly necessary, as well as empirical support. Again, though, these proposals offer hypotheses of the conceptual system that seem sufficiently plausible to be entertained seriously.

Furthermore this approach offers solutions to problems that have been relatively intractable for amodal views. As Barsalou (1999) notes, simulations provide a powerful interface between cognition and perception. Not only does this provide a solution to the symbol grounding problem (Searle, 1980), it explains how conceptual representations can be brought to bear so effortlessly on perception, and how the two can be fused together so easily. This approach also offers a natural account of how the human conceptual system could have evolved from earlier species. It is easy to imagine non-humans having a similar representational system that evolved into ours, whereas it is much harder to imagine how an amodal system could have evolved uniquely for humans. As many theorists have suggested, the major change in humans was a linguistic system that provided powerful control over the same basic sort of conceptual system found in earlier species.

Another outstanding question is whether amodal theories can account for the sorts of findings reviewed in this paper. In principle, they probably can, given their expressive power. As Barsalou (1999) notes, however, these explanations are typically provided post hoc within a framework that is unfalsifiable. Thus these accounts should be viewed cautiously.

Ultimately, the issue boils down to a priori evidence. Empirically and theoretically, what a priori cases can be made for these differing views? The matter is clearly far from being settled at this time.

Nevertheless, one's view of the conceptual system affects how one thinks about the rest of cognition. It is difficult, if not impossible, to think about the cognitive system without committing to a particular theory of concepts. As we saw at the outset, representations in the conceptual system underlie all forms of cognitive activity, including high-level perception, working memory, long-term memory, language, and thought. One's view of the conceptual system affects theorising about all these other activities. As Barsalou (1999, Section 4) shows, viewing conceptual representations as simulations provides a novel view of basic cognitive processes. As recent research further indicates, entertaining the possibility of simulation stimulates new hypotheses that future research can explore. At a minimum, the situated simulation theory has the potential to provoke thinking and research on the nature of the human conceptua(l system, as the field evolves towards increasingly sophisticated theories.

# REFERENCES

Adolphs, R., Damasio, H., Tranel, D., Cooper, G., & Damasio, A.R. (2000). A role for somatosensory cortices in the visual recognition of emotion as revealed by three-dimensional lesion mapping. *Journal of Neuroscience, 20,* 2683–2690.

Ahn, W., & Bailenson, J. (1996). Causal attribution as a search for underlying mechanisms: An explanation of the conjuction fallacy and the discounting principle. *Cognitive Psychology, 31,* 82–123.

Anderson, R.C., & Pichert, J.W. (1978). Recall of previously unrecallable information following a shift in perspective. *Journal of Verbal Learning and Verbal Behavior, 17,* 1–12.

Bar, M., & Ullman, S. (1996). Spatial context in recognition. *Perception, 25,* 343-352.

Barbey, A.K., & Barsalou, L.W. (2003). *Actions interact with conceptual representations during property generation.* Manuscript in preparation.

Barsalou, L.W. (1982). Context-independent and context-dependent information in concepts. *Memory and Cognition, 10,* 82–93.

Barsalou, L.W. (1983). Ad hoc categories. *Memory and Cognition, 11,* 211–227.

Barsalou, L.W. (1985). Ideals, central tendency, and frequency of instantiation as determinants of graded structure in categories. *Journal of Experimental Psychology: Learning, Memory, and Cognition, 11,* 629–654.

Barsalou, L.W. (1987). The instability of graded structure: Implications for the nature of concepts. In U. Neisser (Ed.), *Concepts and conceptual development: Ecological and intellectual factors in categorization* (pp. 101–140). Cambridge: Cambridge University Press.

Barsalou, L.W. (1989). Intraconcept similarity and its implications for interconcept similarity. In S. Vosniadou & A. Ortony (Eds.), *Similarity and analogical reasoning* (pp. 76–121). Cambridge: Cambridge University Press.

Barsalou, L.W. (1991). Deriving categories to achieve goals. In G.H. Bower (Ed.), *The psychology of learning and motivation: Advances in research and theory* (Vol. 27, pp. 1–64).

San Diego, CA: Academic Press. [Reprinted in A. Ram & D. Leake (Eds.), *Goal-driven learning* (1995, pp. 121–176). Cambridge, MA: MIT Press/Bradford Books.]

Barsalou, L.W. (1993). Structure, flexibility, and linguistic vagary in concepts: Manifestations of a compositional system of perceptual symbols. In A.C. Collins, S.E. Gathercole, & M.A. Conway (Eds.), *Theories of memory* (pp. 29–101). Hove, UK: Lawrence Erlbaum Associates Ltd.

Barsalou, L.W. (1999). Perceptual symbol systems. *Behavioral and Brain Sciences, 22,* 577–660.

Barsalou, L.W. (2002). Being there conceptually: Simulating categories in preparation for situated action. In N.L. Stein, P.J. Bauer, & M. Rabinowitz (Eds.), *Representation, memory, and development: Essays in honor of Jean Mandler* (pp. 1–16). Mahwah, NJ: Lawrence Erlbaum Associates Inc.

Barsalou, L.W. (in press). Abstraction as dynamic construal in perceptual symbol systems. In L. Gershkoff-Stowe & D. Rakison (Eds.), *Building object categories.* [Carnegie Symposium Series.] Majwah, NJ: Lawrence Erlbaum Associates, Inc.

Barsalou, L.W., & Barbey, A.K., & Hase, S. (2003). *Spontaneous body movements during property generation for concepts.* Manuscript in preparation.

Barsalou, L.W., & Borghi, A. (2003). *The MEW theory of knowledge: Evidence from concepts for settings, events, and situations.* Manuscript in preparation.

Barsalou, L.W., Huttenlocher, J., & Lamberts, K. (1998). Basing categorization on individuals and events. *Cognitive Psychology, 36,* 203–272.

Barsalou, L.W., Niedenthal, P.M., Barbey, A.K., & Ruppert, J.K. (in press). Social embodiment. in B.H. Ross (Ed.), *The psychology of learning and motivation* (Vol. 43). San Diego, CA: Academic Press.

Barsalou, L.W., & Ross, B.H. (1986). The roles of automatic and strategic processing in sensitivity to superordinate and property frequency. *Journal of Experimental Psychology: Learning, Memory, and Cognition, 12,* 116–134.

Barsalou, L.W., Solomon, K.O., & Wu, L.L. (1999). Perceptual simulation in conceptual tasks. In M.K. Hiraga, C. Sinha, & S. Wilcox (Eds.), *Cultural, typological, and psychological perspectives in cognitive linguistics: The proceedings of the 4th conference of the International Cognitive Linguistics Association* (Vol. 3, pp. 209–228). Amsterdam: John Benjamins.

Barwise, J., & Etchemendy, J. (1990). Information, infons, and inference. In R. Cooper, K. Mukai, & J. Perry (Eds.), *Situation theory and its applications* (pp. 33–78). Chicago: University of Chicago Press.

Barwise, J., & Etchemendy, J. (1991). Visual information and valid reasoning. In W. Zimmerman & S. Cunningham (Eds.), *Visualization in mathematics* (pp. 9–24). Washington, DC: Mathematical Association of America.

Bechtel, W., & Abrahamsen, A. (2002). *Connectionism and the mind: Parallel processing, dynamics, and evolution in networks.* Cambridge, MA: Basil Blackwell.

Biederman, I. (1981). On the semantics of a glance at a scene. In M. Kubovy & J.R. Pomerantz (Eds.), *Perceptual organization* (pp. 213–253). Hillsdale, NJ: Lawrence Erlbaum Associates, Inc.

Black, J.B., Turner, T.J., & Bower, G.H. (1979). Point of view in narrative comprehension, memory, and production. *Journal of Verbal Learning and Verbal Behavior, 18,* 187–198.

Borghi, A.M., & Barsalou, L.W. (2003). *Perspective in the conceptualization of categories.* Manuscript in preparation.

Borkeneau, P. (1990). Traits as ideal-based and goal-derived social categories. *Journal of Personality and Social Psychology, 58,* 381–396.

Bower, G.H., & Morrow, D.G. (1990). Mental models in narrative comprehension. *Science, 247,* 44–48

Bransford, J.D., & Johnson, M.K. (1973). Considerations of some problems of comprehension. In W.G. Chase (Ed.), *Visual information processing*. New York: Academic Press.

Brooks, L.R. (1978). Nonanalytic concept formation and memory for instances. In E. Rosch & B.B. Lloyd (Eds.), *Cognition and categorization* (pp. 169–211). Hillsdale, NJ: Lawrence Erlbaum Associates, Inc.

Buckner, R.L., Petersen, S.E., Ojemann, J.G., Miezin, F.M., Squire, L.R., & Raichle, M.E. (1995). Functional anatomical studies of explicit and implicit memory retrieval tasks. *Journal of Neuroscience, 15*, 12–29.

Bucks, R.S. (1998). *Intrusion errors in Alzheimer's disease*. Doctoral dissertation, University of Bristol.

Caramazza, A., & Shelton, J.R. (1998). Domain-specific knowledge systems in the brain: The animate-inanimate distinction. *Journal of Cognitive Neuroscience, 10*, 1–34.

Chao, L.L., & Martin, A. (1999). Cortical regions associated with perceiving, naming, and knowing about colors. *Journal of Cognitive Neuroscience, 11*, 25–35.

Chao L.L., & Martin A. (2000). Representation of manipulable man-made objects in the dorsal stream. *Neuroimage, 12*, 478–84.

Chaplin, W.G., John, O.P., & Goldberg, L.R. (1988). Conceptions of states and traits: Dimensional attributes with ideals as prototypes. *Journal of Personality and Social Psychology, 54*, 541–557.

Collins, A.M., & Loftus, E.F. (1975). A spreading activation theory of semantic processing. *Psychological Review, 82*, 407–428.

Collins, A.M., & Quillian, M.R. (1969). Retrieval time from semantic memory. *Journal of Verbal Learning and Verbal Behavior, 8*, 240–248.

Conrad, C. (1972). Cognitive economy in semantic memory. *Journal of Experimental Psychology, 92*, 149–154.

Damasio, A.R. (1989). Time-locked multiregional retroactivation: A systems-level proposal for the neural substrates of recall and recognition. *Cognition, 33*, 25–62.

Damasio, A.R., & Damasio, H. (1994). Cortical systems for retrieval of concrete knowledge: The convergence zone framework. In C. Koch & J.L. Davis (Eds.), *Large-scale neuronal theories of the brain* (pp. 61–74). Cambridge, MA: MIT Press.

DeRenzi, E., & Spinnler, H. (1967). Impaired performance on color tasks in patients with hemispheric lesions. *Cortex, 3*, 194–217.

Deschaumes-Molinaro, C., Dittmar, A., & Vernet-Maury, E. (1992). Autonomic nervous system response patterns correlate with mental imagery. *Physiology and Behavior, 51*, 1021–1027.

Donald, M. (1991). *Origins of the modern mind: Three stages in the evolution of culture and cognition.* Cambridge, MA: Harvard University Press.

Donald, M. (1993). Precis of "Origins of the modern mind: Three stages in the evolution of culture and cognition". *Behavioral and Brain Sciences, 16*, 739–791.

Estes, W.K. (1986). Array models for category learning. *Cognitive Psychology, 18*, 500–549.

Farah, M.J. (2000). The neural bases of mental imagery. In M.S. Gazzaniga (Ed.), *The cognitive neurosciences* (2nd edn., pp. 965–974). Cambridge, MA: MIT Press.

Farah, M.J., & McClelland, J.L. (1991). A computational model of semantic memory impairment: Modality specificity and emergent category specificity. *Journal of Experimental Psychology: General, 120*, 339–357.

Fauconnier, G. (1985). *Mental spaces.* Cambridge, MA: MIT Press.

Fauconnier, G. (1997) *Mappings in thought and language.* New York: Cambridge University Press.

Finke, R.A. (1989). *Principles of mental imagery.* Cambridge, MA: MIT Press.

Fodor, J.A. (1983). *The modularity of mind: An essay on faculty psychology.* Cambridge, MA: Bradford Books, MIT Press.

Freyd, J.J. (1987). Dynamic mental representations. *Psychological Review*, *94*, 427–438.

Gainotti, G., Silveri, M.C., Daniele, A., & Giustolisi, L. (1995). Neuroanatomical correlates of category-specific semantic disorders: A critical survey. *Memory*, *3*, 247–264.

Gernsbacher, M.A., Varner, K.R., & Faust, M.E. (1990). Investigating differences in general comprehension skill. *Journal of Experimental Psychology: Learning, Memory, and Cognition*, *16*, 430–445.

Gibbs, R.W., Jr. (1994). *The poetics of mind: Figurative thought, language, and understanding.* New York: Cambridge University Press.

Glass, A.L., & Holyoak, K.J. (1975). Alternative conceptions of semantic memory. *Cognition*, *3*, 313–339.

Glaser, W.R. (1992). Picture naming. *Cognition*, *42*, 61–105.

Glenberg, A.M. (1997). What memory is for. *Behavioral and Brain Sciences*, *20*, 1–55.

Glenberg, A.M., & Kaschak, M.P. (2002). Grounding language in action. *Psychonomic Bulletin & Review*, *9*, 558–569.

Glenberg, A.M., Meyer, M., & Lindem, K. (1987). Mental models contribute to foregrounding during text comprehension. *Journal of Memory and Language*, *26*, 69–83.

Glenberg, A.M., & Robertson, D.A. (2000). Symbol grounding and meaning: A comparison of high-dimensional and embodied theories of meaning. *Journal of Memory and Language*, *43*, 379–401.

Glenberg, A.M., Schroeder, J.L., & Robertson, D.A. (1998). Averting the gaze disengages the environment and facilitates remembering. *Memory and Cognition*, *26*, 651–658.

Gluck, M.A., & Bower, G.H. (1988). Evaluating an adaptive network model of human learning. *Journal of Memory and Language*, *27*, 166–195.

Greenspan, S.L. (1986). Semantic flexibility and referential specificity of concrete nouns. *Journal of Memory and Language*, *25*, 539–557.

Grezes, J., & Decety, J. (2001). Functional anatomy of execution, mental simulation, observation, and verb generation of actions: A meta-analysis. *Human Brain Mapping*, *12*, 1–19.

Hadamard, J. (1949). *The psychology of invention in the mathematical field.* New York: Dover Books.

Hampton, J.A. (1997). Conceptual combination. In K. Lamberts & D. Shanks (Eds.), *Knowledge, concepts, and categories.* (pp. 133–159). Hove, UK: Psychology Press.

Hampton, J.A. (1998). The role of exemplar models in the representation of natural language concepts. Talk presented at a Workshop on Exemplar Models of Category Knowledge, University of Leuven, Belgium, May.

Heit, E. (1998). Influences of prior knowledge on selective weighting of category members. *Journal of Experimental Psychology: Learning, Memory, and Cognition*, *24*, 712–731.

Hinton, G.E. (1989). Learning distributed representations of concepts. In R.G.M. Morris (Ed.), *Parallel distributed processing: Implications for psychology and neurobiology* (pp. 46–61). New York: Oxford University Press.

Hochberg. J. (Ed.) (1998). *Perception and cognition at century's end: Handbook of perception and cognition* (2nd edn.). San Diego, CA: Academic Press.

Hollan, J.D. (1975). Features and semantic memory: Set-theoretic or network model? *Psychological Review*, *82*, 154–155.

Humphreys, G.W., & Forde, E.M.E. (2001). Hierarchies, similarity, and interactivity in object recognition: "Category-specific" neuropsychological deficits. *Behavioral and Brain Sciences*, *24*, 453–509.

Huttenlocher, J., Jordon, N.C., & Levine, S.C. (1994). A mental model for early arithmetic. *Journal of Experimental Psychology: General*, *123*, 284–296.

Intraub, H., Gottesman, C.V., & Bills, A.J. (1998). Effects of perceiving and imagining scenes on memory for pictures. *Journal of Experimental Psychology: Learning, Memory, and Cognition, 24,* 186–201.

Intraub, H., & Hoffman, J.E. (1992). Reading and visual memory: Remembering scenes that were never seen. *American Journal of Psychology, 105,* 101–114.

Jacoby, L. (1983). Remembering the data: Analyzing interactive processes in reading. *Journal of Verbal Learning and Verbal Behavior, 22,* 485–508.

Jacoby, L.L., & Brooks, L.R. (1984). Nonanalytic cognition: Memory, perception, and concept learning. In G.H. Bower (Ed.), *The psychology of learning and motivation: Advances in research and theory* (Vol. 18, pp. 1–47). New York: Academic Press.

Jacoby, L.L., & Hayman, C.A.G. (1987). Specific visual transfer in word identification. *Journal of Experimental Psychology: Learning, Memory and Cognition, 13,* 456–463.

Jeannerod, M. (1995). Mental imagery in the motor context. *Neuropsychologia, 33,* 1419–1432.

Jeannerod, M. (1997). *The cognitive neuroscience of action.* Malden, MA: Blackwell.

Johnson-Laird, P.N. (1983). *Mental models.* Cambridge, MA: Harvard University Press.

Kahneman, D., & Tversky, A. (1982). The simulation heuristic. In D. Kahneman, P. Slovic, & A. Tversky (Eds.), *Judgment under uncertainty: Heuristics and biases* (pp. 201–210). New York: Cambridge University Press.

Kan, I.P., Barsalou, L.W., Solomon, K.O., Minor, J.K., & Thompson-Schill, S.L. (2003). Role of mental imagery in a property verification task: fMRI evidence for perceptual representations of conceptual knowledge. *Cognitive Neuropsychology, 20,* 525–540.

Kaschak, M.P., & Glenberg, A.M. (2000). Constructing meaning: The role of affordances and grammatical constructions in sentence comprehension. *Journal of Memory and Language, 43,* 508–529.

Kellas, G., Paul, S.T., Martin, M., & Simpson, G.B. (1991). Contextual feature activation and meaning access. In G.B. Simpson (Ed.), *Understanding word and sentence.* New York: Elsevier.

Klatzky, R.L., Pelligrino, J.W., McCloskey, B.P., & Doherty, S. (1989). The role of motor representations in semantic sensibility judgments. *Journal of Memory and Language, 28,* 56–77.

Kosslyn, S.M. (1976). Can imagery be distinguished from other forms of internal representation? Evidence from studies of information retrieval time. *Memory and Cognition, 4,* 291–297.

Kosslyn, S.M. (1980). *Image and mind.* Cambridge, MA: Harvard University Press.

Kosslyn, S.M. (1994). *Image and brain.* Cambridge, MA: MIT Press.

Kruschke, J.K. (1992). ALCOVE: An exemplar-based connectionist model of category learning. *Psychological Review, 99,* 22–44.

Lakoff, G., & Johnson, M. (1980). *Metaphors we live by.* Chicago: University of Chicago Press.

Lamberts, K. (1998). The time course of categorization. *Journal of Experimental Psychology: Learning, Memory and Cognition, 24,* 695–711.

Lehrer, A. (1992). Names and naming: A frame approach. In A. Lehrer & E. Kittay (Eds.), *Frames, fields, and contrasts: New essays in semantic and lexical organization* (pp. 123–142). Mahwah, NJ: Lawrence Erlbaum Associates, Inc.

Levine, D.N., Warach, J., & Farah, M.J. (1985). Two visual systems in menal imagery: Dissociation of "What" and "Where" in imagery disorders due to bilateral posterior cerebral lesions. *Neurology, 35,* 1010–1018.

Loken, B., & Ward, J. (1990). Alternative approaches to understanding the determinants of typicality. *Journal of Consumer Research, 17,* 111–126.

Lynch, E.B., Coley, J.D., & Medin, D.L. (2000). Tall is typical: Central tendency, ideal dimensions, and graded category structure among tree experts and novices. *Memory and Cognition, 28,* 41–50.

Mandler, J.M., & Parker, R.E. (1976). Memory for descriptive and spatial information in complex pictures. *Journal of Experimental Psychology: Human, Learning, and Memory, 2,* 38–48.

Mandler, J.M., & Stein, N. (1974). Recall and recognition of pictures by children as a function of organization and distractor similarity. *Journal of Experimental Psychology, 102,* 657–669.

Martin, A., Haxby, J.V., Lalonde, F.M., Wiggs, C.L., & Ungerleider, L.G. (1995). Discrete cortical regions associated with knowledge of color and knowledge of action. *Science, 270,* 102–105.

Martin, A., Ungerleider, L.G., & Haxby, J.V. (2000). Category-specificity and the brain: The sensory-motor model of semantic representations of objects. In M.S. Gazzaniga (Ed.), *The new cognitive neurosciences* (2nd edn., pp. 1023–1036). Cambridge, MA: MIT Press.

Martin, A., Wiggs, C.L., Ungerleider, L.G., & Haxby, J.V. (1996). Neural correlates of category-specific knowledge. *Nature, 379,* 649–652.

McClelland, J.L., & Rumelhart, D.E. (1985). Distributed memory and the representation of general and specific information. *Journal of Experimental Psychology: General, 114,* 159–188.

McCloskey, M., & Glucksberg, S. (1978). Natural categories: Well-defined or fuzzy sets? *Memory and Cognition, 6,* 462–472.

McRae, K., & Cree, G.S. (2002). Factors underlying category-specific deficits. In E.M.E. Forde & G.W. Humphreys (Eds.), *Category specificity in mind and brain* (pp. 211–249). Hove, UK: Psychology Press.

Medin, D.L., & Schaffer, M. (1978). A context theory of classification learning. *Psychological Review, 85,* 207–238.

Minsky, M.L. (1977). A framework for representing knowledge. In P.H. Winston (Ed.), *The psychology of computer vision* (pp. 211–277). New York: McGraw-Hill.

Murphy, G.L. (2000). Explanatory concepts. In R.A. Wilson & F.C. Keil (Eds.), *Explanation and cognition* (pp. 361–392). Cambridge, MA: MIT Press.

Murphy, G.L., & Medin, D.L. (1985). The role of theories in conceptual coherence. *Psychological Review, 92,* 289–316.

Murphy, G.L., & Wisniewski, E. (1989). Categorizing objects in isolation and in scenes: What a superordinate is good for. *Journal of Experimental Psychology, Learning, Memory and Cognition, 15,* 572–586.

Nersessian, N.J. (1999). Model-based reasoning in conceptual change. In Magnani, L., Nersessian, N.J., & Thagard, P. (Eds.) *Model-based reasoning in scientific discovery.* New York: Kluwer Academic/Plenum Publishers.

Newell, A., & Simon, H.A. (1972). *Human problem solving.* Englewood Cliffs, NJ: Prentice-Hall.

Niedenthal, P.M., Brauer, M., Halberstadt, J.B., & Innes-Ker, A.H. (2001). When did her smile drop? Facial mimicry and the influences of emotional state on the detection of change in emotional expression. *Cognition and Emotion, 15,* 853–864.

Nosofsky, R.M. (1984). Choice, similarity, and the context theory of classification. *Journal of Experimental Psychology: Learning, Memory and Cognition, 10,* 104–114.

Nosofsky, R.M., & Palmeri, T.J. (1997). An exemplar-based random walk model of speeded classification. *Psychological Review, 104,* 266–300.

Nyberg, L., Habib, R., McIntosh, A.R., & Tulving, E. (2000). Reactivation of encoding-related brain activity during memory retrieval. *Proceedings of the National Academy of Sciences of the United States of America, 97,* 11120–11124.

Paivio, A. (1986). *Mental representations: A dual coding approach.* New York: Oxford University Press.

Palmer, S.E. (1975). The effects of contextual scenes on the identification of objects. *Memory and Cognition, 3*, 519–526.

Palmer, S.E. (1999). *Vision science: Photons to phenomenology.* Cambridge, MA: MIT Press.

Parsons, L.M. (1987a). Imagined spatial transformations of one's body. *Journal of Experimental Psychology: General, 116*, 172–191.

Parsons, L.M. (1987b). Imagined spatial transformations of one's hands and feet. *Cognitive Psychology, 19*, 178–241.

Pecher, D., Zeelenberg, R., & Barsalou, L.W. (2003). Verifying different-modality properties for concepts produces switching costs. *Psychological Science, 14*, 119–124.

Perani, D., Schnur, T., Tettamanti, M., Gorno-Tempini, M., Cappa, S.F., & Fazio, F. (1999). Word and picture matching: A PET study of semantic category effects. *Neuropsychologia, 37*, 293–306.

Peterson, M.A., & Gibson, B.S. (1994). Must figure-ground organization precede object recognition? *Psychological Science, 5*, 253–259.

Potter, M.C., Kroll, J.F., Yachzel, B., Carpenter, E., & Sherman, J. (1986). Pictures in sentences: Understanding without words. *Journal of Experimental Psychology: General, 115*, 281–294.

Pulvermüller, F. (1999). Words in the brain's language. *Behavioral and Brain Sciences, 22*, 253-336.

Pylyshyn, Z.W. (1973). What the mind's eye tells the mind's brain: A critique of mental imagery. *Psychological Bulletin, 80*, 1–24.

Pylyshyn, Z.W. (1981). The imagery debate: Analogue media vs. tacit knowledge. *Psychological Review, 88*, 16–45.

Pylyshyn, Z.W. (1984). *Computation and cognition.* Cambridge, MA: MIT Press.

Ramachandran, V.S. (1992). Filling in gaps in perception: Part 1. *Current Directions in Psychological Science, 1*, 199–205.

Ramachandran, V.S. (1993). Filling in gaps in perception: Part II: Scotomas and phantom limbs. *Current Directions in Psychological Science, 2*, 56–65.

Reed, C.L., & Vinson, N.G. (1996). Conceptual effects on representational momentum. *Journal of Experimental Psychology: Human Perception and Performance, 22*, 839–850.

Reed, S.K. (1972). Pattern recognition and categorization. *Cognitive Psychology, 3*, 382–407.

Rips, L.J. (1995). The current status of research on concept combination. *Mind and Language, 10*, 72–104.

Roediger, H.L. III & McDermott, K.B. (1993). Implicit memory in normal human subjects. In F. Boller & J. Grafman (Eds.), *Handbook of neuropsychology* (Vol. 8, pp. 63–131). Amsterdam: Elsevier Science Publishers B.V.

Rosch, E. (1975). Cognitive representation of semantic categories. *Journal of Experimental Psychology: General, 104*, 192–233.

Rosch, E., & Mervis, C.B. (1975). Family resemblances: Studies in the internal structure of categories. *Cognitive Psychology, 7*, 573–605.

Rösler, F., Heil, M., & Hennighausen, E. (1995). Distinct cortical activation patterns during long-term memory retrieval of verbal, spatial, and color information. *Journal of Cognitive Neuroscience, 7*, 51–65.

Ross, B.H., & Murphy, G.L. (1999). Food for thought: Cross-classification and category organization in a complex real-world domain. *Cognitive Psychology, 38*, 495–553.

Rumelhart, D.E., Hinton, G.E., & Williams, R.J. (1986). Learning internal representations by error propagation. In D.E. Rumelhart, J.L. McClelland, & the PDP Research Group, *Parallel distributed processing. Explorations in the microstructure of cognition, Vol. 1: Foundations,* (pp. 318–362). Cambridge, MA: MIT Press.

Rumelhart, D.E., Smolensky, P., McClelland, J.L., & Hinton, G.E. (1986). Schemata and sequential thought processes in PDP models. In J.L. McClelland, J.L. & D.E. Rumelhart,

D.E., and the PDP Research Group (1986), *Parallel distributed processing. Explorations in the microstructure of cognition: Vol. 2. Psychological and biological models* (pp. 7–57). Cambridge, MA: MIT Press.

Rumelhart, D.E., & Todd, P.M. (1993). Learning and connectionist representations. In D.E. Meyer & S. Kornblum (Eds.), *Attention and performance 14: Synergies in experimental psychology, artificial intelligence, and cognitive neuroscience* (pp. 3–30). Cambridge, MA: MIT Press.

Samuel, A.G. (1997). Lexical activation produces potent phonemic percepts. *Cognitive Psychology, 32*, 97–127.

Schank, R.C., & Abelson, R.P. (1977). *Scripts, plans, goals, and understanding: An inquiry into human knowledge structures.* Hillsdale, NJ: Lawrence Erlbaum Associates, Inc.

Schooler, J.W., Fiore, S.M., & Brandimonte, M.A. (1997). At loss *from* words: Verbal overshadowing of perceptual memories. *The Psychology of Learning and Motivation, 37*, 291–340.

Schyns, P.G., Goldstone, R.L., & Thibaut, J.P. (1998). The development of features in object concepts. *Behavioral and Brain Sciences, 21*, 1–54.

Searle, J.R. (1980). Minds, brains, and programs. *Behavioral and Brain Sciences, 3*, 417–424.

Shanks, D.R. (1991). Categorization by a connectionist network. *Journal of Experimental Psychology: Learning, Memory and Cognition, 17*, 433–443.

Shepard, R.N., & Cooper, L.A. (1982). *Mental images and their transformations.* New York: Cambridge University Press.

Shiffrar, M., & Freyd, J.J. (1990). Apparent motion of the human body. *Psychological Science, 4*, 257–264.

Shiffrar, M., & Freyd, J.J. (1993). Timing and apparent motion path choice with human body photographs. *Psychological Science, 6*, 379–384.

Simmons, W.K., & Barsalou, L.W. (2003a). *Consistent actions speed visual object categorization.* Manuscript in preparation.

Simmons, W.K., & Barsalou, L.W. (2003b). The similarity-in-topography principle: Reconciling theories of conceptual deficits. *Cognitive Neuropsychology, 20*, 451–486.

Simmons, W.K, Pecher, D., Hamann, S.B, Zeelenberg, R., & Barsalou, L.W. (2003). *fMRI evidence for modality-specific processing in six modalities.* Manuscript in preparation.

Smith, E.E. (1978). Theories of semantic memory. In W.K. Estes (Ed.), *Handbook of learning and cognitive processes* (Vol. 6, pp. 1–56). Hillsdale, NJ: Lawrence Erlbaum Associates, Inc.

Smith, E.E., Osherson, D.N., Rips, L.J., & Keane, M. (1988). Combining prototypes: A selective modification model. *Cognitive Science, 12*, 485–528.

Smith, L.B. & Samuelson, L.K. (1997). Perceiving and remembering: Category stability, variability and development. In Lamberts, K. & Shanks, D.R. (Ed) *Knowledge, concepts and categories.* (pp. 161–195). Hove, UK: Psychology Press.

Smith, L.B., Thelen, E.. Titzer, R., & McLin, D. (1999). Knowing in the context of acting: The task dynamics of the A-not-B error. *Psychological Review, 106*, 235–260.

Solomon, K.O., & Barsalou, L.W. (2001). Representing properties locally. *Cognitive Psychology, 43*, 129–169.

Solomon, K.O., & Barsalou, L.W. (2003). *Perceptual simulation in property verification.* Manuscript submitted for publication.

Spence, C., Nicholls, M. E. R., & Driver, J. (2000). The cost of expecting events in the wrong sensory modality. *Perception and Psychophysics, 63*, 330–336.

Spitzer, M., Kischka, U., Gückel, F., Bellemann, M.E., Kammer, T., Seyyedi, S., Weisbrod, M., Schwartz, A., & Brix, G. (1998). Functional magnetic resonance imaging of category-specific cortical activation: Evidence for semantic maps. *Cognitive Brain Research, 6*, 309–319.

Spivey, M., & Geng, J. (2001). Oculomotor mechanisms activated by imagery and memory: Eye movements to absent objects. *Psychological Research, 65*, 235–241.

Spivey, M., Tyler, M., Richardson, D., & Young, E. (2000). Eye movements during comprehension of spoken scene descriptions. *Proceedings of the 22nd Annual Conference of the Cognitive Science Society* (pp. 487–492). Mahwah, NJ: Lawrence Erlbaum Associates, Inc.

Stanfield, R.A., & Zwaan, R.A. (2001). The effect of implied orientation derived from verbal context on picture recognition. *Psychological Science, 12*, 153–156.

Stevens, J.A., Fonlupt, P., Shiffrar, M., & Decety, J. (2000). New aspects of motion perception: Selective neural encoding of apparent human movements. *NeuroReport, 11*, 109–115.

Tabossi, P. (1988). Effects of context on the immediate interpretation of unambiguous nouns. *Journal of Experimental Psychology: Learning, Memory and Cognition, 14*, 153–162.

Tulving, E. (1972). Episodic and semantic memory. In E. Tulving & W. Donaldson (Eds.), *Organization and memory* (pp. 381–403). New York: Academic Press.

Tulving, E., & Thomson, D.M. (1973). Encoding specificity and retrieval processes in episodic memory. *Psychological Review, 80*, 352–373.

Tversky, B., & Hemenway, K. (1983). Categories of environmental scenes. *Cognitive Psychology, 15*, 121–149.

Tyler, L.K., Moss, H.E., Durrant-Peatfield, M.R., & Levy, J.P. (2000). Conceptual structure and the structure of concepts: A distributed account of category-specific deficits. *Brain and Language, 75*, 195–231.

Vallée-Tourangeau, F., Anthony, S.H., & Austin, N.G. (1998). Strategies for generating multiple instances of common and ad hoc categories. *Memory, 6*, 555–592.

Walker, W.H., & Kintsch, W. (1985). Automatic and strategic aspects of knowledge retrieval. *Cognitive Science, 9*, 261–283.

Wallbott, H.G. (1991). Recognition of emotion from facial expression via imitation? Some indirect evidence for an old theory. *British Journal of Social Psychology, 30*, 207–219.

Warren, R.M. (1970). Perceptual restoration of missing speech sounds. *Science, 167*, 392–393.

Warrington, E.K., & McCarthy, R.A. (1987). Categories of knowledge: Further fractionations and an attempted integration. *Brain, 110*, 1273–1296.

Warrington, E.K., & Shallice, T. (1984). Category specific semantic impairments. *Brain, 107*, 829–854.

Wheeler, M.E., Petersen, S.E., & Buckner, R.L. (2000). Memory's echo: Vivid remembering reactivates sensory-specific cortex. *Proceedings of the National Academy of Sciences of the United States of America, 97*, 11125–11129.

Wisniewski, E.J. (1997). When concepts combine. *Psychonomic Bulletin and Review, 4*, 167–183.

Wu, L., & Barsalou, L.W. (2003). *Perceptual simulation in property generation*. Manuscript submitted for publication.

Yeh, W., & Barsalou, L.W. (2003). *The situated character of concepts*. Manuscript submitted for publication.

Zatorre, R.J., Halpern, A.R., Perry, D.W., Meyer, E., & Evans, A.C. (1996). Hearing in the mind's ear: A PET investigation of musical imagery and perception. *Journal of Cognitive Neuroscience, 8*, 29–46.

Zeki, S. (1993). *A vision of the brain*. Oxford: Blackwell Scientific.

Zwaan, R.A., Stanfield, R.A., & Yaxley, R.H. (2002). Do language comprehenders routinely represent the shapes of objects? *Psychological Science, 13*, 168–171.

Zwaan, R.A., Stanfield, R.A., Yaxley, R.H., & Scheffers, M.K. (2001). Language comprehenders activate implied shapes: Evidence from recognition, naming, and ERP. Paper presented at the 42nd Meeting of the Psychonomic Society, Orlando, FL.

LANGUAGE AND COGNITIVE PROCESSES, 2003, *18* (5/6), 563–582

# Artifacts are not ascribed essences, nor are they treated as belonging to kinds

Steven A. Sloman

*Brown University, Providence, RI, USA*

Barbara C. Malt

*Lehigh University, Bethlehem, PA, USA*

We evaluate three theories of categorisation in the domain of artifacts. Two theories are versions of psychological essentialism; they posit that artifact categorisation is a matter of judging membership in a kind by appealing to a belief about the true, underlying nature of the object. The first version holds that the essence can be identified with the intended function of objects. The second holds that the essence can be identified with the creator's intended kind membership. The third theory is called "minimalism". It states that judgements of kind membership are based on beliefs about causal laws, not beliefs about essences. We conclude that each theory makes unnecessary assumptions in explaining how people make everyday classifications and inductions with artifacts. Essentialist theories go wrong in assuming that the belief that artifacts have essences is critical to categorisation. All theories go wrong in assuming that artifacts are treated as if they belong to stable, fixed kinds. Theories of artifact categorisation must contend with the fact that artifact categories are not stable, but rather depend on the categorisation task at hand.

Psychological essentialism is the hypothesis that object categorisation is a matter of assigning kind membership on the basis of a belief about the true, underlying nature of the object. Most of the discussion of psychological essentialism has concerned judgements about naturally occurring entities and their classification into natural kinds. Strevens

Requests for reprints should be addressed to Steven Sloman, Cognitive and Linguistic Sciences, Brown University, Box 1978, Providence, RI 02912.
Email: Steven_Sloman@brown. edu.

We thank Sergio Chaigneau, Larry Barsalou, Art Markman, James Hampton, an anonymous reviewer and especially Daniel Weiskopf for insightful and helpful comments on the manuscript. This work was funded by NASA grant NCC2-1217 and NIMH Grant MH51271.

http://www.tandf.co.uk/journals/pp/01690965.html     DOI: 10.1080/01690960344000035

(2001a) and Rips (2001) both make convincing cases against an essentialist view of everyday categorisation for naturally occurring entities. Strevens argues instead for a minimalist view. The minimalist view assumes that categorisation is a matter of judging kind membership but that these judgements are based on beliefs about causal laws, not beliefs about true, underlying natures. In this paper, we consider three theories, two essentialist ones and Strevens' minimalist view, and examine their application to artifact categories. Each theory must contend with the fact that artifact categories are not stable, but rather depend on the categorisation task at hand.

## ESSENTIALIST VIEWS OF ARTIFACTS: I. INTENDED FUNCTION AS ESSENCE

Essentialism started life as a theory of word meaning (Kripke, 1972; Putnam, 1975). The original idea was that an individual language speaker using a natural kind term is expressing the term's meaning by appealing to a linguistic convention and not to a mental representation. The arbiter of word usage is an expert (hypothetical or not) who acts as an authority on whether an object is appropriately called by a word. A fundamental requirement of this view of word meaning is that some underlying property or properties that constitute the essence of an individual entity determine the appropriate name for that entity (Gelman & Hirschfeld, 1999). These properties are not necessarily known by an ordinary (lay) speaker and are not even necessarily knowable by such a speaker. Sometimes they are not even fully known by the expert (who may revise his or her beliefs about the essence as scientific knowledge grows). The minimum criterion is only that properties are assumed that an authority could in principle inspect to evaluate whether an object is appropriately labelled by the kind term.

Psychological essentialism, as introduced by Medin and Ortony (1989), concerns not words, but concepts. It is intended as a theory of how people judge an object's kind. Although it does not make a claim about the existence of metaphysical essences, it shares with original essentialism the ideas that people believe entities have essences and that these beliefs provide the basis for their judgements of an object's kind. As such, it makes two assumptions: first, that people treat objects as belonging to stable kinds; second, that people determine kind by appealing to a shared essence. Our discussion concerns both these issues. Like all discussions of psychological essentialism, our focus is psychological, not metaphysical. We are not concerned with whether kinds in the world truly have essences, but with whether beliefs about essences are causally relevant to everyday behaviour. We examine whether beliefs about essences and kinds are causally relevant to judgements about objects' names, properties, and relations to other objects, and not whether those beliefs correspond to metaphysical reality.

According to psychological essentialists (Gelman & Hirschfeld, 1999; Keil, 1995; Medin & Ortony, 1989), people evaluate an object's kind on the basis of their beliefs about the causes of the object's observable properties. They treat the most basic causes, those on which all others depend, as the object's essence. Is it possible to characterise beliefs about such basic causes in the domain of artifacts—human-made entities? If not, doubt is raised about the psychological reality of both essences and, correspondingly, kinds in the domain of artifacts.

One possibility is that artifacts judged to belong to a particular kind all serve a particular function. Something is considered to be a pen if it is used for permanent writing, something is considered to be a boat if it is used for travelling on water. The function would determine the observable properties of the object. Pens are long and thin to fit rigidly in the hand and they contain ink to write with. Boats have a shape that allows them to float while moving forward on water. Therefore, the function of an artifact might be treated as that object's essence, and objects that share that essence will be judged to belong to the same kind. Note, though, that an artifact's function is not actually the most basic cause of its observable properties; in fact, function is usually the effect of an object's observable properties when used by an agent in a certain environment (Barsalou, Sloman, & Chaigneau, in press). The shape of the boat causes it to be able to travel on water. The most basic cause is not its function per se, but its intended function, something in the mind of a user or creator that explains why the object was constructed as it is. So, one essentialist view is that, by virtue of its causal centrality, the intended function of an artifact is treated as its essence (Ahn et al., 2001; Keil, 1989; Rips, 1989).

However, the intended function view of artifact essences suffers from several difficulties:

1. Some groups of objects don't have obvious intended functions, and those that do may not be distinguished from one another by their function.

For some objects, like computers or duct tape, it is hard to say what the intended function is. At best one can state only a very general function, such as "to assist in work" or "to hold things together", functions that do not separate these objects from those that would be called by other names. Even when more detailed functions can be given, such functions may not effectively separate members of contrasting categories (Malt & Johnson, 1992). The intended function of a boat may be to transport people and goods across the surface of the water, but so is the intended function of a raft.

2. An object's intended function is dependent on the particular goals of an agent at a particular time, and on its particular history of use.

Objects can have many intended functions (Barsalou et al., in press). One intended function is that of the artifact's maker (assuming the maker has only one function in mind). But sometimes objects have multiple, independent creators each with a different function in mind, like when a spittoon is turned into an ashtray. The creator of the spittoon has a different intended function for the object than the creator of the ashtray. Furthermore, sometimes the same sort of object is created by different makers for different purposes. For example, broomsticks are usually created with one intended function (to sweep the floor), but sometimes they are created with another (in Harry Potter novels, to fly).

These examples pose a problem for the view that intended function provides the basis for a unique judgement of kind membership for an object. They do not by themselves rule out the possibility that objects can be considered to belong to multiple kinds. Perhaps each intended function of an object places the object in a distinct category. However, as the number of categories that an object is judged to belong to increases, it becomes less plausible that people believe an object has a true, underlying nature that determines its kind membership.

3. When people are asked to judge an object's kind on the basis of either intended function or physical features, physical features are sometimes given more weight.

Malt and Johnson (1992) found substantial use of physical features in decisions about artificial stimuli modelled closely on real artifacts (see also Hampton, 1995; Landau, Smith, & Jones, 1998). Some novel objects having the intended function of a familiar category but divergent physical features were judged not to belong to the category, and some having a novel intended function but normal physical features of the category were judged to belong. This pattern is also seen in everyday life, such as in the case of a pizza cutter, which is distinguished from a knife on the basis of divergent form despite sharing the function of knives, and a frosting knife, which is called a knife on the basis of similar form despite divergent function.

Studies examining how much weight people give to functional versus physical information when naming real objects have found corresponding results. Sloman, Malt, and Fridman (2001) tried to predict the names given to common containers (bottles, jars, jugs, boxes, cartons, etc.) and kitchenware (dishes, plates, and bowls) using similarity judgements and three formal classification models: a prototype model, a nearest neighbour model, and a weighted sum model that combined name and similarity information across exemplars. Predictions were made using each of three types of similarity judgement: functional, physical, or overall. No single type of similarity was consistently better able than any other to account for the category names that people assigned the objects regardless of the classification model used. We also examined the degree to which the names could be accounted for by specific features. Two sets of featural descriptions of the objects were fed into a Bayesian classification model to try to predict the names. Physical features were consistently better than functional features at accounting for names, although not always significantly. Together, these results indicate that function is not given precedence over form in determining what people call common containers.

4. What is the relevant category? Dissociations between naming and similarity judgement imply that beliefs about essences associated with conceptual groupings are not consistent with linguistic categories.

Philosophical essentialism identifies essences with kinds. Change the essence under discussion and the kind changes (by definition); choose a different kind and a different essence is automatically relevant. Such a definition is not susceptible to empirical argument and is not at issue here. Psychological essentialism, however, frames the relation in terms of a judgement process: Beliefs about essences are causally relevant to judgements of category membership; people use their knowledge of essential properties to help them pick out members of a category. Testing such a theory requires two operational definitions: (i) a sufficiently well-formulated definition of essence (e.g., intended function), and (ii) an independent means to decide what people consider to be in the category (the set of actual or hypothetical objects that they take to constitute a kind). Only with both in hand is it possible to test the psychological essentialist hypothesis by seeing if (i) and (ii) correspond. But what should serve as operational definition (ii), what determines a category extension?

A common assumption, pervasive in arguments for psychological essentialism (e.g., Gelman & Hirschfeld, 1999), is that the category comprises all those objects that are given a particular label. Chairs are those objects called "chair". This simple solution fails though because different languages partition the space of artifacts in different ways. Kronenfeld, Armstrong, and Wilmoth (1985) had speakers of English, Hebrew, and Japanese name 11 drinking vessels and found that the languages grouped the objects by name differently. For instance, the Americans gave the same name to a paper drinking vessel and one for drinking tea ("cup"), but the Israelis gave them two different names. In a larger-scale study, Malt, Sloman, Gennari, Shi, and Wang (1999) compared the names for 60 common containers given by speakers of American English, Mandarin Chinese, and Argentinean Spanish, and found that the composition of the categories differed across the three languages. For instance, the 16 objects named "bottle" in English were spread across seven different linguistic categories in Spanish. The Chinese category that contained the 19 objects called "jar" in English also included 13 objects called "bottle" in English and eight called "container", although others called "bottle" or "container" appeared in different Chinese categories. Artifacts do not seem to be grouped into universal linguistic categories; languages categorise them in their own, idiosyncratic ways. Whatever knowledge English speakers draw on in grouping these objects by name, it is not the same as that used by Chinese or Spanish speakers.

Perhaps speakers of different languages just appeal to different essences. This would be fine if the issue at hand were only word use. The linguistic conventions in different languages apparently are different and people could use different criteria in forming beliefs about an object's essence and thereby if the object warranted a particular name. But psychological essentialism is not most directly concerned with word use; it is a theory about concepts. And according to the theory, the essence is what people believe to be the fundamental cause of the object's observable properties. Speakers of different languages surely do not assume different fundamental causes. The causal laws governing a container of soda are bound to be understood in the same way by speakers of English, Chinese, and Spanish. Indeed, similarity judgements of these speakers suggest that they are. Malt et al. (1999) found that, even though the speakers had made different linguistic judgments about the objects, they made almost identical similarity judgements. When asked to sort the objects into piles according to their physical, functional, or overall similarity, the differences between the speaker groups were about the same as the differences within each group. So linguistic categories do not map directly onto the conceptual groupings that underlie similarity judgements, suggesting that if conceptual groupings have essences, and if linguistic groupings have essences, they are not the same. Sloman and Ahn (1999) provide another example of a dissociation between linguistic and non-linguistic task performance.

In sum, the cross-linguistic data indicate that we cannot appeal to labels to decide what comprises the category whose members are believed to share an essence (see Rips, 2001, for a contrasting view). This is a problem for essentialism because there is no clear alternative to appeal to. Obviously, we cannot appeal to objects' functions because that would quickly become circular for the intended function view (the essence of the group of things intended to pound nails is that they were created to pound nails). Can we appeal to objects' inductive potential (as, e.g., Mak & Vera, 1999, and Mandler & McDonough, 1998, do)? Are there conceptual groupings consisting of all and only those things that support similar inductions? The problem here is the lack of an independent basis for determining the relevant inductions. We cannot use just any induction because patterns of induction are property-specific (Heit & Rubinstein, 1994; Sloman, 1994). A grouping of carnivores vs. insectivores supports some inductions (if an owl eats it, that makes it more likely that a bobcat eats it), but not other kinds of inductions (just because an owl has sesamoid bones does not mean a bobcat does). Other groupings (e.g., birds vs. mammals) might support the latter but not the former. So patterns of induction do not provide a unique segregation of objects into kinds.

One might object to our argument as applied to the domain of our example, natural kinds, because natural kinds exhibit clusters of correlated properties (Rosch & Mervis, 1975). To the extent that these correlated properties result in the perception of well-articulated clusters of instances separated by large gaps, then the resulting clusters will support inductions better than any classification that cross-cuts the clusters. What the example shows is that inductive power is gained by considering multiple classification schemes for the same set of objects, and human induction shows this more flexible character. In any case, artifacts show less clustering of ascribed properties than natural kinds do (Keil, 1995; Malt et al., 1999).

Can we determine the relevant groupings by appealing to causal structure (an object belongs to a particular conceptual group if it obeys certain causal laws) as Rips (2001) suggests? Perhaps, but not in a way that is independent of the presumed essence. Essences are defined as fundamental causes, so essentialists already appeal to causal structure to define the notion of essence. Therefore, they cannot also use causal structure to determine what the relevant grouping is because that, again, would be circular. The theory would be predicting merely that the beliefs people hold about the causal structure of objects determine the sets of things that they believe share a causal structure.

In conclusion, the view that intended function constitutes the essence of artifacts does not seem to help explain how people determine an artifact's kind. We next consider a different definition of essence to see if that withstands scrutiny.

## ESSENTIALIST VIEWS OF ARTIFACTS:
## II. CREATOR'S INTENTION AS ESSENCE

Bloom (1996) has offered an alternative essentialist view of judgements of category membership: that people take an object's category to be whatever the maker intended it to be. They classify something as a chair if they believe it was created to be a chair. On this view, people take the maker's intended category membership as the essence of the category. This theory is not vulnerable to Problems 1, 2, or 3 above because it does not rely on function to define the essence. The fact that functions or intended functions are not regularly given priority in naming decisions is not a problem for the same reason. This view does face some difficulties though.

1. Without some independent notion of category identity, the view cannot be tested.

Like the first version of essentialism, testing this view is faced with the problem of circularity. To determine if belief in an essence is the determinant of judged kind membership requires that the essence and category be independently defined. Beliefs about intended function cannot serve to define the relevant categories for the reasons stated in Part I. Nor can we appeal to inductive potential or causal structure, also for reasons given above.

Bloom (1996) often appeals to names, implying that a category is the set of things that a label applies to. But this leads to another problem discussed above: Cross-linguistic differences imply that the essence cannot be associated with a linguistic label unless the essence is understood as something that is language relative. Could beliefs about the maker's intended linguistic category membership for different objects be different in different linguistic communities? Presumably, an American manufacturer of two objects could intend for them both to be labelled "bottle" and a Spanish maker of the same two sorts of objects could intend for them to be called by two different names, e.g., "tarro" and "mamadera". In this case, Bloom would have to say that speakers of the different languages (somehow) understand these different intentions for the same objects. But how would speakers figure out the different intentions? It cannot be via the name they would use for the objects, because that is the thing to be explained. Furthermore, in Malt et al. (1999), the very same set of objects were named differently by speakers of different languages. So it could not possibly be the case that linguistic differences can be reduced to (correct) understanding of different creators' intentions: The events of creation were identical, yet the linguistic categories assigned were different. At best, the linguistic differences might be attributed to mistaken inferences of different intended membership by speakers of different languages. But then the basis for their differing inferences is the crucial point to account for, and it remains unexplained.

Finally, the cross-cultural dissociations between language and similarity reported by Malt et al. (1999) must somehow be accommodated by this view. One possible resolution is that people across cultures share beliefs about makers' intended membership and these beliefs serve as the essence, not of the linguistic categories that vary across cultures, but of the conceptual groupings that our similarity judgements suggest are close to universal. Bloom (1996) is blocked from making this move, however, because his goal is to explain what objects are called, not their nonlinguistic groupings. In any case, nonlinguistic groupings themselves can vary with the nonlinguistic task used (see below).

2. When creator's intended category membership is pitted against other aspects of the objects such as physical structure, kind judgements are sometimes governed by the other aspects.

A second problem for this theory of artifact categorisation was revealed by Chaigneau (2002; see Barsalou, Sloman, & Chaigneau, in press). He considered cases where people have privileged access to the creator's intended category membership by being told it. He pitted such knowledge against other aspects of the object and considered their relative importance in judgements of the appropriateness of a label (as well as judgements of the object's function and the object's causal efficacy). He described scenarios in which one of four aspects of a common object (e.g., a mop) was unusual (different from that of a normal object): its intended category membership, its physical features, the agent's intended use for the object, or the actions performed with the object. To create an unusual intended category membership, Chaigneau described an accidental creation scenario to participants in which the object was not created for any particular purpose. For example, Jane accidentally attached a bundle of thick cloth to a 4-foot long stick and John subsequently used it to wipe up a water spill. To create unusual physical features, a scenario was described in which the object was created to be a mop but was not normal physically. For example, John wiped up water with an object that was made to wipe up spilled water, but the object was a bundle of plastic bags attached to a 4-foot long stick. In the two remaining mop scenarios, the object was intended to be a mop. In one, the agent used the artifact normally but unintentionally (John accidentally pressed the object against a water spill). In the other, the agent performed unusual actions with the object (John pressed the wooden stick rather than the cloth against the water spill).

What Chaigneau (2002) found was that the creator's intended category membership was not the most important variable for any rating task. Most relevant here, changing the creator's intended category membership had less effect on judgements of the goodness of a name than changing the object's physical structure did. A bundle of plastic bags attached to a stick was judged to be less appropriately called a "mop", even though it was intended to be a mop, than an object created by accident that served the wiping up water function very well. People's choice of names were clearly not primarily guided by intended category membership.

These results seem to contrast with those of Gelman and Bloom (2000), Keil (1989), Matan and Carey (2001), and Rips (1989). Rips, for example, asked people whether an object created to be a lampshade but with the physical structure of an umbrella was more likely to be an umbrella or a lampshade. Most people thought it was more likely to be a lampshade, a result that would seem to favour the importance of historical creation over physical structure for kind membership. Those studies differ from Chaigneau's (2002) in several ways. For one, Chaigneau specified the physical structure of his objects precisely (e.g., a 4-foot stick with a bundle of plastic bags attached to one end). In contrast, Rips' descriptions left room for interpretation. For example, one description said the object was "a collapsible fabric dome. It consists of multicolored waterproof fabric stretched taut across six metal struts radiating from a central post in the dome. The metal struts are jointed so that they may be folded and this allows the fabric dome to be collapsed. When fully extended the dome is about three feet wide. [The creator] intended for this object to be used with the inside of the dome facing up as an attachment to ceiling light fixtures ..." Although the description includes a lot of detail and the object is clearly similar to an umbrella, it does not say explicitly that the object has the physical structure necessary to function as an umbrella (e.g., is the fabric permeable?). In contrast, it must have the physical structure necessary to function as a lampshade, because that is what it was intended to be. In Rips' control condition, in which the object clearly does have the physical structure necessary to serve as an umbrella, people were more likely to consider it an umbrella than a lampshade. Hence, the experimental description had just enough ambiguity to allow physical structure to be interpreted in a way consistent with the rest of the story, with the result that the experiment, unlike Chaigneau's, did not directly pit a fixed physical structure against creator's intention. In general, participants' judgements seem to be more closely aligned with the objects' physical structure, or inferred physical structure, than with any other aspect of the object, including its intended category membership.

Like those of Malt et al. (1999) and Sloman and Ahn (1999), Chaigneau's (2002) data show a divergence between naming and conceptual judgements (also see Gennari, Sloman, Malt, & Fitch, 2002). The various scenario aspects showed a different pattern of effects on judgements of naming and judgements of function (as well as judgements of causal efficacy). For example, the agent's actions had more influence on naming than function ratings. This provides further evidence against the possibility that conceptual groupings could be grounded in linguistic ones.

## CONCLUSIONS REGARDING ESSENTIALISM

All in all, psychological essentialism suffers from several critical problems when applied to artifacts. One virtue of essentialism, however, is that it seems to offer a way to think about how people are able to have *modal* beliefs; that is, beliefs about what would be true about an object even if it had properties other than those it actually does have (Rips, 2001). Consider an animal that has all the properties of a giraffe except that it has stripes instead of spots. If you believe that such a beast would be a giraffe, this is a modal belief because presumably no such animal actually exists. What supports this belief? Not direct experience because one cannot have experience of things that do not exist. The essentialist answer is that our belief in essences is what makes such beliefs possible. The belief that giraffes have some true, underlying nature that imparts kind identity and that this nature is the cause of giraffes' observable properties would lead one to conclude, given enough causal knowledge, that spots and stripes are merely observable effects of more fundamental, essential properties. As long as our hypothetical animal retains the essence of the category, it should be judged a category member regardless of its appearance.

But Rips (2001) points out that essentialism is not the only theory available to explain the existence of modal beliefs. A different type of theory appeals, not to intrinsic properties like essences, but to extrinsic relations that objects have with their environments. Modal beliefs could be supported by knowledge of the role that objects play in causal interactions with other things. Something with stripes would still be a giraffe because having stripes would not change the causal relations between the animal and its niche. It could still be its parents' progeny, it could still breathe oxygen, it could still eat leaves high off the ground, etc. And these beliefs about objects' causal interactions with their environments do not depend on beliefs in essences; in fact, often they are mediated by very superficial properties.

## THE MINIMALIST VIEW

Strevens (2001a) makes an argument against essentialism related to Rips' (2001). He points out that essentialism explains categorisation and inductive judgements of biological and chemical categories by positing that people (a) have a belief that the relevant category has an essential property and (b) have causal knowledge about the category. Strevens' argument is that only (b) is actually relevant to explaining what people do on categorisation and induction tasks.

To understand the flavour of Strevens' argument, first consider his analysis of how essentialism explains an experiment reported in Keil (1989) (Strevens actually considers three variants of essentialism). Keil told both children and adults of an animal (e.g., a raccoon) that had been transformed cosmetically to appear just like a different animal (e.g., a skunk, by adding a distinctive odour, white stripe down its back, etc.). When asked if the animal is a skunk or a raccoon, 2nd graders and adults tended to call it a raccoon (though kindergartners tended to call it a skunk). The essentialist account of the older participants' responses posits that people use causal knowledge to decide which of an object's features are most likely to be direct causal consequences of being a category member. The most direct causal consequences have the most influence in categorisation decisions because they are the least defeasible. Explaining how a raccoon could have a stripe on its back is easier (because someone could have painted it there) than explaining how a skunk could have begun life as a raccoon. Because the causal inference explaining how this strange creature could be a raccoon is easier to construct than the one explaining how it could be a skunk, we call it a raccoon. In general, properties are given more weight in the categorisation decision to the extent they are causally central (Ahn, 1998) because the ease of explaining away a property is inversely proportional to its centrality (Sloman, Love, & Ahn, 1998). Note that essence plays no role in the explanation of the data. Keil examined not only animal transformations but also transformations of one artifact to another (e.g., a kitchen pipe that is turned into a flute). He found that all participants were more likely to say that a kitchen pipe with holes that can be used to make music is more likely to be a flute than a kitchen pipe. This can also be explained by appealing to defeasibility conditions derived from a causal analysis of object properties. An explanation for why something with holes that can be used to make music would be a flute is easier to generate than for why it would be a kitchen pipe.

Essentialism provides a related account of how inductions about generic, unfamiliar properties are made. A property is projected from one entity to another to the degree that a causal analysis leads to certainty that the properties of the two entities have a common source (a claim like this is made, for example, by Gelman, 1988).

Strevens (2001a) makes two important points. First, he argues that causal knowledge comes in the form of universal categorical assertions that he calls K-laws. K-laws have the form "All Ks have P" in which K is a natural kind and P is an observable property (e.g., all raccoons have raccoon parents by virtue of the causal process of reproduction). Second, he argues that K-laws do all the work in explaining categorisation and induction, that any further assumption that categories have essences is superfluous and unnecessary. He therefore posits a non-essentialist theory of categorisation that he calls minimalism, that categorisation and induction are driven by knowledge of K-laws (no essence required).

Strevens (2001b) is not willing to extend his argument to artifacts. His unwillingness could arise for several reasons. We consider four possibilities: (i) There is a dearth of clear causal laws governing artifacts. Many properties of artifacts are arbitrary, unconnected to any causal system inherent to the object. The colour and texture of telephones, refrigerators, cups, etc. are independent of the other properties of those objects. More generally, many properties of artifacts concern aesthetics and design and can be selected with minimal consideration of the object's causal properties and therefore are unrelated to a causal system specific to the object. (ii) Relatedly, artifacts—individually or in groups—support fewer inductions than natural kinds because their properties do not occur in such tightly clustered sets. For instance, the fact that a screwdriver has some property or component is a weak reason to project the property to any other artifact because the property or component is likely to be specific to activities involving the screwdriver, or it may be there for aesthetic reasons. (iii) Many artifacts have little or no internal structure. The structure of a plate or a table is simple and does not lend itself to much causal analysis. (iv) Finally, members of natural kinds tend to evolve or develop in a specific niche, governed by fixed causal laws. In contrast, artifacts can emerge in multiple environments in multiple ways and can serve many roles, sometimes simultaneously. To illustrate, jars have emerged in many forms (ceramic, tin, glass) in many societies, often to serve different functions (to store wine, to carry water, even to bake cakes). With so many roles to play, there may not be a fixed set of causal laws governing them.

But all of these arguments concern matters of degree, not fundamental differences between artifacts and natural kinds. We consider each possibility in turn. (i) Many properties of artifacts are arbitrary, but many are not. The colour of a telephone may be arbitrary, but it should have a microphone and a speaker, and these should be positioned to allow use by someone with a mouth and an ear in the specific locations that one finds them on the human head. Pens should be graspable, and they should extrude ink at a constant rate. (ii) Most artifacts support fewer inductions than natural kinds, but all support some. In fact, Farrar, Raney, and Boyer (1992) and Sloman (1998) found no difference between the number of inferences drawn from artifacts and natural kinds. Even if all one knows is that an object is a paperweight, one can induce that its mass is within a certain range. Moreover, some artifacts allow more inductions than some natural kinds. Knowing the properties of cars offers many hints about the properties of trucks. Not many of the properties of clouds, a natural kind, generalize to other entities. (iii) Most artifacts do not have much internal structure, but some have a great deal (cars, rocketships, computers, clocks, player pianos, etc.). More importantly, artifacts have critical causal structure, namely the relations between their parts and operations and the function they serve to the external agent who uses them (or even just appreciates them). (iv) Although some artifacts have a variety of functions, others do not (e.g., an atomic clock). And even for those that do, a multiplicity of functions does not imply that the object is not governed by a fixed set of causal laws. The laws may vary with the function, but that just means they are context-specific, not absent. Often a minimal set does carry over from context to context. In the example above of a jar, the causal laws related to containment apply throughout. In sum, we see no principled reason to limit any theory of how people categorise to natural kinds or artifacts alone. The two domains differ in central tendency, but they overlap (Keil, 1989; Markman, 1989).

If minimalism does apply to artifacts as much as natural kinds, then Strevens' (2001a) argument against essentialism should apply to artifacts as much as to natural kinds. The claim of such an argument would be that, once assumptions about causal knowledge are made, no assumption about essence is necessary to explain how people group or make inductions about artifacts. Presumably, the relevant causal knowledge for artifacts would be twofold. First, it would concern how creators' intentions get realised in physical media such that objects are created to perform certain functions. Second, it would concern how agents use objects to actually perform particular functions. Once this causal knowledge and its relation to judgement is spelled out (as it is in Barsalou et al., in press), no notion of essence—of a true underlying nature that confers kind identity—does further explanatory work because there is no more work to do.

## HOW DOES THE MINIMALIST VIEW FARE WITH ARTIFACTS?

Minimalism describes the causal knowledge enabling categorisation in terms of K-laws, universally quantified relations between kinds and properties. Applying the theory to artifacts, an example of a K-law might be "all hammers pound nails", where *hammers* refers to a kind and *pound nails* to a property that is a causal effect afforded by being a hammer.

But do we need to assume that the causal beliefs people use to make judgements and to reason about objects are beliefs about a relation of causal properties to kinds per se? A theory even more minimal than minimalism may be sufficient to explain most nonlinguistic judgements about artifacts. Such a superminimalist theory would dispense not only with the assumption that judgements about kinds are determined by an essence as minimalism does (Strevens, 2001c), but also with the assumption that causal beliefs about artifacts are organised around kinds at all.

One suggestion of the Malt et al. (1999) work is that common containers do not have a single natural partitioning, but rather different tasks and different languages partition them in different ways. These partitionings depend on the demands of the specific categorisation task and historically derived conventions about how to perform the task. Other studies have shown that inductions are not governed by a fixed category structure but rather depend on specific task demands (Heit & Rubinstein, 1994; Sloman, 1998).

Such task relativity suggests that objects of the type we have studied are not perceived as belonging to any one kind of thing; their classification depends on the purpose of the task. Different tasks have different goals and people excel at learning to attend to properties and structural relations that satisfy their goals. The relativity of category structure is consistent with McCloskey and Glucksberg's (1978) finding that people vary considerably in their category judgements from day to day. In their data, 25% of instances received a different category assignment (measured as the name given) from the same participant a month later.

In science, causal powers are carried by properties, not by objects per se. Diamond cuts granite because of their relative hardnesses. If a piece of granite were sufficiently hard, diamond would not cut it. Indeed, causal laws in science describe relations between properties, not kinds (e.g., $F = ma$ can be construed as a causal relation amongst three properties that hold regardless of which object is in motion). The fact that science organises causal knowledge around properties, not kinds, suggests—at minimum—that that is a good way to understand things. People may take advantage of this organisational principle, at least for artifacts. In other words, even if causal knowledge is not organised around kinds, causal laws may still govern judgement about artifacts (if it is impermeable to water, it can store liquids; if it is sufficiently flat, it can be used to serve food). But these are not K-laws because they do not relate kinds to properties; instead they relate properties to properties.

Organising causal knowledge around properties rather than kinds supports flexibility and task relativity because the properties relevant to a task can usually be selected and attended to with relative ease. Massive task relativity does not make as much sense for living things as it does for artifacts. The notion of kind is critical to folk classification and induction of living things, which tend to be consistent across cultures (López, Atran, Coley, Medin, & Smith, 1997; Malt, 1995; note however that McCloskey & Glucksberg's, 1978, data show equal variability across time in category judgements between natural kinds and artifacts and Sloman, 1998, showed systematic neglect of category structure in inductions over living things). This is a consequence of biology; many important generalisations apply to living things at levels more abstract than those that apply to artifacts (e.g., for all living things: if its parents are of kind X, then it is an X; if it is of kind X, then it has a particular physical structure). The kinds relevant to these abstract inference rules are stable enough, and the inferences are important enough in our daily lives, that they are part of our inventory of everyday inference rules.

These abstract inference rules that take kinds as arguments are more prevalent and provide more inductive power in biology than in the artifact domain. Relatively few abstract inference rules apply to artifacts, especially very general rules. Even apparently strong ones like "if it is a vehicle, then it transports people or things" admit of many exceptions (junkyards are full of them). Another difference between natural kinds and artifacts, as we have already noted, is that many natural kinds, especially those encompassing living things, cluster more tightly in similarity space with larger gaps between clusters than artifacts do (though cf. Malt, 1994, on water). As a result, natural kinds are likely to show less divergence across tasks and cultures than artifacts.

## CONCLUSION

We conclude that psychological essentialism and minimalism are both underdetermined by the evidence in the artifact domain. Psychological essentialism suffers from inadequacies in the characterisation of essence either as intended function or in terms of creators' intention. Also, the task relativity of judgement makes the theory untestable because no independent, acceptable method exists to determine whether people assign an object to a "kind". Both types of theory make unnecessary assumptions, namely that categorisation is determined by a belief in essences (essentialism) and that people group artifacts into stable clusters constituting kinds (essentialism and minimalism). These assumptions are unnecessary because both essentialism and minimalism require further assumptions about causal knowledge relating properties to one another to explain how people make classification and induction judgements, and those further assumptions are sufficient to explain the judgements.

Both essentialism and minimalism go wrong in assuming that people represent artifact kinds with a stable set of beliefs separate and distinct from the tasks used to classify objects. We propose that there are no fixed artifact categories in the head. Artifact categories have no fixed boundaries, even fuzzy ones. Of course, objects cluster in particular contexts; they are more or less similar to one another in those contexts. However, to say that objects cluster in some conceptual space is not to say that objects must be understood as of one kind or another. The fact that judgements of similarity are notoriously labile means that an appeal to similarity cannot impart confidence in the stability of category structure. Similarity judgements depend on a host of contextual factors (knowledge of the judge, the set being judged, the nature of the similarity judgement task; Sloman & Rips, 1998; see Medin, Goldstone, & Gentner, 1993, for a review). Induction tasks impose their own structure on objects. In the case of induction, that structure depends on a causal analysis of the specific property being projected. Other tasks may result in yet other groupings. For instance, it is an open question how the space of objects would be cut up by recognition memory. Confusions in recognition can be construed as a measure of similarity, but they can differ systematically from explicit similarity judgements (e.g., Gennari et al., 2002). One reason is that recognition is known to be sensitive to frequency, whereas similarity is less so.

Therefore, artifact categories depend on how the categories are elicited—on the categorisation task at hand. Naming is one categorisation task that cuts up the space of artifact objects, but different languages do it differently. And the way each does it is conventionalised, depending on the specific history and structure of the language. Naming is also governed by the specialised purpose of language—to communicate—and the communicative context may have specific effects on the names people choose (e.g., Brennan & Clark, 1996; Malt & Sloman, 2001). Obviously, people use language to learn about the properties of artifacts and indeed linguistic labels are sometimes given priority in the inductive process even by young children (e.g., Gelman & Markman, 1986). Presumably, this is because linguistic cues are extremely effective pointers to the existence of shared structure between objects. But this does not mean that linguistic categories are mirrored by non-linguistic mental representations that underlie object knowledge. It merely means that words used appropriately in context can be effective pointers to non-linguistic structure. Surely non-linguistic structure exists. For example, artifacts share more or less causal structure with one another. And such structure is indeed correlated with the names we give things. But the correlation is far from perfect because we do different things with it as required by specific tasks. Moreover, tasks add their own constraints. We have argued that causal knowledge is organised around property relations and not around kinds for exactly that reason: so that different tasks can pick out the relevant bits of knowledge. A well-designed conceptual system should not have fixed boundaries when the knowledge plays a variety of different roles. Allowing different tasks to partition objects differently according to their demands enhances the system's flexibility.

Our conclusion is inconsistent with theories other than just essentialism and minimalism. It is inconsistent with any theory that assumes that kinds are fundamental, such as theories that assume defining features for category membership or theories that explicitly impose category boundaries in their representation (e.g., Ashby, 1992). It is also inconsistent with exemplar theories that assume that exemplars are stored with a single category label because the labels impose an implicit boundary (Kruschke,

1992; Nosofsky, 1988). A different type of exemplar model would remain tenable though, one that does not store a label with each exemplar. Labels could either be stored independently or multiple labels might be stored with each object. Such a representation could allow category boundaries to vary with the task by differentially weighting exemplars to generate a response, with the weighting depending on task demands. Of course, how causal structure can be abstracted from an exemplar representation remains an open (and difficult) question.

Our claim that artifacts do not come in kinds violates a strong intuition. It seems right to say that a hammer is a hammer, it is not a nail; the two objects are of fundamentally different kinds. How can we say otherwise? Relatedly (but not equivalently), how can we say that essences do not matter when people feel so sure that they do? Remember that the cross-linguistic data we have described indicate that the linguistic intuition must be separated from the conceptual one. We agree that an object that all English speakers would call a "hammer" should almost never be called a "nail". Not only would that violate Gricean maxims of cooperativeness, nobody would know what you were referring to. Our claim is not that objects do not have better or worse names in a particular language. Patterns of naming do yield linguistic category boundaries. However, those linguistic categories are a function of particular linguistic and cultural histories (Malt et al., 1999) and objects' roles in systems of relations (Barsalou et al., in press; Markman & Stillwell, 2001; Rips, 2001) as much as of inherent properties of the objects. Our claim is that talking about an artifact's kind does not help us much to explain how people perform everyday conceptual classification and inductive judgement tasks. This claim can be true even if people believe that artifacts come in kinds. People can hold beliefs about essences and beliefs about how essences relate to kind membership without those beliefs having any causal relation to judgements that put object knowledge to use.

Why do people have such strong intuitions about kinds? We suspect that the intuition derives at least in part from the ease and automaticity with which people represent knowledge using language. People do have knowledge about artifacts, such as causal knowledge about how properties relate to other properties, and giving an object a name is often intended to convey that knowledge. If my uncle points at a machine across the street and says "that's a trencher", he is asserting that he knows it is for digging trenches, that he knows enough about its parts and their relations to determine its function, and that he knows the English convention for labelling the machine. It is a small step from the ability to use language to demonstrate our knowledge of objects to the belief that the successful use of a name for an object reflects a category membership that the object must hold by virtue of its properties.

# REFERENCES

Ahn, W. (1998). Why are different features central for natural kinds and artifacts? The role of causal status in determining feature centrality. *Cognition, 69,* 135–178.

Ahn, W-K., Kalish, C., Gelman, S.A., Medin, D.L., Luhmann, C., Atran, S., Coley, J.D., & Shafto, P. (2001). Why essences are essential in the psychology of concepts. *Cognition, 82,* 59–69.

Ashby, F.G. (1992). Multidimensional models of categorization. In F.G. Ashby (Ed.). *Multidimensional models of perception and cognition.* Hillsdale, NJ: Lawrence Erlbaum Associates, Inc.

Barsalou, L.W., Sloman, S.A., & Chaigneau, S.E. (in press). The HIPE theory of function. In L. Carlson & E. van der Zee (Eds.), *Representing functional features for language and space: Insights from perception, categorization and development.* New York: Oxford University.

Bloom, P. (1996). Intention, history, and artifact concepts. *Cognition, 60,* 1–29.

Brennan, S.E., & Clark, H.H. (1996). Conceptual pacts and lexical choice in conversation. *Journal of Experimental Psychology: Learning, Memory, and Cognition, 22,* 1482–1493.

Chaigneau, S.E. (2002). Studies in the conceptual structure of object function. Doctoral dissertation, Department of Psychology, Emory University, Atlanta, GA.

Farrar, M.J., Raney, G.E., & Boyer, M.E. (1992). Knowledge, concepts, and inferences in childhood. *Child Development, 63,* 673–691.

Gelman, S.A. (1988). The development of induction within natural kind and artifact categories. *Cognitive Psychology, 20,* 65–95.

Gelman, S.A., & Bloom, P. (2000). Young children are sensitive to how an object was created when deciding what to name it. *Cognition, 76,* 91–103.

Gelman, S.A., & Hirschfeld, L.A. (1999). How biological is essentialism? In D.L. Medin & S. Atran (Eds.), *Folkbiology.* Cambridge, MA: MIT Press.

Gelman, S.A., & Markman, E.M. (1986). Categories and induction in young children. *Cognition, 23,* 183–209.

Gennari, S.P., Sloman, S.A., Malt, B.C., & Fitch, W.T. (2002). Motion events in language and cognition. *Cognition, 83,* 49–79.

Hampton, J.A. (1995). Testing the prototype theory of concepts. *Journal of Memory and Language, 34,* 686–708.

Heit, E., & Rubinstein, J. (1994). Similarity and property effects in inductive reasoning. *Journal of Experimental Psychology: Learning, Memory, and Cognition, 20,* 411–422.

Keil, F.C. (1989). *Concepts, kinds, and cognitive development.* Cambridge, MA: MIT Press.

Keil, F.C. (1995). The growth of causal understanding of natural kinds. In D. Sperber, D. Premack, & A.J. Premack (Eds.), *Causal cognition: A multidisciplinary approach* (pp. 234–262). New York: Oxford University Press.

Kripke, S. (1972). *Naming and necessity.* In D. Davidson & G. Harman (Eds.), *Semantics of natural language* (pp. 253–355). Dordrecht, Netherlands: D. Reidel Publishing.

Kronenfeld, D.B., Armstrong, J.D., & Wilmoth, S. (1985). Exploring the internal structure of linguistic categories: An extensionist semantic view. In J.W.D. Dougherty (Ed.), *Directions in cognitive anthropology* (pp. 91–113). Urbana, IL: University of Illinois Press.

Kruschke, J.K. (1992). ALCOVE: An exemplar-based connectionist model of category learning. *Psychological Review, 99,* 22–44.

Landau, B., Smith, L., & Jones, S. (1998). Object shape, object function, and object name. *Journal of Memory and Language, 38,* 1–27.

López, A., Atran, S., Coley, J.D., Medin, D.L., & Smith E.E. (1997). The tree of life: Universal and cultural features of folkbiological taxonomies and inductions. *Cognitive Psychology, 32,* 251–295.

Mak, B.S.K. & Vera, A. (1999). Motion-based categorization in young children. *Cognition, 71,* B11–B21.

Malt, B.C. (1994). Water is not $H_2O$. *Cognitive Psychology, 27,* 41–70.

Malt, B.C. (1995). Category coherence in cross-cultural perspective. *Cognitive Psychology, 29,* 85–148.

Malt, B.C., & Johnson, E.C. (1992). Do artifact concepts have cores? *Journal of Memory and Language, 31,* 195–217.

Malt, B.C., & Sloman, S.A. (2001). *Beyond conceptual pacts: Enduring influences on lexical choice in conversation.* Manuscript under review.

Malt, B.C., Sloman, S.A., Gennari, S.P., Shi, M., & Wang, Y. (1999). Knowing versus naming: Similarity and the linguistic categorization of artifacts. *Journal of Memory and Language, 40,* 230–262.

Mandler, J.M., & McDonough, L. (1998). Studies in inductive inference in infancy. *Cognitive Psychology, 37,* 60–96.

Markman, A.B., & Stillwell, C.H. (2001). Role-governed categories. *Journal of Experimental and Theoretical Artificial Intelligence, 13,* 329–358.

Markman, E.M. (1989). *Categorization and naming in children.* Cambridge, MA: MIT Press.

Matan, A., & Carey, S. (2001). Developmental changes within the core of artifact concepts. *Cognition, 78,* 1–26.

McCloskey, M., & Glucksberg, S. (1978). Natural categories: Well-defined or fuzzy sets? *Memory and Cognition, 6,* 462–472.

Medin, D.L., Goldstone, R.L., & Gentner, D. (1993). Respects for similarity. *Psychological Review, 100,* 254–278.

Medin, D.L., & Ortony, A. (1989). Psychological essentialism. In S. Vosniadou & A. Ortony (Eds.), *Similarity and analogical reasoning.* New York: Cambridge University Press.

Nosofsky, R.M. (1988). Similarity, frequency, and category representation. *Journal of Experimental Psychology: Learning, Memory, and Cognition, 14,* 54–65.

Putnam, H. (Ed.) (1975). The meaning of 'meaning'. In *Mind, language, and reality: Philosophical papers, Vol. 2.* Cambridge: Cambridge University Press.

Rips, L.J. (1989). Similarity, typicality, and categorization. In S. Vosniadou & A. Ortony (Eds.), *Similarity and analogical reasoning.* New York: Cambridge University Press.

Rips, L.J. (2001). Necessity and natural categories. *Psychological Bulletin, 127,* 827–852.

Rosch, E., & Mervis, C.B. (1975). Family resemblances: Studies in the internal structure of categories. *Cognitive Psychology, 7,* 573–605.

Sloman, S.A. (1994). When explanations compete: The role of explanatory coherence on judgments of likelihood. *Cognition, 52,* 1–21.

Sloman, S.A. (1998). Categorical inference is not a tree: The myth of inheritance hierarchies. *Cognitive Psychology, 35,* 1–33.

Sloman, S.A., & Ahn, W. (1999). Feature centrality: naming versus imagining. *Memory and Cognition, 27,* 526–537.

Sloman, S.A., Love, B.C., & Ahn, W. (1998). Feature centrality and conceptual coherence. *Cognitive Science, 22,* 189–228.

Sloman, S.A., Malt, B.C., & Fridman, A. (2001). Categorization versus similarity: the case of container names. In M. Ramscar, U. Hahn, E. Cambouropolos, & H. Pain (Eds.), *Similarity and categorization.* Cambridge: Cambridge University Press.

Sloman, S.A., & Rips, L.J. (1998). Similarity as an explanatory construct. *Cognition, 65,* 87–101.

Strevens, M. (2001a). The essentialist aspect of naive theories. *Cognition, 74,* 149–175.

Strevens, M. (2001b). Only causation matters: reply to Ahn et al. *Cognition, 82,* 71–76.

Strevens, M. (2001c). Further comments on Ahn et al. Website: http:/www-csli.stanford.edu/ ~strevens.

LANGUAGE AND COGNITIVE PROCESSES, 2003, *18* (5/6), 583–624

# On the conceptual basis for the count and mass noun distinction

Edward J. Wisniewski, Christopher A. Lamb and
Erica L. Middleton

*University of North Carolina at Greensboro, USA*

The English language makes a grammatical distinction between count nouns and mass nouns. For example, count nouns but not mass nouns can occur in plural form and can appear with the indefinite article. A number of scholars have suggested that to a fair degree this distinction is an arbitrary convention of language. An alternative view is based on the cognitive individuation hypothesis: count nouns refer to entities that speakers conceptualise as kinds of individuals whereas mass nouns refer to entities that they conceptualise as non-individuated. We propose a third view in which the use of count-mass syntax is often systematically related to a conceptual distinction in the minds of speakers. In other cases, though, speakers may use a count or mass noun in a way that does not reflect its typical conceptual basis, because of competing communicative functions of language. We describe research from a variety of domains including superordinates (e.g., clothing, vehicle), aggregates (e.g., rice, toothpicks), sounds and sensations, as well as developmental work that supports to a large degree a cognitive individuation view of the count-mass distinction. However, we also provide some preliminary evidence suggesting other reasons for count-mass syntax use (based on competing linguistic functions) that are not predicted by the cognitive individuation hypothesis.

---

Requests for reprints should be addressed to Edward J. Wisniewski, University of North Carolina, Department of Psychology, P.O. Box 26164, Greensboro, NC 27402, USA. E-mail: edw@uncg.edu.

We thank Emily Clancy and three anonymous reviewers for trenchant comments on a previous draft, and Mutsumi Imai, Paul Bloom, Barbara Malt, and Gregory Murphy, for input on some of the issues addressed in the paper. The first author thanks Bob Dylan for providing some of the inspiration for this work. This research was supported by National Science Foundation grant BCS-9975198 given to the first author.

http://www.tandf.co.uk/journals/pp/01690965.html    DOI: 10.1080/01690960344000044

A small but growing number of people in strife-torn Pakistan deal with their woes by *smoking scorpions* ... Users dry the scorpion's stingers, grind them up, light the powder, and suck the smoke. "When I *smoke scorpion*," said Ghulam Raza, "then the heroin is like nothing to me."[1]

The English language makes a distinction between count nouns and mass nouns. In general, a number of syntactic properties distinguish these two types of nouns. To illustrate some of these properties, consider the count noun "dog" and the mass noun "mud". Count nouns but not mass nouns can be pluralised and preceded by numerals (e.g., "three dogs" but not "three muds"). On the other hand, mass nouns can be preceded by the indefinite quantifiers "much" and "little" (e.g., "much mud" but not "much dog") whereas plural count nouns can be preceded by the indefinite quantifiers "many" and "few" (e.g., "few dogs", but not "few muds"). Count nouns but not mass nouns take the indefinite determiner "a" (e.g., "A dog ate the chicken", but not "A mud covered the chicken").[2]

In English, count nouns as well as mass nouns are used to name diverse entities. Physical objects (such as dog) are primarily labelled by count nouns but so are some abstract entities (e.g., idea, wish), events (e.g., party, explosion), and superordinate categories (i.e., broad categories of perceptually diverse things such as animal and vehicle). Substances (such as mud) are primarily labelled with mass nouns but so are some abstract entities (e.g., evidence, insanity), events (e.g., sleep, running), and superordinate categories (e.g., furniture, clothing). In addition, both count and mass nouns can name very similar entities. For example, pebbles is a count noun and gravel a mass noun even though they appear to refer to very similar things. Furthermore, the same kind of entity can sometimes be labelled using either count or mass syntax (e.g., "I'll go buy a cake", versus "I want cake for dessert").

This paper addresses the question of why people use count and mass nouns in language. One answer is that the grammatical distinction between count and mass nouns corresponds to a conceptual distinction in the minds of speakers. That is, when speakers use count nouns (or mass nouns) to refer to entities they implicitly have something in mind that they are trying to convey which is common across all such uses. On this view, the grammatical distinction between count and mass nouns is systematically related to a conceptual distinction between the referents of count and mass nouns.

---

[1] Quote from Yahoo-Reuters news source, November 7, 2001.

[2] Some nouns are neither count or mass nouns, including proper nouns and pluralia tantum (e.g., groceries, coffee grounds, soapsuds). The latter do not appear in the singular form and are grammatically intermediate between mass nouns and count nouns (Wierzbicka, 1988).

A second answer is that this grammatical distinction is, to a very large degree, semantically opaque. In general, a person must learn the correct syntax for each noun as a matter of grammatical convention, and not by understanding why it has that syntax. A conceptual distinction between count and mass nouns seems clear when one is talking about physical objects (e.g., dog, chair) which are named by count nouns and substances (e.g., mud, water) which are named by mass nouns. However, it seems quite unclear for most other kinds of nouns (e.g., facts versus knowledge, garments versus clothing, plants versus vegetation). A number of researchers have suggested that the count-mass distinction is primarily arbitrary, unprincipled, or idiosyncratic (e.g., Bloomfield, 1933; Gleason, 1969; McCawley, 1975; Markman, 1985; Palmer, 1971; Quine, 1960; Ware, 1979; Whorf, 1962).

One can draw an analogy between this situation and learning the gender marking of nouns. Languages such as Spanish and French make a grammatical distinction between nouns with masculine and feminine gender. For example, in Spanish, masculine nouns take the determiner "el" and often end in "o" but feminine nouns take the determiner "la" and often end in "a". The conceptual basis for gender seems obvious when one considers nouns referring to entities with a natural gender, such as "mujer" (woman), "muchacha" (girl), "tia" (aunt) and "hombre" (man), "muchacho" (boy), and "tio" (uncle). However, there seems to be no rhyme or reason for why "pluma" (pen), "tonada" (tune), and "playa" (beach) are feminine but "libro" (book), "codo" (elbow), and "favor" (favour) are masculine. Thus, for many nouns, the gender distinction may be semantically opaque and learned as a matter of grammatical convention.[3]

A third possibility, and the one that we propose in this paper, is that the use of count-mass syntax is often systematically related to a conceptual distinction in the minds of speakers. However, for some (probably small) proportion of nouns, it may not at all be apparent why they have the syntax that they do. In other cases, speakers may use a count or mass noun in a way that does not reflect its typical conceptual basis, because of *competing communicative* functions of language.

We begin by describing an hypothesis for the conceptual basis that motivates the use of count and mass nouns, called the *cognitive*

---

[3] However, there is evidence that children acquire gender on the basis of morphological properties of nouns (e.g., Levy, 1988; Braine, 1987) and on the basis of correlations with other grammatical constructions (e.g., Maratsos, 1988). Also, to some extent there is a semantic basis for non-natural gender terms. For instance, Zubin and Kopcke (1986) provide evidence that neuter gender in German applies to nouns referring to heterogenous classes and that feminine and masculine gender apply to nouns referring to homogeneous classes.

*individuation* hypothesis. According to this hypothesis, a speaker uses a count noun or mass noun when conceptualising some aspect of reality as an individual or a non-individuated entity, respectively. Focusing on studies of American, English-speaking subjects, we present evidence from a variety of fields that is consistent with this hypothesis. Much of this evidence comes from studies conducted in our laboratory. We also describe uses of count-mass syntax that appear to violate the cognitive individuation hypothesis. Some of these violations evidently arise because of the competing communicative functions of language. Finally, we discuss several broader issues—the relationship between individuation and other aspects of cognition and the cross-linguistic status of the count-mass noun distinction. With respect to the latter issue, we address the extent to which individuation is systematically reflected in the grammars of other languages—including those that do not have the distinction (e.g., numeral classifier languages such as Japanese).

## THE COGNITIVE INDIVIDUATION HYPOTHESIS

According to the cognitive individuation hypothesis, whether a person uses a count or a mass noun to refer to some aspect of reality depends on whether they interpret the referent as an individual or as a non-individuated entity (Bloom, 1990, 1994, 1996; Bloom & Kelemen, 1995; Imai, 1999; Langacker, 1987; Mufwene, 1984; Wierzbicka, 1988; Wisniewski, Imai, & Casey, 1996). For example, physical objects are prototypical individuals in being discrete, bounded entities that are separate from other aspects of the world. Substances are prototypical non-individuated entities in being continuous, unbounded, and arbitrarily divisible (e.g., mud divided into any-sized portion is still mud). Not surprisingly, physical objects are almost always labelled with count nouns (e.g., a cat, a computer, a coffee cup) and substances with mass nouns (e.g., clay, honey, jelly).

However, the notion of individual is more abstract than the notion of prototypical object and includes many types of individuals that are not objects, such as bounded substances (e.g., a puddle), parts of objects (e.g., a finger), sounds (e.g., a knock), physical events (e.g., a party), mental events (e.g., a nightmare), emotional states (e.g., a fear), and collections of objects (e.g., an army) (Bloom & Kelemen, 1995). Thus, what is common to the referents of all count nouns is that speakers view them as distinct individuals. Analogously, the notion of a non-individuated entity is more abstract than the notion of substance and includes entities such as sounds (e.g., thunder), physical events (e.g., sleep), mental events (e.g., reasoning), emotional states (e.g., anxiety), and even categories consisting of diverse objects (e.g., ski gear). Thus, the commonality among mass noun referents is that speakers view them as non-individuated entities.

## Scope of predication

Of course, this hypothesis raises the question of what one means by an individual versus a non-individuated entity. Our working hypothesis is that the distinction between an individual and a non-individuated entity is determined by its *scope of predication*. In particular, people will consider some aspect of reality as an individual if they are able to predicate important properties to that aspect which do not also apply to arbitrary portions of that aspect. In contrast, people will consider some aspect of reality as non-individuated if they are able to predicate important properties to that aspect as well as to arbitrary portions of that aspect. To make this notion concrete, consider a cat and glue. Many important properties characterise a cat that neither characterise a portion of the cat or multiple cats together. For example, "is a pet", "eats cat food", "is alive", "meows", and "has a tail" do not apply to an arbitrary portion of a cat. By the same token, such properties cannot be attributed to a group of cats of arbitrary size. For example, neither "has a tail" or "is alive" applies to a group of cats. Instead, these properties are true of each separate cat. One can say "those cats have tails", or "those cats are alive" but people mean that these characteristics apply separately to each of the cats.[4] In contrast, important properties of glue include: "sticky", "viscous", "sticks things together". Such properties apply to arbitrary portions of glue. The notion of scope of predication is consistent with various observations of philosophers and linguists that the referents of mass terms but not count terms are arbitrarily divisible and refer cumulatively (e.g., Quine, 1960), uncountable (Wierzbicka, 1988) and unbounded (Langacker, 1987). However, this notion may explain these observations.

In asserting this working hypothesis, some caveats are in order. First, we have not defined what we mean by "important properties". Roughly speaking, they are properties that are central to an entity "being what it is", such that it would very difficult to imagine that entity existing without such properties. (See Sloman, Love, and Ahn (1998) for a candidate operational definition of this idea.) Second, this view does not preclude all properties of a count noun referent from applying to arbitrarily divisible portions of that referent. It only assumes that there are central properties of the referent that do not apply to arbitrary portions of that referent. For

---

[4] Important properties can be predicated of a group of the same entities. However, we would argue that such a group would then be conceptualised as an individual (e.g., a choir sings, a family takes a vacation).

example, "has a functioning heart" is much more central to being a cat than is "furry". One cannot predicate "has a functioning heart" of arbitrary portions of a cat, whereas "furry" could apply to (some) arbitrary portions of cat. Conversely, this view does not preclude properties that apply to a mass noun referent from failing to apply to all possible portions of the referent. Third, our working hypothesis seems intuitively plausible when applied to prototypical objects and substances. As noted, however, people construe many entities as individuated or as non-individuated, which are neither prototypical objects or substances. At this point, the generality of our hypothesis is unclear. Later, we present some evidence that differences in scope of predication predict whether people individuate entities that are non-prototypical objects and substances.

## Construal

A central aspect of the cognitive individuation hypothesis is the process of *construal*. In particular, a person's interpretation of some aspect of reality can be a product primarily of either expectations or the physical input, or both. As a result, whether a person construes that reality as an individual or as a non-individuated entity is to some extent flexible. For example, in most contexts people interpret a bench as a distinct individual and hence refer to it as "a bench". The physical input readily gives rise to the perception of a discrete, bounded object that is distinctly separate from other aspects of the situation, which is then reflected in the use of bench as a count noun. However, in certain contexts, people's expectations can lead them to selectively attend to different perceptual characteristics of the bench and hence to a construal of the bench as a non-individuated entity. For example, consider a situation in which a person wants to sit down on a crowded bench and tells those sitting to "move over and give me some bench". In this case, the person is construing the bench as a non-individuated entity (i.e., a flat expanse of space) which is reflected in the use of bench as a mass noun.

Another example of an expectation is one generated from the use of count-mass noun syntax itself. The act of a speaker referring to an aspect of reality with count or mass syntax may lead the listener to construe that reality as individuated or non-individuated, respectively. Thus, the relationship between conceptualisation and syntax is bi-directional. That is, conceptualisation can affect the choice of syntax or syntax can affect the type of conceptualisation. We will present evidence of this bi-directional influence as well as show that how people interact with physical entities can affect their construal as individuated or non-individuated.

This notion of construal includes two general mechanisms, one that allows people to construe any non-individuated entity as an individual and a second that achieves the converse. As many scholars have pointed out, by viewing a typically non-individuated entity as a *type* or *kind*, people construe the entity as an individual (e.g., "a fine wine", Langacker, 1987; "What breads have you got today?", Quirk, Greenbaum, Leech, & Svartvik, 1972). (See Langacker, 1987, for an account of why this type of construal leads to an entity being individuated.) On the other hand, by selectively attending to a quantifiable dimension associated with a typically individuated entity, people construe the entity as non-individuated. Examples cited in the literature include the construal of an entity as a spatial dimension (e.g., "There's not enough table for everyone to sit at", Allan, 1980; "We still have quite a lot of road ahead of us", Mufwene, 1984) and as a substance (e.g., "Emmy finds squashed spider more nauseating than the thing alive", Allan, 1980). (See also the quote that opens this paper.) However, a web search revealed a number of construals involving other quantifiable dimensions that we determined from the surrounding context (e.g., "... they are too much dog for most novice owners" [care]; "... it really is a lot of telescope for the money" [value]; "A long instrumental part, featuring a lot of piano, was played" [piano music]; "lots of jump rope" [the activity of jumping rope]).[5]

In questioning the conceptual basis for the count-mass distinction, many scholars cite pairs of count and mass nouns whose referents are perceptually similar (oats vs. wheat, Bloomfield, 1933; rice vs. beans, Gleason, 1969; pebbles vs. gravel, Markman, 1985; noodles vs. spaghetti, McCawley, 1975; foliage vs. leaves, Palmer, 1971; footwear vs. shoes, fuzz vs. cop, shit vs. turd, fruit vs. vegetable, Ware, 1979). According to these scholars, how can there be a conceptual distinction between the referents of these count and mass noun pairs if they are so perceptually similar? However, this question does not address differences in how people construe perceptually similar entities (see also Bloom, 1990; Langacker, 1987; Mufwene, 1984; Wierzbicka, 1988). In the next section, we provide evidence showing that people construe perceptually similar entities differently and that such differences are related to the count-mass distinction.

In summary, proponents of the cognitive individuation hypothesis argue that speakers are not passive observers of perceptual characteristics that dictate whether an entity is named by a count or mass noun. Rather, a cognitive agent takes an active role in conceptualising an entity either as an individual or non-individuated entity (which is then reflected by whether the entity is labelled with a count or mass noun, respectively). We now turn to evidence that supports the cognitive individuation hypothesis and the process of construal.

---

[5] We thank Suzanne Adams for conducting this web search.

## EVIDENCE FOR THE COGNITIVE INDIVIDUATION HYPOTHESIS AND A CONCEPTUAL BASIS FOR COUNT/MASS SYNTAX

In this section we describe evidence from a number of disciplines suggesting that speakers conceptually distinguish between the referents of count and mass nouns. This evidence falls into three categories that vary in terms of how strongly they support a conceptual distinction view. In one approach, researchers use their intuitions to identify conceptual distinctions that they presume hold between familiar count and mass nouns. This type of evidence provides relatively indirect support for a conceptual distinction because it does not establish that the layperson knows these distinctions or has such distinctions in mind when using count and mass nouns. In another approach, researchers also hypothesise conceptual distinctions between the referents of familiar count and mass nouns but then establish that the layperson knows such distinctions. This evidence constitutes stronger but still indirect support for a conceptual distinction. It does not establish that the layperson actually makes these distinctions when using familiar count and mass nouns. A third approach provides stronger, more direct evidence. Again, the researcher hypothesises conceptual distinctions between the referents of familiar count and mass nouns but then designs an experiment in which participants must label novel stimuli with novel count or mass nouns. The stimuli are constructed in such a way that their perceptual characteristics or participants' interactions with the stimuli are systematically related to the conceptual distinctions. If participants have such knowledge of this systematic relationship, then they should be able to productively apply it in labelling stimuli with novel count or mass nouns.

### Wierzbicka's analysis of count and mass nouns

Wierzbicka (1988) examined count and mass nouns across 14 classes of language terms, arguing that for each class the count-mass distinction is conceptually motivated. Her analysis primarily focused on English, although she occasionally examined the use of count-mass syntax in Russian and Polish. In her extensive analysis of these classes, Wierzbicka suggested that the conceptual basis for the count-mass distinction is a function of a number of factors, the most important of which are: perceptual conspicuousness, arbitrary divisibility, heterogeneity, and how people interact with an entity. Below, we briefly describe these factors and how they relate to count-mass syntax.

Perceptual conspicuousness refers to how easy it is to see or perceive an entity. According to Wierzbicka, this factor helps explain why some *aggregates* are named by count nouns but others by mass nouns.

Aggregates are collections of multiple, similar constituents, such as rice, sand, and noodles. For instance, the constituents of noodles are more conspicuous than those of rice because they are larger. Thus, noodles refer to collections of separate individuals and are named with a count noun. In contrast, rice refers to non-individuated "stuff" and is named with a mass noun.

An entity is arbitrarily divisible if it can be divided into portions of any size and each portion can still be classified as the original entity. Arbitrarily divisible entities (such as liquids and substances) tend to be named by mass nouns. For example, butter is arbitrarily divisible because one can divide butter into any number of different-sized portions and each portion is still considered "butter".

Heterogeneity refers to whether the entities making up a group are of different kinds. According to Wierzbicka, the entities making up such a group cannot be counted and as a result are named with mass nouns. For example, the mass noun ski gear refers to a group of entities that may include skis, goggles, and ski poles. Wierzbicka suggests that when people use such a term they are not thinking of the entities comprising the group as one kind of thing, but rather as different kinds which can be used for a similar purpose (e.g., skis, ski poles, and goggles help people to ski).

Finally, the ways that people interact with an entity can have a variety of effects on whether it is named by a count or mass noun. For example, Wierzbicka suggests that the count, mass, or dual status of fruits and vegetables in Russian systematically varies as a function of how Russian speakers typically interact with such entities. In particular, berry-sized fruits are all mass nouns, because they are handled and consumed in quantity. Medium-sized fruits are count nouns because they are typically eaten whole and uncooked. Large fruits that are too big to be held individually while eating and are eaten on a single occasion can be either mass or count nouns, depending on the context. On the other hand, medium-sized vegetables are dual status nouns. They can be named by mass nouns because they are typically eaten chopped and cooked (and so take on properties of a substance). They also can be named with count nouns because they are relatively large and can be seen as individuals.

Wierzbicka's analysis reveals that for a number of language classes people appear to interact with the referents of count and mass terms in different ways. Also, the referents of these terms appear to differ in their perceptual characteristics. She plausibly interprets these differences as suggesting that people conceptualise the referents of count and mass nouns as distinct individuals and non-individuated entities, respectively. However, her analysis does not show that people are aware of these differences (either implicitly or explicitly) or that people conceptually distinguish the referents of count and mass nouns on the basis of these differences.

Further, Wierzbicka typically examined a relatively small number of count and mass terms in each language class. It is not clear if her samples are representative and thus whether her conclusions generally apply within a domain. Nevertheless, Wierzbicka's analysis contains many insightful and provocative hypotheses about the factors that influence individuation. Her work provides the starting point and motivation for several sets of studies that we describe next.

## Superordinate categories

Superordinates are broad categories of perceptually diverse things (e.g., furniture, animal, exercise equipment, clothing). In English and in many other languages, superordinates divide into mass terms and count terms (see Table 1). Prima facie, the referents of both count and mass superordinates appear to be discrete objects–prototypical, individuated entities. For example, the referents of *shirt*, *coat*, and *sweater* are typically conceptualised as distinct individuals and are named by count nouns (consistent with the cognitive individuation hypothesis). Yet, these entities are also considered *clothing* (a mass noun). Why are there both count and mass superordinates if their members are themselves considered distinct individuals?

Largely because of this paradox, researchers have suggested that the distinction between count and mass superordinates is not conceptually based (Gordon, 1985; McPherson, 1991; Murphy & Wisniewski, 1989; Ware, 1979). In addition, studies of natural categories mix mass and count superordinates together, implicitly assuming that conceptual differences do not exist between them (e.g., Gelman & O'Reilly, 1988; Jolicoeur, Gluck, & Kosslyn, 1984; Murphy & Brownell, 1985; Rosch, Mervis, Gray, Johnson, & Boyes-Braem, 1976; Tversky & Hemenway, 1984; Waxman, 1990; Waxman & Gelman, 1986; Wisniewski & Murphy, 1989).

However, Wisniewski et al. (1996) provide evidence that people construe the referents of count and mass superordinates differently. In particular, people conceptualise a count superordinate term as referring to one or more distinct entities named by that term. Thus, "vehicle" might refer to a single car. Or, "vehicles" might refer to a luggage truck and a plane—with each entity thought of as separately being a vehicle. But, they conceptualise a mass superordinate term as referring to a non-individuated group. For instance, clothing might refer to a shirt, jacket, and sweater, *together* as clothing, with each entity *not* being thought of as separately being an item of clothing. Wisniewski et al. (1996) noted that people can and often think of entities associated with mass superordinates as distinct individuals. However, when *using a mass superordinate term*, this way of conceptualisation does not apply. As we detail shortly, a consequence of this difference in construal is that mass superordinates are not true taxonomic categories (unlike count superordinates; see also Bloom, 1990; Wierzbicka, 1988).

Wisniewski et al. (1996) hypothesized that this conceptual difference arises because of differences in how people interact with the entities associated with count and mass superordinates. People typically interact with a single member of a count superordinate on a particular occasion. However, they interact with multiple, co-occurring entities associated with a mass superordinate. For example, one typically interacts with a single vehicle (e.g., driving a car to work, taking a plane to another city, bicycling in the park) but usually interacts with multiple items of clothing at the same time (e.g., dressing, undressing, washing, wearing). On this view, people consider members of count superordinates to be individuals because important properties of the superordinate apply *separately* to each entity. In contrast, people treat entities associated with mass superordinates as non-individuated because important properties apply to multiple items *together as a whole*. Furthermore, to a large extent, such properties appear to apply to arbitrary-sized groups (e.g., one can wash a varying amount of clothing at any one time).

Wisniewski et al. (1996) present a number of studies that provide converging evidence for this view. They involved a relatively large number of superordinates—more than in any studies of superordinates in the cognitive and developmental literature (the range was from 28 to 40, except for one study that used 22 superordinates; see Table 1). In all studies but one, the proportions of natural kind and artifact count superordinates were equal or approximately equal to the proportions for mass superordinates. In the studies that we describe, all the experimental results were stastically reliable.

One set of studies examined whether items of mass superordinates are more likely to co-occur than the members of count superordinates. Clearly, if people more often interact with multiple items of a mass superordinate on a particular occasion than they do with count superordinate members, then mass superordinate items should more often co-occur. In three studies, we randomly selected pairs of high frequency items from mass superordinates and pairs of high frequency items from count super-ordinates. Then, on a series of trials, subjects saw a pair of items from a count superordinate along with a pair of items from a mass superordinate. (They were not given the superordinate category names.) The subject decided which pair of things was more often seen together. (In addition, they picked the pair of things that was more similar. The rationale for collecting these judgements will become apparent later.) Across the three studies, subjects selected the items of the mass superordinate as more often co-occurring on 67% of the trials; 100 of 101 subjects picked a majority of

TABLE 1
Count and mass superordinates used in
Wisniewski et al. (1996)

| Count nouns | Mass nouns |
| --- | --- |
| animal | camping equipment |
| beverage | clothing |
| building | exercise equipment |
| disease | food |
| fruit | furniture |
| household appliance | glassware |
| insect | hardware |
| kitchen utensil | jewelry |
| machine | livestock |
| mammal | money |
| mineral | office supplies |
| musical instrument | poultry |
| pet | precipitation |
| plant | produce |
| scientific instrument | reading material |
| ship | silverware |
| tool | ski gear |
| vegetable | sports equipment |
| vehicle | tableware |
| weapon | vegetation |
|  | waterfowl |
|  | wildlife |

items of mass superordinates as more often co-occurring. Further, for 78% of superordinates, more mass items were selected as occurring together than count members.

Another experiment showed that subjects are more likely to interact with single members of count superordinates but with multiple items of mass superordinates. In a property inference task, subjects listed properties that were likely to be true of a superordinate category. They often listed common activities involving humans interacting with the superordinate categories (e.g., "eat" for food, "get sick from" for disease, "you play" for musical instrument). A different group of subjects then judged whether each of these activities involved mostly one or mostly more than one member of the superordinate, on a particular occasion. There was also an in-between option—sometimes with one and sometimes with more than one. Subjects more often interacted with multiple items of mass superordinates. The average proportion of time that activities were judged to involve mostly multiple items was .48 for mass superordinates versus .25 for count superordinates. In contrast, subjects more often interacted with single members of count categories. The average proportion of time that activities were judged to involve mostly a single item was .43 for count categories versus .22 for mass superordinates.

Taken together, these results suggest that people are more likely to interact with multiple items of a mass superordinate on the same occasion, but are more likely to interact with a single member of a count superordinate on a particular occasion. Wisniewski et al. (1996) suggested that these differences lead people to conceptualise count and mass superordinates differently. However, these results do not directly show that people actually conceptualise the referents of count and mass superordinates differently.

Other studies provide evidence for these hypothesised differences in conceptualisation. Returning to the property inference task, subjects listed a greater proportion and number of object parts as properties of count superordinates than of mass superordinates. Object parts are prototypical properties that apply separately to an individual rather than to a group. For example, the property "has a pair of windshield wipers" does not apply to a group of vehicles as a whole but to each separate vehicle. Likewise, the property "has a label" does not apply to a group of clothing as a whole but to each item of clothing. Subjects listed twice as many object parts for count superordinates than for mass superordinates. One would expect such a finding if people conceptualised the referent of a count superordinate to be one or more entities that individually belonged to the superordinate category but conceptualised the referent of a mass super-ordinate to be a non-individuated group of entities that belonged as a whole to the superordinate category. These differences between count and mass superordinates are also consistent with the hypothesised differences in scope of predication between individuals and non-individuated entities that we suggested earlier.

In another property inference task subjects were presented with a number of categories and listed the four things "that were most essential to knowing about the category". The categories were typical and atypical items of count and mass superordinates. If people think of entities as separately belonging to count superordinate categories (but not to mass superordinate categories) then they should more often list "membership in a superordinate category" as an important property of the entity. So, if people think of a single car as an individual vehicle then they should list "is a vehicle" as an important property of car. However, if people do not think of a single shirt as an individual clothing but rather shirt, pants, and socks together as clothing then they should be less likely to list "is clothing" as an important property of shirt. Subjects listed the superordinate category much more often for items belonging to count superordinates than to mass superordinates (38% vs. 10%, respectively) and were more than twice as likely to list the count superordinate for its atypical members than to list the mass superordinate for its typical members (32% vs. 13%).

A final task examined category verification times for a single member versus multiple members of a superordinate category. Subjects more quickly verified that a single item belonged to a count superordinate than to a mass superordinate (1285 vs. 1444 m) but were slightly faster to judge that several items belonged to a mass superordinate than to a count superordinate (1467 vs. 1496 m). For example, subjects were faster to judge sentences such as "A bomb is a kind of weapon" (single member, count superordinate) than ones such as "A chair is a kind of furniture" (single item, mass superordinate) However, they were slightly faster to verify sentences such as "Chair and table are furniture" (several items, mass superordinate) than ones such as "A gun and a bomb are weapons" (several members, count superordinate). Again, these results are consistent with the view that people conceptualise members of a count superordinate as individually belonging to that category, but they conceptualise a group of entities together as belonging to a mass superordinate category.

There are several important implications of these findings. First, the results suggest that count superordinates but not mass superordinates are taxonomic categories. By definition, the entities associated with a taxonomic category are each a member of the category. Further, the entities can inherit properties of the category which apply to each individual member. For example, if you are told that an opprobine is a vehicle, then you can infer that a particular opprobine probably has a steering wheel, is operated by one or two people, goes from one location to another, etc. However, "members" of mass superordinates are groups of entities (often of arbitrary size) and properties of the superordinate characterise the group rather than applying separately to each entity of that group. Thus, it is misleading to refer to one or more entities as individually belonging to a mass superordinate category. Figure 1 illustrates these conceptual differences between count and mass superordinates. In contrast, the dominant view in cognitive and developmental psychology assumes that all superordinate categories are taxonomic. Our findings are also inconsistent with Markman's (1985) view of the developmental importance of mass superordinates—namely that they facilitate a child's learning of taxonomies (see Wisniewski et al., 1996 for more details).

Second, our results are relevant to previous views of the conceptual basis for count and mass superordinates. Both Bloom (1990) and Wierzbicka (1988) also hypothesised that the conceptual distinction reflected one between individuals and non-individuated entities. However, their accounts of this distinction differ from Wisniewski et al. (1996). In brief,

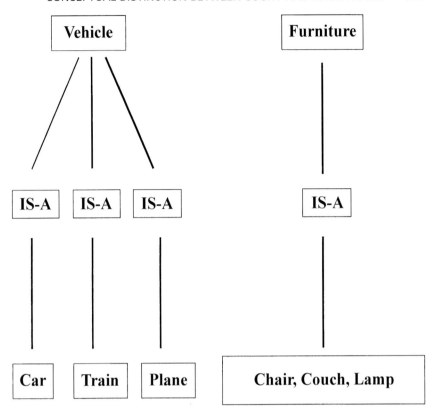

**Figure 1.** The different conceptual structures of count and mass superordinates.

Bloom suggested that mass superordinates are non-individuated because their members co-occur and are more similar than those of count superordinates (see Bloom, 1990, for some evidence). Thus, the combination of spatial contiguity and similarity of the items conspires to de-emphasise the individuality of any particular item, leading people to construe the items as a non-individuated group. On the other hand, Wierzbicka suggested that people do not individuate the objects associated with a mass superordinate because they are of *different* kinds (and thus cannot be counted). Bloom's view predicts that items from mass super-ordinates should be more similar to each other than should those from count superordinates whereas Wierzbicka's view predicts the opposite result. But, recall that Wisniewski and his colleagues had subjects make a series of judgements in which they selected which of two pairs of items was more similar (a pair from a mass superordinate versus a pair from a count superordinate). In three studies using this method, there was no statistically reliable difference between the within-category similarity of count superordinates and that of mass superordinates. This finding suggests that neither Bloom or Wierzbicka's view provides a general account of the conceptual difference between mass and count super-ordinates. However, for a given class of language terms, a variety of factors could affect the conceptualisation of their referents with respect to individuation (Wierzbicka, 1988; Bloom, 1996). Homogeneity and/or heterogeneity of superordinate categories could play a role in whether they are conceptualised as individuals or as non-individuated entities. Further work is needed to assess this possibility.

Finally, the results also underscore the importance of the cognitive agent in determining the reference of a term. Prima facie, the referents of both count and mass superordinates appear equivalent in being distinct entities. This apparent equivalency is one reason for the view that the count-mass noun distinction between superordinates is not conceptually motivated. However, these results suggest that people's conceptualisations of these entities are different, arising from differences in how the cognitive agent interacts with the entities in achieving goals.

## Aggregate terms

Aggregates refer to entities consisting of multiple, co-occurring, relatively small, homogeneous constituents. Even though they have these simila-rities, aggregates can be divided into those named by plural count nouns (e.g., grapes, toothpicks, tacks) and those named by mass nouns (e.g., rice, grass, confetti). Furthermore, a number of pairs of count and mass nouns refer to aggregates consisting of very similar constituents (e.g., oats and wheat, pebbles and gravel, snow flurries and snow, pills and aspirin, coins and change). Given these similarities among aggregates, is there a conceptual basis for why some are named by count nouns and others by mass nouns?

Wierzbicka (1988) hypothesised several reasons for such a conceptual distinction. First, she suggested that differences in how speakers interact with the constituents of an aggregate determine whether they will individuate those constituents, which in turn will be reflected in the syntax of the language. For example, Wierzbicka notes that in Polish, groups of berry-like fruits (e.g., raspberries, currants, strawberries, and plums) are named by plural count nouns because Polish people usually interact with the constituents one by one (e.g., when picking them or eating them). In contrast, Polish farmers selling their wares at a market setting commonly refer to such fruits with mass nouns because they interact with them as quantities and not as individual entities. Wierzbicka also suggested that the ease of distinguishing the constituents of an aggregate influences whether a speaker construes those constituents as individuals. For example, she argues that "beans" is a plural count noun and "rice" a mass noun because beans are more perceptually distinguishable than individual grains of rice. Thus, people construe each bean as a distinct individual but rice as a non-individuated group.

Recently, we and some of our colleagues tested Wierzbicka's hypothesis (Middleton, Wisniewski, Trindel, & Imai, 2003). Several undergraduates and naïve research assistants generated a list of aggregates. From this list, we selected a large and representative sample of aggregates consisting of 112 items—42 named by mass nouns and 70 named by count nouns. They included both natural kind (e.g., dirt, fleas, hail, pebbles) and human-made aggregates (e.g., dominoes, paper clips, keys, Q-tips). The sample contained a greater proportion of count items than mass items, reflecting the proportions of the initial pool of items. We also selected the sample so that it contained a diverse set of entities.

In one study, 25 subjects rated how easy it is to see or distinguish the individual elements that compose each aggregate, using a scale from 1 to 9, with "1" indicating that the elements were extremely easy to see and distinguish and "9" indicating that the elements were extremely hard to see and distinguish. Each count aggregate was presented in the format "a(n) X" (e.g., a bean) and every mass aggregate was presented in the format "a unit of X" (e.g., a unit of rice). The referents of these phrases are single elements of an aggregate. For each element, subjects were instructed to visualise a typical group of that element before making their rating. We used this procedure to minimise the effects of count-mass syntax on subjects' judgements. For example, subjects' judgements about the size of the elements of "rice" or of "beans" might be influenced by their knowledge that rice is a mass noun and beans is a count noun, respectively. Although this issue may be of theoretical interest, it was not the focus of this study. Prior to the rating task, subjects saw all the items randomly presented twice so that they were aware of the range of the perceptibility of the items.

The results showed that the rated ease of distinguishing the elements of an aggregate was systematically related to whether the aggregate was named by a count or mass noun. In particular, subjects gave lower ratings to count aggregates ($m = 3.00$) than to mass aggregates ($m = 4.03$). (Lower ratings indicate that subjects judged the elements of an aggregate as more easy to distinguish perceptually.) This difference was highly reliable, $t(23) = 5.81, p < .001$ (participants); $t(110) = 4.05, p < .001$ (items). These data support Wierzbicka's hypothesis: aggregates consisting of easily perceptible elements are more often named with count nouns whereas aggregates consisting of harder to perceive elements are more often named with mass nouns.

In a second study, 24 subjects rated how often they interacted with or used one or a few of the elements of an aggregate using a scale from 1 to 9, with "1" indicating that they frequently interacted with one or a few of the individual elements and 9 indicating that they rarely interacted with one or a few of the individual elements of the aggregate. The procedure was identical to that of the previous study except for the type of rating that subjects gave.

The results showed that the rated likelihood of interacting with one or a few elements of an aggregate was systematically related to whether the aggregate was named by a count or mass noun. In particular, subjects gave lower ratings to count aggregates ($m = 4.55$) than to mass aggregates ($m = 5.59$). (Lower ratings indicate higher judgements of the likelihood of interacting with one or a few elements of an aggregate.) This difference was highly reliable, $t(23) = 4.27, p < .001$ (participants); $t(110) = 4.65, p < .001$ (items). Again, these data support Wierzbicka's hypothesis: compared with mass aggregates, count aggregates consist of elements that people are more likely to interact with on an individual basis.

## Exceptions

We examined whether there were aggregates whose ratings failed to conform to both the predictions of the distinguishability judgement task and those of the interaction judgement task. In particular, for each task we rank ordered from lowest to highest, the mean ratings of all 112 aggregates. If the ratings perfectly predicted the count-mass syntax of all the aggregates, then the mean ratings for all 70 of the count aggregates should be higher than the mean ratings for all 42 of the mass aggregates. Exceptions to our predictions were any count aggregates that were ranked lower than 70th in both rating tasks and any mass aggregates that were ranked higher than 70th in both rating tasks. We did not include borderline cases as true exceptions (i.e., those count aggregates whose mean ratings were among the 10% of rankings below the 70th ranking on either or both tasks, and those mass aggregates whose mean ratings were among the 10% of rankings above the 70th ranking on either or both tasks).

By this procedure, we identified 18 exceptions (10 count and 8 mass aggregates). Some of the exceptions may be explained by other factors that influence whether an entity is individuated or not. For example, four of the count exceptions are animate (e.g., fleas, bacteria, maggots, and lice). Animacy may be a third factor that causes people to individuate the elements of an aggregate. Compared with perceptual distinguishability and how people interact with aggregates, animacy may be given more weight in determining whether people conceptualise the elements of an aggregate as individuals or as non-individuated. As another example, the mass exception "mail" appears to be composed of less homogeneous elements than our other stimuli. In particular, it may refer to a collection of *different kinds* of things (i.e., magazines, letters, bills, brochures, etc). As suggested by Wierzbicka (1988; see also Bloom & Kelemen, 1995), one uses a plural (count) noun to refer to multiple things of the *same kind* (e.g., three beans) but a mass term to refer to things of a different kind.

On the other hand, two of the mass exceptions, 'aspirin' and 'bacon' appear to have retained the syntax that reflects how their original referents were conceptualised. According to the *Oxford English Dictionary*, aspirin was formerly manufactured and administered as a powder whereas bacon previously referred to fresh pig meat (pork). Thus, they previously referred to things that are prototypical non-individuated entities. Today, though, aspirin are tablets and people typically interact with them one or a few at a time (as we found in the interaction study). Still, people call them aspirin (cf. vitamins). Likewise, bacon now refers to a cured slab that is pre-sliced and people typically eat one or a few at a time (as we found in the interaction rating task). Yet, people call them bacon (cf. french fries). It is unclear why English speakers have retained the mass syntax of these aggregates. (See Middleton et al., 2003, for discussion about the other exceptions.)

In general, the results are consistent with Wierzbicka's (1988) hypothesis that ease of distinguishing the elements of an aggregate as well as interaction with one element of an aggregate at a time lead people to construe the aggregate as a collection of distinct individuals. Hence, they refer to the aggregate with a plural count noun. In contrast, when the elements of an aggregate are harder to distinguish and people do not interact with one element of the aggregate at a time, then people construe the aggregate as a non-individuated group. Hence, they refer to the aggregate with a mass noun.

Why do these two factors lead people to construe the elements of aggregates as individuals or as non-individuated groups? Clearly, elements that are easier to distinguish from each other are perceived as more separate from each other. Further, interaction with a single element of an aggregate physically separates that element from the others (thus making the element more distinguishable from the others). Thus, it should be more likely that they will be considered individuals.

Importantly, people's interactions with count aggregates often involve using a single element to achieve a particular function. Thus, people consider count aggregates to refer to distinct individuals because a salient property (i.e., function) applies separately to each element of the aggregate rather than to the aggregate as a whole (e.g., the function "for cleaning teeth" does not apply to a group of toothpicks at the same time but to each toothpick one at a time, "buttoning" does not apply to a group of buttons at the same time but to each button one at a time). In contrast, people's interactions with mass aggregates often involve functions that require multiple elements at the same time. Thus, people consider a mass aggregate to refer to a non-individuated entity because a salient property does not apply to each element separately but to a group of elements as a whole (e.g., the function "for flavouring food" does not apply to each element of pepper one at a time but to a group of pepper at the same time, "tossing into the air" does not apply to each element of confetti one at a time but to a group of confetti at the same time). Furthermore, the size of the group appears to be somewhat arbitrary. For example, one could flavour food with varying amounts of pepper.

Note that these differences in how people interact with count versus mass aggregates parallel the differences in how people interact with count versus mass superordinates. Further, they again illustrate that the count-mass distinction is related to differences in scope of predication. In particular, important functional properties of count aggregates apply to each individual whereas they apply to multiple elements of a mass aggregate (and to a large extent, such properties apply to arbitrary-sized groups of such elements).

These findings show that if asked the appropriate questions, people reveal that they are aware of differences between the referents of count and mass aggregates. Further, we can plausibly interpret these differences as suggesting that a count aggregate refers to multiple, distinct individuals and a mass aggregate refers to a non-individuated group. However, the findings do not provide strong evidence that people actually conceptualise the referents of count and mass aggregates in these different ways when they use such terms. To obtain more direct evidence for differences in conceptualisation, we conducted two other experiments in which subjects mapped novel count and mass nouns onto novel aggregates.

In one experiment, we varied the perceptual distinguishability of the elements making up the aggregate. In particular, 32 subjects saw a series of pairs of novel aggregates accompanied by a phrase containing either a novel count or mass noun. (Pictures of novel aggregates were actually used.) Each pair of aggregates differed either in the size of their constituents, in the spatial proximity of their constituents, or along both dimensions. Figure 2 presents examples of each pair along with a count or mass noun phrase that was presented with the pair (equal numbers of subjects saw each pair with either a count noun phrase or a mass noun phrase). We assumed that the greater size of elements and the greater distance between elements increases their distinguishability. A subject's task was to read the phrase below the pair of pictures and to assume that someone had said the phrase when talking about one of the two pictures. The subject was to pick the picture that this someone was talking about.

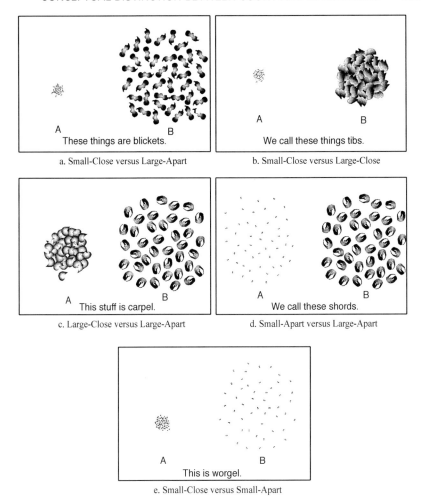

**Figure 2.** Examples of trials involving artificially constructed aggregates paired with novel count and mass noun phrases (Middleton et al., 2003).

The results showed a strong effect of spatial contiguity. Consistent with our hypothesis, subjects frequently chose count nouns as names for aggregates with non-contiguous elements and chose mass nouns as names for aggregates with contiguous elements. For example, Figure 2e shows an aggregate with small elements close together (Small-Close) on the left and an aggregate with small elements relatively far apart (Small-Apart) on the right. Subjects tended to choose the aggregate on the right for phrases containing novel count nouns (e.g., "These things are blickets") but they tended to choose the aggregate on the left for phrases containing novel mass nouns (e.g., "This stuff is blicket"). Overall, 26 of 32 participants showed this pattern of responding for the majority of the trials involving stimulus pairs in which spatial contiguity was varied ($p < .001$, by a binomial test). Further, the effect obtained for 15 of the 16 stimulus pairs ($p < .001$, by a binomial test). On the other hand, "size did not matter". That is, subjects did not show a tendency to pick aggregates with large elements over those with small elements when a phrase contained a count noun (and vice versa, when a phrase contained a mass noun). In hindsight, we noticed that the elements of the small non-contiguous aggregates are physically separate and can be seen as distinct from each other, even though they are relatively small. This factor may explain the lack of a size effect for the small-apart versus large-apart comparison (Figure 2d). Conversely, for the small-together versus large-together comparison, it appears difficult to perceptually separate the elements in either aggregate, whether they are large or small (Figure 2b). This factor may explain the lack of size effect for this comparison.

A final experiment examined whether interaction with a novel aggregate would change the way people construe the aggregate. In a baseline condition (not involving interaction), 28 subjects examined an aggregate consisting of yellow, coarse-grain sugar formed into a circular-shaped pile inside an open box. The aggregate was novel in the sense that it was generally unfamiliar to undergraduates, especially given the experimental context. Subjects were given a response sheet with one phrase containing a novel count noun (e.g., "We call these blickets") and another containing a novel mass nouns (e.g., "We call this blicket"). They were told to circle the phrase that they believed someone might say when referring to the contents of the box. Sixty-one per cent or 17 of 28 participants selected a mass noun phrase as best describing the aggregate.

In the interaction condition, 26 other subjects saw the same yellow coarse-grain sugar presented in the same box as in the baseline condition. However, they also interacted with single elements of the sugar. In particular, a subject was given a board with holes big enough for a grain of sugar to be dropped through and a small metal implement that enabled the subject to pick up a single grain of sugar and to drop it through one of the holes. The experimenter illustrated the task by carrying it out herself for 2 min and then signalling the subject to begin with their own board. The experimenter and subject then carried out the task for 15 min. Afterward, the subject completed the same labelling task as in the baseline condition. In contrast to the baseline condition, 69% or 18 of 26 participants selected a novel count noun phrase as best describing the aggregate even though they observed the same identically displayed aggregate as did subjects in the baseline condition. The difference between the baseline and interaction conditions was highly reliable, $\chi^2 (1) = 4.86$, $p < .03$.

This study provides direct evidence that how people interact with an aggregate affects their construal of that aggregate as individuated or as non-individuated. Observing an aggregate consisting of many very small, spatially contiguous elements led subjects to construe the aggregate as an non-individuated group. In turn, given a choice between labelling the aggregate with a count or a mass noun, subjects chose a mass noun. However, interacting with the elements of this aggregate one at a time led subjects to construe the aggregate as a collection of distinct individuals. In turn, given a choice between labelling the aggregate with a count or a mass noun, subjects chose a count noun. Thus, conceptualisation can affect the choice of count-mass syntax that people use to refer to an entity. Below, we present further evidence for the influence of conceptualisation on syntax as well as the influence of syntax on conceptualisation.

Taken together, the studies of aggregates provide evidence that people conceptualise the referents of count and mass aggregates differently. They construe the referent of count aggregate as a collection of distinct individuals but the referent of a mass noun aggregate as a non-individuated group. The studies using novel aggregates show that these differences in construal are caused by differences in how people interact with the constituents of aggregates and by differences in the ease of distinguishing the constituents. Furthermore, these differences in distinguishability and mode of interaction generally characterise many familiar aggregates. Thus, the studies support Wierzbicka's (1988) hypothesis about the conceptual basis for a distinction between count and mass aggregates. At the same time, differences in distinguishability and interaction did not perfectly predict the count-mass syntax of aggregates. We attribute this less than perfect relationship to some arbitrariness in the language and to other factors that might affect the conceptualisation of aggregates, which we did not investigate in these studies (e.g., animacy).

Finally, as in the studies with superordinates, the results underscore the importance of the active role of the cognitive agent in determining the reference of a term. Differences in how a person interacts with an aggregate's constituents affect whether they construe the aggregate as a collection of distinct individuals or as non-individuated group. As a result, people may construe the referents of aggregates differently even though they may share similar perceptual characteristics (or identical perceptual characteristics as in the last experiment that we described).

## Sounds and sensations

Many entities are characterised by their temporal properties. Events, sounds, and sensations are types of entities that occur over a period of time and whose existence is relatively short-lived compared with objects, substances, and many organisms. Such temporal entities can be referred to by count nouns (e.g., "a shriek") and by mass nouns (e.g., "yelling"). Little empirical work has examined the conceptual basis for the use of count and mass nouns that name temporal entities. One exception is a study by Bloom (1990) which examined whether people's use of count and mass syntax was sensitive to temporal properties of novel sounds and sensations. In particular, undergraduates read descriptions of two types of novel sounds and two types of novel sensations which were produced by machines. A description either described the sound (sensation) as consisting of discrete intervals separated by silence (absence of sensation) or as a continuous interval, as indicated below:

> *Sound-discrete intervals*: John attached the moop-producer to his stereo and switched it on. It started off very loud and then was silent. Then loud, then silent. This went on for many hours.

> *Sound-continuous interval*: John attached the moop-producer to his stereo and switched it on. It started off very loud and stayed loud, the volume never changed. This went on for many hours.

> *Sensation-discrete intervals*: The mad scientist attached the wug-producer to John's head. John felt the oddest sensation, something that was uncomfortable but not really painful and then it was gone. Then the sensation returned and a second later it was gone. This went on for many hours.

> *Sensation-continuous interval:* The mad scientist attached the wug-producer to John's head. John felt the oddest sensation, something that was uncomfortable but not really painful. The intensity of the feeling did not change. This went on for many hours.

After reading each description, subjects saw two sentences, one using the novel noun as a plural count noun (e.g., "The machine produced a lot of moops") and one using it as a mass noun (e.g., "The machine produced a lot of moop"). They judged each sentence on a 7-point scale, in terms of whether the sentence was terrible (1) or perfect (7). For descriptions of discrete sounds and sensations, subjects judged the sentence containing the novel count noun as better than the one containing the novel mass noun. The reverse finding obtained for descriptions of continuous sounds and sensations.

These results suggest that people construe temporal events differently, depending on their physical properties. When sounds and sensations occur as a series of discrete events interspersed with periods in which the event is absent, people construe them as a series of distinct individuals and thus select a count noun as most appropriately characterising the referent. But when temporal events are continuous and of long duration, people conceptualise them as non-individuated entities and select a mass noun as most appropriately characterising the referent. Thus, as in the Middleton et al. study on interaction with aggregates, conceptualisation can affect the choice of count-mass syntax that people use to refer to an entity.

Further, the temporal properties that distinguish individuated versus non-individuated sounds and sensations appear to have analogs with aggregates in the spatial domain. In particular, a series of sounds or sensations interspersed with a period of silence corresponds to a set of spatially non-contiguous entities. In both cases, the entities can be perceived as more separate from each other and hence as individuals. In contrast, a continuous sound or sensation corresponds to a set of spatially contiguous elements. In both cases, the entities are difficult to perceive as separate individuals.

Clearly, further work could be done in these domains. For example, other temporal properties may be related to individuation. For instance, the duration of each sound in a series relative to the duration of the intervening silences may be important (the sound-continuous interval in the Bloom study is a limiting case). It would also be important to assess the generality of such factors by comparing the temporal properties of familiar sounds and by examining actual sounds rather than their descriptions.

## Developmental research

A number of studies have examined the count-mass noun distinction in early development (e.g., Bloom, 1990; Brown, 1957; Gathercole, 1985, 1986; Gordon, 1985; Imai & Gentner, 1997; Macnamara, 1982; Soja, 1992; Soja, Carey, & Spelke, 1991). Much of this work concerns how children acquire the grammatical distinction between count and mass nouns and the corresponding conceptual distinction. On one account, children first acquire the grammatical distinction and only later learn the conceptual distinction (e.g., Gathercole, 1985; Gordon, 1985; Quine, 1960, 1969). On another view, children have the conceptual distinction prior to learning the grammatical distinction (e.g., Bloom, 1990). A third position is that children initially have a conceptual distinction but it differs from that of the adults in being narrower. That is, children distinguish objects from non-solid substances and then learn to map this distinction onto count and mass nouns (e.g., McPherson, 1991; Macnamara, 1982). Several studies suggest that children distinguish objects from non-solid substances prior to mastery of count-mass syntax (Soja, Carey, & Spelke, 1991; Soja, 1992). As stronger evidence for such conceptual distinctions prior to grammatical distinctions, Imai and Gentner (1997) showed that Japanese children as young as 2 distinguish objects from non-solid substances (the Japanese language does not have count and mass nouns).

More relevant to this section is research showing that young children can construe novel count and mass nouns as referring to individuated and non-individuated entities, respectively—including entities other than proto-typical objects and substances. Bloom (1990) showed that 3- to 5-year-old children were able to construe the same aspect of reality as either an individuated or non-individuated entity, depending on whether it was labelled with a count or mass noun, respectively. Children saw examples of food (lentils or coloured pieces of spaghetti) and sounds (two series of bell rings with different pitches that occurred at a fast rate of speed). These stimuli are ambiguous in that they can be conceptualised as either individuals or as non-individuated entities. For example, one could interpret the bell rings as a series of discrete, individual sounds or as undifferentiated noise.

The experiment began with a learning phase. For each child, the experimenter referred to one of the food stimuli with a series of novel count noun phrases (e.g., "There really are a lot of feps here") and the other with novel mass noun phrases (e.g., "There really is a lot of fep here"). Likewise, the experimenter referred to one of the sound stimuli with count noun phrases and the other with mass noun phrases. In a test phase, a puppet requested a food from the child using the syntax previously associated with that food (e.g., "Please give me a fep", if that food had been previously labelled with count syntax). Or, the puppet asked the child to make a sound (e.g., "Please make fep for me", if that sound had been previously labelled with mass syntax). For both age groups, children who heard stimuli labelled with count noun phrases more often gave the puppet one object and more often made one sound than for the stimuli that were labelled with mass noun phrases. But, for stimuli labelled with mass noun phrases, children more often gave the puppet multiple objects and more often made multiple sounds than for the stimuli that were labelled with count noun phrases. Thus, the results show that syntax can influence conceptualisation of foods and sounds as either individuated or non-individuated entities.

More recently, Bloom and Kelemen (1995) showed that children as young as 5 could construe the referent of a novel count noun as of an individual that is more abstract than a whole object. In one study, children saw pictures depicting novel objects (either five identical animals or five identical machines). For one group of children, the experimenter referred to each set of objects using a novel plural count noun (e.g., "These are fendles"). For a second group, the experimenter referred to each set of the (same) objects using a novel singular count noun (e.g., "This is a fendle"). They were then shown another picture of the same five objects in a different configuration as well as a picture of one of the objects. A puppet named Big Bird then asked a child "Can you show me a fendle?". Children who heard the plural count noun tended to point to the single entity but those who heard the singular count noun pointed to the group of entities.

A second study produced a similar result using actual objects. Thus, 5-year-old children hearing a novel singular count noun construed its referent as a *single* individual more abstract than a whole object, namely one analogous to collections of entities such as "a family", "a choir", etc. In contrast, children hearing this same aspect of reality labelled with a novel plural noun construed its referent as a number of distinct individuals. Again, these results show that syntax influences conceptualisation.

Taken together, these findings by Bloom and his colleagues present evidence suggesting that young children have a conceptual distinction between individuated and non-individuated entities that is broader than the distinction between physical objects and substances. Thus, they conceptualise a sound as either individuated or non-individuated and a collection of discrete objects as a single individual. Also, they have general knowledge about how count/mass syntax maps onto this broader distinction, and can flexibly construe the same aspect of reality in a way that is consistent with the syntax.

## Summary

In this section, we presented evidence from a variety of areas that supports the cognitive individuation hypothesis. This evidence suggests that people tend to use count nouns when they have distinct individuals in mind but mass nouns when they have non-individuated entities in mind. We also provided evidence of a bidirectional influence of syntax and conceptualisation. Several studies showed that how people conceptualise an entity systematically influences their choice of whether to refer to it with a count or mass noun, in a way that is consistent with the predictions of the cognitive individuation hypothesis. Likewise, several studies showed that labelling an entity with either a count or mass noun (or with either a singular or plural count noun) systematically influences how people conceptualise that entity, in a way that is consistent with the predictions of the cognitive individuation hypothesis. Importantly, we presented findings showing a conceptual basis for the count-mass distinction among language terms for which a conceptual basis was thought not to exist (e.g., superordinate categories).

At the same time, our findings and those of other researchers do not show a perfect relationship between conceptualisation and count-mass syntax. One reason for a lack of a perfect relationship is that for any class of language terms, there may be multiple conceptual factors related to individuation (Bloom, 1996; Wierzbicka, 1988). Cognitive agents may weight these factors differently in how they conceptualise an entity. For instance, as we suggested with aggregates, people may consider animacy to be more important with respect to individuation than perceptual distinguishability and mode of interaction. Thus, they may conceptualise an aggregate such as "maggots" as composed of multiple individuals even though maggots are relatively small and people do not interact with them one or a few at a time.

Nevertheless, the count-mass syntax associated with some entities does not seem explainable on the basis of conceptual factors related to individuation. We previously noted that aspirin and bacon are mass terms even though people may conceptualise these entities as individuated. As another example, a major proponent of the cognitive individuation hypothesis has said:

> I have no doubt that I think of a piece of toast as a singular individual, but—due to a quirk of English—I have to talk about it using the word 'toast,' a mass noun. So I ask you, 'Do you want more toast?' while thinking of a singular entity.[6]

Furthermore, in naming entities, speakers may focus on other important aspects of the entity besides whether the entity is individuated or not. As a result, the name for the entity may have a syntax that conflicts with its conceptualisation. In the next section, we discuss examples of this phenomenon.

## THE INTERACTION BETWEEN USE OF COUNT-MASS SYNTAX AND OTHER COMMUNICATIVE ASPECTS OF LANGUAGE

The cognitive individuation hypothesis predicts that when speakers conceptualise an entity as individuated, they should refer to that entity with a count noun. Likewise, when conceptualising an entity as non-individuated they should refer to it with a mass noun. In doing so, speakers convey to listeners an entity's status with respect to individuation. We call this aspect of communication the *individuation function*. Evidently though, speakers sometimes communicate about other aspects of an entity in ways that take precedence over the individuation function. As a result, speakers may refer to an entity using count-mass syntax that does not reflect how they are conceptualising the entity with respect to individuation (cf. the quote above about "toast"). In this section, we present examples of how other communicative aspects of language interact with the individuation function. We are unaware of any systematic investigations of this issue. Thus, our discussion is speculative. However, whenever possible we draw on research to support our view.

---

[6] Paul Bloom (personal communication, July, 2002).

Food is a domain in which communicating about other aspects of an entity take precedence over the individuation function. Various kinds of foods undergo transformations that change their status from individuals to non-individuated entities as a result of chopping, dicing, mashing, scrambling, etc. For example, people dice tomatoes, chop peanuts, scramble eggs, and mash potatoes. These transformations destroy the integrity of the individuals and produce substances. Yet, the syntax of the names for these entities does not reflect this change to a non-individuated entity. For example, American English-speakers refer to potatoes that have been mashed as "mashed *potatoes*", and to eggs that have been scrambled as "scrambled *eggs*". However, we seriously doubt that people are construing them as multiple individuals, as the syntax would imply.

Perhaps speakers base their names for these substances on information that characterises how the substances originated. In particular, the names "mashed potatoes" and "scrambled eggs" may reflect the type of transformation and type of entity to which the transformation was applied. For example, we may refer to a yellowish, fluffy, edible substance with the plural count noun phrase "scrambled eggs" because the scrambling was applied to multiple individuals (i.e., eggs). Thus, the name for the resulting substance inherits the count-mass syntax of the entity that was transformed to produce that substance. Note also that people may be reluctant to use the mass noun phrase "scrambled egg" because it would incorrectly imply that the scrambling was applied to a substance. As support for this view, a web search found that the percentage of hits for "scrambled eggs" or "some scrambled eggs" compared with "scrambled egg" or "some scrambled egg" was 89% (out of 38 374 hits). Likewise, the percentage of hits for "mashed potatoes" or "some mashed potatoes" compared with "mashed potato" or "some mashed potato" was also 89% (out of 116 620 hits).

Presumably, in coining the phrases "mashed potatoes" and "scrambled eggs", information about the origin of and process that produced the substance was more important to convey about the entity than its individuation status. Furthermore, the count syntax of these phrases may not present a problem to the listener in determining reference—even though the referents of these phrases are non-individuated. The meaning of such phrases implies that their referents are non-individuated. For instance, the first few times that listeners hear "mashed potatoes", they may infer that it refers to a substance-like entity produced by mashing potatoes. For subsequent mentions of "mashed potatoes", listeners can simply retrieve the meaning of "mashed potatoes" in determining its referent.

To examine the generality of using count nouns to name foods transformed into substances, we analysed the names for small- and medium-sized fruits and vegetables (and the legume peanut) that undergo transformations to substances. These fruits and vegetables are typically named by count nouns in their untransformed state. We searched the web for count and mass noun references to the substance forms of these fruits and vegetables. For each fruit or vegetable, we computed the percentage of hits for plural count versus mass noun phrases involving the adjectives mashed, diced, and chopped. For example, for radish, we computed the sum of the number of hits for plural count phrases "chopped radishes", "some chopped radishes", "diced radishes", some diced radishes", "mashed radishes", and "some mashed radishes", and the sum of the number of hits for mass noun phrases "chopped radish", "some chopped radish", "diced radish", "some diced radish", "mashed radish", and "some mashed radish".[7]

Table 2 presents our findings. For peanut and all the fruits and vegetables except one (lemon), people primarily refer to the transformed entity (i.e., the substance) with a plural count noun phrase. Consistent with our analysis of scrambled eggs and mashed potatoes, this finding suggests that the names of fruit-vegetable substances provide information about the type of transformation and type of entity (i.e., multiple individuals) to which the transformation was applied. As a result, the name for the substance inherits the count noun syntax of the multiple individuals that were transformed into that substance.

Beyond the food domain, we have identified more cases in which communicating about other aspects of an entity takes precedence over the individuation function. For instance, speakers use the count noun phrases "eyedrops" and "artificial tears" to refer to a variety of liquids contained in small bottles (and manufacturers have labelled the bottles with these names). When referring to one of these liquids with a plural count noun we seriously doubt that people are construing the liquid as a collection of individual drops of liquid or tears. Instead, these names have dual reference. They refer to actual drops of liquid or tear-like liquid as well to the liquid contents of small bottles. The names seem to reflect important functions of these liquids (i.e., placing *drops* of liquid into the eyes to correct various eye problems). Evidently, naming the actual liquid was based on function and took precedence over naming based on the individuation function.

Another possible example, involving naming based on resemblance, is illustrated by the phrase "pine needles". The phrase was originally coined

---

[7] Some of the hits for the mass noun phrases involved adjectives instead of nouns (e.g., in some cases "chopped lemon" was part of the phrase "chopped lemon peel"). We excluded such phrases. Specifically, for each mass noun phrase, we examined a random sample of 20 phrases and determined the proportion of adjective uses. We then reduced the number of hits for that phrase by that proportion.

TABLE 2
Percentage of occurrences of phrases referring to fruits and vegetables transformed into substances

|  | (some) | mashed Xs<br>diced Xs<br>chopped Xs | (some) | mashed X<br>diced X<br>chopped X |
|---|---|---|---|---|
| *Small* | | | | |
| apricot | | 90% | | 10% |
| blueberry | | 97% | | 3% |
| cherry | | 97% | | 3% |
| cranberry | | 99% | | 1% |
| grape | | 91% | | 9% |
| pea | | 96% | | 4% |
| peanut | | 100% | | 0% |
| radish | | 69% | | 31% |
| raspberry | | 93% | | 7% |
| *Medium* | | | | |
| apple | | 68% | | 32% |
| banana | | 66% | | 5% |
| beet | | 100% | | 0% |
| carrot | | 75% | | 25% |
| lemon | | 33% | | 67% |
| orange | | 53% | | 47% |
| parsnip | | 100% | | 0% |
| peach | | 96% | | 4% |
| pear | | 89% | | 11% |
| plum | | 96% | | 4% |
| tomato | | 83% | | 17% |

to refer to leaves of a pine tree that resemble needles (they are also prickly to some extent like needles). Actual needles are good examples of individuals. People frequently interact with them one at a time and the important properties of needles are predicated of each individual needle (e.g., for sewing a button, for drawing blood, for administering a vaccine). In contrast, pine needles are a good example of a non-individuated entity. They occur as multiple entities found on the ground in very close proximity which are difficult to perceive as separate individuals. People also interact with multiple pine needles at a time (when using them as mulch). Further, individual pine needles are not seen falling from a tree as is the case with other leaves. As noted in our studies of aggregates, these characteristics are associated with non-individuated entities. Evidently, whoever named pine needles "pine needles" was struck by their resemblance to needles, and retained the count syntax of needle at the expense of the individuation function.

Yet another possible example of the interaction of communicative functions is described by Clark (1993). She suggests that speakers of a language adhere to the principle of contrast in which the use of a different word marks a difference in meaning. With respect to the count-mass distinction, Clark (1993; page 69) notes that prior to the Normandy invasion, animal terms in English were dual status—they referred to both the animal (a count noun) and its meat (a mass noun). After the Normandy invasion, English acquired French terms for animals that were also dual status. As a result, English contained different words with the same meaning. The English and French animal terms were differentiated by assigning the animal meanings to the English terms (e.g., calf, deer) and the meat meanings to the corresponding French terms (e.g., veal, venison).

At a general level, the view that a speaker's use of count-mass syntax is sometimes a function of factors other than cognitive individuation is consistent with recent work by Malt, Sloman, Gennari, Shi, and Wang (1999) on naming across cultures. They found that speakers of English, Chinese, and Spanish show substantially different patterns of naming for common containers (bottles, cans, boxes, jars, etc). This result obtained even though the different cultures tended to agree on how similar the containers are (as measured by ratings of their physical, functional, and overall similarity).

To account for these findings, Malt et al. (1999; see also Malt, 1993) suggest that naming is influenced by a variety of communicative and social factors besides similarity. In some cases, these factors result in entities being given different names even though they are conceptualised as similar, or being given the same names even though they are conceptualised as different. For example, one factor is pre-emption (see also Clark, 1993). People may avoid using a name for a novel entity that they otherwise would have used if it had not already referred to an existing entity. For instance, Malt et al. (1999) suggest that "a soup tureen (for serving soups) may have been named 'tureen' even though people conceptualise its features as falling within the range of objects called 'bowl' or 'pot' because calling it a soup bowl or soup pot would create referential confusion with vessels for eating or cooking things" (page 236). Malt et al. (1999) also emphasise that a person may accept a name for an entity because it facilitates communication and thus focus less on its similarity to other entities in that category. For instance, someone may adopt a product name provided by an advertiser because it is known to and used by others. With respect to the count-mass noun distinction, a recent example is "egg beaters". This name refers to processed egg white *substance*. Evidently, manufacturers based its name on function, which took precedence over naming based on the individuation function. (It is called "egg beaters" because it "beats" the cholesterol problem associated with eggs.)

In closing this section, we note one more example of how other language factors may interact with the individuation function. Consider the quote that began our paper. Why when apparently referring to the same entity, does the journalist reporting this story use the phrase "smoking scorpions" whereas the Pakistani drug addict who does the smoking uses the phrase "smoking scorpion"? One possibility, consistent with the cognitive individuation hypothesis, is that the journalist and drug addict differ in how they interact with scorpions which in turn affects how they construe scorpions. However, another possibility is that the reporter is trying to introduce a novel idea to readers. Yet, before explaining the novel use of scorpions, the reporter must introduce the referent in its common syntax to prevent confusion on the reader's part. On the other hand, the addict is under no such obligation and refers to the scorpion with mass syntax, which is congruent with its construal as a substance made of scorpion stingers.

## THE CROSS-LINGUISTIC STATUS OF THE COUNT–MASS NOUN DISTINCTION

We and others have suggested that the count–mass distinction reflects a basic, fundamental cognitive process—that of conceptualising aspects of reality either as individuated or non-individuated. As a result, one would think that the count-mass distinction in other languages should also reflect this difference in conceptualisation. Furthermore, one should expect cross-linguistic agreement on the count-mass status of nouns that refer to the same entities.

Languages also vary in how and to what extent they signal individuation. In particular, numeral classifier languages (e.g., Japanese, Chinese, Korean, Mayan) lack the count-mass distinction and show less tendency to explicitly signal individuation (Imai & Gentner, 1997; Lucy, 1992; Mufwene, 1984). Does this difference between count–mass and classifier languages have implications for how cultures conceptualise the world? In this section, we discuss cross-linguistic research on the count–mass distinction as well as possible effects of language differences on cognition.

### Cross-linguistic studies of the count–mass distinction

As far as we know, little systematic research has examined the use of count and mass nouns cross-linguistically. Some evidence suggests that the classification of English superordinate terms into count and mass nouns agrees to a fair extent across languages. In an examination of 18 languages from a variety of language families, Markman (1985) had native speakers judge whether each of 25 superordinates was a mass or count noun in their native language (or functioned like a count or mass noun if the language did not make such a distinction.) They made this judgement by deciding whether the term could be quantified directly (e.g., two vehicles) or required a quantificational phrase (e.g., two pieces of furniture). Native speakers also made these judgements for 48 basic-level categories that were subsets of the superordinate categories—two basic-level categories per superordinate (e.g., dollar and penny which were subsets of the superordinate money).

For the count-mass classification of the basic-level categories, Markman found an overall agreement across languages of more than 99%. There was considerably less agreement for superordinates. However, our examination of her results reveals that the English count-mass classification of 10 of the 25 superordinate terms agrees with the classification of 16 of the 18 languages (Markman, 1985, Table 1, page 37).[8] In a more detailed analysis of Markman's data, Bloom (1990) found that for 15 of the 18 languages, there was a positive correlation between the count-mass status of the superordinates in that language and those in English. (Ten of the correlations were statistically reliable.)[9]

Although these findings show a systematic relationship between count and mass noun usage in English and other languages, it is not close to perfect. A variety of factors could contribute to inconsistency across cultures in the use of count and mass nouns. First, in any valid cross-linguistic comparison of count-mass noun agreement, one must determine that the nouns in different cultures involve categories that are familiar to both cultures and have extensions that significantly overlap. For example, one of the superordinates in the Markman study was silverware. However, in Japanese (one of the languages investigated), there is no comparable term for the category of silverware in English, as the Japanese traditionally do not use forks and spoons. In Japanese, "silverware" could be translated as "ginseihin". However, this category is much broader than the English silverware category and includes many things made of silver (Imai & Wisniewski, 2003).

Importantly, one also must establish that cultures *interact* with category members in similar ways. We have emphasised that the type of interaction affects the conceptualisation of a category's members. For example, many aspects of reality can be construed either as individuated or non-individuated (e.g., some cake versus a cake, too much curiosity versus a

---

[8] These terms were toy, building, musical instrument, flower, vehicle, tree, animal, and bird (count nouns), and money and food (mass nouns).

[9] The 15 languages with positive correlations were Afrikaans, Dutch, German, French, Greek, Polish, Ukranian, Urdu, Finnish, Hungarian, Turkish, Arabic, Guro, Nzema, and ASL. The exceptions were Japanese, Korean, and Hebrew.

curiosity). For entities with alternative construals, cultures could differ in terms of the importance of the interactions that they have with those entities. In turn, these differences could be reflected in whether the culture names an entity with a count or mass noun. One culture may mostly interact with an entity in a way that leads it to be primarily construed as individuated, whereas another culture's most common way of interacting with that entity leads it to be primarily construed as non-individuated. Thus, one culture would name the entity with a count noun and the other with a mass noun—leading to an apparent discrepancy. Perhaps though, a culture may occasionally use the other syntactic form of the noun or some other language construction to capture the less common construal. For instance, English speakers can use a variety of partitives to individuate the referents of mass nouns (e.g., an item of clothing, a slice of meatloaf, a puddle of blood).

Inconsistency across cultures in count-mass usage also may arise if languages differ in the number of terms used to refer to alternative construals of some aspect of reality. For example, in many languages, animal terms such as cow, calf, and deer are dual status: they are used either as a count or a mass noun to refer to the animal or its meat, respectively. However, in English, these terms are count nouns. Without other knowledge of English, one might consider this observation as evidence against a systematic relationship between count-mass syntax and conceptualisation that holds across cultures. Of course, English uses such animal terms to refer to the animal and has separate mass nouns that refer to their meat (beef, veal, and venison, for cow, calf, and deer, respectively). As previously noted, these mass terms arose because of competing linguistic functions in English.

## Count–mass versus numeral classifier languages

A large family of languages called numeral classifier languages do not make the grammatical distinction between count and mass nouns (e.g., Japanese, Chinese, Korean, Yucatec Mayan). In these languages, when speakers refer to a number of entities, the name of that entity must be preceded by a numeral and a *classifier* (hence, the name "numeral classifier language"). In general, classifiers mark nouns as members of certain broad categories (such as shape or form). An example of a classifier in Japanese is *hon* which typically refers to relatively long, thin things (i.e., things which are prominent along only a single dimension, such as chopsticks and golf clubs).

Although numeral classifier languages do not have the count–mass distinction, other aspects of their grammar signal individuation. However, compared with English and related languages, they are less likely to explicitly mark the status of an entity with respect to individuation. To illustrate this point, consider some differences between Japanese and English.[10] When English speakers introduce a referent in a discourse setting, they very often use either count or mass syntax. For example, in showing a picture of a dog to a young child, an adult might say, "This is a dog". If instead the picture depicted mud, the adult might say, "This is mud". However, the corresponding Japanese equivalents would be "This is dog" and "This is mud", respectively. Also, English speakers must use the singular-plural distinction to indicate whether they are referring to one or multiple distinct individuals of the same kind. However, Japanese does not make the singular-plural distinction. In the absence of context, someone hearing "This is dog" would not know if the speaker was referring to one or multiple distinct individuals. As a third example, English syntactically marks individuated and unindividuated entities with the pairs of adjectival quantifiers *many/much* and *few/little*. Here, *many* and *few* refer to a relatively large or small number of distinct individuals, respectively. *Much* and *little* refer to a relatively large or small amount of some non-individuated quantity, respectively. In contrast, Japanese does not syntactically distinguish a large number from a large amount or a small number from a small amount. Rather, they use the same term *takusan* in both contexts in which English speakers use *much* and *many* and the same term *sukoshi* or *chotto* (colloquial) in both contexts in which English speakers use *few* and *little*.

Japanese does mark individuation when speakers find it necessary to count entities. Like other numeral classifier languages, it uses classifiers together with numerals for this purpose. Using this mechanism, Japanese individuates entities in a way that is somewhat analogous to how English uses discrete unit terms to individuate substances (e.g., a *stick* of butter, two *bottles* of water, three *piles* of sand). For example, one can count butter by preceding it with a numeral and *hon* (as in, "buttaa o 2 *hon* totte". Literally, this phrase means "[Please] get me two long, thin things of butter". Japanese must also use such classifiers in referring to discrete entities. For example, to refer to the number of golf clubs, pencils, or chopsticks, one must also use *hon* together with a numeral. A few classifiers appear only with certain nouns that name discrete objects (prototypical individuated entities), such as *nin* (for humans) and *dai* (for large machines). Thus, some classifiers may mark especially prototypical examples of individuals.

---

[10] We are grateful to Mutsumi Imai for providing us with this information about the Japanese language.

Importantly, Japanese does not generally require the use of classifiers. Only in contexts in which a mention of the number of an entity is important would a Japanese speaker use a numeral coupled with an appropriate classifier. Thus, one would say "Ringo o *1 ko* totte kudasai" when explicitly requesting a single apple because a recipe calls for one apple. (The classifier *ko* typically refers to things in which one dimension does not dominate relative to the others, such as an apple.) It is more common to refer to entities without indicating their number and form via a numeral and classifier. Thus, it is very acceptable to say "Ringo o totte kudasai" (literally, "Please give me apple"). In this case the listener must use contextual cues to determine whether the speaker wants a whole apple, a slice of an apple, a few apples, etc. As a result, this request does not syntactically cue the status of the entity with respect to individuation. In contrast, English speakers probably would make a more specific request and one that signals individuation (e.g., Please give me *an* apple).

Some evidence suggests that the difference in the degree to which count–mass and classifier languages signal individuation leads to small differences in cognitive processing. That is, although one would expect cultures to share the same basic cognitive processes, these processes might differ at a very subtle level (e.g., in the relative ease of remembering a certain kind of information indicated by the grammar, Hunt & Agnoli, 1991). In a developmental study involving 2-year-olds, 4-year-olds, and adults, Imai and Gentner (1997) compared how American and Japanese subjects construe novel stimuli consisting of complex objects, simple objects, and substances. Subjects saw a series of stimulus triads consisting of a standard and two alternatives. The standard was either a complex object, simple object, or substance (formed into a shape of a complex object). The *shape* alternative had the same shape as the standard, but was made of a different material. The *material* alternative was made of the same material as the standard but did not have the same shape. On each trial subjects saw the standard, labelled with a simple phrase containing a novel noun. In English, whether the noun was a count or mass noun was indeterminate (e.g., "Look at this dax"). Subjects then selected the alternative that best matched the standard.

The results showed both cross-linguistic similarities and differences in construal. When the standard was a complex object, Japanese and American subjects tended to select the shape alternative. However, when the standard was the simple object, American subjects tended to select the shape alternative whereas adult Japanese subjects preferred the material alternative. (Japanese children tended to respond at chance.) For substance trials, Japanese subjects tended to select the material alternative whereas American subjects tended to respond at chance. Imai and Gentner (1997) concluded that, "linguistic structure affects the weighting of dimensions and the way in which speakers classify entities into different categories" (page 196). That is, English-speaking subjects attend relatively more to shape and Japanese speakers more to material. In turn, English-speaking subjects are more likely to construe solid substances formed into simple shapes as individuated objects whereas (adult) Japanese speakers are more likely to construe these entities as non-individuated. Further, Japanese subjects are more likely to construe nonsolid substances formed into complex shapes as non-individuated entities.

Lucy (1992) also found cross-cultural differences in attention to material versus shape and in the tendency to individuate entities. In one study, adult Mayan and American men saw stimulus triads composed of three inanimate physical objects. Each trial consisted of a standard stimulus (e.g., sheet of paper) that had the same shape as one alternative (e.g., sheet of plastic) and the same material composition as the other alternative (e.g., book). Subjects were instructed to choose the alternative that was most like the standard. Mayan subjects primarily selected the material alternative whereas American subjects primarily chose the shape alternative. Consistent with Imai and Gentner's results, English-speaking subjects attended relatively more to shape in considering the similarity between objects whereas Mayan speakers attended relatively more to material.

In a variety of other studies, Mayan and American subjects described pictures of scenes, judged their similarity, and were tested on their recognition memory for the scenes. One finding concerned subjects' sensitivity to the number of discrete, inanimate objects of the same type present in a scene (e.g., the number of buckets in a scene). American subjects were more likely to: (a) mention the number of such objects in describing a scene, (b) judge scenes that varied in the number of such objects as less similar, and (c) produce fewer false alarms in recognition tests for scenes which differed only in the number of such objects present in the original scenes.[11]

Lucy (1992) interpreted these findings as support for the view that language differences lead to differences in cognitive processing. In particular, Mayan speakers do not use plural terms when referring to more than one discrete, inanimate object of the same type. In contrast, English speakers must use plural terms. As a result, English speakers attend more to and have better memory for the number of distinct individuals of the same type.

---

[11] There were other findings in these studies that we do not report because of page limitations and expository reasons. Also, for some of these studies, Lucy did not report statistical analyses examining the differences between Mayan and American subjects. See Lucy (1992, Chapter 3) for more details.

In conclusion, languages vary in the degree and extent to which their grammar indicates whether an entity is individuated. These language differences are reflected in subtle differences in how cultures process information in their environments. To date, research has only examined this issue with respect to objects and substances—prototypical individuated and non-individuated entities, respectively. Future work might address the effects of language with respect to less prototypical entities (e.g., those named by superordinate terms or by abstract terms). These entities may have properties that lend themselves to either type of construal. For example, although mass superordinates refer to non-individuated groups, those groups consist of discrete objects that can be seen as individuals. Thus, language may exert more influence on the conceptualisation of less prototypical entities (cf. Imai and Gentner's findings with simple objects).

## INDIVIDUATION AND ITS ROLE IN COGNITION

The process of construing an entity as individuated or non-individuated appears to be a very basic process that pervades all of cognition. For example, counting requires that one individuates some number of entities. Categorising entities requires that they be individuated or treated as non-individuated, depending on the type of entity. For example, categorising some entity as a cat requires that one construe the cat as a distinct individual, and to categorise something as sand one must construe that sand as non-individuated.

As suggested by the cross-linguistic research that we reviewed, the process of individuation also affects memory and attention. As another example, consider differences in how people might attend to a non-individuated entity like a substance versus an individuated entity such as a physical object. Construing something as a non-individuated substance suggests that its texture and colour are important and that shape is irrelevant. In contrast, construing something as an individuated physical object suggests that shape is important and that texture and colour are less relevant. As a result, people might attend to different features in the two cases that in turn could affect memory for these features.

Individuation also affects the types of inferences that people draw about the environment. For example, the inferences that one makes when hearing "some chicken" versus "a chicken" can be dramatically different. The former can refer to a non-individuated substance-like entity that is likely to be found in a kitchen, have an expiration date, and be cooked and eaten. The latter can refer to a live bird and hence is likely to be found on a farm, have wings, fly, be alive, etc. These different inferences depend on specific knowledge about chickens. However, it is the count-mass syntax, by indicating whether the chicken refers to an individuated or non-individuated entity, that enables people to access the appropriate information. Sometimes differences in inferences can be quite subtle. For example, if you heard someone say, "I heard some noise in the kitchen" versus "I heard a noise", you might infer that the former was of longer duration. Or, hearing "that girl had too much curiosity" versus "that girl was a curiosity" leads one to infer that the girl was in a mental state of curiosity in the former sentence but was the cause of the curiosity in the latter sentence.

## SUMMARY AND CONCLUSIONS

Philosophers, linguists, and psychologists have long debated why English and other languages have a count-mass noun distinction. On our view, the debaters fall into two camps. One camp maintains that the distinction is primarily an arbitrary convention of language. The other camp maintains that the distinction is primarily conceptually motivated. They account for any apparent arbitrariness by postulating that the referents of count and mass nouns cannot always be identified on the basis of their obvious perceptual characteristics. Rather, speakers can flexibly construe the referents of count and mass nouns as individuated and non-individuated entities, respectively. We have described a range of evidence that supports this conceptually motivated distinction. At the same time, this view must be qualified. Other functions of language sometimes override the individuation function conveyed by count/mass syntax.

## REFERENCES

Allan, K. (1980). Nouns and countability. *Language, 56,* 541–547.

Bloom, P. (1990). *Semantic structure and language development.* Unpublished doctoral dissertation. Massachusetts Institute of Technology, Cambridge, USA.

Bloom, P. (1994). Possible names: The role of syntax-semantics mappings in the acquisition of nominals. *Lingua, 92,* 297–329.

Bloom, P. (1996). Possible individuals in language and cognition. *Current Directions in Psychological Science, 5,* 90–94.

Bloom, P., & Kelemen, D. (1995). Syntactic cues in the acquisition of collective nouns. *Cognition, 56,* 1–30.

Bloomfield, L. (1933). *Language* (pp. 266–268). New York: Holt & Co.

Braine, M (1987). What is learned in acquiring word classes: A step toward an acquisition theory. In B. MacWhinney (Ed.), *Mechanisms of language acquisition* (pp. 65–87). Hillsdale, NJ: Lawrence Erlbaum Associates, Inc.

Brown, R. (1957). Linguistic determinism and the parts of speech. *Journal of Abnormal and Social Psychology, 55,* 1–5.

Clark, E.V. (1993). *The lexicon in acquisition.* Cambridge: Cambridge University Press.

Gathercole, V.C. (1985). 'He asks too much hard questions': The acquisition of the mass-count distinction in *much* and *many. Journal of Child Language, 12,* 395–415.

Gathercole, V.C. (1986). Evaluating competing linguistic theories with child language data: The case of the mass-count distinction. *Linguistics and Philosophy*, *9*, 151–190.

Gelman, S.A., & O'Reilly, A.W. (1988). Children's inductive inferences within superordinate categories: The role of language and category structure. *Child Development*, *59*, 876–887.

Gleason, H.A. (1969). *An introduction to descriptive linguistics*. London: Holt, Rinehart, & Winston.

Gordon, P. (1985). Evaluating the semantic categories hypothesis: The case of the count/mass distinction. *Cognition*, *20*, 209–242.

Hunt, E., & Agnoli, F. (1991). The Whorfian hypothesis: A cognitive psychology perspective. *Psychological Review*, *98*, 377–389.

Imai, M. (1999). Constraint on word-learning constraints. *Japanese Psychological Research*, *41*, 5–20.

Imai, M., & Gentner, D. (1997). A cross-linguistic study of early word meaning: Universal ontology and linguistic influence. *Cognition*, *62*, 169–200.

Imai, M., & Wisniewski, E.J. (2003). *A cross-linguistic examination of superordinate categories*. Manuscript in preparation.

Jolicoeur, P., Gluck, M.A., & Kosslyn, S.M. (1984). Pictures and names: Making the connection. *Cognitive Psychology*, *16*, 243–275.

Langacker, R.W. (1987). Nouns and verbs. *Language*, *63*, 53–94.

Levy, Y. (1988). On the early learning of formal grammatical systems: Evidence from studies of the acquisition of gender and countability. *Journal of Child Language*, *15*, 179–187.

Lucy, J.A. (1992). *Grammatical categories and cognition*. Cambridge: Cambridge University Press.

Macnamara, J. (1982). *Names for things: A study of human learning*. Cambridge, MA: MIT Press.

Malt, B.C. (1993). Concept structure and category boundaries. In D. Medin, R. Taraban, & G. Nakamura (Eds.), *The psychology of learning and motivation*, *Vol. 29*: *Acquisition, representation, and processing of categories and concepts*. Orlando, FL: Academic Press.

Malt, B.C., Sloman, S.A., Gennari, S.P., Shi, M., & Wang, Y. (1999). Knowing versus naming: Similarity and the linguistic categorization of artifacts. *Journal of Memory and Language*, *40*, 230–262.

Maratsos, M. (1988). *The acquisition of formal word classes*. In Y. Levy, I. Schlesinger, & M. Braine (Eds.), *Categories and processes in language acquisition* (pp. 31–44). Hillsdale, NJ: Lawrence Erlbaum Associates, Inc.

Markman, E.M. (1985). Why superordinate category terms can be mass nouns. *Cognition*, *19*, 31–53.

McCawley, J. (1975). Lexicography and the count-mass distinction. *Berkeley Linguistic Society*, *1*, 314–321.

McPherson, L.P. (1991). A little goes a long way: Evidence for a perceptual basis of learning for the noun categories COUNT and MASS. *Journal of Child and Language*, *18*, 315–338.

Middleton, E.L., Wisniewski, E.J., Trindel, K.A., & Imai, M. (2003). *Separating the chaff from the oats: Evidence for a conceptual distinction between count and mass noun aggregates*. Manuscript submitted for publication.

Mufwene, S. (1984). The count mass distinction and the English lexicon. In D. Testen, V. Mishra & J. Drogo, (Eds.), *Papers from the parasession on lexical semantics*. Chicago: Chicago Linguistic Society.

Murphy, G.L., & Wisniewski, E.J. (1989). Categorizing objects in isolation and in scenes: What a superordinate is good for. *Journal of Experimental Psychology: Learning, Memory, and Cognition*, *15*, 572–586.

Murphy, G.L., & Brownell, H.H. (1985). Category differentiation in object recognition: Typicality constraints on the basic category advantage. *Journal of Experimental Psychology: Learning, Memory and Cognition, 11*, 70–84.

Palmer, F.R. (1971). *Grammar* (pp. 34–35). Harmondsworth, UK: Penguin Books.

Quine, W.V. (1960). *Word and object.* Cambridge, MA: MIT Press.

Quine, W.V. (1969). *Ontological relativity and other essays.* New York: Columbia University Press.

Quirk, R., & Greenbaum, S., Leech, G., & Svartvik, J. (1972) *A grammar of contemporary English* (pp. 169–171). New York: Seminar Press.

Rosch, E., Mervis, C.B., Gray, W.D., Johnson, D.M., & Boyes-Braem, P. (1976). Basic objects in natural categories. *Cognitive Psychology, 8*, 382–439.

Sloman, S.A., Love, B.C., & Ahn, W. (1998). Feature centrality and conceptual coherence. *Cognitive Science, 22*, 189–228.

Soja, N.N. (1992). Inferences about the meanings of nouns: The relationship between perception and syntax. *Cognitive Development, 7*, 29–45.

Soja, N.N., Carey, S., & Spelke, E.S. (1991). Ontological categories guide young children's inductions of word meaning: Object terms and substance terms. *Cognition, 38*, 179–211.

Tversky, B., & Hemenway, K. (1984). Objects, parts and categories. *Journal of Experimental Psychology: General, 113*, 169–913.

Ware, R. (1979). Some bits and pieces. In F. Pelletier (Ed.), *Mass terms: Some philosophical problems* (pp. 15–29). Dordrecht, Holland: Reidel.

Waxman, S.R. (1990). Linguistic biases and the establishment of conceptual hierarchies: Evidence from preschool children. *Cognitive Development, 5*, 123–150.

Waxman, S.R. & Gelman, R. (1986). Preschoolers' use of superordinate relations in classification and language. *Cognitive Development, 1*, 139–156.

Whorf, B.L. (1962). In J. Carroll (Ed.), *Language, thought, and reality* (pp. 140–141). New York/London: John Wiley & Sons.

Wierzbicka, A. (1988). *The semantics of grammar.* Amsterdam: John Benjamins.

Wisniewski, E.J., Imai, M., & Casey, L. (1996). On the equivalence of superordinate concepts. *Cognition, 60*, 269–298.

Wisniewski, E.J., & Murphy, G.L. (1989). Superordinate and basic category names in discourse: A textual analysis. *Discourse Processes, 12*, 245–261.

Zubin, D.A., & Kopcke, K. (1986). Gender and folk taxonomy: The indexical relation between grammatical and lexical categorization. In C. Craig (Ed.), *Noun classes and categorization* (pp. 139–180). Amsterdam: John Benjamins.

LANGUAGE AND COGNITIVE PROCESSES, 2003, *18* (5/6), 625–662

# Object recognition under semantic impairment: The effects of conceptual regularities on perceptual decisions

Timothy T. Rogers and John R. Hodges
*MRC Cognition and Brain Sciences Unit, Cambridge, UK*

Matthew A. Lambon Ralph
*University of Manchester, Manchester, UK*

Karalyn Patterson
*MRC Cognition and Brain Sciences Unit, Cambridge, UK*

Although patients with semantic deficits can sometimes show good performance on tests of object decision, we present evidence that this pattern applies when nonsense-objects do not respect the regularities of the domain. In a newly designed test of object-decision, 20 patients with semantic dementia viewed line drawings of a real and chimeric animal side-by-side, and were asked to decide which was real. The real animal was either more typical (*real > nonreal*) or less typical (*nonreal > real*) than the chimera. Performance was significantly better in the *real > nonreal* condition, and success in both conditions was modulated by patients' degree of semantic impairment. A similar effect of item typicality was revealed in a subset of items selected from a standard test battery. Object-decision scores were highly correlated with other pictorial and verbal assessments of conceptual knowledge, suggesting that impaired performance on all tasks resulted from the degradation of a unitary underlying system.

What is the relationship between perceptual knowledge and conceptual or semantic knowledge? How do the perceptual representations and processes that negotiate our experience with the environment give rise to our conceptual knowledge of it; and how in turn does conceptual knowledge influence perceptual recognition?

Requests for reprints should be addressed to Dr Timothy Rogers, Medical Research Council Cognition and Brain Sciences Unit, 15 Chaucer Road, Cambridge CB2 2EF, UK.

http://www.tandf.co.uk/journals/pp/01690965.html    DOI: 10.1080/01690960344000053

Answers to these questions have tended to fall into one of two camps. The first follows a research tradition extending back to Lissauer (1890, cf. Humphreys & Riddoch 1999) and heavily influenced by Marr (1982), in which a stimulus object or word must be recognised before its meaning can be accessed. "Recognition" in turn is construed as the process of matching a perceptual representation of the stimulus item to stored representations of previously encountered stimuli (or representations derived from these). Such stored "structural" representations are understood to be qualitatively different from the "semantic" representations that store meanings—they do not encode explicit semantic content, but capture information about visuo-spatial structure in the case of visual object recognition (see for example Biederman, 1987) or lexico-morphological structure in the case of word recognition (see Coltheart, Rastle, Perry, Langdon, & Ziegler, 2001). For example, the dual-route cascaded (DRC) model of word-reading posits phonological and orthographic "lemma" representations that facilitate spoken- and written-word recognition, but which do not capture word meaning (Coltheart et al., 2001). Similarly, the interactive activation (IAC) model of object naming posits visual "structural descriptions" which permit the recognition of objects from vision prior to retrieval of explicit information about their functional and associative properties (Humphreys, Riddoch, & Quinlan, 1988). Both models distinguish representations that encode explicit meanings from those that subserve stimulus recognition.

The second view also has a long provenance in cognitive science, extending at least back to Wernicke and other neuropsychologists of the late nineteenth century (see Eggert, 1977). Here, semantic knowledge does not reside in representations that are separate from those that subserve perception and recognition, but emerges from the learned associations amongst such representations in different modalities (e.g., Allport, 1985; Warrington & McCarthy, 1987; Humphreys & Forde, 2001). Neuroanatomically, the semantic system (on this view) consists in those cortical tracts and regions that permit the interaction of perceptual representations in different modalities, which need not be construed as capturing explicit, inherently meaningful semantic content (Rogers et al., in press; Rogers & McClelland, in press; Rogers & Plaut, 2002). Instead, meanings inhere only in the distributed patterns of activity provoked by a stimulus item or event across regions of cortex that are dedicated to the representation of modality-specific information: what things look like, how they move, the sounds they make, the words that describe them. This approach has found recent widespread endorsement in the interpretation of findings from functional neuroimaging (e.g., Chao, Haxby, & Martin, 1999; Damasio, Grabowski, Tranel, & Hichwa, 1996; Kellenbach, Brett, & Patterson, 2001), EEG (e.g., Pulvermuller, 1999), and neuropsychology (e.g., Plaut, 2002), as well as in many contemporary theories of conceptual knowledge (e.g., Barsalou, this issue; Smith, 2000; Quinn, Johnson, Mareschal, Rakison, & Younger, 2000; Rogers et al., in press).

The critical difference underlying the two approaches may be summarised thus: the former view differentiates between two kinds of representation—those that encode *semantic content*, or "meanings", and those that encode structural information sufficient to support stimulus recognition in a given modality of input. The second view does not distinguish between content-bearing semantic representations and content-free structural representations, but emphasises that semantic memory *serves a particular function*—namely, the association in memory of modality-specific perceptual representations. Accordingly, we will refer to the former view as a *content-based* approach to semantics, and to the latter view as a *process-based* approach.

In the current paper we examine one line of evidence relevant to this debate from the study of object recognition, which has heretofore been taken to support content-based approaches to semantics: specifically, reports of cases in which brain-damaged patients appear able to recognise line-drawings of objects as familiar, despite being unable to retrieve semantic information about them. Such cases appear to provide some of the most convincing evidence that stimulus recognition is supported by a process that is functionally independent of semantic knowledge (Humphreys et al., 1988; Coltheart, Inglis, Michie, Bates, & Budd, 1998). We will suggest an alternative explanation for the apparent preservation of visual object recognition under semantic impairment, more in keeping with a process-based approach to semantics, and will describe three experiments designed to test the explanation. The results suggest to us that the ability to recognise objects from vision always draws upon semantic resources, as required by process-based approaches, but that the consequences of disruption to the semantic system are only apparent in certain predictable stimulus conditions. In the general discussion we will consider implications of the current results for contemporary theories of semantic memory.

## PAST RESEARCH ON VISUAL OBJECT PROCESSING

In the neuropsychological literature, the idea that visual object recognition is subserved by representations and processes that are functionally independent of semantics stems primarily from studies of object decision (Hillis & Caramazza, 1995; Humphreys & Riddoch, 1987, 1993; Rumiati & Humphreys, 1997; Stewart, Parkin, & Hunkin, 1992). In the typical experiment, participants are shown a series of single line drawings depicting either a real object, or a non-real object (a *chimera*) constructed from the parts of real items (e.g., a turtle's body with the head and neck of a snake). The participant's task is to accept the real objects and reject the chimeras. Because the individual parts from which the chimeric objects are built are all real (and familiar), and the chimeras themselves are as visually complex and well-formed as the real objects, accurate performance requires participants to make their judgements with reference to stored knowledge about whole familiar objects (Humphreys et al., 1988; Humphreys, Lamote, & Lloyd-Jones, 1995). Object decision has become an important means of assessing the integrity of visual object recognition in the face of semantic and other kinds of neuropsychological disorders (Humphreys & Forde, 2001; Rumiati & Humphreys, 1997). When used together with tests of higher-level visual perception which do not draw on stored knowledge about real objects (such as the unusual-views matching test), and with tests of semantic memory, object decision is often interpreted as providing a tool for determining the locus of a visual processing impairment.

Take, for example, the seminal study of patient J.B. (Riddoch & Humphreys, 1987) who, despite substantial impairments in retrieving semantic information from visual presentation of objects, performed within the normal range on "easy" and "difficult" tests of object decision (from the Birmingham Object Recognition Battery, or BORB; see Riddoch & Humphreys, 1993). J.B. performed relatively well on tests of higher-level object perception (such as the view-matching task, which requires participants to decide which two of three photographs depict the same object from different viewpoints) and on purely verbal tests of semantic memory (such as naming to definition). Humphreys et al. (1988) concluded that J.B.'s difficulty did not lie in visual perception, visual object recognition, or semantics. Instead it resulted from damage to the tracts by which visual representations of known objects (*structural descriptions*) activate the functionally independent semantic representations that store meanings. Since this report, there have been a handful of similar cases (Hillis & Caramazza, 1995; Sheridan & Humphreys, 1993; Stewart et al., 1992), supporting the conclusion that visual object recognition does not depend upon intact communication with semantics, and must therefore be subserved by an independent recognition system.

Studies of patients with generalized semantic impairments complicate this picture to some extent. Particularly informative in this regard are studies of patients with semantic dementia: a neurodegenerative condition characterized by progressive atrophy of the anterior temporal lobes bilaterally (Garrard & Hodges, 2000; Hodges, Garrard, & Patterson, 1998). Patients with semantic dementia typically present with a moderate to severe anomia, accompanied by general impairment on a wide range of semantic tasks including category fluency, word to picture matching, sorting both words and pictures into conceptual categories, semantic matching tasks such as the Pyramids and Palm Trees test, concept definition to both words and pictures, sound-picture matching, demonstrating object use, drawing, and so on (e.g., Bozeat et al., 2003; Bozeat, Lambon Ralph, Patterson, & Hodges, in press; Hodges, Graham, & Patterson, 1995; Snowden, Goulding, & Neary, 1989; Warrington, 1975). These deficits are not typically category- or modality-specific, and the degrees of impairment measured in different semantic tasks are typically highly correlated (Bozeat, Lambon Ralph, Patterson, Garrard, & Hodges, 2000), although patients with predominantly left temporal atrophy often have greater difficulty with verbal relative to non-verbal semantic tasks (Lambon Ralph, McClelland, Patterson, Galton, & Hodges, 2001).

Despite these often severe semantic impairments, other cognitive faculties appear to be remarkably spared well into the progression of the disorder. For example, speech remains grammatical and (apart from word-finding difficulties) fluent, patients are well-oriented in time and place, and perform within the normal range on tests of episodic memory such as delayed recall of the Rey figure, and tests of mechanical problem-solving (Hodges et al., 1999a; Hodges, Spatt, & Patterson, 1999b; Hodges, Bozeat, Lambon Ralph, Patterson, & Spatt, 2000) and executive function (e.g., Wisconsin card-sorting, see Perry & Hodges, 1999).

Patients with semantic dementia typically perform within the normal range on tests of visual object and spatial perception well into the disease progression. For example, they achieve normal scores in subtests of the Visual Object and Space Perception battery (VOSP; Warrington & James, 1991); on tasks of matching the same object photographed from different views (see Hovius, Kellenbach, Graham, Hodges, & Patterson, 2003); on tests of recognition memory for pictures of objects or faces (Graham, Simons, Pratt, Patterson, & Hodges, 2000); and in the immediate and delayed conditions of the Rey figure copy (Hodges et al., 1999a,b).

Despite these spared abilities, the semantic impairment that characterises this syndrome can express itself in purely visual tasks that tap the participant's knowledge about real objects. For example, when patients are required to reproduce drawings of real objects from memory after a 10-second delay, they show consistent, striking impairments. Increasingly with disease progression, they tend to omit the distinguishing and idiosyncratic visual properties of objects (such as the horns and udder on the cow); and to incorrectly add properties typical of a given category to atypical category members (e.g., adding four legs to a drawing of a seal; see Rogers et al., in press). The same patients are well able to copy the same drawings, so long as the stimulus remains present for them to consult—suggesting (together with their generally good performance on other visual tests) that the disorder spares visual object perception. Furthermore, the patients' relatively preserved scores on delayed-copying of non-meaningful stimuli (such as complex geometric shapes or the Rey figure) suggest visual, executive, and episodic memory resources that are sufficient to the copying task under delay conditions. Only when required to reproduce drawings of meaningful objects after a delay do they show substantial deficits (Bozeat et al., 2003).

The pattern of errors observed in delayed copying mirrors the general pattern of impaired performance observed across a range of different semantic tasks (Rogers et al., in press; Tyler, Moss, Durrant-Peatfield, & Levy, 2000), including naming (Hodges et al., 1995), sorting, property verification (Warrington, 1975), word-picture matching (Funnell, 1996), and drawing to name (Lambon Ralph & Howard, 2000). In all of these tasks, patients with semantic dementia demonstrate (a) a relative preservation of knowledge about properties that objects tend to share with their semantic neighbours, (b) rapid deterioration of knowledge about idiosyncratic or distinguishing object properties, (c) robust preservation of broad semantic distinctions (e.g., animal versus artifact) with declining sensitivity to narrower distinctions (e.g., pig versus goat), and (d) over-extension of names and properties from typical category exemplars to their semantic neighbours (e.g., calling a pig a "dog"; drawing four legs on a picture of a seal). The pattern of errors observed in the delayed copy task neatly reflects these tendencies as well, suggesting that this task may be susceptible to the same underlying semantic impairment that disrupts performance on such clearly semantic tasks as naming, word-sorting, and word-picture matching.

The empirical data thus pose a certain puzzle. Studies of patients like J.B. suggest that the visual knowledge that supports visual object recognition is independent of semantic knowledge, as stipulated by content-based approaches to semantic memory (e.g., Humphreys et al., 1995; Coltheart et al., 1998). By contrast, studies of delayed copying in patients with semantic dementia suggest that impairments to semantic memory also compromise visual representations of meaningful objects, as required by process-based approaches to semantics.

The experiments we will describe here suggest a possible resolution to the apparent incongruity of these data. We suggest that the general robustness of knowledge about the shared and typical properties of semantically related objects may provide the basis for seemingly preserved performance in the object decision test under semantic impairment, owing to the fashion in which target and distractor stimuli are usually constructed. If the real-object targets in the test corpus consist mainly of items that share many visual attributes with their semantic neighbours, whereas most of the chimeric distractors include unusual and idiosyncratic visual features, patients may perform well simply by accepting typical-looking items and rejecting atypical-looking items. Put differently, the increasing restriction of their conceptual knowledge to general and typical features may lead the patients to accept any item whose properties are consistent with the regularities that are still relatively robust in the degraded system, and to reject or guess randomly on any unusual item whose properties violate those regularities.

Several previous studies of semantic dementia have included assessments of object decision, with discrepant outcomes ranging from virtually perfect performance (Lambon Ralph & Howard, 2000) to scores no better than chance (Hodges, Patterson, & Tyler, 1994). Of particular note, one case with an unusual category-specific pattern of semantic dementia was impaired at recognising natural kinds (especially fruits and vegetables), in line with his generally poorer semantic performance for natural kinds (Barbarotto, Capitani, Spinnler, & Trivelli, 1995).

It is difficult, however, to draw any general conclusions regarding object decision performance in semantic dementia, because most reports so far are from single-case studies of patients with widely varying degrees of semantic deterioration and also tested with different sets of stimulus materials. The purpose of the present study was to obtain case-series data on object decision in semantic dementia, using materials designed to assess the impact of regularities in the real and non-real objects. In Experiment 1, we discuss a new object-decision test designed to measure the influence of conceptual regularities on object decision performance in a forced-choice paradigm. In Experiment 2, we investigate the influence of conceptual over-regularisation in the classic object-decision paradigm; and in Experiment 3 we consider the extent to which semantic task deficits and object decision deficits may be construed as arising from the same central semantic impairment in semantic dementia. The results of these experiments will then be discussed with reference to process- and content-based approaches to semantics.

## EXPERIMENT 1: THE OVER-REGULAR ANIMAL TEST (OAT)

We tested object decision performance using a two-alternative forced-choice design, in which the participants were shown line drawings of a real animal and a chimera side-by-side, and were asked to decide which was real. Half of the stimuli were constructed so that the chimera was effectively more prototypical than the real animal (the *nonreal > real* condition)—for example, the patient might see a picture of a camel paired with a chimeric camel which had no hump. The remaining stimuli were constructed such that the chimera was atypical relative to the real animal (the *real > nonreal* condition)—for example, the patient might see a donkey paired with a chimeric donkey with a hump added to its back. By "typicality", we mean the propensity for an item to be composed predominantly of parts that are shared by familiar items in the same semantic category. For example, most familiar animals have tails and ears, whereas relatively few have humps on their backs or horns on their snouts. Thus, when shown a lion with or without a tail, and asked to decide which is real, the correct choice (the lion with a tail) is also the most typical stimulus. However when shown a gorilla with and without a tail, the correct choice (the gorilla without a tail) is the less typical stimulus. Sixteen such stimulus pairs were created in each condition, making 32 items in the test all together. Examples are shown in Figure 1. If object decision is supported purely by intact visual recognition processes, and if semantic dementia is a selective deficit of conceptual knowledge, then patients should be able to match the real-animal targets to stored visual representations, and should perform well in both conditions. On the other hand, if their visual recognition processes are contaminated by the over-regularisation that results from degraded semantic processing, they should perform well in the *real > nonreal* condition (in which chimeras are atypical relative to targets), but poorly in the *nonreal > real* condition (in which chimeras are more prototypical than targets).

In this experiment, we employed only animal items, simply because the domain of animals has strong typicality structure, with many properties tending to be shared by well-known exemplars—artifact categories by contrast tend to have less apparent typicality structure (Garrard, Lambon Ralph, Hodges, & Patterson, 2001; Tyler et al., 2000; Cree & McRae, 2002; Rogers et al., in press). Patients with semantic dementia almost always show equivalent impairment for animal and artifact domains (Garrard,

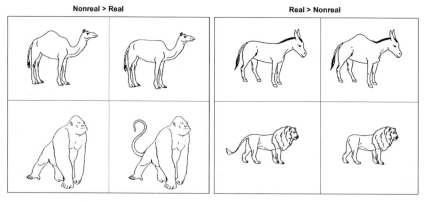

**Figure 1.** Examples of stimuli in the *nonreal > real* and *real > nonreal* conditions of the Over-regular Animal Test (OAT).

Lambon Ralph, & Hodges, 2002; Rogers & Plaut, 2002), and we expect that the results obtained in the present experiment would extend well to artifact categories that have an equally strong degree of typicality structure.

To assess our manipulation of visual typicality, we asked 10 normal control subjects to judge the relative typicality of the visual features that differentiated real and chimeric stimuli in the OAT stimulus pairs. For example, participants were asked to judge whether the typical animal has a hump on its back or no hump on its back, long ears or short ears, four legs or two legs, etc. The volunteers were further instructed that in some cases the choice might be difficult to make, but that they should rely upon their own idea of what a "typical animal" might look like to make their decision. For all but four of the properties, participants unanimously judged as more typical the property that was consistent with our intended manipulation—for example, judging that the typical animal was unlikely to have a hump on its back, was likely to have a tail, was more likely to have four rather than two legs, etc. For the remaining properties (squat legs vs. long legs; short ears vs. long ears; straight neck vs. curved neck; crest on the head vs. no crest on the head) the majority of participants chose the property that was consistent with the intended manipulation.

## Methods

*Participants.*    Data were collected from 15 control participants from the MRC-CBU volunteer subject panel (age- and education-matched to the patient group) and from 20 patients with semantic dementia: 16 recruited through a Memory and Cognitive Disorders Clinic at Addenbrooke's Hospital, Cambridge; and 4 through the Neurology Department of the Royal United Hospital (RUH) in Bath, and the Research Institute for Care of the Elderly (RICE), St. Martin's Hospital in Bath. All patients matched the profile of semantic dementia that has been documented at length elsewhere (see Patterson & Hodges, 2000, for a recent review). Scores on a range of standard neuropsychological tests (along with demographic data) are shown in Table 1. All patients were administered a semantic battery, and all showed mild to severe difficulty with picture naming, word-picture matching, and both verbal and visual variants of the Pyramids and Palm Trees test. In this and subsequent experiments, all data from a given individual were collected within a 6-month period. Scores on these tests are also shown in Table 1. In this and all subsequent tables and figures, patients are rank-ordered according to their scores on a 10-alternative forced-choice word-picture matching task which provides a general index of the extent of their semantic impairment (Hodges et al., 1995).

## TABLE 1
### Scores from 20 semantic dementia patients on a range of semantic and non-semantic neuropsychological tests

| Test | AC | WM | AN | EO | JP | ATe | MA | JC | DA | GO | SL | EK | AT | KH | GT | JG | DC | PD | JH | MK |
|---|---|---|---|---|---|---|---|---|---|---|---|---|---|---|---|---|---|---|---|---|
| Age | 58 | 53 | 64 | 75 | 65 | 65 | 63 | 58 | 75 | 62 | 52 | 59 | 60 | 59 | 70 | 68 | 77 | 72 | 62 | 66 |
| Education | 13 | 13 | 9 | 12 | 10 | 13 | 13 | 10 | 16 | 9 | 12 | | 10 | 9 | 9 | 11 | 9 | 13 | 10 | 10 |
| Sex | M | F | M | F | M | M | M | M | M | M | F | F | M | M | F | F | F | F | F | F |
| Clinical | | | | | | | | | | | | | | | | | | | | |
| MMSE (/30) | 30 | 24 | 28 | 15 | 27 | 25 | 29 | 15 | 9 | 19 | 24 | 27 | 26 | 24 | 26 | 19 | 15 | 13 | 7 | 21 |
| Rey | | | | | | | | | | | | | | | | | | | | |
| Copy | 36 | 36 | 36 | 25.5 | 36 | 36 | 36 | 31 | 34 | 34 | 30 | 34 | 23.5 | 36 | 34 | 34 | 29 | 36 | 34 | 30 |
| Immediate recall | 24 | 23 | 29 | 0.5 | 24 | 23 | 17.5 | 8.5 | 16 | 26 | 16 | – | – | 12 | – | 3.5 | 3 | – | 5 | – |
| Delayed recall | 23 | 25 | 27.5 | – | 24 | 24 | 6.5 | 8 | 17 | 18.5 | 14 | – | 3 | 12.5 | – | 4 | 4 | – | 0 | – |
| Digit span | | | | | | | | | | | | | | | | | | | | |
| Forw | 8 | 8 | 8 | 6 | 5 | 8 | 6 | 7 | 3 | 6 | 5 | 6 | 5 | 4 | 6 | 6 | 5 | 7 | 6 | 5 |
| Back | 7 | 5 | 6 | 3 | 4 | 4 | 3 | 3 | 2 | 3 | 4 | 7 | 4 | 3 | 4 | 4 | 3 | 5 | 5 | 4 |
| VOSP | | | | | | | | | | | | | | | | | | | | |
| Screen (/20) | 20 | 20 | – | 20 | 19 | 20 | – | 16 | 18 | 20 | 20 | 20 | 18 | 20 | 20 | 19 | 17 | 19 | 17 | 17 |
| Incomplete letters (/20) | 19 | 19 | 20 | 12 | 19 | 20 | 19 | 17 | 17 | 19 | 20 | 20 | 13 | 19 | 18 | 20 | – | 3 | – | 10 |
| Dot count (/10) | 10 | 10 | – | 10 | 10 | 10 | 10 | 8 | 9 | 10 | 9 | 10 | 10 | 10 | 10 | 10 | 10 | 10 | 10 | 10 |
| Position discrimination (/20) | 20 | 11 | 20 | 17 | 20 | 20 | 20 | – | 19 | 20 | – | 20 | 16 | 19 | 20 | 20 | 18 | 16 | 19 | 17 |
| Number location (/10) | 10 | 10 | 10 | 5 | 10 | 9 | 10 | 2 | 10 | 10 | – | 10 | 3 | 10 | 10 | 10 | 10 | 9 | 10 | 6 |
| Cube (/10) | 10 | 10 | 10 | 1 | 10 | 10 | 10 | 10 | 8 | 10 | 10 | 10 | – | 10 | 10 | 10 | 4 | 5 | 9 | 6 |
| Object decision (/20) | 15 | 19 | 20 | 16 | 17 | 19 | 16 | 16 | 18 | 16 | 13 | 12 | 12 | 17 | 12 | 16 | 14 | 6 | 17 | 9 |
| Semantic | | | | | | | | | | | | | | | | | | | | |
| WP-Match (/64) | 63 | 63 | 63 | 59 | 59 | 58 | 57 | 56 | 50 | 49 | 48 | 46 | 46 | 44 | 32 | 29 | 19 | 17 | 16 | 11 |
| PPT (/52) | | | | | | | | | | | | | | | | | | | | |
| Words | 49 | 39 | 48 | 48 | 48 | 44 | 48 | 36 | 41 | 34 | 38 | 36 | 33 | 41 | 32 | 28 | 33 | 26 | – | 26 |
| Pictures | 49 | 44 | – | 44 | 49 | 47 | 41 | 40 | 39 | 42 | 44 | 35 | 29 | 35 | 37 | 38 | 25 | 26 | 30 | 33 |
| Naming (/64) | 50 | 57 | 62 | 30 | 57 | 10 | 13 | 33 | 18 | 7 | 18 | 17 | 20 | 30 | 11 | 6 | 3 | 4 | 5 | 2 |

*Note*: Patients are ordered by their scores in the word-picture matching task.

*Procedure.* Participants were told that they would see a series of picture pairs depicting similar-looking animals. They were instructed that the two pictures would differ in some important way, and that they must decide which picture showed a "real" animal. The participants were then shown the series of 32 test items in the same random order. For each item, the experimenter pointed out the difference between the real and chimeric animal, without referring to either the animal or the animal's parts by name. For example, the experimenter might say, "This one looks like this, and this one looks like this", while gesturing toward the feature that differentiated the real animal from the chimera. The participant was then prompted to decide which animal was real.

## Results

Control participants performed well in both conditions of the task. In the *real > nonreal* condition, all controls performed perfectly. In the *nonreal > real* condition, performance ranged from 14–16 correct (of 16). This may seem to indicate that the *nonreal > real* condition was somewhat more difficult, but an item analysis revealed that all controls scored perfectly for all but two stimulus items in this condition. The two troublesome items were the raccoon and the gorilla, on which only about half of the control subjects made the correct choice. Dropping these two difficult items and their partners in the *real > nonreal* condition from the analysis of patient data does not change the results of interest. In the following report of the results, the figures show the data from the entire set; but in our statistical analyses we will report results for both the complete set and the set with these items excluded.

The proportions correct in the two conditions are shown in Figure 2, for each individual patient and for the patient group as a whole. As noted earlier, the patients are ordered according to the magnitude of their semantic impairment as assessed by word-picture matching, with milder patients toward the left and more severe patients toward the right. Accuracy in both object-decision conditions declined to some extent with severity of semantic impairment, and significant correlations with the word-picture matching task were observed in both conditions ($r = .66, p < .001$ for the *real > nonreal* condition; $r = .77, p < .001$ for the *nonreal > real* condition). For all except the mildest patients (whose scores were relatively good in both conditions), however, performance was worse for *nonreal > real* items than for *real > nonreal* pairs. For some cases, the discrepancy in performance is quite dramatic—for example, both A.T. and P.D. scored below chance for *nonreal > real* items, but above 80% correct when the real item looked more typical.

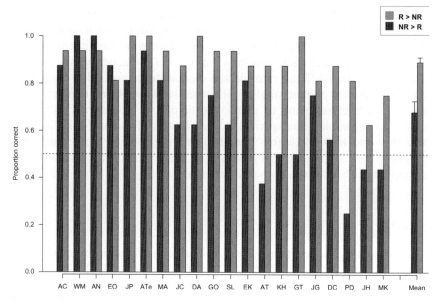

**Figure 2.** Proportion correct for *nonreal > real* and *real > nonreal* conditions of the OAT, for each of 20 semantic dementia patients, ordered by degree of semantic impairment. The dotted line indicates chance performance.

The data were subjected to an arcsine transformation and tested with a repeated-measures ANOVA using (transformed) proportion correct as the dependent measure, and item condition as the within-subject independent measure. The ANOVA confirmed that patients performed reliably better on *real > nonreal* than *nonreal > real* stimulus items, $F_1(1, 19) = 18.23$, $p < .0001$ for the complete set; $F_1(1, 19) = 7.74$ $p < .02$ for the set with the two difficult items and their partners removed. The difference was also significant by items in both analyses, $F_2(1, 30) = 17.6$, $p < .001$ for analysis with all items; $F_2(1 , 27) = 12.1$, $p < .003$ for analysis dropping difficult items.

## DISCUSSION

Experiment 1, introducing a new test of object decision (the OAT), demonstrates that object decision performance in a forced-choice paradigm under semantic impairment is highly sensitive to the structure of the target and distractor stimuli. When real target objects (animals in this test) are typical-looking and chimeric distractors are atypical, object decision may seem to be spared even in patients with severe semantic deficits. For example, P.D. scored correctly on only 17 of 64 items (27% correct) in the word-picture matching task, but chose correctly for 13 of 16 items (82% correct) in the *real* > *nonreal* condition of the OAT. When target objects are unusual and chimeras are typical-looking, however, the picture changes dramatically: even patients with relatively mild semantic deficits may perform poorly. For example, J.C. exhibited a mild semantic impairment in the word-picture matching task (56/64, or 87% correct), but chose correctly for only 10 of 16 *nonreal* > *real* items in the OAT (67% correct). This difference is particularly striking when one considers that chance performance is 10% in the word-picture matching task, but 50% in the object decision task. Considering *nonreal* > *real* items in isolation, patients like J.C. may seem to have an object-decision deficit with only mildly degraded semantic knowledge; and considering *real* > *nonreal* items alone, patients like P.D. may seem to have spared object recognition with substantially degraded semantic knowledge. Considering the two conditions together, we can see that these differences are a factor of the stimulus properties, and not of the neuropsychological profiles of the two patients.

One of the patients (J.G.) seemed to perform disproportionately well in the *nonreal* > *real* condition of the OAT, given the degree of her semantic impairment. From comments made during the test session, it was clear that one of J.G.'s correct choices in this condition, and at least two of her choices in the *real* > *nonreal* condition, arose from her confusion about the identity of the different animal parts. When shown pictures of a normal horse and a chimeric horse with an udder added, J.G. chose the chimera and laughingly said, "It's a horse, isn't it—a *male* horse". Apparently she had mistaken the udder for male genitalia. When shown the matched stimulus in the alternate condition (a cow with and without an udder), she again picked the animal with an udder (this time correctly), and again commented that it must be a male. Finally, when shown the deer with four or with six legs, she incorrectly chose the chimera, but commented that it "had too many legs". Since the real and chimeric items differed only in the number of legs, it is not clear on what basis J.G. made her decision. The discrepancy in performance between the two conditions was small in J.G.'s case; but in light of these comments it is difficult to conclude that J.G. succeeded in object recognition. Nevertheless we will consider J.G.'s object decision performance in further detail in Experiment 2, to determine whether she constitutes a counter-example to our claim that semantic impairment necessarily compromises visual object recognition.

Three further points are of interest. First, the patients' poor performance in the *nonreal* > *real* condition cannot be attributed to any deficit of episodic memory. In past work, it has been difficult to rule out the possibility, however unlikely, that deficits observed in the delayed-copy task actually reflect a subtle episodic memory impairment in semantic dementia. However, the current task does not require participants to retain visual information in memory over a delay, and in any case the demands of the two conditions are identical—hence it is difficult to explain the data with reference to episodic memory problems.

Second, because each stimulus item consists of a real and a chimeric animal side-by-side, participants were always faced with a correct option when making their decision in the current experiment. It therefore seems an inescapable conclusion that the patients were failing at recognition. If the patients had intact "structural descriptions", and if the processes that activate such representations were functionally independent of semantics, the patients should have recognised the real animal target in each stimulus pair. The results thus suggest either that visual object recognition processes are not independent of semantics, or that the non-semantic visual representations and processes that support recognition are conjointly impaired along with semantic memory in these cases. We will return to this issue in Experiment 3.

Finally, the discrepancy in performance between the two conditions is consistent with the account of spared object-decision in the face of semantic impairment that we sketched out in the introduction. The more impaired patients in Experiment 1 were likely to accept prototypical-looking animals and reject unusual-looking animals, regardless of whether they were real. The finding suggests that patients with semantic impairments will seem to have intact object recognition in the standard object-decision procedure if real targets are more prototypical than chimeric distractors. We investigate this possibility further in the next experiment by comparing patient performance on the OAT with performance on the BORB.

## COMPARING THE OAT AND THE BORB

We designed Experiment 2 to fulfil two aims. First, although results from the OAT are strongly suggestive, it is difficult to know how the data from this task relate to object decision performance in the standard single-item yes/no procedure. In contrast to the usual task, the forced-choice procedure required participants to direct their attention to two different stimuli, to select one as a suitable target for the response, and to refrain from acting on the other. It is possible that these differences tax executive and attentional systems in ways that the standard procedure does not. It is therefore useful to evaluate the degree of impairment evident in the two conditions of the OAT with reference to well-known tests of object decision such as the BORB. Thus in Experiment 2a, we compare performance on the OAT and the short version of the BORB employed by Riddoch and Humphreys (1993) for 13 of the 20 semantic dementia patients described above.

Second, we were interested to know whether the regularity effects witnessed in Experiment 1 might also be observed in the standard object-decision procedure. To this end, we collected data on the long version of the BORB from four of our participants in Experiment 2b. From this battery we culled a subset of very prototypical and very atypical real animals and chimeric distractors, and assessed performance on these as a function of typicality and stimulus type (real or chimeric).

## Experiment 2a: Comparing the magnitude of impairment in BORB and OAT

*Procedure.*    Nine of the 20 semantic dementia patients described above were tested on the short version of the BORB object decision task, and four patients were tested on the complete version. The long form of the task consists of 128 line drawings, half depicting real objects and half chimeric objects matched for visual complexity. Though most of the items in the BORB object decision task are animals, this battery also includes a set of artifact items. The BORB is administered in four blocks of 32 items each (half real and half chimeric). Two blocks include relatively easy stimuli (as judged by university undergraduates) and two contain some-what harder items. The short version consists of one easy block and one hard block from the complete test. In this experiment we will consider the performance of all 13 patients as a group on the items from the short version of the task.

The usual object decision paradigm employed in the BORB proceeds as follows. Patients are instructed that they will see a series of line drawings, some depicting real objects and some not. For each item, the participants are to indicate whether or not they think it is real. Items are presented in the same randomly generated order for all participants.

## Results

The left-hand panel of Figure 3 displays the means and standard errors of the proportion correct for all 13 patients on the short 64-item BORB object decision and on the two conditions of the OAT from Experiment 1. Performance on the BORB task fell mid-way between the two conditions of the OAT. Average performance was also reflected in the individual data: proportion correct on the BORB fell between performance on the two conditions of the OAT for 11 of 13 patients. For the two exceptions (E.K. and J.G.) performance on the BORB was worse than performance on either of the OAT conditions.

The middle and right-hand panels of Figure 3 shows the same data calculated separately for milder and more severe patients, as determined by a median split on word-picture matching scores across the 13 patients.

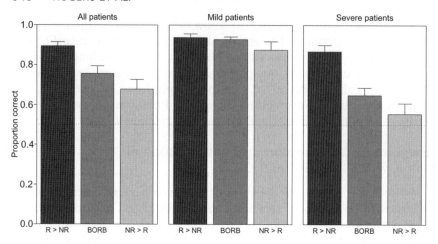

**Figure 3.**   Mean proportion correct for *real > nonreal* OAT (*R > NR*), the short version of the BORB object decision, and *nonreal > real* OAT (*NR > R*) for all patients (left panel), and separately for milder (middle) and more severe (right) patients, as measured by a median split on word-picture matching. Error bars indicate the standard error of the mean for the different factor levels.

The pattern described above is clearly influenced by the severity of semantic deficit. Milder patients (scoring 75% or better on the word-picture matching test) performed well in all three tasks, with only small differences apparent across them (although in the predicted direction). The performance of the more severe patients (scoring less than 75% correct on the word-picture matching test), by contrast, varied substantially across the three conditions, with the *nonreal > real* condition of the OAT near chance, the BORB somewhat better, and the *real > nonreal* condition of the OAT yielding better than 80% correct. The data from the more severe group demonstrate that the very same set of semantically impaired patients may show object-decision scores that do not differ from chance (*nonreal > real* OAT); are better than chance but substantially off ceiling (BORB); or are only a little off ceiling (*real > nonreal* OAT). Whether the patients appear to have a deficit of object recognition thus depends upon which test is used.

We tested the statistical reliability of these observations with a repeated-measures analysis of covariance, in which testing condition (*nonreal > real* OAT, BORB, or *real > nonreal* OAT) was treated as a within-subject factor, and severity of impairment as assessed by the word-picture matching task was treated as a between-subjects covariate. Scores on the different object-decision tasks were converted to proportions and subjected to an arcsine transformation prior to conducting the ANCOVA. The results revealed significant main effects of both severity of impairment, between-subjects effect $F(1, 11) = 20.86$, $p < .001$ for all data; $F(1, 11) = 7.86$, $p < .001$ for the reduced OAT set with difficult items removed, and test condition, within-subjects effect $F(2, 22) = 9.33$, $p < .001$; $F(2, 22) = 18.98$, $p < .001$ for the reduced OAT set. Post-hoc contrasts of the condition effect revealed that, across all patients, performance on the *real* > *nonreal* condition was reliably better than performance on the other two conditions ($p < .01$ in full and reduced OAT sets), but that performance on the BORB was not significantly better than on the *nonreal* > *real* condition of the OAT ($p = $ *n.s.* in both OAT sets). The interaction of these factors was also significant, $F(2, 22) = 3.86$, $p < .04$ for all data; $F(2, 22) = 6.07$, $p < .04$ for reduced OAT set, indicating that the differences among test conditions were greater for the severe patients than for the milder patients, as Figure 3 suggests.

To determine how scores for milder and more substantially impaired patients compare with chance performance, we divided the 13 patients into "mild" and "severe" groups using a median split on their word-picture matching scores, and calculated 95% confidence intervals on the transformed mean proportion correct for all three object-decision measures. These confidence intervals were then reverse-transformed to derive appropriate intervals in the original proportion-correct measure. Amongst the mild patients, the confidence intervals for the three test conditions overlapped: for the *nonreal* > *real* OAT the estimate ranged from 0.71–0.95; for the BORB, from 0.87–0.95; and for the *real* > *nonreal* OAT, from 0.91–0.96. Amongst the severe patients, the estimate for the *nonreal* > *real* OAT ranged from 0.42–0.67, meaning that severe patients did not perform reliably better than chance in this condition. For the BORB, the 95% confidence interval ranged from 0.56–0.69 which is reliably better than chance, even though not reliably better than performance in the *nonreal* > *real* condition of the OAT. Finally, in the *real* > *nonreal* condition of the OAT the confidence interval for severe patients ranged from 0.81–0.91, reliably better than both other conditions.

Finally, we note that J.G., the patient who performed unusually well in the *nonreal* > *real* condition of the OAT, chose correctly on only 63% of the items in the BORB. The two patients closest to J.G. in the extent of their semantic impairment (G.T. and D.C.) scored 67 and 66% correct, respectively. Thus there is no indication from the BORB that J.G.'s object recognition is disproportionately spared given the degree of her semantic impairment.

*Comment.*    The results of Experiment 2a show that performance in the standard object decision task can be compromised under semantic impairment, just as is performance on the OAT. Moreover, the magnitude of the deficits on the short version of the BORB is just what one might expect from these patients' OAT scores, assuming that BORB stimuli were selected without regard for the degree to which targets and distractors are typical-looking. One can view the two subsets of the OAT as exemplifying polar stimulus conditions: one in which targets are always more typical than distractors, and one in which the reverse is true. If object decision deficits arise primarily from sensitivity to typicality in semantic dementia, these conditions should represent the upper and lower bounds of performance under semantic impairment, as they appear to do. Because items in the BORB were not designed to manipulate typicality, performance on this task should fall somewhere between these bounds, as indeed it did both in the average patient data and in all but two of the individual cases.

## Experiment 2b: Over-regularisation in the BORB

Is there more direct evidence that a preference for typicality in semantic dementia can influence performance in the standard object decision task? To answer this question, we examined the performance of four patients (E.K., P.D., G.T., and M.K.) on a subset of real and chimeric items from the BORB, selected to be either highly typical-looking, or highly atypical. The four patients considered were those recruited in Bath, who were tested on the full complement of items in the long version of the BORB (whereas the remaining patients from Cambridge completed just the 64 items in the shorter version). As indicated in Table 1, all four fall in the severe end of the disease spectrum.

*Procedure.* We examined the 128 stimulus items from the full complement of the BORB object decision test, initially searching for chimeric stimuli that had the typical properties of four-legged land animals. We counted as "typical" those chimeras that met the following criteria. First, they had to share the properties of animals that are preserved in delayed-copy and drawing tasks by patients with semantic dementia: four legs, a body, a tail, a head, and eyes. Second, they could not include parts from animals spanning grossly different animal categories; for example, we rejected chimeras made from mammal and bird parts. Third, they had few distinguishing or idiosyncratic features. Of the 64 chimeric stimuli in the BORB, 11 met these criteria—7 from the "hard" stimulus set, and 4 from the "easy" stimulus set. We next selected 11 typical-looking real animal drawings (7 from the hard and 4 from the easy set) to match these, using the same criteria for selection and avoiding the high-frequency items *cat*, *dog*, and *horse*.

We then selected 11 atypical chimeras and 11 atypical real animals from the BORB, choosing 7 from the hard set and 4 from the easy set in each case. By "atypical", we mean items that violated the constraints described above: animals with idiosyncratic features, or animals without tails, four legs, etc. Thus these 44 items in the BORB constitute a subset in which two factors—real or chimeric, and typical or atypical—are fully crossed; and within each cell, difficulty is approximately matched.

## RESULTS

Figure 4 shows the mean proportion correct across patients in each factor cell, as well as the data for each patient individually. Amongst the typical-looking items, patients were near ceiling for the real targets and near floor for the chimeric distractors. In other words, when confronted with a typical-looking stimulus, whether real or chimeric, patients usually judged that it was a real animal—thereby scoring correctly for real items and incorrectly for non-real items. By contrast, amongst the atypical items, patients behaved somewhat more randomly for both real and chimeric stimuli.

These observations were confirmed by statistical analysis in a within-subjects ANOVA treating proportion correct for each stimulus condition as the dependent measure, and typicality (high or low) and stimulus type (real or chimeric) as within-subjects factors. As Figure 4 would lead one to expect, there was no significant main effect of typicality: participants were effectively at chance overall for both typical and atypical stimuli (both by subjects and by items, $F < 1$). Patients tended to be more accurate when the item was real than when it was chimeric, $F_1(1, 3) = 6.1, p < .1; F_2(1, 40) = 22.8, p < .001$. As the figure shows, however, this effect is entirely due to the fact that the patients scored so well for real items and so poorly for chimeras in the typical condition, by virtue of almost always deciding that typical-looking items were real. Accordingly, the interaction between stimulus type and typicality was reliable by subjects and by items, even

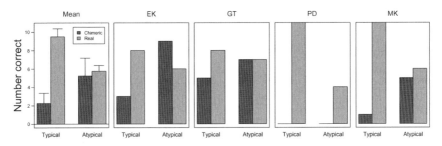

**Figure 4.**   Performance on the subset of typical and atypical BORB stimuli averaged across four semantic dementia patients. Error bars indicate standard error of the mean in each condition.

with this small number of participants, $F_1(1, 3) = 26.3, p < .02; F_2(1, 40) = 17.4, p < .001$. On average, patients tended to accept typical-looking stimuli as real, regardless of whether or not they were; and when confronted with an unusual-looking animal, patients guessed at random for both real and chimeric stimuli.

The interaction of interest is apparent by inspection in each individual patient's data—in all four cases the difference in performance between real and chimeric items was larger (and positive) for typical stimuli than for atypical stimuli. The interaction is even apparent in patient P.D., who was strongly biased to accept most stimuli (rejecting only a handful of atypical-looking real animals). An analysis of log odds ratios revealed that this interaction was statistically significant for two of the four individuals (E.K., $z = 2.28, p < .01$, and M.K., $z = 1.98, p < .05$). It should be noted that with only 11 observations in each cell, there is little power to detect significant interactions in individual patients—the reliable effects observed in E.K. and M.K. reflect the large magnitude of the effect in these cases. From the graphs in Figure 4, it is apparent that the significant effect revealed in the group analysis is not carried solely by E.K. and M.K.—the interaction is in the same direction in all four cases, which is why the ANOVA yields a significant result, despite the small sample size.

*Comment.* Experiment 2b provides good evidence that the behaviour of semantically impaired patients in the object decision task is strongly influenced by the typicality of the target and distractor stimulus items used in the BORB. Patients with severe semantic deficits accepted typical-looking items as real, and guessed randomly in response to atypical-looking items. If typicality is controlled in the stimulus set, this pattern of behaviour will yield chance performance, as it did for four patients across the subset of items we examined. However, chance performance may not be observed even for such severe patients when stimulus items in the test are not balanced in this way. If most of the real animals in the BORB are typical-looking, semantically impaired patients will be likely to score correctly for these items. If most of the chimeras in the test are atypical-looking, patients guessing randomly will choose correctly for half of these stimuli. Across such an unbalanced set, then, patients who are completely unable to discriminate real from chimeric animals when typicality is controlled may be expected to exceed chance in the test, as did the four severely semantically impaired patients described here.

A second point of interest is the finding that the four patients in Experiment 2b did not consistently reject atypical items, but instead seemed to guess randomly when faced with an unusual-looking stimulus. That is, the patients were willing to accept most typical-looking stimuli (including chimeras) as real; but were not willing to reject most atypical-looking items as nonreal. Why was typicality almost uniformly alluring, when atypicality was not uniformly off-putting?

One possibility is that the stimulus items in the matched subset did not perfectly capitalise on the visual regularities that constrain impaired performance in the task. Though past studies of drawing to name and delayed copying suggest that visual attributes common to items in the semantic domain are more likely to be preserved than are more idiosyncratic properties, it is difficult to know precisely which aspects of visual object knowledge will prove robust to substantial semantic impairment. Perhaps the visual structure of some proportion of both real and chimeric stimulus items in the "atypical" subset was sufficient to permit chance performance on this set overall (as opposed to below-chance performance for atypical real animals, and above-chance performance for atypical chimeras).

A more interesting possibility is that this pattern reflects some spared knowledge about the potential for variability within the domain of animals. Though the patients clearly have degraded knowledge about the visual appearance of particular unusual-looking animals, they may retain the more general knowledge that it is *possible* for animals to deviate substantially from the visual prototype that characterises their state of knowledge about the domain generally. On this view, patients feel confident that typical-looking animals are likely to be real, because such stimuli conform to the knowledge that they retain about animals. Unusual-looking animals do not conform to this robust knowledge, and hence do not offer tempting targets; but patients guess randomly for these items, because they remember that there are some unusual-looking real animals in the world, even if they do not know whether the item facing them is one of these.

## COMPARING OBJECT DECISION AND SEMANTIC TASKS

We have demonstrated that patients with semantic dementia show consistent deficits in object decision, which mirror the pattern of semantic impairment revealed in other tasks. Specifically, as conceptual knowledge deteriorates, patients increasingly tend to accept (as "real") objects constituted of parts that are robust to semantic impairment—those that are typical of a semantic category or domain—and to reject or guess randomly when faced with items that violate such regularities. These data are at least consistent with the view that the processes supporting visual object recognition and those supporting semantic memory are highly interactive.

It is difficult, however, to rule out the possibility that the observed deficits in object decision arise, not solely from impairment to a unitary and interactive semantic system, but from the conjoint impairment of functionally independent semantic and visual recognition systems. The patients we have discussed perform quite well on tests of visual perception, such as the non-semantic subtests of the VOSP and the immediate copying of abstract and real-object stimuli. However, these tests do not eliminate the possibility that there exists an intermediate level of visual processing, functionally independent of earlier vision and later semantics, which corresponds to a stage of pre-semantic visual recognition and which is gradually compromised in semantic dementia.

In Experiment 3 we sought further evidence for our preferred hypothesis, by examining the degree to which performance on various uncontroversially semantic tasks covaries with performance on different forms of object-decision. Consider what one might expect to find if visual object recognition and semantic processes are functionally independent but conjointly impaired. Across individuals, the degree to which each independent system is compromised by the disease process will likely vary to some small extent, even if both systems are affected together from the beginning. In this case, the magnitude of the correlation between tasks that tap object-recognition processes on the one hand and those that tap semantics on the other may be high; but it should not be as high as the degree of intercorrelation within various different semantic tasks, or various different object-recognition tasks. On the other hand, if object-recognition deficits and semantic deficits result from the same central impairment, we might expect the correlations between the two kinds of tasks to be as great as the intercorrelations among different versions of the same kind of task. The goal of Experiment 3 was to measure the extent to which scores on different object decision tasks correlate with one another, with other semantic tasks that tap visual and/or verbal semantic knowledge, and with other non-semantic tasks.

## Method

The 20 semantic dementia patients described in Experiment 1 were tested on a further well-known object-decision task (the object-decision component of the VOSP), so that, together with the data from Experiments 1 and 2, we were able to examine scores on four varieties of object decision (the two conditions of the OAT, the BORB, and the VOSP). The same patients were also tested on five semantic and eight non-semantic tasks.

The semantic tasks varied in the extent to which they required intact visual recognition and verbal comprehension skills. They were as follows.

*Pyramids and Palm Trees Test.*    A semantic matching task in which participants are required to match one of two candidate response items to a sample stimulus on the basis of semantic relatedness (Howard & Patterson, 1992). For example, the participant is shown a picture of a pyramid as the sample, and asked to decide which of a pine tree or a palm tree best matches it. The test consists of 52 items and may be administered with either picture or word triads. We conducted both versions for purposes of comparison to object decision. Note that the picture version requires intact semantics and visual object recognition, but does not require verbal comprehension; whereas the word version requires verbal comprehension, but does not tap visual object recognition.

*Camel and Cactus Test.*   A test designed on the same principle as the Pyramids and Palm Trees Test above, but with a larger number of items (64), and with four response choices rather than two. It may also be administered with pictures or words as stimuli; both are reported here. See Bozeat et al. (2000) for further detail.

*Word-Picture Matching.*   This is a 10-alternative forced-choice word-picture matching task in which the participant is given the spoken name of an object and is asked to which of 10 real-object line drawings (1 target and 9 foils) it refers. Sixty-four target stimuli were drawn from six semantic categories, half living things and half non-living things (land animals, birds, fruits, household objects, vehicles, or tools). Distractors were drawn from the same category as the target (see Bozeat et al., 2000, for further details). The word-picture matching task requires intact verbal comprehension, semantics, and visual object recognition.

The eight non-semantic tasks consisted of three tasks that draw upon frontal/executive resources (the Rey figure copy, forward digit span, and backward digit span); and five subcomponents of the VOSP designed to test visual perception (dot counting, position discrimination, incomplete letters, cube drawing, and number location; see Warrington & James, 1991).

Most patients were able to complete most tasks, but we were unable to obtain data from all patients for 5 of the 17 tasks. Each patient completed the tests within an 8-month time window. To determine how performance covaried across the various tests, we first considered the pairwise correlation coefficients for all pairs of tests. We then conducted a confirmatory factor analysis to determine how best to explain the observed patterns of covariation.

## Results: Analysis 1

The left-most panel of Figure 5, labelled "Within task", shows the correlation coefficients for all pairs of object-decision tests ("Obj Dec"), all pairs of tasks requiring visual object recognition and semantics ("Vis-

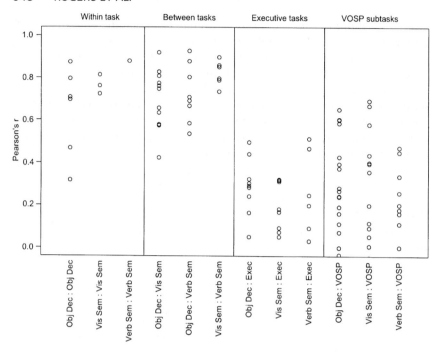

**Figure 5.** Correlation coefficients for pairs of similar tasks (left-most panel); between object-decision, visual, and verbal semantic tasks (second from left panel); and between these tasks and frontal/executive tasks (second from right) and tests of visual perception (rightmost panel).

Sem"), and the two verbal-semantic tests ("Verb-Sem"). The next panel (labelled "Between task") reflects the correlation coefficients for all pairings of tests between these groupings. As the illustration makes clear, the degree of association is of comparable magnitude for between-task comparisons and within-task comparisons. Two of the three lowest correlation coefficients occurred between different varieties of object decision (the correlation between the two conditions of the OAT, and between *real > nonreal* OAT and the VOSP); and two of the four highest correlation coefficients observed were between an object decision task (the BORB) and the two purely verbal semantic tasks (the word-only versions of the Camel and Cactus test and the Pyramids and Palm Trees test; $r = .88$ and .93 respectively).

The two right-hand panels in Figure 5 show how the object-decision, visual-semantic, and verbal-semantic tasks correlate with the tasks that draw upon frontal-executive resources (second panel from right) or visual perception (rightmost panel). Here correlations are relatively low, and importantly, the semantic and object-decision tasks show similar degrees of association with the sets of non-semantic tasks. The results indicate that the impairments in semantic and object-decision tasks, and the high degree of association among these, do not result from a global deficit that affects all cognitive domains.

## Analysis 2

The relatively small number of cases over which these correlation coefficients were calculated (ranging from 10 to 20), as well as the fairly large number of potential comparisons, limit the power to detect reliable differences among the various correlation coefficients. Our hypothesis stipulates that the magnitude of correlation within object-decision and within semantic tests should be no greater than the degree of correlation between these types of tests; hence this lack of statistical power poses a particular difficulty in testing our hypothesis.

In the second analysis we addressed this issue by conducting a confirmatory factor analysis designed to contrast three different models of the factors underlying object decision and semantic task performance in our patient sample, using a subset of the observed variables. The relatively small sample size is also a serious concern in this case; however, by restricting the number of observed measures to 5 we found that we were able to fit the various models and come near to the statistical rule of thumb advocated by Bryant and Yarnold (1995), which states that the ratio of subjects to variables should not fall below 5.

From the object-decision and semantic tasks listed above, we employed five observed measures in the factor analysis: the proportion correct for the complete OAT (i.e., the sum of *nonreal* > *real* and *real* > *nonreal* conditions divided by 32), the VOSP object decision task, word-picture matching, Pyramids and Palm Trees with pictures, and Pyramids and Palm Trees with words. Of these five measures, two require object-recognition alone (OAT and VOSP), two require object-recognition as well as semantic capabilities (WP-Match and PPT-pictures), and one requires semantic but not object-recognition abilities (PPT-words). All five variables were tested for multivariate normality. Two variables (WP-Match and VOSP) deviated significantly from normal and were submitted to an arcsin transformation, bringing them well within accepted standards, WP-Match: $W(18) = 0.95$, $p < .37$, VOSP: $W(18) = 0.96$, $p < .56$.

Data from the 20 participants were then fitted to each of the three models illustrated in Figure 6, using AMOS, a standard structural equation modelling software package. Each model in the figure depicts an alternative hypothesis about the factors that underlie the observed variation and covariation of the five measures. Latent factors are represented with ovals, and observed variables are represented with

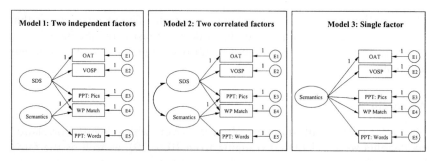

**Figure 6.** Structural equation models for three confirmatory factor analyses, comparing three different hypotheses about the factors underlying performance on object-decision and semantic tasks in semantic dementia.

boxes. Single-headed arrows represent the causal relations among latent and observed variables stipulated by the hypothesis in question, whereas double-headed arrows indicate that the factors they connect may be correlated. Circles labelled with an "E" indicate sources of variation in the observed variables not accounted for by the latent factors in the model—for example, measurement error, or other influences not represented in the model. Finally, numbers indicate parameters of the model that are fixed to a constant value in advance (i.e., parameters that are not estimated from the observed data). The model-fitting procedure requires that one of the free parameters associated with each latent variable (either the variance, or one of the factor loadings) be fixed. We have fixed one of the factor loadings for each latent variable to unity as is the standard custom.

   With these conventions in mind it is possible to interpret the hypotheses embodied by each of the three models in our comparison. Model 1 posits that variation in the observed measure arises from two underlying factors. The first (labelled *SDS* for "structural description system") is the sole contributor (apart from the error term) to the object-decision tasks, and it also contributes to the two semantic tasks that require object recognition (WP-Match and PPT-pictures). The second factor (labelled *Semantics*) contributes to all of the semantic tasks, but not to the object-decision tasks. The absence of a double-headed arrow between *Semantics* and *SDS* indicates that, in this model, the two factors are constrained to be uncorrelated. We know from the previous analyses that this is unlikely to be a good model—the hypothesised underlying systems, even if they are functionally independent, must be conjointly impaired (i.e., correlated in the model) in order to explain the observed correlations between object-decision performance and semantic-task performance. However we include this model specification in the current comparisons in order to determine whether we have the statistical power to reject what we know, a priori, to be a bad model of the data.

Model 2 is almost identical to Model 1, but it includes an additional parameter: it allows Semantics and the SDS to be correlated (as indicated by the double-headed arrow). This model thus corresponds to the alternative hypothesis outlined above, that object-decision and semantic tasks are subserved by two functionally independent systems, which are conjointly impaired in semantic dementia and therefore might be correlated. Fitting of this model will allow us to determine whether we have the statistical means to differentiate this plausible model from the implausible Model 1; and to estimate just how correlated the deterioration of Semantics and the SDS must be to achieve optimal explanation of the observed data.

Model 3 represents our hypothesis about the factors underlying object decision and semantic task performance in semantic dementia. Here, all observed variation and covariation is explained with reference to a single underlying factor. A comparison of this model with Model 2 allows us to determine whether it is necessary (or preferable) to invoke two functionally independent but correlated factors to explain the observed data.

Models 1 and 3 may be viewed as more constrained hypotheses falling within the space of possibilities represented by Model 2. Model 2 treats the correlation between the two latent factors, as well as their variances, as free parameters to be estimated from the data. Model 1 differs from Model 2 only in that it fixes one of these free parameters, constraining the correlation between the two underlying factors to 0. Model 3 differs from Model 2 by treating the two underlying factors as identical—which is equivalent to fixing their correlations to 1, and constraining their variances to be equal. Thus Models 1 and 3 may be viewed as more specific sub-cases of Model 2—that is, they are *nested* within Model 2. The difference in degree of fit for two nested models is distributed as $\chi^2$, with degrees of freedom equivalent to the difference in degrees of freedom in the models being compared. Hence, it is easy to compare the goodness-of-fit for nested models.

Each of the three models shown in Figure 6 was fitted to the data from the five measures of interest. Two cells of data were missing; hence the models were fitted using the maximum-likelihood algorithm as required by AMOS. All models converged in less than 30 iterations.

## Results

Model fit indices are given in Table 2. The $\chi^2$ statistic reflects the discrepancy between observed and model-predicted covariance matrices, with high values indicating a poor fit. The $p$ values associated with these indicate the probability with which the model should be rejected as a

TABLE 2
Fits for three models of the factors underlying performance
on object-decision and semantic tasks

| Fit Stat | Model 1 | Model 2 | Model 3 |
|---|---|---|---|
| $\chi^2$ | 17.0 | 0.091 | 2.49 |
| df | 3 | 2 | 5 |
| $p$ | 0.001 | 0.95 | 0.77 |
| Relative Fit Index (RFI) | 0.761 | 0.998 | 0.979 |
| Comparative Fit Index (CFI) | 0.959 | 1.00 | 1.00 |
| Parsimony-adjusted CFI | 0.192 | 0.133 | 0.33 |
| Akaike Information Criterion (AIC) | 51 | 36 | 32 |

possible explanation of the data. Reassuringly, Model 1 is rejected with likelihood $p < .001$, demonstrating that even with our relatively small sample size there is sufficient power to reject an inappropriate model. Neither Model 2 nor Model 3 is near to being rejected; however it is important to exercise caution in interpreting such a null result—the likelihood of failing to reject an inappropriate model is much greater when sample sizes are small.

The Relative Fit Index (RFI) reflects the normalised ratio of the model $\chi^2$ to that of a null-hypothesis-model in which all parameters are fixed to zero, adjusted for discrepancies in degrees of freedom. This measure varies considerably with sample size. The Comparative Fit Index (CFI) is more robust to such variation. Statistical rules-of-thumb dictate that a model should be rejected if either measure falls below 0.95. On these grounds, Model 1 is again rejected, and Models 2 and 3 remain viable.

The parsimony-adjusted CFI and the Akaike Information Criterion (AIC) are measures that penalise models with more free parameters. Models with a higher adjusted CFI or a lower AIC may be understood to provide a more parsimonious account of the data. Model 3 performs slightly better than Model 2 on these measures.

Because Model 3 is nested within Model 2, it is possible to test the null hypothesis that the two models are identical by calculating the difference in the model $\chi^2$ fits, and testing this againt a $\chi^2$ distribution on 3 degrees of freedom (i.e., df for Model 3 − df for Model 2). A difference of 7.82 or greater is necessary to reject the null hypothesis with $p < .05$. The observed difference of $\chi^2 = 2.40$ does not exceed this criterion; hence we cannot reject the null hypothesis that the estimated best fit for Model 2 is identical with the more constrained hypothesis represented by Model 3. In other words, the best fit to Model 2 given the data is one in which the latent factors correlate perfectly and have the same variance—a model in which they are treated as the same factor.

## Discussion

The results of Experiment 3 are only suggestive. Analysis 1 illustrated that the correlations within various object decision and semantic tasks are no greater than the correlations between these task types; and that these associations are not due to a global cognitive impairment. These results are qualitative—the relatively small size of our sample precluded strict comparison of all pairs of correlation coefficients. Analysis 2 provided a more quantitative examination of three hypotheses regarding the factors underlying performance on the various tasks, but the small sample size remains a concern here as well. In particular, low sample sizes inflate the likelihood of a Type II error: failure to reject a poor model. It is reassuring in this regard that we were able to reject a model known a priori to be unlikely. Nevertheless we cannot confidently determine, without considerably more cases, whether the two theoretically interesting models provide equally good accounts of the data.

With these caveats in mind, we would like to make two points. First, our analyses provide no evidence to support the rival hypothesis, that object recognition and semantic tasks draw upon functionally independent systems that are conjointly impaired in semantic dementia. Qualitatively, there was no indication that within-task correlations are higher than between-task correlations—indeed, the highest correlation observed was between an object-decision task (the BORB) and a verbal semantic task (the word version of the Camel and Cactus Test). The comparative factor analysis indicated that, given our limited data set, the best fit for a model with two covarying latent factors is one in which the two factors are effectively collapsed into one. Although interpretation of these results must remain tentative pending a larger sample, the suggestion they offer up is that performance on object-decision and semantic tasks in semantic dementia is governed by a single underlying factor.

Second, the two lowest correlations observed in Analysis 1 were among different object-decision tasks (specifically, the correlation of the *real > nonreal* OAT with the BORB and with the *nonreal > real* OAT). In light of Experiments 1 and 2, this is not very surprising—those results demonstrated that even very severe patients can perform well on the *real > nonreal* condition of the OAT. The finding of relatively low correlations between different varieties of object decision is also consistent with recent work described by Hovius et al. (2003), which revealed that object-decision scores can vary considerably under semantic impairment depending upon the particular measure chosen. We believe that our account provides an explanation of this variability across task type. If object-decision and semantic task performance draw upon the same resources, then the same factors that compromise semantic task performance should also affect object-decision. In the current work we have seen that, just as patients with semantic dementia tend to retain knowledge about the typical and shared properties of objects in a domain, so too do they tend to endorse drawings of animals that have many shared and typical animal parts—regardless of whether these are real. From this we may conclude that two measures of object-decision will not correlate well if the stimulus items they employ differ considerably in typicality. More generally, the current results suggest that the variation of performance on object-decision tasks under semantic impairment is best explained with appeal to the typicality structure of the test stimulus items, rather than to the degree of impairment in a functionally independent visual recognition system.

## GENERAL DISCUSSION

We opened the paper by differentiating two common hypotheses about the nature of semantic knowledge. The first, which we have described as a *content-based* approach, distinguishes between two qualitatively different forms of representation: semantic representations, which encode explicit semantic content; and structural representations, which support stimulus recognition but do not capture semantic content. Such a view implies that semantic content—meanings—consist in something other than knowledge about familiar objects' shapes, familiar word forms, and other surface properties, and the links among them. The second hypothesis, which we have termed a *process-based approach*, suggests that meanings emerge from the interactions of such surface representations in different modalities. On this view, semantic memory is best defined with reference to its function: to capture associations between the various modality-specific surface representations that encode explicit content, such that experiencing a concept in one modality can activate its corresponding representations in other modalities.

One of the primary sources of evidence for content-based theories of semantics stems from case studies of patients who, despite impaired access to meaning from visually presented objects, appear to succeed at object-decision tasks (e.g., Riddoch & Humphreys, 1987). Such findings seem to suggest that the representations and processes that support visual object recognition do not depend upon intact communication with semantics— and therefore that these representations and processes are not constituents of the system of knowledge that encodes meanings, but are functionally separable from it. Process-based theories of semantics are challenged to explain how, if visual and semantic representations and processes are mutually interdependent, semantic impairment can possibly spare visual object recognition.

In the current paper, we have addressed this challenge by suggesting that good performance on object-decision tasks can still obtain under semantic impairment if, and only if, targets in the task respect the surface structure of the domain and distractors do not. When chimeric distractors are unusual and real-animal targets are typical-looking, patients perform well even in the face of severe semantic impairment. When real-animal targets are unusual and chimeric distractors are typical-looking, the same patients show a degree of impairment approximately commensurate with the magnitude of their semantic deficits. These results were observed both in a novel two-alternative forced-choice test of object decision, and in the more usual object-decision paradigm on a subset of stimuli from the standard test that we selected as fulfilling these typicality characteristics.

We suggest that the observed deficits are a consequence of a general amodal semantic impairment in semantic dementia, which arises with damage to the brain regions that mediate interactions among high-level perceptual representations in different modalities, as suggested by process-based theories of semantic memory. There are three observations from the present data we would like to offer in support of this hypothesis.

First, the object-decision deficits that we have chronicled parallel the general pattern of impairment observed previously in semantic dementia, in a broad range of different semantic tasks including drawing and copying (Bozeat et al., 2003; Lambon Ralph & Howard, 2000), word-picture matching (Rogers et al., in press), and even purely verbal tasks such as attribute verification (Warrington, 1975), definition of concept names (Lambon Ralph, Graham, Patterson, & Hodges, 1999), and word sorting (Hodges et al., 1995). All of these tasks suggest that the degradation of semantic memory in semantic dementia entails the dissolution of knowledge about the detailed properties of objects that differentiate them from their semantic neighbours, with relative sparing of knowledge about properties that are generally characteristic of objects in the domain. As we have seen, object decision is no different: participants endorse items with many typical and few idiosyncratic visual properties, and reject items composed primarily of atypical or unusual properties. This influence of typicality was observed in both the novel test described in Experiment 1 and a subset of items from the familiar BORB object-decision test (Experiment 2).

Second, the degree of impairment in the *nonreal* > *real* condition of the OAT correlates strongly with the overall degree of semantic impairment, as does performance in the BORB object-recognition task (see Hovius et al., 2003, as well as the current results). Indeed, object-decision performance on various different versions of the task correlated as well with semantic tasks as with one another (Experiment 3). The symmetry of the current findings with past results in other semantic tasks, coupled with the finding of generally high correlations between object-decision and semantic tasks, together suggest that the system supporting visual object recognition is part and parcel of the general system of semantic knowledge that deteriorates in semantic dementia.

Third, the factor analysis described in Experiment 3 revealed that the best-fitting parameterisation of a two-factor model explaining the observed covariances among two object-decision and three semantic tasks is one in which the two latent factors are effectively collapsed into one. Although this result is not conclusive given the small sample size, the analysis does not compel us to invoke more than a single underlying factor to explain performance on these different tasks.

Thus the present data are at least consistent with a theory of semantic memory in which semantic knowledge emerges from the interactive activation of perceptual representations in various sensory and verbal modalities. We might further inquire whether there are other empirical or theoretical reasons for preferring a process-based theory of semantics to content-based approaches. This is of course a subject of controversy with a scope that extends beyond the neuropsychological considerations addressed here. There are, however, two points that we would like to make with respect to this question.

First, we believe that our data call into question one of the primary reasons for differentiating between "meaningful" semantic representations and "non-meaningful" structural representations. Several key researchers in the field have strongly emphasised the importance of data from both object- and word-recognition under semantic impairment for motivating this distinction (see Humphreys et al., 1988; Coltheart et al., 1998; Lauro-Grotto, Piccini, & Shallice, 1997). We have offered an alternative explanation for the apparent sparing of object recognition under semantic impairment, which depends upon assumptions about the structure of interacting representations rather than upon claims about the functional architecture of separate recognition and semantic systems. It is almost certainly possible to explain our results within a more functionally segregated framework; but we suggest that our data begin to challenge one of the primary reasons for presupposing such segregation in the first place. Further research will be necessary to determine whether a similar account might extend to explain other puzzling phenomena, such as the apparent sparing of word-recognition under semantic impairment (e.g., Ward, Stott, & Parkin, 2000), though preliminary results in this endeavour are encouraging (see Rogers, Lambon Ralph, Hodges, & Patterson, in press).

Second, we do not believe that alternative approaches that have heretofore differentiated meaningful from structural representations would lose any of their appeal were they to discard the distinction. Our reasoning derives from a consideration of one of the best-known neuropsychological models of naming from vision—the interactive-activation (IAC) model proposed by Humphreys and colleagues (Humphreys et al., 1988, 1995)—and how it has evolved in recent years (Humphreys & Forde, 2001).

The IAC model consists of three processing layers that locally represent different kinds of information. Structural descriptions are coded in one layer, knowledge about the functional or associative semantic properties of objects is stored in a second layer, and lexical/phonological representations of known words are stored in a third. Visual stimuli excite stored structural descriptions of known objects in parallel, in proportion to the degree of structural overlap between the stimulus and the stored representations. Activation then cascades forward to semantic representations, which explicitly encode information about the functional and associative properties of objects, and from there to lexical or phonological representations of words.

In its original formulation (Humphreys et al., 1988), the IAC model included only feed-forward connections from structural descriptions to semantics. Because activity in the semantic system did not feed back to influence activity in the structural description system, disruption of communication between structural descriptions and semantics had no consequence for the activation of the structural descriptions themselves. The model's ability to explain data from patients like J.B. (who showed poor access to semantic information from vision, but relatively good object-decision performance) thus relied upon what amounts to a theoretical claim about the functional independence of visual object recognition and semantic processes.

As originally described, the IAC model exemplifies a content-based approach to semantics. The representations that encode visual structural information are cast as being separate from those encode semantic content; and the processes that support visual recognition and semantic memory, far from being mutually interdependent, are posited to be functionally independent.

Later instantiations of the theory, including an implemented computational model described by Humphreys et al. (1995), altered the original design by incorporating feedback connections from semantic to structural description representations. Semantic representations were still cast as encoding a qualitatively different kind of information than structural descriptions but, more in line with process-based approaches, the two systems were described as interacting. This alteration did not compromise the model's ability to explain the time-course of processing in various kinds of semantic tasks, or other appealing aspects of the theory (Humphreys & Forde, 2001). Not surprisingly, however, it did compromise the functional independence of structural descriptions and semantics. Because the states of semantic units in this implementation can influence the activation of structural descriptions, one would expect degraded semantic processing to have consequences for the resolution of competition at the level of structural descriptions (and, therefore, for object recognition).

In the most recent incarnation of the IAC approach (the HIT model; see Humphreys & Forde, 2001), the authors propose that each modality of perception contains its own perceptual recognition stores, akin to the structural description system in vision, which interact with one another either directly or via Damasio's "convergence zones". Here, separate semantic representations that code the meanings of words and objects have effectively disappeared from the picture—the retrieval of information about objects arises from the interaction of these different perceptual knowledge stores. The theory is, in fact, just the process-based approach to semantics that we have been advocating in the present work; and as the authors note, it obviates the notion that semantic knowledge resides in a separate semantic store (with the possible exception of "encyclopaedic" information about objects).

In moving away from functionally separable structural and semantic stores, and toward a more interactive and process-based approach, the HIT framework raises the same question that the IAC model was intended to address: how are patterns of impairment such as J.B.'s possible? If semantic knowledge arises simply from the interactive activation of modality-specific representations, why should the degradation of these interactions spare visual object recognition? This is, after all, the issue that prompted claims of functional separability between meaningful and structural representations in the first place.

The current work allows us to see how apparent dissociations of object recognition and semantic knowledge might arise as a consequence of representational structure in a recurrent, interactive and distributed system, such as the one we have described elsewhere (Rogers et al., in press). Deficits such as J.B.'s do not lay bare the functional separability of two independent systems, but simply reflect sensitivity to the same factors that govern impaired performance in all semantic tasks. Indeed, one version of the HIT framework described by Humphreys and Forde (2001)—the version that incorporates convergence zones (see Figure 4 in that paper)—is similar in many respects to a computational model we have used to explain a range of phenomena in semantic dementia (Rogers, Lambon-Ralph, Patterson, McClelland, & Hodges, 1999). We view our model as similar in spirit (if different in some of the details) to this version of the HIT framework; and the family of distributed and interactive semantic models as alternative implementations of a similar, process-based theory of semantics.

# REFERENCES

Allport, D.A. (1985). Distributed memory, modular systems and dysphasia. In S.K. Newman & R. Epstein (Eds.), *Current perspectives in dysphasia*. Edinburgh: Churchill Livingstone.

Barbarotto, R., Capitani, E., Spinnler, H., & Trivelli, C. (1995). Slowly progressive semantic impairment with category specificity. *Neurocase, 1*, 107–119.

Barsalou, L.W. (this issue). Situated simulation in the human conceptual system. *Language and Cognitive Processes, 18*, 513–562.

Biederman, I. (1987). Recognition-by-components: A theory of human image understanding. *Psychological Review, 94*, 115–147.

Bozeat, S., Lambon Ralph, M.A., Graham, K.S., Patterson, K.,Wilkin, H., Rowland, J., Rogers, T., & Hodges, J.R. (2003). A duck with four legs: Investigating the structure of conceptual knowledge using picture drawing in semantic dementia. *Cognitive Neuropsychology, 20*, 27–47.

Bozeat, S., Lambon Ralph, M.A., Patterson, K., Garrard, P., & Hodges, J.R. (2000). Nonverbal semantic impairment in semantic dementia. *Neuropsychologia, 38*, 1207–1215.

Bozeat, S., Lambon Ralph, M.A., Patterson, K., & Hodges, J.R. (in press). When objects lose their meaning: what happens to their use? *Cognitive, Affective, and Behavioral Neuroscience*.

Bryant, F.B., & Yarnold, P.R. (1995). Principal components analysis and exploratory and confirmatory factor analysis. In P.R. Grimm & L.G. Grimm (Eds.), *Reading and understanding multivariate analysis*. Washington, DC: American Psychological Association Books.

Chao, L.L., Haxby, J.V., & Martin, A. (1999). Attribute-based neural substrates in temporal cortex for perceiving and knowing about objects. *Nature Neuroscience, 2*, 913–919.

Coltheart, M., Inglis, L., Michie, P., Bates, A., & Budd, B. (1998). A semantic subsystem of visual attributes. *Neurocase, 4*, 353–370.

Coltheart, M., Rastle, K., Perry, C., Langdon, R., & Ziegler, J. (2001). DRC: A dual route cascaded model of visual word recognition and reading aloud. *Psychological Review, 108*, 204–256.

Cree, G., & McRae, K. (2002). Factors underlying category-specific deficits. In E.M.E. Forde & G.W. Humphreys (Eds.), *Category specificity in brain and mind*. Hove, UK: Psychology Press.

Damasio, H., Grabowski, T.J., Tranel, D., & Hichwa, R.D. (1996). A neural basis for lexical retrieval. *Nature, 380*, 499–505.

Eggert, G.H. (1977). *Wernicke's works on aphasia: A sourcebook and review* (Vol. 1). The Hague: Mouton.

Funnell, E. (1996). Response biases in oral reading: An account of the co-occurrence of surface dyslexia and semantic dementia. *Quarterly Journal of Experimental Psychology, 49A*, 417–446.

Garrard, P., & Hodges, J.R. (2000). Semantic dementia: Clinical, radiological, and pathological perspectives. *Journal of Neurology, 247*, 409–422.

Garrard, P., Lambon Ralph, M., & Hodges, J.R. (2002). Semantic dementia: A category-specific paradox. In E.M.E. Forde & G.W. Humphreys (Eds.), *Category specificity in brain and mind* (pp. 149–179). Hove, UK: Psychology Press.

Garrard, P., Lambon Ralph, M.A., Hodges, J.R., & Patterson, K. (2001). Prototypicality, distinctiveness and intercorrelation: Analyses of the semantic attributes of living and nonliving concepts. *Cognitive Neuroscience, 18*, 125–174.

Graham, K.S., Simons, J.S., Pratt, K.H., Patterson, K., & Hodges, J.R. (2000). Insights from semantic dementia on the relationship between episodic and semantic memory. *Neuropsychologia, 38*, 313–324.

Hillis, A.E., & Caramazza, A. (1995). Cognitive and neural mechanisms underlying visual and semantic processing: Implications from "optic aphasia". *Journal of Cognitive Neuroscience, 7*, 457–478.

Hodges, J.R., Bozeat, S., Lambon Ralph, M.A., Patterson, K., & Spatt, J. (2000). The role of conceptual knowledge in object use: Evidence from semantic dementia. *Brain, 123*, 1913–1925.

Hodges, J.R., Garrard, P., & Patterson, K. (1998). Semantic dementia and pick complex. In A. Kertesz & D. Munoz (Eds.), *Pick's disease and pick complex*. New York: Wiley Liss.

Hodges, J.R., Garrard, P., Perry, R., Patterson, K., Bak, T., & Gregory, C. (1999a). The differentiation of semantic dementia and frontal lobe dementia from early alzheimer's disease: A comparative neuropsychological study. *Neuropsychology, 13*, 31–40.

Hodges, J.R., Graham, N., & Patterson, K. (1995). Charting the progression in semantic dementia: Implications for the organisation of semantic memory. *Memory, 3*, 463–495.

Hodges, J.R., Patterson, K., & Tyler, L.K. (1994). Loss of semantic memory: Implications for the modularity of mind. *Cognitive Neuropsychology, 11*, 505–542.

Hodges, J.R., Spatt, J., & Patterson, K. (1999b). What and how: Evidence for the dissociation of object knowledge and mechanical problem-solving skills in the human brain. *Proceedings of the National Academy of Sciences, 96*, 9444–9448.

Hovius, M., Kellenbach, M., Graham, K.S., Hodges, J., & Patterson, K. (2003). What do tests of object decision measure? Evidence from semantic dementia. *Neuropsychology, 17*, 100–107.

Howard, D., & Patterson, K. (1992). *Pyramids and palm trees: A test of semantic access from pictures and words*. Bury St. Edmunds, UK: Thames Valley.

Humphreys, G.W., & Forde, E.M.E. (2001). Hierarchies, similarity, and interactivity in object-recognition: On the multiplicity of 'category-specific' deficits in neuropsychological populations. *Behavioral and Brain Sciences, 24*, 453–509.

Humphreys, G., Lamote, C., & Lloyd-Jones, T.J. (1995). An interactive activation approach to object processing: Effects of structural similarity, name frequency, and task in normality and pathology. *Memory, 3*, 535–586.

Humphreys, G.W., & Riddoch, M.J. (1987). *To see but not to see: A case-study of visual agnosia*. Hove, UK: Lawrence Erlbaum Associates Ltd.

Humphreys, G.W., & Riddoch, M.J. (1993). Interactions between object and space systems revealed through neuropsychology. In D.E. Meyer & S. Kornblum (Eds.), *Attention and Performance XIV: Synergies in experimental psychology, artifical intelligence, and cognitive neuroscience*. Hillsdale, NJ: Lawrence Erlbaum Associates, Inc.

Humphreys, G.W., & Riddoch, M.J. (1999). Impaired development of semantic memory: Separating semantic from structural knowledge and diagnosing a role for action in establishing stored memories for objects. *Neurocase, 5*, 519–532.

Humphreys, G.W., Riddoch, M.J., & Quinlan, P.T. (1988). Cascade processes in picture identification. *Cognitive Neuropsychology, 5*, 67–103.

Kellenbach, M., Brett, M., & Patterson, K. (2001). Large, colorful or noisy? Attribute- and modality-specific activations during retrieval of perceptual attribute knowledge. *Cognitive, Affective and Behavioral Neuroscience, 1*, 207–221.

Lambon Ralph, M., Graham, K.S., Patterson, K., & Hodges, J.R. (1999). Is a picture worth a thousand words? Evidence from concept definitions by patients with semantic dementia. *Brain and Language, 70*, 309–335.

Lambon Ralph, M.A., & Howard, D. (2000). Gogi-aphasia or semantic dementia? Simulating and assessing poor verbal comprehension in a case of progressive fluent aphasia. *Cognitive Neuropsychology, 17*, 437–465.

Lambon Ralph, M.A., McClelland, J., Patterson, K., Galton, C.J., & Hodges, J. (2001). No right to speak? The relationship between object naming and semantic impairment: Neuropsychological evidence and a computational model. *Journal of Cognitive Neuroscience*.

Lauro-Grotto, R., Piccini, C., & Shallice, T. (1997). Modality-specific operations in semantic dementia. *Cortex, 33*, 593–622.

Lissauer, H. (1890). Ein fall von seelenblindheit nebst einem beitrage zur theorie derselben. *Archiv fur Psychiatrie und Nervenkrankheit, 21*, 222–270.

Marr, D. (1982). *Vision*. San Francisco, CA: W.H. Freeman.

Patterson, K., & Hodges, J. (2000). Semantic dementia: One window on the structure and organisation of semantic memory. In F. Boller & J. Grafman (Eds.), *Handbook of neuropsychology: Vol. 2. Memory and its disorders* (2nd edn., pp. 313–333). Amsterdam: Elsevier Science.

Perry, R.J., & Hodges, J.R. (1999). Attention and executive deficits in Alzheimer's disease: A critical review. *Brain, 122*, 383–404.

Plaut, D.C. (2002). Graded modality-specific specialisation in semantics: A computational account of optic aphasia. *Cognitive Neuropsychology, 19*, 603–639.

Pulvermuller, F. (1999). Words in the brain's language. *Behavioral and Brain Sciences, 22*, 253–336.

Quinn, P., Johnson, M.H., Mareschal, D., Rakison, D., & Younger, B.A. (2000). Understanding early categorization: One process or two? *Infancy, 1*, 111–122.

Riddoch, M.J., & Humphreys, G.W. (1987). Visual object processing in optic aphasia: A case of semantic access agnosia. *Cognitive Neuropsychology, 4*, 131–185.

Riddoch, M.J., & Humphreys, G.W. (1993). *BORB: Birmingham Object Recognition Battery*. Hove, UK: Psychology Press.

Rogers, T.T., Lambon-Ralph, M., Garrard, P., Bozeat, S., McClelland, J.L., Hodges, J.R., & Patterson, K. (in press). The structure and deterioration of semantic memory: A computational and neuropsychological investigation. *Psychological Review*.

Rogers, T.T., Lambon-Ralph, M., Hodges, J.R., & Patterson, K. (in press). Natural selection: The impact of semantic impairment on lexical and object decision. *Cognitive Neuropsychology*.

Rogers, T.T., Lambon-Ralph, M., Patterson, K., McClelland, J.L., & Hodges, J.R. (1999). A recurrent connectionist model of semantic dementia. In *Cognitive neuroscience society annual meeting program 1999*. Retrieved from http://cognet.mit.edu/posters/poster.tcl?publication_id=3664

Rogers, T.T., & McClelland, J.L. (in press). *Semantic cognition: A parallel distributed processing approach*. Cambridge, MA: MIT Press.

Rogers, T.T., & Plaut, D.C. (2002). Connectionist perspectives on category specific deficits. In E. Forde & G. Humphreys (Eds.), *Category specificity in mind and brain*. Hove, UK: Psychology Press.

Rumiati, R., & Humphreys, G.W. (1997). Visual object agnosia without alexia or prosopagnosia: Arguments for separate knowledge stores. *Visual Cognition, 4*, 207–217.

Sheridan, J., & Humphreys, G.W. (1993). A verbal-semantic category-specific recognition impairment. *Cognitive Neuropsychology, 10,* 185–200.

Smith, L.B. (2000). From knowledge to knowing: Real progress in the study of infant categorization. *Infancy, 1,* 91–97.

Snowden, J.S., Goulding, P.J., & Neary, D. (1989). Semantic dementia: A form of circumscribed cerebral atrophy. *Behavioral Neurology, 2,* 167–182.

Stewart, F., Parkin, A.J., & Hunkin, N.M. (1992). Naming impairments following recovery from herpes simplex encephalitis: Category specific? *Quarterly Journal of Experimental Psychology, 44A,* 261–284.

Tyler, L., Moss, H.E., Durrant-Peatfield, M.R., & Levy, J. P. (2000). Conceptual structure and the structure of concepts: A distributed account of category-specific deficits. *Brain and Language, 75,* 195–231.

Ward, J., Stott, R., & Parkin, A.J. (2000). The role of semantics in reading and spelling: Evidence for the 'summation hypothesis'. *Neuropsychologia, 38,* 1643–1653.

Warrington, E.K. (1975). The selective impairment of semantic memory. *Quarterly Journal of Experimental Psychology, 27,* 635–657.

Warrington, E.K., & James, M. (1991). *Visual Object and Space Perception battery.* Bury St. Edmunds, UK: Thames Valley Test Company.

Warrington, E.K., & McCarthy, R. (1987). Categories of knowledge: Further fractionation and an attempted integration. *Brain, 110,* 1273–1296.

LANGUAGE AND COGNITIVE PROCESSES, 2003, *18* (5/6), 663–692

# Categorisation, causation, and the limits of understanding

Frank C. Keil

*Yale University, New Haven, CT, USA*

Although recent work has emphasised the importance of naïve theories to categorisation, there has been little work examining the grain of analysis at which causal information normally influences categorisation. That level of analysis may often go unappreciated because of an "illusion of explanatory depth", in which people think they mentally represent causal explanatory relations in far more detail than they really do. Naïve theories therefore might seem to be irrelevant to categorisation, or perhaps they only involve noting the presence of unknown essences. I argue instead that adults and children alike effectively track high-level causal patterns, often outside awareness, and that this ability is essential to categorisation. Three examples of such pattern-tracking are described. The shallowness of our explanatory understandings may be further supported by a reliance on the division of cognitive labour that occurs in all cultures, a reliance that arises from well-developed abilities to cluster knowledge in the minds of others.

Categorisation is influenced by a wide range of types of information creating a diversity and richness that is often underestimated and which poses challenges for how we are to understand our abilities to have effective mental representations of categories. We have long recognised the importance of frequency and correlational information in influencing our formation and use of categories, and there is a temptation to reduce all of categorisation to such patterns through appeals to parsimony. This perspective, however, has been challenged in more recent times by those who argue that "theory-based" information also plays a critical role above and beyond that played by tabulations of frequencies and correlations.

Requests for reprints should be addressed to Frank Keil, Department of Psychology, Yale University, P.O. Box 208205, 2 Hillhouse Avenue, New Haven, CT 06520-8205, USA. E-mail: frank.keil@yale.edu.

Preparation of this paper and some of the research described therein was supported by National Institutes of Health Grant R01-HD23922 to Frank Keil. Many thanks to Paul Bloom, James Hampton, and three anonymous reviewers for comments on earlier versions of this paper and to Lisa Webb for help in manuscript editing.

http://www.tandf.co.uk/journals/pp/01690965.html    DOI: 10.1080/01690960344000062

I will consider how causal information supports theory-based effects. The complexity and variety of causal patterns, in turn, will make it clear that people cannot possibly track all causal patterns associated with categories. Moreover, people grossly overestimate their own and others' abilities to know causal relations. This "illusion of explanatory depth" might be taken as an indication of the empty and ineffectual nature of intuitive theories. I will argue, however, that there is a different, often more implicit way in which people track causal structure, that powerfully influences concepts and categorisation.

## CAUSATION, COMPLEXITY, AND CATEGORISATION

The process of learning about most categories critically involves noticing how often various properties occur and co-occur. Frequencies of instances of categories and of properties can have a powerful influence on later judgements of category membership, both in terms of the speed of such judgements and in terms of one's confidence about category membership (Hampton, 2001; Smith & Medin, 1981). In some cases, however, equally frequent properties seem to be weighed quite differently from each other, and in others, equal correlations are treated differently. One way of understanding such effects is to assume that our perception of the importance of features and correlations is also influenced by our understanding of how and why features and features clusters occur as they do (Murphy & Medin, 1985). This perspective has become popular in the cognitive science literature and has been called the "theory theory" (Gopnik & Wellman, 1994).

In the theory theory, concepts and the categorisation behaviour arising from them are both influenced by theories about how features are related. For example, blackness is probably a more frequent property of tyres than is roundness (given the many flat and partially deflated tyres in the world), yet roundness seems much more central to the concept of a tyre. This notion of theoretical centrality has been invoked to explain a wide variety of experimental results concerning concepts and categories (Murphy & Medin, 1985; Lin & Murphy, 1997; Murphy & Allopenna, 1994; Rehder & Hastie, 2001; Wisniewski & Medin, 1994; Ahn & Kalish, 2000; Sloman, Love, & Ahn, 1998; Murphy, 2002). Theory influences seem to be further supported by arguments that patterns of conceptual change across the development and the history of a science must be understood in terms of the theories in which concepts are embedded (Kuhn, 1977; Keil, 1989; Carey, 1991; Barrett, Abdi, Murphy, & Gallagher, 1993).

Although disagreements remain about the extent to which theory-like or explanatory relations do influence membership decisions about categories and the speed with which one makes such decisions, most acknowledge some degree of influence. The challenge lies in describing the nature and extent of the relevant theoretical or background knowledge. For this discussion, I focus primarily on knowledge of causal relations. It is certainly possible to have theories that discuss no causal relations (e.g., in mathematics, or in some mathematical models of physical phenomena); but much of science, and most folk science, centers on causal relations.

There are at least three ways in which concepts might be related to theories: concepts are theories themselves, concepts are parts of theories, or concepts are influenced by theories (Prinz, 2002). Viewing concepts as theories has the attractive feature of explaining how conceptual change and theory-change are linked. Seeing concepts as parts of theories saves one from difficult issues concerning the compositionality of concepts. Finally, having concepts influenced by theories is the most conservative claim, capturing an influence effect that is implicit in the other two views but making no additional commitments. The arguments of this paper require no more than this third view.

If causal relations influence how we weight a property, how deeply must we master those causal relations? My concept of dogs might include the idea that they have hair to insulate them against cold. But that explanation, in turn, depends on an explanation of why hair was the means for insulation as opposed to blubber, or another way of insulation. That issue, in turn, could lead to questions about the nature of insulating materials, how they work, and how they might be produced in the most efficient fashion by a biological organism. Other questions might arise as to whether mammals are subject to different constraints concerning insulation needs and methods for providing insulation when compared with other animals. Still further questions occur about the distinctive natures of mammals, of ecological niches and thermodynamics. Full theoretical understanding creates a problem of causal explanatory holism, in which almost all the natural sciences in all their details seem to be required to fully explain any particular explanatory belief.

This problem of an ever-expanding chain of supporting explanations is clearly surmounted in both folk and laboratory science. Virtually no practicing scientists claim to understand all the causal chains behind the phenomena that they study. They adopt certain ideas, such as, that hair is good insulator, and then use those ideas in further reasoning without requiring a deeper understanding of how hair insulates. Moreover, this practice appears to be effective, given that the sciences do improve in their abilities to make predictions. In the biological and cognitive sciences, and in much of engineering, we seem to decompose a phenomenon or system into functional units and then analyse how those units interact to create the phenomenon in question. This functional-analytical approach (Lycan,

2002) succeeds because, in most cases, the functional units do not need to be further decomposed for an explainer to gain genuine insight.

The level of incompleteness of intuitive theories may also vary considerably across individuals. There are surely large individual differences in terms of how well people know the causal pathways underlying phenomena such as diseases, kinds of living things, or complex devices, with a corresponding potential for substantial disagreements over the relevant members of categories. If all of one's theoretical knowledge relevant to an entity influenced one's concept-learning and use, there should be more variation among individuals in categorisation than is normally observed. Thus, a nuance in a person's understanding of causal factors for a disease might cause him to reject a set of symptoms as an instance of a disease while another person would accept them as a member of that disease category.

The theory theory therefore offers a way of choosing among equally high frequencies and of deciding which correlations are causally meaningful (e.g., Murphy & Medin, 1985). However, its ability to simplify categorisation appears to be compromised when there is no clear way to decide how much and what type of causal understanding is needed. This problem is one reason why Fodor, in his criticism of cognitive science's approach to concepts, is so dubious of the concepts-as-theories view (Fodor, 1998). Theory-based influences are potentially unbounded, raising questions about how theories could be an effective structure for concepts if all causal relations are brought to bear. In addition, people vary considerably in the depth of their causal understandings, yet that variation does not map neatly onto individual differences in category use (see also Prinz, 2002).

The existing literature rarely considers the details of the theories that influence concept-acquisition and use and categorisation; and, when examples are provided, their lack of detail is illuminating. One frequently employed example suggests that features of birds such as wings, hollow bones, and feathers are mentally linked because they are understood as converging to support flight (e.g., Murphy & Medin, 1985). Similarly, curvedness is perceived as more important to boomerangs than to bananas because it is thought to be more causally central to explaining the nature of boomerangs (Medin & Shoben, 1988). In all these cases, however, the real level of the causal analysis is often surprisingly shallow, in comparison to what one thinks it is. Shape is important to boomerangs because it is considered causally critical to explaining their unique patterns of flight. This shape centrality seems to be a widespread "theoretical belief" (Medin and Shoben, 1988). Yet, very few people could explain why the bent shape of a boomerang actually makes it more likely to return than a straight one (see Walker, 1979, for a fuller explanation). People do not really have a complete theory of boomerang flight; instead, they have a conviction that shape will be central to any such account. Similarly, in knowing that wings enable the flight of birds, people use very simple ideas of wings "holding the bird up" without really understanding how the wing shape achieves lift (Murphy, 2002). In most cases, people use simple causal schemas to guide their judgements about categories, and these schemas seem quite distant from theories, as explained in a science class.

Only a fraction of the potential causal understandings associated with categories and their members may be routinely invoked to constrain category-learning and use. Moreover, that fraction may show considerably more commonality across most people. Thus, there may be a skeletal set of causal patterns that most people use in similar ways, but that look little like fully detailed theories. However, we often mistake these sketchy relationships for richer intuitive theories because of certain illusions about what we really know.

## BLESSED IGNORANCE

One way to better understand the importance of intuitive theories is to examine more closely the level of causal information that people normally track in the world around them. Surprisingly, the grain at which causal information is encoded has rarely been examined directly, with the result that the literature contains a large range of views ranging from those who argue that we have rich and powerful naïve theories (e.g., Vosniadu & Brewer, 1992) to those who argue that we detect only the weakest fragments of real world patterns (e.g., di Sessa, 1993). Thus, it seems clear that some data reduction must occur in our tracking of causal relations in the world around us; the question is just how much reduction and of what type.

One cannot exhaustively assess all causal patterns that people notice both because there are too many domains to examine and because we have no easy way to quantify the full range of what might be known and compare it to what is known. We can, however, ask how well people's first impressions of what information they know corresponds to what they really know in local domains. We have conducted a series of studies examining people's initial self-assessments of their knowledge and their re-assessments after a series of experimental manipulations. Those studies focus on judgements about knowledge of explanatory relations and contrast them to judgements about knowledge in several other domains, most notably knowledge about procedures, narratives, and facts (Rozenblit & Keil, 2002).

In tasks assessing explanatory understanding, people are presented with a large list of phenomena and devices and are asked to judge how well they think they understand each of them. For example, they might be asked to judge how well they think they know how a helicopter works. Before they start rating their understanding, they are trained extensively on the use of a seven-point rating scale showing them that "level 1" would barely go beyond knowing the phenomenal properties of the device or phenomena (e.g., helicopters are things that fly up and down as well as sideways and use big blades on top and do not have wings), while "level 7" would be a fully detailed mechanistic understanding (e.g., a full description of the workings of a helicopter that captures the workings of all its parts).

After people have been trained on the scale, they rate a large set of initial items. Next, they give responses for a small subset of the items from that initial list. For each item there are several stages of responses. First, the participants are asked to write out the fullest description they can of how the device works or why the phenomenon is the way it is. Then, based on their self-perceived success of writing that explanation, they are asked to re-rate their initial understanding. Next, they are asked a critical diagnostic question requiring deep understanding (e.g., tell me how a helicopter goes from hovering to flying forward). They are subsequently asked to again re-rate their initial understanding in light of their answer to the diagnostic question. Finally, they are presented with a concise expert explanation of how the device works or why the phenomenon exists and are asked once again to re-rate their initial understanding.

People in these tasks consistently show a large drop in the ratings of their own knowledge after seeing an expert description, often with strong emotional reactions. They are often astounded at how little they knew compared to what they thought they knew. They do not say that they had misunderstood the scale; they are genuinely taken aback at how badly they overestimated their knowledge. The drops in ratings are found in several different populations and in different task manipulations, including one in which participants know they will be asked the follow-up questions.

The illusion of knowing is not seen for many other kinds of knowledge. Ask people to estimate how well they know certain facts, such as the capitals of countries, or certain procedures, such as how to make an international phone call, or certain narratives, such as the plot of a popular movie, and they are usually well calibrated. We have conducted a series of studies in the domains of facts, procedures, and narratives, and we repeatedly find either a much smaller drop in ratings or no drop whatsoever in comparison to explanatory understanding. Because the illusion of knowing is particularly powerful for explanatory knowledge, as opposed to knowledge of other types, we have called it the "illusion of explanatory depth" or IOED, meaning that people think they understand how things work and why phenomena exist in far greater depth than they actually do.

There seem to be several reasons why the IOED is so strong for causal information relative to other kinds of knowledge. One factor is a confusion of information that is stored in the head with information that can be recovered from phenomena that are in front of an observer. I may think I fully understand how a bicycle derailleur works because, when one is in front of me, I can puzzle out in real-time what all its parts do and why. But I may have mentally represented only a small fraction of the working arrangements and will be completely unable to recreate them without the object in front of me. This failure is analogous to at least one sense of situated cognition, where the cognitive capacities of individuals are said to be heavily dependent on the contexts in which they are situated (Brown, Collins, & Duguid, 1989).

We have found evidence for this factor by engaging in analyses of where the miscalibrations are largest for explanations of devices. There is a large drop in self-ratings for devices relative to other domains, but within the set of devices, there is also considerable variation. To understand the causes of this variation, we asked judges to rate several properties relating to each device, including familiarity with the device, the total number of parts in the device, the ratio of visible to hidden parts, and the number of parts for which a judge knew specific names. The strongest predictors of the drops in self-ratings were the ratio of visible to hidden parts and the number of parts for which judges knew names. By contrast, neither judged-familiarity of the item nor the total number of judged-parts-predicted drops (Rozenblit & Keil, 2002). It seems that the more visible parts an object has, the more one is lulled into thinking one has remembered those parts and internalised their working relations. Thus, visual clues that might be indicative of better causal reasoning when an object is present are confused as being indicative of richer mental representations. Knowing names for parts also seems to create an impression that one knows how they work.

The confusion of internally represented information with environmentally available information is similar to an effect frequently noted in the change blindness literature, where an observer of a scene may recall strikingly few details of a scene just observed while being convinced that she has internally represented far more. Indeed, follow-up studies show that people have a powerful "change blindness blindness", in which they are unaware of the limitations (Levin, Momen, Drivdahl, & Simons, 2000). The similarity may reflect a common error of underestimating the extent to which one revisits a scene or a device to extract further information as needed rather than storing it all initially. In practice, why try to store extensive details about scenes or devices if it is easy enough to examine them again for further information when needed?

Three other factors converge to create a strong IOED relative to other domains: the difficulty of self-testing the quality of one's explanations, the smaller likelihood of having given them in the past, and a tendency to confuse insights gained at one level of analysis with details at a lower level.

Self-testing can be quite difficult because the end-state of an adequate explanation is often unclear. In asking myself how a helicopter flies, I may evaluate some misconceptions as evidence for detailed knowledge because I do not realise they are misconceptions until I have to provide a full explanation or am asked to answer a critical question about the phenomenon.

People also rarely provide comprehensive explanations for most phenomena and devices around them and it is therefore difficult to examine one's past successes and failures. By contrast, one often has a larger knowledge base of past procedures one has successfully completed or of facts one has recalled, or even of stories one has told, all of which can aid self-ratings of the relevant knowledge.

The confusion of one level of analysis with a lower one is a third factor. Most complex systems consist of functional units that interact in lawful ways. These units, in turn, have subunits that interact in functional ways as well. People may confuse genuine insight at one level (e.g., a cylinder lock works because the key makes the bolt go in or out when you turn it) with insight at a lower level (e.g., the key pushes up a series of pins in such a way that their ends are aligned with the edge of a cylinder which is then free to turn, thus enabling rotation that can move a bolt in or out). Most natural and artificial systems have nested sets of such stable subassemblies (Simon, 1981), and the rush of insight that comes with the understanding of high-level functional units may be mistaken for having an understanding of lower level units. This structural property of systems, for which we make causal explanations, is not present for facts and appears to be considerably weaker for procedures and narratives. Many procedures, such as how to make an international phone call, are a chain of steps with few or no embedded sub-steps. While narratives can have hierarchical structures (Mandler & Johnson, 1977), one tends to tell them as a chain of events at the lowest level and may therefore inspect one's knowledge more reliably and consistently at that level. A related factor may be the confusion of high level functions with lower level mechanisms, suggesting that the illusion of knowing might not be as strong for explanatory knowledge in domains with no functional concepts, such as those of non-living natural phenomena like the tides or earthquakes. We have some suggestive evidence that the IOED is somewhat weaker in those cases in contrast to devices or living systems (Rozenblit & Keil, 2002).

The IOED is different from classic overconfidence effects. For example, in the judgement and decision-making tradition, the disparity between people's average confidence levels for their answers to almanac questions and the proportion of correct answers is used to calculate an overconfidence measure (Fischhoff, 1982; Lichtenstein & Fischoff, 1977; Yates, Lee, & Bush, 1997; Yates, Lee, & Shinotsuka, 1996). However, that method assesses people's estimates of their performance on a task, not their differences in self-ratings over time from first impressions to having already attempted to generate the knowledge, to after being given the correct knowledge. In addition, much of that overconfidence literature remains controversial because people are asked to make probability estimates about single events. When they are asked to make frequency judgements, in fact, overconfidence effects sometimes disappear (Gigerenzer, Hoffrage, & Kleinboelting, 1991). Asking someone how likely it is that they just made a correct judgement is very different from asking them about the quality and detail of their knowledge.

Overconfidence is also found in studies of text comprehension, in which people often do not detect their own failures to understand a passage of text (Glenberg & Epstein, 1985; Glenberg, Wilkinson, & Epstein, 1982; Lin & Zabrucky, 1998). These studies, however, have people assess knowledge that they have just learned. In contrast, our IOED studies examine long-standing knowledge that people bring with them into the laboratory. The IOED is also not a phenomenon confined to arrogant students in an elite university. Indeed, when broader populations are examined, if anything, the illusion seems stronger in less-educated participants (Rozenblit & Keil, 2002). (See also Krueger & Dunning, 1999 for a related finding.)

One ongoing study in our laboratory suggests another important contrast to overconfidence effects related to self-image. Several studies have documented a self-enhancement effect, in which most people think they are above average on most positive traits (e.g., Krueger, 1998; Paulhus, 1998). This effect is a logical impossibility that apparently arises from inflated estimates of one's own abilities relative to others. The ongoing study on the IOED is suggesting that no such self–other difference exists for judgements of the depth of explanatory understanding; that is, judges are just as miscalibrated in their estimates of the abilities of others to offer explanations as they are of themselves. Thus, the IOED patterns vary differently across the self–other divide than do most other self-ratings.

The selectivity of the IOED for explanatory forms of understanding also seems to be present throughout much of development. Using the same paradigm as with adults, but simplifying the language and the examples, it has been possible to show drops in self-ratings over time in young elementary school children with a comparable specificity to that seen in adults for explanations, as opposed to other kinds of knowledge, such as procedures (Mills, Skinner, Goldenberg, & Keil, 2001). Thus, the structural properties of explanatory understanding that create the strength and specificity of the IOED are already at work from an early age. Younger children also show higher levels of confidence for all kinds of knowledge but the selective illusion for explanatory understanding remains.

Most laypeople, and presumably many cognitive scientists as well, assume that ordinary folks' intuitive theories are much richer and more detailed than they really are. Since most cognitive scientists have been vague about the details of intuitive theories it is harder to demonstrate their capture by the IOED. It seems likely, however, that cognitive scientists fall prey to the same biases as most other people. Presumably, no cognitive scientist thinks that the average person knows every one of the several hundred thousand components of a 747 jet and all their functional roles. Many researchers, however, by incorrectly assessing their own knowledge of jets, may assume significantly more detail than normally is present in laypeople.

## ESSENCES—WHAT LIES BENEATH?

Perhaps all the work supposedly done by theories can really be done in shorthand by beliefs in underlying essences. Beliefs in essences are said to guide many cognitive activities of both adults and children (Medin & Ortony, 1989; Gelman, 1999; Keil, 1986; Braisby, Franks, & Hampton, 1996; Gelman, 2003). In this view, being an essentialist means positing unseen features and properties that are assumed to be more at the core or "essence" of what an entity is than what is available through direct inspection. These essentialist beliefs are said to have a placeholder function for essential entities that are not explicitly known but which are assumed at the core of a category. For some, this view raises a concern as to whether the essentialism bias captures anything different about category knowledge (e.g., Gärdenfors, in press; Malt, 1994). If it just encompasses more features, then those features, once known to a person, might work in exactly the same psychological manner as prior more apparent features, thus making any theory/feature frequency contrast irrelevant. The placeholder function of the essentialist bias could be relegated to a relatively minor role of saying that one's feature list is incomplete and that one should hedge one's bets in making category-based judgements.

If essences are simply understood as defining features, or what Gelman (2003) refers to as "sortal essences", then an essentialist bias might indeed be little more than a feature-weighting and hedging function. There is a difference sense, however, of "causal essentialism" (ibid.) that has much stronger implications for the nature of theory-like influences. Essences are not simply assumed to be defining features, but also the causal reason behind the manifestation of surface features. The essence of gold, whatever it may be, is assumed to be causally responsible for all the phenomenal properties of gold, and so also for tigers, roses, and all other natural kinds. It is not necessary that beliefs in essences be correct (Medin, 1989). Indeed, essentialist biases about race (Hirschfeld, 1996), species (Wilson, 1999), and gender (Taylor, 1996) are almost certainly mistaken and detrimental (Gelman, 2003). The causal essentialist bias therefore attributes to children and adults alike not only the assumption that many categories have hidden essences but also the belief that those essences are the reason behind many of the features of a category. Interestingly, the causal essentialist bias does not usually include any sense of how it is that the essence is causally linked to the surface, just the notion that it is.

In many cases, however, a belief in essences may entail more than merely believing they are responsible for surface features. It may also include some sense of the kinds of unseen causal patterns that are responsible for surface properties. A belief in essences might also include cases in which there are no hidden features at all as part of the essentialist bias, but only hidden patterns. In such cases, the bias assumes that there is a pattern of causal relations between the features that is responsible for their presence and/or their stable occurrence together. One example might involve the principles that lead to the formation of a solar system. One might easily observe all the components of a solar system but assume a set of non-obvious causal relations that explain its stability and which represent its true essence. There is no inner "stuff" to point to as the essence, just particular patterns of causation.

A second example might occur in the sophisticated biologist's concept of species. Understanding species as a fixed set of hidden properties, such as a specific DNA sequence, is not an option for biologists since many species are distributions of such sequences where quite possibly no two members of that species (if it is one that does not have monozygotic twinning) have the same DNA. The scientist could simply assume the essence is a family resemblance of DNA types or the scientist could also assume that a particular set of causal relations creates a complex of related DNA types that, while capable of drifting over time, has great stability relative to other DNA sequences that are not governed by those causal relations. The stability itself may be the essence of the species and indeed current biology contains fascinating debates about the relative roles of the causal patterns of evolution, development, and reproduction in weighting various sequences of DNA in decisions about species (Wilson, 1999).

With laypeople, for natural kinds at least, there may be more of a tendency to assume a set of fixed essential properties; but even, in those cases, it seems likely that those essential properties are understood in terms of their causal roles in creating and maintaining phenomenal properties. Laypeople may often think of hidden properties as the peak of an upside-down pyramid, where the base is the set of surface manifestations that arise from a complex matrix of causal forces that make up the volume of the pyramid. It may be rare for an essence to be understood merely as invisible essential features without any concomitant idea not only of the essence's enormous causal influence but also of the ways it might have that influence. The implication here is that the essential feature must have a property that is plausibly causally connected to the surface features. If there is no reasonable causal pathway linking the essence to the surface, it will be ruled out, even if other data are equally supportive of it.

The nature of an essence varies considerably as a function of the kind of thing involved and people's invocations of the relevant causal patterns will be correspondingly different. For living kinds, it is relatively easy to envision a causal process internal to a species that is largely responsible for the creation of manifest surface properties. In contrast, some have argued that artifacts have no essence at all (Schwartz, 1977; Sloman & Malt, this issue); others maintain that their essence lies in the intentions of their creators (Bloom, 1996). Thus, if essences exist for artifacts, they are not a set of properties and causal relations inside the artifact; they are instead the external goals of intentional agents. But in many cases, a disembodied intention as essence may be inadequate and we may also invoke the set of causal forces that explain a consistent intention to create them. It may not be enough to have an intention to create $X$ for something to be $X$. The intention may have to come about in a reasonable manner.

For example, imagine that Adam wanders into a surgical suite of his neighbourhood hospital and sees an array of surgical instruments lying on a table. He is particularly intrigued by one instrument, which has a label on it calling it a "re-seater" which he pockets and takes home. Adam is a skilled machinist and carefully duplicates the re-seater for sale on the black market. Adam's clear intention is to make a surgical tool, yet unfortunately for Adam, the object he copied happened to be a plumber's tool that was accidentally left on the table by a plumber who had just fixed a faucet in the surgical suite. We do not think the thing Adam created is a surgical tool despite his clear intention of doing so because the broader context that explains the intention suggests otherwise. In many cases, laypeople may embed notions of intention in such larger contexts when they make judgements about artifacts.

Similarly, in viewing a novel object that we assume is an artifact, we often attempt to divine the intention of the object's creator from inferences about its preferred function and then use that intention as the basis for categorisation. But that set of inferences may often contain assumptions about reasonable ways in which intentions give rise to artifacts and not be so compelled by implausible ways such as the unwitting copier of the plumbing tool. Much of this awaits empirical studies on people's intuitions of how intentions influence categorisation across different contexts that vary the causal roles the intentions play. Here I want to raise the possibility that beliefs in essences usually involve some grasp of larger causal systems, even for artifacts.

Essences may therefore often presuppose much more causal relational structure than is obvious at first glance. To the extent that they do, they are not shorthand for intuitive causal theories but a reflection of them. They may rarely be pure placeholders. At the same time, this putative knowledge of causal relations is almost never that of detailed mechanism. What else might it be?

## SHALLOWNESS AS A VIRTUE

The relevance of causal structure to essence only intensifies concerns about how the supposed influences of knowledge of causal structure can be reconciled with the IOED. The IOED suggests that our folk theories are much coarser than we think. Is there enough structure and substance left to those theories to enable them to have their supposed influences on concepts and categorisation?

There are many ways we can track causal patterns that occur far above the level of concrete mechanisms. In what follows I describe three such ways in which we do monitor causal relations, starting with the coarsest, causal relevance, followed by causal powers, followed by coding of high level interactions among stable subassemblies. I will then further argue that the information that we do successfully track in these cases has significant influences on categorisation.

### Causal relevance

Coding of causal relevance does not encode specific patterns of causal interactions but rather a sense of what properties matter most in a particular domain. Consider, for example, encountering a novel artifact and being told it is a kind of hand tool. Despite its having a distinctive colour and pattern of surface markings, one is inclined to discount those properties in developing a concept of the category to which that tool belongs. In contrast, one is inclined to count quite heavily the shape of the tool and its size. With a plant, however, the colour and surface pattern might be seen as quite central to the category with size being somewhat less important. This kind of knowledge, called "causal relevance", can be elicited in a variety of ways and yields distinctive profiles for high-level categories such as tools, furniture, animals, and plants (Keil, 1994; Keil et al., 1998). Causal relevance is information about what kinds of properties are likely to matter in a domain but does not specify precisely how those properties will matter or even which property in particular will matter. Thus, causal relevance may indicate that colour and surface texture are important for understanding living kinds but may not specify which colour or texture in particular.

There are individual exceptions. For example, some tools, such as measuring tapes, have surface markings that are essential to their nature. But overall default expectations about causal relevance remain. We have demonstrated these expectations in a series of studies with adults and children. Thus, if one is learning about a novel tool, plant, or animal, one tends to weight different kinds of properties as more important in the learning process, even though one knows little about the details of how those properties work (ibid.). For example, if participants are told about a novel hand tool that has a certain colour, shape, size, and surface pattern but are provided no other details, they are inclined to categorise new tools that have the same shape and size but different colour and surface patterns as more likely members of that category than other new tools that have different shapes and sizes but similar colours and surface patterns. By contrast, for novel flowers, they are more likely to weight all dimensions about the same. Similarly, in an induction task, if taught that a particular novel tool has a certain property, such as a distinctive colour or shape, participants are more likely to induce that other members of the same category have the same shape than the same colour. The pattern of inductions results in a very different relevancy profile for novel biological kinds, where colour is projected much more strongly to other members of the same kind.

We have default expectations about what sorts of properties are likely to do important causal work in such broad domains as animals, plants, hand tools, and furniture. At lower levels, such as insects vs. mammals, an inventory of the most causally relevant properties reveals them to be essentially identical. Thus, to the extent that specific colour is considered causally important for most mammals, it is considered causally important for most insects. Similarly, colour is seen as the same in importance for most farm tools and most scientific instruments. In all cases, a person may think that a kind of property is important, such as colour for animals, but have no idea of its particular causal role.

Recently, we have explored an influence of causal relevancy intuitions on the judged quality of explanations. We have given several descriptions of pairs of people who both claim to be experts on a particular class of things. The descriptions contain vague statements of the kinds of properties the person thinks are critical to understanding the class of things. Thus, we might be told that there are two people who claim to know all about phlebots, which are a kind of surgical instrument. Person A says the most important things to know about phlebots are that they are mostly black, have diagonal stripes on much of their surface, and have 23 parts. Person B says that the most important things to know are that they are typically about the size of a shoe, are crescent shaped, and are quite fragile. If asked who is more likely to be the real expert, adult judges strongly prefer person B for artifacts. When the phlebot is described as a kind of mammal participants either find both experts about equally compelling or prefer case A. Children as young as 5-years old show these same preferences. The judged quality of explanatory understanding therefore appears to be strongly influenced by one's general default assumptions about what properties are mostly likely to be causally central, with the expectation that good explanations will emphasise the more causally relevant features.

Causal relevancy normally has a different directionality for artifacts as opposed to natural kinds. The causally relevant properties for artifacts tend to be ones that have direct consequences for the use of the artifact. By contrast, with plants, for example, not all causally relevant properties are seen as having strong causal consequences; instead, properties are causally relevant because they are assumed to be indicative of core causal factors. For example, I may not attribute any causal role to the white colour of a certain mushroom or to its surface dot pattern, but I likely will assume that the colour and pattern are tightly causally linked to the chemical makeup of that mushroom and that a differently coloured and patterned mushroom is not likely to be of the same kind. Perhaps the most salient causal aspect of the mushroom is that it is highly poisonous. I may have no beliefs about its surface pattern causing it to be poisonous; but I may well believe that the genetic processes that give rise to its surface patterns are closely linked to those that give rise to its poisonous properties. For a group of naturally occurring mushrooms to systematically vary from the target in colour and surface pattern, I assume they probably also vary in deep ways that also cause variations in their poisons.

In short, sometimes a property like colour can play a direct causal role for a living kind, such as camouflage or mate attraction; but other times it can be seen as tightly causally linked to the entity's essence in such a way that it is implausible for a member of that kind to exist with a radically different colour and surface pattern while maintaining all other properties unchanged. It may well not be true for some living kinds, which can show tremendous variations of colour (such as some species of flowers); but there is a clear general bias to think that whether something is an animal, a plant, or an inorganic substance, its colour is more directly causally linked to its most important properties than it is for a hand tool, a piece of furniture, or a farm implement. The nature of its linkage, however, does not need to be specified by notions of causal relevancy. As seen earlier, a causally relevant property can either be one that has a causal impact of its own or is judged as tightly causally linked to other features that do have such impacts.

Tracking of such causal relevancy notions may be one of the most basic and primitive aspects of noticing causal patterns in the world. Not only are the same relevancy profiles found at a wide range of ages, recent work suggests something like such profiles in other primates, including cotton top tamarins, a group of New World monkeys with a very modest brain size that is only a small fraction of that found in humans. In those studies, the tamarins generalise tool concepts on the basis of shape relative to colour but do the opposite for classes of foodstuffs, putting more of an emphasis on colour (Santos, Hauser, & Spelke, 2001). Given such findings in other species, it is perhaps not surprising that this sort of knowledge is usually implicit. Thus, in our studies, after adults generate their causal relevancy profiles, in debriefing, they often note that they had never explicitly thought of such systematic relations between classes of properties and high-level classes of things.

## Causal powers

A more detailed manner of tracking causal structure extends beyond noting that particular property types likely have important causal roles in a specific domain, to encompass notions of their particular roles. This is one sense of the notion of "causal powers" (Harré & Madden, 1975). Thus, I may know not only that shape is important to the class of artifacts known as boomerangs; I also may believe that their distinctive shape gives them the ability to return in flight. Similarly, I may know not only that colour is important for bears; I also believe it helps conceal them as predators. This kind of knowledge may not contain any further explanations about causal roles. I know that magnets have the ability to exert an attractive force on various metals but may know little about magnetism and the reasons that some metals make good magnets while others do not. We can think of this level as the first level at which distinct causal roles are attributed to properties. There may be a relatively small set of causal relations such as: contain, prevent, support, and launch that are at this first level of coding. Above that level of understanding, we simply know that a property is causally relevant for a kind. Notions of causal powers do not require any interrelations among properties in a coherent system; they may simply be isolated causal attributions to kinds. Magnets have the power of attracting certain metals, chairs of supporting human agents, and knives of cutting. How they come to have these powers may remain unspecified. Beliefs in causal powers therefore need not include any sense of mechanism.

## Causal relations

A final, somewhat richer, but still abstract, way of tracking causal patterns is in terms of functional relations among stable subassemblies (Simon,

1981). In terms of coarse encodings, the stable subassemblies with all their constituent causal processes are treated as single entities in causal pathways with no tracking of their internal processes. We do encounter new questions concerning the definition of stable subassemblies and whether certain kinds of stability are especially prone to being treated as non-decomposable units; but that set of issues seems tractable and an important way of understanding how we do handle complex causal information. Thus, if a set of elements forms a stable unit with a clear function, we are inclined to encode only the unit as a whole and its functions, even if its internal structure works at the same level of complexity. For example, in understanding a complex mechanical watch, all parts are explained in terms of simple mechanics, but in many cases it may be useful to focus on interactions among larger subassemblies, such as the oscillator, the mainspring, the escapement, and the display. Understanding complex systems only at the highest level of functional interactions can lead us into trouble in some difficult cases but works well enough much of the time.

Knowledge of the coarsest functional relations in a domain may amount to little more than knowing the function of an entity as a whole and just a few of its largest constituents. For many people, their mental representations of the causal relations for cars may largely be confined to knowing that they convey people from place to place on roads, that they are propelled by an engine whose output is increased by pressing on an accelerator, and that they are slowed down by brakes. For an unfamiliar vehicle, only the notion of transport and some means of controlling speed may be present.

Collectively, these coarse representations of the world's much richer causal structure play a major role in how we learn and use knowledge about categories. They guide our attention and weighting of features and consequently our identification of new members of categories (Ahn, Kim, Lassaline, & Dennis, 2000). This coarseness may be one reason, however, why there is so much controversy concerning the role of theories in guiding concept structure and use. If theories are to be thought of as detailed mechanistic models of the world around us, at most we know local fragments that may differ considerably from person to person. But those mechanistic fragments may not be the central factors that influence our concepts and categorisation. Instead, the more skeletal frameworks of understanding may be much more universal and invariant across people.

All three of the coarse interpretations of reality just described frequently seem to operate at an implicit level. In our laboratory studies, participants clearly track causal patterns but often are unaware of those patterns until their set of responses are shown to them. I have already noted that people have sharply contrasting causal relevancy profiles for animals, machines, and non-living natural kinds; yet this understanding seems to be implicit unless it is explicitly pointed out. Similarly, causal powers are often sensed and not explicitly mentioned. Finally, the highest-level causal functional roles of objects are often grasped but not discussed. We often use this kind of knowledge as a lens to interpret reality and, in looking through this lens, are often unaware of the ways in which it guides us to track some sorts of causal relations more effectively than others. While detailed mechanistic understandings are usually explicit and verbalisable, much of the coarser ways of tracking the world seems to occur outside awareness. This implicit aspect of causal understanding may be a key reason why developmental patterns are often described in such different ways. If there is a focus on ability to provide explicit accounts of how things worked or why phenomena exist, younger children often seem to be incompetent. By contrast, if one considers their patterns of judgement and the information needed to drive those judgements, young children can be highly competent in being sensitive to high-level causal patterns associated with broad domains.

## DEPENDENCY AND DEFERENCE

A problem with only having coarse encodings of causal structure is that, when pressed, one runs into huge gaps in knowledge. Most of the time these gaps do not bother us, for two reasons: either we do not notice them because of the IOED, or we do notice them but assume that someone to whom we can have access knows them. More than 25 years ago, this dependence on others was pointed out in Hilary Putnam's essay on the meaning of meaning, in which he invoked a "division of linguistic labour" to explain how we successfully use terms like *gold* without knowing anything at all about the atomic makeup of gold (Putnam, 1975). In short, we succeed because we believe there is a relevant group of experts to whom we can defer when we encounter gaps in our own knowledge. In the case of *gold*, Putnam argued that we believe experts have knowledge of the true essence of gold. Putnam's proposal, combined with that of others (e.g., Burge, 1979), has led to a vigorous debate in cognitive science over "narrow" versus "wide" content, that is, whether meanings can be individuated solely by referring to internal mental states or whether they are also bound to the external world (Segal, 2000; Fodor, 1998). Such a debate affects claims about the nature of concepts, but it is less relevant to questions about factors that influence categorisation. One might be unsure about whether concepts have theories as part of their structure, while still maintaining that certain kinds of causal explanatory relations influence categorisation. Similarly, one might maintain that the division of linguistic labour influences judgement about word usage, while being unsure whether word meanings intrinsically depend on such a division.

The division of linguistic labour is a special case of a more general division of cognitive labour that occurs in all cultures. Just as we rely on specialisation of physical labour to provide us with resources that we cannot produce ourselves, we rely on a specialisation of intellectual labour to provide us with underpinnings to knowledge where we have none. Virtually every human group of any size develops different sub-communities that have different clusters of specialised knowledge and deeper explanatory understanding. But this reliance on other's knowledge is a far more subtle and complex ability than it appears at first and links in powerful ways to our tracking of causal patterns in the world.

Consider, for example, variations in knowledge about trees. I am profoundly ignorant about different types of trees and know little beyond the distinction between trees with needles and trees with leaves. Thus, when confronted with a particular tree and asked whether it is an elm, a beech, or a basswood tree, I would have no idea. Yet, I firmly believe that there are such categories and that there are people who could tell me why trees belong in each category and something about how they are related in a larger system of classification. Moreover, I do not necessarily believe that the best expert is simply someone who has looked at a lot of trees. There are hikers who may go through a wood almost every day for years and be highly experienced with various trees; but that experience may be with landmarks on a trail and not with trees as a species. The hikers may be able to recognise individual trees in those woods better than almost any one, but they may not have any sense of tree categories; or perhaps they have a sense of categories in terms of tree types that show tree blazes the most clearly. In deciding where to allocate my dependence on other's knowledge, I would put my trust in someone who I think could explain all the various surface properties of trees and their "behaviours" over the seasons. I would assume that a person could do so because she knew something about the deep relations between certain classes of trees.

To pick the right experts, I need to have some sense of biology and perhaps of plants as well. I need a skeletal sense of the kinds of relations that are central to a domain such that a person who grasped those relations would be much more likely to explain surface phenomena in the domain as well. To benefit from the division of cognitive labour, I need to have a sense of what the key principles are in broad domains, such as animals, plants, and tools, such that a person who grasped those principles would be able to guide me to proper judgements about categorisation.

Trees are an especially interesting case because they illustrate how one's assumption about the division of cognitive labour may be wrong. Thus, the global category of "trees" does not agree well with western biological sciences, which would instead classify an apple tree as more similar to a daisy than to a pine tree. In turn, a pine tree would be seen as more similar to a fern than to an oak (Dupre, 1981). I may be correct in assuming there are molecular and evolutionary reasons that shed insight into the differences between elms and beeches but wrong in assuming that there are any molecular reasons for trees being a separate category from other plants. There are, however, evolutionary arguments that the appearance of tree-like structures is due to the biomechanical constraints of obtaining adequate light for large free-standing plants to survive (e.g., Niklas, 1996), though these accounts reveal no common molecular relations. There are yet other causal systems in which trees may be embedded that are quite different from those of western science but which may well have their own groups of experts who are especially tuned to those kinds of causal structures, e.g., trees that are particularly good hosts for certain kinds of fauna versus those that create environments that are especially hospitable to certain kinds of plants (López, Atran, Coley, Medin, & Smith, 1997). These alternatives could suggest a "promiscuous realism" in which there are an indefinitely large number of such categories, since they reflect the boundless nature of human creativity (Dupre, 1981). The alternative view favoured here allows many natural and artificial objects to be parts of several different stable causal systems but not an indefinitely large set. These systems could each have their own experts and ways of construing categories but would be limited to a relatively small number of real world stable causal systems that embed those kinds (Keil, 1989).

By this account, categorisation may be heavily influenced by causal interpretations that not only tell us what properties and kinds of relations are likely to be relevant, but also what kinds of experts could provide us with further details. For such an account to be plausible, however, it is important to show that people have reliable intuitions about the division of cognitive labour that at least show some consistency within cultural groups. In a recent series of studies, we have explored such intuitions by asking both adults and children to tell us if a person who understood phenomenon A was more likely to understand phenomenon B or C. This is a very natural task even for preschoolers (Lutz & Keil, 2002). In adults, the task is most sensitive when set up as a triad of the following sort:

> John knows all about why gasoline is poisonous to people. Because of this, what else is he likely to know a lot about?
>> Why horses perspire when they get hot, or
>> Why a heavy person must sit closer to the middle on a seesaw.

Both adults and children will pick the alternative about perspiration most often, even though the first and third sentences refer to people whereas the second refers to horses. They often do not know the details of the answers at all, but can nonetheless be quite confident in their judgement. If adults are asked to provide a rationale, many say that the person is a biology expert. Others who have more difficulty voicing a reason are still confident in their choice. Children, however, often cannot give a reason, even though they show the same clusterings of biology with biology and physical mechanics with physical mechanics. When children do offer justifications, they usually refer to different relational patterns. For example, one child said, "John knows about how people and animals work, what their insides do" "... the other thing is about how things move".

The knowledge that drives these judgements creates distinctions like many of the major natural and social science departments in universities: physics, chemistry, biology, psychology, political science, and economics. These judgements happen in younger children who have no awareness of these labels or the departments. With adults and older children, further subdivisions such as molecular biology vs. ecology are also understood without explicit labels for those disciplines. Thus, people have a sense of what sorts of phenomena are likely to be clustered together because they can be explained by some common set of principles. A person who really understood one phenomenon in that cluster would also tend to understand others that arose from the same principles, even if they were radically different on the surface

Laypeople in fact do not intuitively know the principles of modern physics, chemistry, or biology but instead have more schematic notions that approximate the domains of a science. Physics is understood as being about moving solid objects and their interactions with other solids, chemistry as the ways objects change state or mix with others, and biology as the basic functions of living kinds. It is possible to reveal these approximations by presenting phenomena that are technically problems in physics, chemistry, or biology but which may elude children and many adults because they do not fit these simple schemata. For example, if a child's schema dictates that physics involves bounded objects in motion, a phenomenon involving static forces, such as those holding a suspension bridge, may not be clustered with other physics problem.

These studies on the division of cognitive labour suggest that young children link together phenomena that they think are governed by the same causal patterns with particular groups of experts. Even for preschoolers, it is very natural to see such groups of experts as mapping onto causal patterns in the world. Put differently, to solve the above problems, children and adults alike need to have some sense of how the world is causally structured into different domains. They do not need to know the details of how things work in each domain, such as the principles of respiration or reproduction for biology; they merely need to have enough of a sense of the causal patterns distinctive to that domain. That skeletal sense of causal patterns may well be the same as the coarse level of representing causal relations that was discussed earlier. In short, people do track large-scale causal patterns in coarse terms that may explain both theory-like influences on categorisation and intuitions about how causal understandings are clustered in other minds.

## THE COGNITIVE CONSEQUENCES OF KNOWING WHO KNOWS WHAT

If children as young as 4 years have reliable notions of how knowledge is distributed in other minds, and if several of those notions are based on their tracking of high-level causal patterns, what do people do with this knowledge? In particular, to what extent do implicit models of the division of cognitive labour influence categorisation? One influence may involve arbitration of marginal cases or the enabling of conceptual change when an initial category structure is missing key relations. In such cases, people often show deference to experts by adjusting their categories when told that an expert has a particular view of category membership. The extent of this deference, however, may vary across contexts and may not always include the most appropriate uses of experts. Thus, in some cases, people might defer on a natural kind categorisation decision to a group described as shoppers as much as they do to a group described as scientists (Braisby, 2001). The opinions of both experts and non-experts do matter to our decisions about category membership but perhaps not in a simple manner that has the opinions of the most relevant scientists always being the most influential. In addition, if the views of the experts are discordant enough with all other known cases of expert influence (e.g., a group of experts who claim that cats are really remotely controlled robots) deference will not be nearly as strong as with a more mundane but more ordinary case (e.g., an iris is really a kind of orchid).

Adults are not usually confronted with an expert opinion that causes them to radically change category assignments. When we do make revisions they are most often to quite nearby categories. Even with nearby categories, wholesale reassignments are rare, e.g., the discovery that panda bears were not really bears. Larger reassignments may be more common in children, e.g., learning that whales are not fish, but such dramatic revisions may not be the norm even in childhood.

Notions of the division of cognitive labour normally work in a more subtle and incremental manner during category learning. Consider how an adult might learn about a new category, such as a new disease agent. He might have heard the term "prion" mentioned a few times in relation to mad cow disease. As he learns more about prions and the disease, he needs to weigh different bits of information that he encounters, ranging from the panicked remarks of a caller to a radio talk show to the remarks of a molecular biologist. If the caller and the biologist both ascribe a property to prions, the caller likely will weigh the biologist's ascription more heavily. New information about a category that comes from more qualified sources is more likely to be given more weight. The process is, of course, fallible, and urban myths about any number of categories arise from such fallibilities; but there is a general effect of favouring knowledge from appropriate experts. The relevant expert also clearly varies as a function of the kinds of categories and relations involved. I weigh the molecular biologist's statements heavily in gathering information about prions, but when the biologist starts talking about economic recessions brought about by diseases, I weigh that information less heavily in developing knowledge of a category of recessions.

One can therefore think of the division of cognitive labour as providing a spotlight on the most relevant features when thinking about a category. It can serve both to make features salient that might not have been otherwise noticed and to weight salient ones more heavily as causally central. These influences are not confined to the occasional novel category and, in fact, are at work for some of our most mundane and familiar categories. Consider, for example, my understanding of the category of dogs. For years I have noticed statements about the similarities and differences between dogs and wolves, but until recently these statements had been made mostly by dog owners, people with dog phobias, and authors of various novels involving ferocious dogs. Because I regarded all those sources as non-experts, I had not used them much to adjust my understanding of dogs. A few months ago, however, I came across an article on the evolution of dogs, in which biologists discussed the relatively short time frame in which dogs have emerged from the wolf category and the extraordinary overlap in their genetic material. That article caused me to weigh somewhat differently many of the features of dogs and their causal roles. I may have been mistaken in making such adjustments, but they occurred because I believed the information came from credible experts. Such a re-weighting does not cause me to label major groups of dogs, such as Labradors and poodles, differently, but they may influence cases at the margin. Thus, if I see a creature with wolf-like and dog-like features, I would be more likely to accept a more wolf-like creature as a dog.

Children's categorisation may be just as heavily influenced by their own quite well developed senses of the division of cognitive labour. As they learn about new categories or elaborate on recently acquired ones, they might well weight information differently based on its sources. In an ongoing line of research in our lab, we are finding that elementary school children discount or favour the same information as a function of who provided the information. Thus, to the extent that information about a new category is learned through social transmission, the ways that information affects categorisation will be influenced by our understandings of the division of cognitive labour.

The impact of a sense of the division of cognitive labour is not just on information acquired through social transmission; it can work directly on information acquired from real time, direct experience. If some prior encounter with a body of expertise causes one to weight certain kinds of properties or causal relations as more central, that effect will carry forth to new encounters with potential instances of a category. In my own case, the features and causal relations that I encounter in novel canines will be encoded differently because of my beliefs about prior information that came from experts vs. novices.

In many cases, there is a cycle of interaction between notions of the division of cognitive labour, our tracking of causal structures, and the impact on categorisation. When encountering a novel phenomenon, I will notice certain high level causal patterns, such as those of relevancy, causal power, and schematic patterns, and will use them to pick out a relevant domain of expertise. Identifying the phenomenon as in the domain of biology will lead me to further consider what I have heard from experts in that domain in terms of key relations and properties. That information, in turn, will guide my more detailed analysis of the phenomenon and my attempts to form relevant categories.

A division of labour framing of information seems to promote searches for deeper causal relations. Thus, in a series of studies (Keil & Rozenblit, 1997), we compared adult ratings of the similarities of various phenomena, such as "water is transparent to light", "water is a frequent source conflict between nations", and "televisions get static buildup on their screen" in cases where they were presented as "bare facts" with cases where they were embedded in a division of cognitive labour frame (e.g., "This expert knows all about why water is transparent to light"). Adults categorised the phenomena quite differently when presented in their raw form versus when embedded in a division of cognitive labour frame in which clustering by similar experts is requested. In the explanation frame case adults see a much stronger similarity between the two cases that share more similar underlying causal patterns (in this case those of physics). Embedding phenomena in a frame that invokes the division of cognitive labour increases sensitivity to their underlying causal patterns and principles. Moreover, preliminary findings from an ongoing study with children suggest that this division of cognitive labour framing causes a corresponding shift in their similarity judgements.

Our sense of the division of cognitive labour also allows us to be more confident in our understandings when there are large gaps in our knowledge. Put differently, that sense tells us what sorts of causal patterns and properties are likely to be explanatorily relevant in a domain and, at the same time, likely to be known in much more detail by experts. We can therefore be more confident if we believe that experts would be as well. Thus, I weight some properties more heavily because I both sense their important roles in causally central relations in that domain and because I believe that relations of that sort drive successful expertise. The division of cognitive labour helps give us a sense of relevant properties and relations within a domain. It may be analogous to the role of a guardrail on a narrow, curving mountain road. Drivers on such roads very rarely touch the guardrails, but most feel vastly more confident and willing to drive on roads with guardrails as opposed to those without and may use the guard rail to guide their driving speed and vigilance. The division of cognitive labour is a comparable guiding and supporting backdrop for categorisation.

## CONCLUSIONS

When we leave laboratory categorisation tasks, which have a few neatly defined features, we give up the elegance of clear control over our stimuli. However, we then start to confront one of the most basic problems of real world categorisation: the immensity of information that is associated with most categories in our daily lives. Many features and feature correlations help create this immensity; however, another major contributor is the massive set of causal patterns, which are responsible for the creation and continued existence of members within a category and are critical to understanding which features are likely to be most central to that category. Fortunately, much of the time, typicality, correlation, and causation converge. The most frequent two features are usually highly correlated and usually play important causal roles for members of a category. Furthermore, patterns of variation of property types and values and property kinds within and across categories can be powerful clues to causal relations.

There are also cases of mismatch, in which causality and typicality are not correlated. For many artifacts, highly typical colours can be such properties, such as washing machines being white. For natural kinds, highly typical but low causally central features seem less common because one assumes an efficiency in which functionally irrelevant features are discarded. Indeed, for biological kinds, there may even be a bias to attribute important causal roles to structures when in fact none exist and they are mere byproducts of other structures (Gould & Lewontin, 1979). Still, even in biology, some features may be clearly irrelevant even if they are consistent with all known instances. For instance, I recently moved to a neighbourhood where a parasite had attacked a special kind of evergreen I had not seen before. Virtually every tree of this kind has huge blotches of brown needles instead of a uniform green. I did not, however, attribute those properties as important to that class of trees, presumably because of beliefs about normal structure/function relations in plants.

An appreciation of causal relations does appear to be essential to understand categorisation in the real world. That appreciation, however, is not in the form of well-developed theories that provide blueprints of various devices and phenomena. One's knowledge does not come close to allowing one to recreate a working system, only to appreciating some central causal patterns that are collectively unique to a broad domain in which that object is a member. This coarse level of encoding is powerful enough to narrow down the complexity of what one must track, but also shallow enough to allow quick and efficient processing. Shallowness is a real virtue in this sense of navigating the causal complexities of the world around us. Thus, we extract the causal "gist" to ascertain enough detail within a particular domain so that we can detect the most salient features without being overwhelmed. In this view, the relevance of causal understandings to concepts and categorisation is a basic aspect of our cognition seen as early as humans can notice causal patterns for large-scale domains, something that quite young infants notice for such domains as intentional versus inanimate agents. What develops is an appreciation of ever-finer patterns and better ways of linking cause to typicality and correlation.

Causal information is valuable to understanding classes of objects around us, both in terms of predicting patterns and in terms of encoding relations and helping guide exploration. But, causal information threatens to swamp us with its complexity. It has been popular to invoke intuitive theories as a mechanism for significantly reducing the number of features and correlations we have to examine. However, this claim does not help us understand a two-faceted problem for theories: Which of the countless theories for a set of relations do we pick, and at what level of detail?

There has been little attention given to the problem of finding the minimal amount of information about a theory required to "get by" in tasks such as categorisation and induction. Our studies on the Illusion of Explanatory Depth (IOED) show that adults and children alike have a particularly strong illusion of knowing explanatory relations in far more detail than they really do. Moreover, this illusion is a distinct phenomenon from other overconfidence effects and is much stronger for explanatory knowledge as opposed to several other types.

One should not interpret the IOED studies as supporting the idea that intuitive theories of concepts and categorisation are too ephemeral and sketchy to be of any use. Rather, we effectively track high-level coarse causal patterns, which tell us what sorts of causal relations are central to a given domain. That level of causal interpretation, however, is very different from concrete mental models of how things work and rarely includes notion of specific mechanisms. Indeed, it is often implicit and works outside of normal awareness and discourse about phenomena and devices. Such coarse representations become evident when one specifically looks for people's abilities to track causal patterns and explores how that information can guide explanation preferences and notions about the division of cognitive labour. I have also suggested that coarse under-standings guide category-learning and use and may be the real basis for many theory-like effects on categorisation. I have further argued that our sensitivity to causal patterns is often heightened when we consider phenomena from the viewpoint of how such patterns might map onto domains of expertise.

A final note concerns the generative nature of explanatory under-standing. One major factor creating the IOED is confusion between what one mentally represents and what is decipherable from a pattern that is present for inspection. People are often quite adept at figuring out causal relations and patterns on the fly when in information-rich environments. Thus, I may not store in my head detailed theories of desert, arctic, and jungle vehicles but, when confronted a series of vehicles and environments, I may quickly sort them into categories in which their feature clusters mesh nicely with these three environments. I come to the situation with schematic expectations about causal patterns in artifact domains and perhaps for vehicles as well, and I use those to help create a much more transient, detailed theory on the fly. Like "ad hoc categories" (Barsalou, 1983), much of the detail of our everyday theories may be fleeting and controlled primarily by local and, immediate contexts.

It may be more appropriate to think of what a person brings to a situation, not as involving just broad causal gists, but also involving a set of specialised toolboxes for constructing theories. That is, the plumber, the electrician, and the carpenter bring quite different sets of tools when making house calls, tools that embody expectations about the kinds of problems that will be encountered and which are designed to be most causally effective for those situations. We also tend to bring a conceptual toolbox that best embodies expectations about the most relevant kinds of causal patterns for each particular domain of phenomena. Such a toolbox would contain schemata that are most likely to be central to that domain and perhaps some information on how they work together in a larger system. In this manner, rapidly constructed ad hoc causal explanations may also show theory-like effects on categorisation that supersede broader, more abstract expectations.

# REFERENCES

Ahn, W., & Kalish, C. (2000). The role of mechanism beliefs in causal reasoning. In F.C. Keil & R.A. Wilson (Eds.), *Cognition and explanation* (pp. 199–225). Boston: MIT Press.

Ahn, W., Kim, N.S., Lassaline, M.E., & Dennis, M.J. (2000). Causal status as a determinant of feature centrality. *Cognitive Psychology, 41*, 361–416.

Barrett, S.E., Abdi, H., Murphy, G.L., & Gallagher, J.M. (1993). Theory-based correlations and their role in children's concepts. *Child Development, 64*, 1595–1616.

Barsalou, L.W. (1983). Ad hoc categories. *Memory and Cognition, 11*, 211–227.

Bloom, P. (1996). Intention, history, and artifact concepts. *Cognition, 60*, 1–29.

Braisby, N.B. (2001). *Deference in categorization: Evidence for a division of linguistic labor?* Paper presented at the 2001 Congress of the European Society for Philosophy and Psychology, August 8–11, 2001. Fribourg, Switzerland.

Braisby, N., Franks, B., & Hampton, J. (1996). Essentialism, word use, and concepts. *Cognition, 59*, 247–274.

Brown, J.S., Collins, A., & Duguid, P. (1989). Situated cognition and the culture of learning. *Educational Researcher, 18*, 32–42.

Burge, T. (1979). Individualism and the mental. In P. French (Ed.), *Midwest studies in philosophy IV: Studies in metaphysics* (Vol. 4, pp. 73–122). Minneapolis: University of Minnesota Press.

Carey, S. (1991). Knowledge acquisition: Enrichment or conceptual change? In S. Carey & R. Gelman (Eds.), *The epigenesis of mind: Essays on biology and cognition* (pp. 257–291). Hillsdale, NJ: Lawrence Erlbaum Associates, Inc.

di Sessa, A. (1993). Towards an epistemology of physics. *Cognition and Instruction, 10*, 105–225.

Dupre, J. (1981). Natural kinds and biological taxa. *Philosophical Review, 90*, 66–90.

Fischhoff, B. (1982). Debiasing. In D. Kahneman, P. Slovic, & A. Tversky (Eds.) *Judgement under uncertainty: Heuristics and biases* (pp. 422–444). Cambridge: Cambridge University Press.

Fodor, J.A. (1998). *Concepts: Where cognitive science went wrong.* New York: Oxford University Press.

Gärdenfors, P. (in press). Concept modeling, essential properties, and similarity spaces. *Behavioral and Brain Sciences.*

Gelman, S.A. (1999). *Essentialism.* Retrieved August 1, 2002 from MIT Encyclopedia of the Cognitive Sciences site http://cognet.mit.edu/MITECS/Entry/ kornblith.

Gelman, S.A. (2003). *The essential child.* London: Oxford University Press.

Gigerenzer, G., Hoffrage, U., & Kleinboelting, H. (1991). Probabilistic mental models: A Brunswikian theory of confidence. *Psychological Review, 98*, 506–528.

Glenberg, A.M., & Epstein, W. (1985). Calibration of comprehension. *Journal of Experimental Psychology: Learning, Memory, and Cognition, 11*, 702–718.

Glenberg, A.M., Wilkinson, A.C., & Epstein, W. (1982). The illusion of knowing: Failure in the self-assessment of comprehension. *Memory and Cognition, 10*, 597–602.

Gopnik, A.A., & Wellman, H.M. (1994). The theory theory. In L.A. Hirschfeld & S.A. Gelman (Eds.), *Mapping the mind: Domain specificity in cognition and culture* (pp. 257–293). Cambridge: Cambridge University Press.

Gould, S.J., & Lewontin, R.C. (1979). The spandrels of San Marco and the Panglossion paradigm: A critique of the adaptationist programme, *Proceedings of the Royal Society of London B, 205*, 581–598.

Hampton, J.A. (2001). The role of similarity in natural categorization. In U. Hahn & M. Ramscar (Eds.), *Similarity and categorization.* Oxford: Oxford University Press.

Harré, R., & Madden, E.H. (1975). *Causal powers.* Oxford: Blackwell.

Hirschfeld, L.A. (1996). *Race in the making: Cognition, culture, and the child's construction of human kinds.* Boston: MIT Press.

Keil, F.C. (1986). The acquisition of natural kind and artifact terms. In W. Demopoulos & A. Marras (Eds.), *Language learning and concept acquisition: Foundational issues* (pp. 133–153). Norwood, NJ: Ablex.

Keil, F.C. (1989). *Concepts, kinds, and cognitive development.* Cambridge, MA: Bradford Books/MIT Press.

Keil, F.C. (1994). Explanation based constraints on the acquisition of word meaning. *Lingua, 92,* 169–196.

Keil, F.C. & Rozenblit, L. (1997). *Knowing who knows what.* Paper presented at the 1997 meeting of the Psychonomics Society, Philadelphia.

Keil, F.C., Smith, C.S., Simons, D.J., & Levin, D.T. (1998). Two dogmas of conceptual empiricism. *Cognition, 65,* 103–135.

Kuhn, T.S. (1977). *The essential tension: Selected studies in scientific tradition and change.* Chicago, IL: University of Chicago Press.

Krueger, J. (1998). Enhancement bias in the description of self and others. *Personality and Social Psychology Bulletin, 24,* 505–516.

Krueger, J., & Dunning, D. (1999). Unskilled and unaware of it: How difficulties in recognizing one's own incompetence lead to inflated self-assessments. *Journal of Personality and Social Psychology, 77,* 1121–1134.

Levin, D.T., Momen, N., Drivdahl, S.B., & Simons, D.J. (2000). Change blindness blindness: The metacognitive error of overestimating change-detection ability. *Visual Cognition, 7,* 397–412.

Lichtenstein, S., & Fischhoff, B. (1977). Do those who know more also know more about how much they know? *Organizational Behavior and Human Decision Processes, 20,* 159–183.

Lin, E.L., & Murphy, G.L. (1997). The effects of background knowledge on object categorization and part detection. *Journal of Experimental Psychology: Human Perception and Performance, 23,* 1153–1169.

Lin, L., & Zabrucky, K.M. (1998). Calibration of comprehension: Research and implications for education and instruction. *Contemporary Educational Psychology, 23,* 345–391.

López, A., Atran, S., Coley, J.D., Medin, D.L., & Smith, E.E. (1997). The tree of life: Universal and cultural features of folkbiological taxonomies and inductions. *Cognitive Psychology, 32,* 251–295.

Lutz, D.J., & Keil, F.C. (2002). Early understanding of the division of cognitive labor. *Child Development, 73,* 1073–1084.

Lycan, W.G. (2002). Explanation and epistemology. In Paul Moser (Ed.) *The Oxford handbook of epistemology.* Oxford: Oxford University Press.

Malt, B.C. (1994). Water is not $H_2O$. *Cognitive Psychology, 27,* 41–70.

Mandler, J.M., & Johnson, N. (1977). Remembrance of things parsed: Story structure and recall. *Cognitive Psychology, 9,* 111–151.

Medin, D.L. (1989). Concepts and conceptual structure. *American Psychologist, 44,* 1469–1481.

Medin D.L., & Ortony, A. (1989). Psychological essentialism. In S. Vosniadou & A. Artony (Eds.), *Similarity and analogical reasoning.* Cambridge: Cambridge University Press.

Medin, D.L., & Shoben, E.J. (1988). Context and structure in conceptual combination. *Cognitive Psychology, 20,* 158–190.

Mills, C., Skinner, H., Goldenberg, D., & Keil, F. (2001). *Thinking you know more than you do: Children's assessment of their own knowledge and explanations.* Poster presented at 2001 Cognitive Development Society Conference, October 26–27. Virginia Beach, VA.

Murphy, G.L. (2002). *The big book of concepts.* Cambridge, MA: MIT Press.

Murphy, G.L., & Allopenna, P.D. (1994). The locus of knowledge effects in concept learning. *Journal of Experimental Psychology: Learning, Memory, and Cognition, 20*, 904–919.

Murphy, G.L. & Medin, D.L. (1985). The role of theories in conceptual coherence. *Psychological Review, 92*, 289–316.

Niklas, K.J. (1996). How to build a tree. *Natural History, 105*, 48–52.

Paulhus, D.L. (1998). Interpersonal adaptiveness of trait self-enhancement: A mixed blessing? *Journal of Personality and Social Psychology, 74*, 1197–1208.

Prinz, J.J. (2002). *Furnishing the mind: Concepts and their perceptual basis.* Cambridge, MA: MIT Press.

Putnam, H. (1975). The meaning of "meaning". In K. Gunderson (Ed.), *Language, mind, and knowledge* (Vol. 2, pp. 131–193). Minneapolis: University of Minnesota Press.

Rehder, B., & Hastie, R. (2001). Causal knowledge and categories: The effects of causal beliefs on categorization, induction, and similarity. *Journal of Experimental Psychology: General, 130*, 323–360.

Rozenblit, L.R. & Keil, F.C. (2002) The misunderstood limits of folk science: An illusion of explanatory depth, *Cognitive Science, 26*, 521–562.

Santos, L.R., Hauser, M.D., & Spelke, E.S. (2001). The representation of different domains of knowledge in human and non-human primates: Artifactual and food kinds. In M. Beckoff, C. Allen, & G. Burghardt (Eds.) *The cognitive animal.* Cambridge, MA: MIT Press.

Schwartz, S. (1977). *Introduction to naming, necessity, and natural kinds.* Ithaca, NY: Cornell University Press.

Segal, G.M.A. (2000). *A slim book about narrow content.* Cambridge, MA: Bradford Books/ MIT Press.

Simon, H.A. (1981). *The sciences of the artificial*, 2nd edn. Cambridge, MA: MIT Press.

Sloman, S.A., Love, B.C., & Ahn, W. (1998). Feature centrality and conceptual coherence. *Cognitive Science, 22*, 189–228.

Sloman, S.A., & Malt, B.C. (this issue). Artifacts are not ascribed essences, nor are they treated as belonging to kinds. *Language and Cognitive Processes, 18*, 563–582

Smith, E.E., & Medin, D.L. (1981). *Categories and concepts.* Cambridge, MA: Harvard University Press.

Taylor, M. (1996). The development of children's beliefs about social and biological aspects of gender differences. *Child Development, 67*, 1555–1571.

Vosniadou, S., & Brewer, W.F. (1992). Mental models of the earth: A study of conceptual change in childhood. *Cognitive Psychology, 24*, 535–585.

Walker, J. (1979). The amateur scientist. *Scientific American, 240*, 162–172.

Wilson, R.A. (1999). *Species: New interdisciplinary essays.* Cambridge, MA: MIT Press.

Wisniewski, E.J., & Medin, D.L. (1994). On the interaction of theory and data in concept learning. *Cognitive Science, 18*, 221–281.

Yates, J.F., Lee, J.W., & Bush, J.G. (1997). General knowledge overconfidence: Cross-national variations, response style, and "reality". *Organizational Behavior and Human Decision Processes, 70*, 87–94.

Yates, J.F., Lee, J.W., & Shinotsuka, H. (1996). Beliefs about overconfidence, including its cross-national variation. *Organizational Behavior and Human Decision Processes, 65*, 138–147.

LANGUAGE AND COGNITIVE PROCESSES, 2003, *18* (5/6), 693–723

# Concepts, language, and privacy: An argument "vaguely Viennese in provenance"

David K. Levy

*King's College, London, UK*

I consider two notable recent philosophical theories of concepts (Fodor and Peacocke) in relation to some challenges set by Wittgenstein in his notorious private language argument. The challenge is formulated in terms of contraints on the explanation of the relation between thought and language. I try to show how these theories of concepts relate to constraints that arise from this challenge. I also relate the challenge to a recent contribution in the debate about narrow and broad content. In so doing I try to illuminate how this philosophical debate bears on some issues in cognitive psychology. In particular, I suggest it bears on nativism about concepts, the relation between an adequate notion of public language and thought, and the idea that concepts are "in" *mentalese*, a Language of Thought. Accommodating these considerations requires increasing the consideration of linguistic evidence and the linguistic character of concepts in laboratory research if distinctively human thought is to be explained.

## INTRODUCTION

I am a philosopher, here writing principally for psychologists, aware that some psychologists are very uncertain about how philosophy can interact with psychology. Of course to the extent that philosophy and psychology have diverged, they have done so quite recently. Perhaps 125 years ago psychology moved more towards the methods of empirical science while philosophy retained its emphasis on conceptual analysis, renewing an interest in the logical structure of language. However, the gap waxes and

Requests for reprints should be addressed to David K. Levy, Department of Philosophy, King's College, London, The Strand, London WC2R 2LS. E-mail: david.levy@kcl.ac.uk.

I am grateful to Jon Barton for many corrections and suggestions, Nicholas Shea for detailed, critical, and constructive comments, and Gregor Stewart for helpful and protracted discussions of content, as well as the editors and two anonymous reviewers for *Language and Cognitive Processes*.

http://www.tandf.co.uk/journals/pp/01690965.html    DOI: 10.1080/01690960344000080

wanes. Today a majority of philosophers and cognitive psychologists share the functionalist view of mind, that mental phenomena can be broadly individuated by their functional role in the lives and behaviour of people. Philosophy and psychology have a mutual interest in concepts, the analysis of which has haunted Western thinking for over two thousand years. Two millennia later, we have some consensus on some specific concepts but rather less on *general* theories of concepts and their relation to thought and language.

In the last century, philosophy has focused increasingly on the distinctive relationship between language and thought in human life. Central to these developments were the idea of Ludwig Wittgenstein, native of Vienna. No less a personage than Jerry Fodor has said:

> there is rumoured to be an argument, vaguely Viennese in provenance, that proves that 'original', underived intentionality must inhere, *not* in mental representations *nor* in thoughts, but precisely in the formulas of public language. I would be very pleased if such an argument actually turned up, since then pretty nearly everything I believe about language and mind would have been refuted ... (Fodor, 1998a, p. 9)

He continues though, "Unfortunately, however, either nobody can remember how the argument goes, or it's a secret that they're unprepared to share with me". Never mind that Fodor seemed to have a good idea of the argument some years ago (Fodor, 1975, pp. 55–98; Fodor & Chihara, 1965), I shall go *part* way toward sharing the argument with him. After sketching some reasonably common ground with respect to concepts, I shall describe one facet of Wittgenstein's argument *against* the possibility of a private language. Language is to be understood broadly so as to include any behaviour which might reasonably be incorporated into the pragmatics of a theory of meaning, including gestures, grunts, whistles, etc. The argument is designed to show that there is something *essentially* public and external about language and also thought. It is suggested that this public dimension controls our understanding and theorising about language and thought. Then I outline Peacocke's theory of concepts and relate it to Wittgenstein's argument. I then do the same with Fodor's theory of concepts. Following that I recount the basics of a debate about content, two of whose participants, Putnam and Burge, are congenial to the direction of Wittgenstein's argument. I shall conclude by speculating whether the conflict I have outlined is real or merely apparent, or whether it lies in the nature of the explanations proffered and is therefore salutary for research programmes in this area.

I am engaged in trying to illuminate a question of relevance to philosophers and psychologists. Do Wittgenstein's arguments for the publicity of language, thought, or concepts constrain the theories of concepts we develop and the explanations those theories underwrite? I shall argue that if Wittgenstein's arguments are correct then the answer is more or less "yes" depending on the kind of explanation one tries to give of human thoughts. The discussion of Fodor's and Peacocke's theories is intended to provide examples of different explanations. If this is to be of relevance to cognitive psychologists then philosophical theorising will need to bear on psychological theorising, even as one is generally conducted by means of conceptual analysis and the other by means of empirical laboratory work. In so far as psychology is a science, the considerable work done in the philosophy of science will bear on it. In the case of physics and biology for instance, philosophers have applied their strengths in conceptual analysis to help scientists produce more systematic, distinct, and sophisticated explanations (and theories) of their work. This, ideally, feeds back into the experimental process and produces better focused and more productive laboratory results. The process has worked both ways with, for instance, discoveries about the plasticity of neural function motivating the move from early identity theories of mind to more sophisticated functionalist theories. Philosophical theories of language are very rich, and the constraints stemming from Wittgenstein that I shall highlight are only one facet of that bounty. If some of these theories are right, they ought to constrain how psychologists understand that part of our behaviour that is saturated with language. The close connection between concepts, word meanings, sentences and inferences suggest that the study of concepts is one such area. For psychologists this bears on the way experiments involving concepts are conceived. For instance, it appears that the work on kind concepts has been very heavily oriented toward *categorisation* tasks; or the degradation of *recognition* abilities due to lesions. Much less work appears to have been done on inferential relations among kinds and concepts, or on how concepts are used in tasks other than categorisation. Yet these are central to concept use in discussion and reasoning. Keil (this issue) provides an example of how much progress can be made with traditional difficulties in conceptual theories if for instance the causal content of concepts is emphasised. In what follows I will highlight some examples of how philosophical theories of concepts relate to psychological theorising.

## Wittgenstein and psychology

If the interaction essayed above is generally right, the constraints stemming from Wittgenstein's arguments bear on some discussions in psychology. He argues for the impossibility of a logically private language—a language no one else could know or could have reason to think they knew. We shall need to distinguish between logical privacy and naive privacy. Something is naively private if a person has a special access to it, for instance one's own thoughts. This is not a very strong kind of privacy since although only I can gain access to my thoughts by simple introspection, others can learn of them by other means. For instance we may know that a boxer is preparing a straight right because he always drops his left hand before throwing a straight right. Indeed, it can sometimes be the case that we know what someone is thinking before they do (or if they do) merely because for instance we are paying closer attention to certain cues. Logical privacy is stronger. Something is logically private if someone has a unique access to it such that no one else could ever be warranted in thinking they had obtained access to it. An ideolect could be logically private. That is, having warrant for believing we had understood or characterised someone's ideolect might be impossible. Certain conscious states might be logically private, for instance someone's experience of Kandinsky's *Composition VII*. This bears on Nativism when nativists are committed to a pre-linguistic language of thought (or something similar) by which we acquire or translate public language. Such a pre-linguistic language might on some accounts be logically private. It bears on the Whorfian Hypothesis (Whorf, 1956) if that is understood as supporting languages that are logically private between social groups (logically private sociolects). Wittgenstein's Private Language Argument denies the possibility of logically private languages. The Private Language Argument is one part of a larger argument that public language is explanatorily primary in our understanding of ourselves.

A strong indication of the *essentially* public character of language would *seem* to undermine nativism about the mind, particularly of a radical kind, if it were further argued as Wittgenstein does that public language is in an important sense arbitrary and contingent.[1] Nativists generally posit domain-specific knowledge or innate capacities for the acquisition of such knowledge where 'innate' means non-psychological, or primitive.[2] Indeed, there are unrestricted references to *mentalese* in cognitive science and psychology literature as if we had an unproblematic notion of a private *language* of thought (e.g., Carey 2001).[3] If Wittgenstein is right about the essentially public character of language then it will be important to ask *how* we can characterise this innate knowledge in a way which neither assumes possession of a language, nor makes circular reference to *public* linguistic notions in its explanation, yet is still sufficiently language-like to underwrite the idea (even within a scientific theory) of translating from

---

[1] Wittgenstein 1953, section 497 and *passim*.

[2] The nativism debate is nicely characterised in Samuels (2002); I use 'primitive' following him.

[3] I take it the '-ese' is evidence of an intended linguistic connotation even when it is not used in the context of a specific theory.

*mentalese* to English as we do Russian to English. If the nativist position is undermined or constrained by Wittgensteinian considerations, then an increased research focus on the plasticity of concepts under socio-linguistic pressure may be warranted, in contrast to the focus on uncovering putatively universal concepts, categories, or taxonomies. I discuss this further below.

The central aim of psychology today is, roughly, the scientific explanation of the behaviour of creatures with minds, especially humans. Different accounts of the role of language and concepts will bear on the character of behavioural explanations that can be accepted. Fodor's and Peacocke's theories both have consequences for psychological explanation. Similar work has been done for Wittgensteinian theories across the spectrum of research areas (e.g., Geach, 1957; Hopkins, unpubl. manuscript; Malcolm, 1959; Thornton, 1998). One virtue of this work is that it has gone some way toward closing the gap between the methods of psychoanalysis and cognitive psychology. One way of expressing a central tenet in these theories is given by Dummet. He has argued, in part from Wittgensteinian considerations, to the claim that language is prior to thought in the order of explanation (Dummett, 1991, p. 315)—a claim he calls "the priority thesis". If this is right, any explanation of thought needs to advert at least in principle to an explanation of language. I will discuss this last point further below.

## CONCEPTS

The word "concept" is not essentially a term of art. We use it in describing our thoughts, often as a loose synonym for idea. We say of a child that he does not yet have the concept of property, that he is unaware that toys belong to others. We may say of someone that they have no concept of integration in mathematics, that they would neither recognise integration if they saw it, nor be able to carry it through themselves. Or we may disagree about what is a just distribution of wealth in society. In this case, I would not ordinarily attribute to you an incapacity, rather I may say that we must have different concepts (or conceptions) of 'justice'. This may ramify further. We may *agree* that things are unjust, but only one of us may be moved to action *only* by its being so. We may wish to put this down to conceptual difference too. I shall take it as uncontentious then that concepts are integral to the subject matter of our thoughts. By thoughts I mean cognitive states we would describe as my understanding of property, my belief in the efficacy of integration, my wish for justice, etc.

Concepts feature in our explanation of what our thoughts are about, which we may call the content of our thoughts. Such content is cognitive insofar as it features in our explanations of our cognition. Following Segal

(2000), I will refer to the content of these thoughts as *cognitive content*. For him, cognitive content is averted to in psychological explanations. For example, I explain the content of Mary's present beliefs (e.g., about society) by reference to her antecedent beliefs (e.g., about the nature of justice). So too, I explain her actions by reference to her desires or commitments, say. Content here is a loose notion in that it is not tied to a particular sematics, truth predicate, or conditions for attribution. Content, while based on common sense or folk psychology, is meant to extend, as Segal neatly puts it, to

> ... any branch of scientific psychology that recognises contentful states, and to all such states, including perceptual states, states of the Freudian unconscious, tacit cognition of language, neonate cognition, animal cognition and so on. (Segal, 2000, p. 5)

Talk of thought contents has sometimes appeared to proceed from the assumption that concepts are used to think of what J.L. Austin called "medium size dry goods"—things that we can see, touch, and organise. Indeed, the supposed classical definition of concepts taken from Plato seems to support this view with its talk of necessary and sufficient conditions for something to fall under a concept, independent of its being judged to do so. However, in Plato's analysis of concepts he emphasised the skill or craft (*tekne*) and the *abilities* one had when one had an understanding of a concept.[4] So, for example, my grasp or possession of the concept of (mathematical) integration is in part responsible for my ability to carry out integration. Similarly, it is plausibly my distinctive concept of "justice" that explains my moving from the fact of injustice to action against it. The link between thought and action should be integral in our theorising about concepts. I shall proceed with this general picture of concepts in hand.

## WITTGENSTEIN AND THE PRIVATE LANGUAGE ARGUMENT

Wittgenstein is often thought to be the source of prototype or exemplar theories of concepts because of remarks he made about family resemblance in "language-games". (Wittgenstein 1953, sections 65–78) However it would be wrong to say that Wittgenstein ever had a theory of concepts or indeed of content. He was too anti-theoretical for that. Rather he had distinctive views on language and our "life with language".[5] It is

---

[4] The philosophical *locus classicus* for the classical view is usually given as *Euthyphro*. However, dialogues like *Theaetetus*, *Republic*, *Meno*, and *Gorgias* all emphasise the skills one has when one understands a concept, often in analogy with a doctor.

[5] I borrow the phrase from Cora Diamond (1991).

premiss of his macro argument that language is essential to distinctively human thought. It is further premiss that a key feature of distinctively human thought is our ability to share meanings, and thus social life. How can it be that we share meanings? Consider these possibilities:

1. We each have private languages and we learn to relate our private languages to each other, often through public language.
2. Our language is aligned with independent features of the world, and when it is well aligned (i.e., tracking well), then we track the same things. Our shared meanings are a function of tracking the same things well.
3. In sharing language and life together, we track each other, and meaning depends on our doing so. So, analysis of meaning depends in the first instance on analysis of our shared language and life.

The third is roughly Wittgenstein's view, which he argues for mainly by arguing against the first two views. The second is a popular view in cognitive science and is the target of a set of Wittgenstein's arguments called the Rule Following Considerations (Wittgenstein 1953, approximately sections 138–202). It is central to securing Wittgenstein's view, but I cannot reprise it here. The first view is held in various ways by philosophers and psychologists. It is the target of the public language argument. This is often what is meant when people speak of Wittgenstein's insisting on the "publicity" of meaning. His private language arguments (hereafter, collectively PLA) are intended to show that there could not be such a thing as a private meaning, or indeed a private language. Private here means *logically* private in the sense above: no one could even *in principle* learn the language.[6] A common example of an imagined private language is one that I use to describe the contents of my own mental states, of how things seem to me. There has been a tremendous amount written about the PLA and I cannot begin to summarise either all the original arguments and their interrelation or the secondary literature.[7] However, I hope to bring out the structure of a primary strand in the argument by considering some of the original elements of the argument.

The argument in brief is this. A private language cannot support a distinction between what *is* right and what *seems* right to the private linguist. But *facts* are independent from how things seem to one. So, a private language cannot support the *independence* required to be fact

---

[6] Wright (2001) weakens this to the claim that no one could have warrant for asserting that they had *understood* another's private language. My presentation of the PLA here owes a great deal to Wright.

[7] It is easy enough to recommend Kripke (1982) and Wright (2001) on the PLA and the Rule Following Considerations, though there are dozens more.

stating. And as it does not state a fact, a statement in a putative private language can be neither true nor false. It is not even a candidate for truth/falsity—it is not "truth-apt". But since the truth and *meaning* of our statements depend on facts—on how things are—it follows that a private language is neither truth-apt nor meaningful. And now it becomes pointed whether there remains any reason to call it a *language* at all. This lends support to the *conclusion* that if there is *meaning* (intentionality), then it inheres in the public formulas of language. This conclusion serves as a premiss in the larger argument above. In the strand of argument given here, the question of whether *reference* depends on the publicity of language (which is implicitly a component of the second view above) is not directly addressed.

In order to bring out the dialectic between Wittgenstein and his imagined interlocutor, the text of the extracts from *Philosophical Investigations* (Wittgenstein 1953, hereafter "PI") has been broken down and italicised. Wittgenstein's hypothetical interlocutor's view is italicised, while Wittgenstein's is not. Each of the four extracts targets a way of conceiving of a private language and attempts to undermine that conception. They are in brief:

PI 258 The Private Diarist. It is not within my powers to create meanings, even referring to private objects.

PI 265 The Private Dictionary. A private dictionary is dependent on something independent for its authority, if it is to be about the world.

PI 268 The Private Society. I cannot replicate the formulas of public language within my own mental "community".

PI 237 The Inscrutable Geometer. A private language would be explanatorily inert in sharing meanings, and concepts and our world.

## PI 258

*Let us imagine the following case. I want to keep a diary about the recurrence of a certain sensation. To this end I associate it with the sign "S" and write this sign in a calendar for every day on which I have the sensation.*
I will remark first of all that a definition of the sign cannot be formulated.
*But still I can give to myself a kind of ostensive definition.*
How? Can I point to the sensation?
*Not in the ordinary sense. But I speak, or write the sign down, and at the same time concentrate my attention on the sensation—and so, as it were, point to it inwardly.*
But what is this ceremony for? [F]or that is all it seems to be! A definition surely serves to establish the meaning of a sign.

701 CONCEPTS, LANGUAGE, AND PRIVACY

*Well that is done precisely by the concentration of my attention; for in this way I impress on myself the connexion between the sign and the sensation.*

But "I impress it on myself" can only mean: this process brings it about that I remember the connexion *right* in future. But in the present case I have no criterion of correctness. One would like to say: whatever is going to seem right to me is right. And that only means that here we can't talk about 'right'.

This section is a critique of the idea of private definition or association, in this case personally defining "S" to stand for a sensation of jealousy I have. Wittgenstein first observes that we cannot make an *internal* ostensive association by pointing as we do when we point to something *external* to us (something essentially *public*). Nevertheless, second, he points out that any such definition cannot do the work expected of it, because it establishes no fact allowing comparison between my current use of "S" and the definitional use of "S". My "ceremony" of impressing it on myself will not *guarantee* that "S" really will henceforth refer to that which I allegedly made internal ostensive reference. I may after all be mistaken. Worse still, any error will be undetectable since the *only* criterion of whether a particular use of "S" *is* right is whether *I* think "S" is right. If someone were to insist that there is a fact of the matter as to whether my present use of "S" is the same as the defining one, we should ask what sort of fact it is? Specifically, is it a meaning-fact, i.e., a fact about which we could have reason to agree or disagree? Suppose it is a fact about a *type* of brain state, observable using a brain scanner. First, if this is the fact then it is a *public* one (i.e., only naively private) since anyone can see that "S" denotes this brain type by looking at the scanner also. Second, if the type of brain state is something other than one-which-I-think-is-"S" (the unusable criterion), then it will be false that the definition of "S" was established by my inward pointing. Rather it will have been fixed by the criteria for being that type of brain state, e.g., what we all take as criteria of jealousy, say unreasonable anger (or the presence of some neurochemical).[8] These criteria are good ones because I am not authoritative about them. I can be mistaken. I cannot redefine them at will. But that is because they are public, not private.

## PI 265

Let us imagine a table (something like a dictionary) that exists only in our imagination. A dictionary can be used to justify the translation of a word X

---

[8] Although this too is problematic since there is a question about what is authoritative in a case of conflict between the presence of the chemical, and the subject's insistence contrary to what the chemical putatively indicates.

by a word Y. But are we also to call it a justification if such a table can only be looked up in the imagination?
*Well yes; then there is a subjective justification.*
But justification consists in appealing to something independent.
*But surely I can appeal from one memory to another. For example, I don't know if I have remembered the time of departure of a train right and to check it I call to mind how a page of the time-table looked. Isn't that the same here?*
No; for this process has got to produce a memory which is actually *correct*. If the mental image of the time-table could not itself be *tested* for correctness, how could it confirm the correctness of the first memory? ([A]s if someone were to buy several copies of the morning paper to assure himself that what it said was true.)
Looking up a table in the imagination is no more looking up a table than the image of the result of an imagined experiment is the result of an experiment.

This section critiques the idea that our use of our private language could be regulated by an internal dictionary. One doubt is that such a dictionary is possible in the absence of (private) *facts* of usage to which the dictionary could be faithful. The question here is: in what facts would the correctness of the dictionary consist? In the case of the train time-table, my memory of the time-table is correct only in so far as it corresponds to the actual time-table, and is therefore correctable by comparison. But in the case of a private dictionary, all that could be a corrective is *my* memory that I used word X to translate word Y. The challenge is not one of being certain or reliable. The challenge asks on what basis could my memory be independently correct, since my *impression* of the consistency of my memories is not independent of what is at issue, viz. the putative facts of previous usage. The point about buying multiple copies of the newspaper is that the *consistency* with which they are *produced* (printed) is yet no guarantee of their truth. That is dependent on the world they report, not that every copy says the same thing. Just as a thought experiment lacks the right sort of independence to be an experiment revelatory of the world (of empirical facts), so too the idea of a mental dictionary. But where the dictionary translates words of the private language with words of a public language, the (logical) privacy of the private language is vitiated. This critique anticipates the difficulties in grounding symbols (or relations) within systems given by Harnad (1990) and McCarthy and Hayes (1969).

## PI 268

Why can't my right hand give my left hand money?—My right hand can put it into my left hand. My right hand can write a deed of gift and my left hand a receipt.—But the further practical consequences would not be those of a gift. When the left hand has taken the money from the right, etc., we shall ask: "Well, and what of it?" And the same could be asked if a person had given himself a private definition of a word; I mean, if he has said the word to himself and at the same time has directed his attention to a sensation.

We often say things like, "I am talking to myself". It is a recurrent temptation to read this as suggesting that there are two people within me. The example of lending is meant to give the lie to taking this suggestion literally. It is true that I can move money from one hand to the other while saying that by this I am lending the money. But it cannot really be a case of lending because hands are not the sorts of things that *can* have obligations to return what they borrow, that can spend money, that participate in the practice of lending. These things are done by people only, not by body parts. Similarly then there can be *no* sense in the idea that at the personal level part of me *defines* the use of words in the private language, another *uses* the words, and still another *regulates* definition and usage. There is only one person, even though it may be useful sometimes to speak metaphorically of more than one person. Practically, the requisite *independence* necessary for statements cannot be had by appeal to this metaphor. This argument also undermines the idea that there is some (autonomous) independent private language mechanism whose output I consult.[9]

## PI 237

> Imagine someone using a line as a rule in the following way; he holds a pair of compasses, and carries one of its points along the line that is the 'rule', while the other one draws the line that follows the rule. And while he moves along the ruling line he alters the opening of the compasses, apparently with great precision, looking at the rule the whole time as if it determined what he did. And watching him we see no kind of regularity in this opening and shutting of the compasses. We cannot learn his way of following the line from it. Here perhaps one really would say: "The original seems to *intimate* to him which way he is to go. But it is not a rule."

This section highlights the interdependence between publicity and intelligibility. We are asked to imagine an *apparently* meaningful project executed by a geometer whose behaviour is apparently responsive to his understanding of what the "rule" (i.e., line used as a guide) "intimates" to him in his operation of the compasses. We are told that we cannot *discern* how the rule governs his behaviour, that we cannot *learn* his rule. But in

---

[9] First, if it were truly independent, the consulting part of me would need a language within which to understand the mechanism's output. Second, this would make my knowledge of the meaning of my own words a matter of consultation about which I could be wrong—a highly counter-intuitive result. Third, consultation need not be essentially private. Fourth, it remains a nice question in what the correctness of this system would consist such that it remained private. Blackburn (1984) pursued a strategy on this tack.

this case, it is unclear on what basis we should still call his behaviour "following a rule"—that there *is* a fact (rule) of meaning to which he is responding? Suppose there is a private rule about how to use the line as a guide that only he knows perhaps because it is logically private. If it were the case that we could by observation come to understand his rule, then the rule is not private in the sense in which we are interested. However, if his rule is truly *inscrutable* (i.e., logically private) and he decided to teach us the rule, it is not clear what sort of *demonstration* he might make by way of instruction since *ex hypothesi* no amount of observation would reveal his rule. So, the putative private "rule" remains both unintelligible and incommunicable, raising again the question of its status as a rule—or anything at all.

I hope these threads of the argument are sufficient to give an idea of how the considerations offered in the PLA are supposed to undermine the first view of shared meanings mentioned above. By itself the PLA only goes part of the way to supporting the view that intentionality inheres in the "formulas of public language". As stated earlier, the second view considered is the subject of related but distinct arguments: the Rule Following Considerations.[10] The PLA does urge the explanatory priority of public language in any discussion of thought and its content. If concepts constitute cognitive content, then that further motivates a constraint that an explanation of concepts will in the first instance need to proceed from the role those concepts have in public language, in human linguistic communication. That constraint applied to theory is the topic of the following sections.

## PEACOCKE

### Theory of concepts

Concepts are not merely the means by which our thoughts refer, they are also integral to the cognitive relations between thoughts themselves, not necessarily the things to which they refer. In this sense, concepts are abilities to think about things, e.g., apples, as well as to think about the relations between thoughts, e.g., that A follows from B, as when we infer from the fact that all men are mortal, that if Socrates is a man, then Socrates is mortal. Thought contents are what our thoughts are about (e.g., my being hungry), sometimes the things to which they refer (e.g., the apple I see), sometimes to the *kinds* of things we think about (e.g., apples ordinarily being red). Our thoughts are usually at least partially composed of conceptual constituents. For this reason, content is generally taken as

---

[10] The Rule Following Considerations have been discussed at length in Kripke (1982) and Wright (2001), further debate is collected in Miller and Wright (2002).

conceptual, that is composed of elements understood to be instances of certain concepts (viz. myself, hunger, apples.). One further important property of concepts in this context is their *compositionality*. Compositionality is the property concepts have such that a concept functions in a similar way in different thoughts. So a thinker who understands the one concept "love" can think the different thoughts "A loves B" and "B loves A", even though they are composed differently, in this case reversed.

Inferential Role Theories of concepts attempt to individuate concepts by the transitions between thoughts they explain. So, two concepts will be distinct if they play different inferential roles. For instance, if we differ in inferring that an apple is edible from our belief that it is an apple, that may be explained by a difference in our concept of "apple". They are different precisely because of the different inferences they permit. Peacocke has developed a theory of concepts and their relation to language, rationality, and knowledge (Peacocke, 1992) whose principal thesis is that a concept is individuated by its possession conditions. That is, two concepts will be distinct if they have different possession conditions. For a thinker to possess the concept they must meet the possession conditions for the concept. These conditions generally refer to *canonical* ways of coming to accept contents composed of the concept in question; or of canonical judgements that follow from those contents. These canonical ways are in other words the inferences the concept permits, so Peacocke's theory is a species of inferential role theory. Put simply, on Peacocke's theory we say someone possesses the concept of an apple if they react in certain canonical ways to a particular cognitive content (i.e., a thought) with that concept as an element (e.g., "that is an apple"). These canonical ways include being able to recognise it, the apple, when perceptually presented; or to draw canonical conclusions, such as that it is edible, when asked. This approach has sometimes received a baffled response, especially from psychologists. However, it is not such an unfamiliar approach. Bowerman (1978) sought precisely canonical, or at least characteristic, elements in her analysis of how children learn such words as "moon", "aha!", "open" and "close". The expression Peacocke gives is somewhat abstract compared with Bowerman. For example (Peacocke, 1992, p. 108):

Possession Condition for the Concept *Square*. For a thinker to possess the concept *square* (C)

S1: He must be willing to believe the thought $Cm_1$ where $m_1$ is a perceptual demonstrative, when he is taking his experience at face value, the object of the demonstrative $m_1$ is presented in an apparently square region of his environment, and he experiences that region as having equal sides and as symmetrical about the bisectors of its sides (I summarise this by saying that "the object has appearance $\Sigma$"), and

S2: for an object thought about under some other mode of presentation $m_2$, he must be willing to accept the content $Cm_2$ when and only when he accepts that the object presented by $m_2$ has the same shape as perceptual experiences of the kind in (S1) represents objects as having.

Peacocke's formulation is somewhat abstract because he is aiming for precision, and because he is attending to constraints stemming from other philosophical considerations. However, work toward this precision is consonant with beginning as Bowerman does. The formulation does not yet say anything of *how* the possession conditions are met in a particular thinker. Whatever *realises* our possession of a concept gives us the ability to know how the world must be for our thought to refer when it is true, i.e., have a semantic value consistent with the world. The precision Peacocke seeks may also be necessary if we are (eventually) to pursue the scientific investigation of the neural correlates that realise specific thoughts or concepts.

Nor has it been said why the concepts we have are about the things in the world to which the possession conditions refer, e.g., apples. That is, it does not explain how a theorist determining the possession conditions for a concept can get it right when he does, and know that he is right when he is. It is important that concepts have this connection to the world to avoid investigating bogus concepts such as phlogiston and cosmic aether which do not refer to anything. (Of course, psychologists may wish to investigate how we came to have such concepts.) Peacocke thinks that this connection is effected by means of a *determination theory* that describes how a content has its referential properties (roughly, its *semantic value*), i.e., refers to things in the world. The determination theory describes the way the semantic value of a concept is *fixed* by its possession conditions. When all goes well, the fact that our meeting the possession conditions for a concept allows us to refer to things in the world, and thus think potentially true thoughts, is explained by the determination theory. Roughly, the determination theory explains why it is that meeting *those* possession conditions allows us to refer to *those* things in the world. Peacocke argues from this connection that *possessing* a concept can be identified with *knowing* what it is for something to be the semantic value of the concept. It is this knowledge that explains or fills out what it is about possessing a concept that enables us, for instance, to understand how concepts combine differently in different contexts or contents. It is the link with determination theories that brings scientific and philosophical investigations into alignment.

It might seem that concepts are merely terminological entities since they are individuated solely on the basis of the *formulations* (descriptions) we give of their possession conditions in our theories. However, the determination theory and the possession conditions work together to allay this worry. For any putative concept—individuated by a particular *formulation* of it possession conditions—there must exist a determination theory related to that formulation. The putative concept's formulation will be incomplete in the absence of its determination theory; and in its absence the formulation has no chance of picking out a genuine concept. Similarly, if we discover an error in the determination theory, or discover that no determination theory is possible, then we shall have to conclude their related possession conditions are for a bogus concept. Bogus concepts cannot be used to think true (or false) thoughts, although we may not realise a concept is bogus and so imagine we are thinking a true thought. Peacocke states that concepts are abstract objects, like numbers. However, he argues that an ontology of abstract objects is no cause for concern if the ontology is elaborated and legitimated by application to classifying the non-abstract world. The simple thought is that no one is concerned that numbers are abstract objects since we think that the number nine really is the number of actual planets in our solar system. Peacocke offers a similar elaboration of legitimacy for his theory of concepts as abstract objects.

Here is an example of a concept with which to orient oneself (Peacocke, 1992, pp. 136–138).

> Possession Condition for *Plus*. Plus is that concept C to possess which a thinker must find transitions of the form
>
> $$\frac{(m\ C\ k)\ is\ n}{(m\ C\ s(k))\ is\ s(n)}$$
>
> primitively compelling (where $m$, $n$, $k$ are senses that obviously refer to the natural numbers; and $s$ is a successor function on the natural numbers), and he must find them compelling because they are of that form. Similarly for the principle $(m\ C\ 0)\ is\ m$.

> SV/*plus*. The semantic value of *plus* is the function on the natural numbers that makes the general transition [above] always truth-preserving and makes [the] principle [above] always true.

## Relating philosophy and psychology

Still it may be very difficult for a psychologist to recognise any of the foregoing as providing a theory of concepts as they understand them in the "laboratory" or in the "wild". Peacocke takes it as a virtue of his theory that it demarcates boundaries between philosophy and psychology. It is a question for philosophy *and* psychology to explain our ability to think, and know contents. For Peacocke, psychologists answer the question of *how* this is possible, and do so in terms of the *sub-personal* realisation of our cognitive abilities. But that explanation can only be offered after we have characterised such abilities, in personal (rational, reason-involving) terms. This is in part a methodological point about the need to individuate concepts prior to explaining them. More precisely, concepts must be individuated before it can be explained how we have them. That said, Peacocke fully expects these sub-rational realisers of our abilities to be explained causally, perhaps involving mental representations or a Language of Thought, (Peacocke, 1992, ch. 7). Indeed, he says that the *form* of the transition given for plus is "primitively compelling" where that means that it is not "inferred" from anything else, is compelling, and its "correctness" is not "answerable" to any other *ground* than that it has that form; also that we are *causally* "influenced" in making the transition by the form (Peacocke, 1992, pp. 6, 135). Whether "plus" is a primitively compelling concept might be challenged but in any case Peacocke argues that *some* concepts must be primitively compelling.

Another example of Peacocke's conception of how philosophy and psychology work together in his model is given in Peacocke (2000). There he discusses Johnson-Laird's account of modality (Johnson-Laird, 1978). Johnson-Laird has proposed that one understands modality (necessity) by starting from some base knowledge of modality. This is applied to a specific circumstance so as to represent possibilities as sequels from the circumstance. Such sequels can include an admixture of non-modal knowledge, e.g., of the law, of physics. In essence though, it represents our knowledge of necessity as being constructed out of quite ordinary beliefs. Peacocke thinks this account is insufficient as far as it goes since it leaves unclear precisely what needs explaining, viz. in what our under- standing of modality consists. There are good reasons to think that such understanding cannot be constituted by quite ordinary beliefs about how things are since we are concerned to know either how they must be or how they might be. He introduces his own "principles of possibility"—in a form harmonious with his theory of concepts—to augment Johnson-Laird's account. These principles of possibility are comprised in part by concepts relating to what we might call specifically modal relations and entities. Specifying the possession conditions for these sets constraints on what the content Johnson-Laird's hypothesised moral knowledge could be.

## Peacocke and private language

Peacocke's theory is an example of a theory which is constructed in full awareness of certain Wittgensteinian challenges. Peacocke says his account is consistent with a Wittgensteinian "major insight" that an account of "what is involved in employing one concept rather than another" must "mention what thinkers employing the concept are inclined to believe" (Peacocke, 1992, p. 13). Indeed, Peacocke later proffers a Discrimination Principle that states.

> For each content a thinker may judge, there is an adequately individuating account of what makes it the case that he is judging that content rather than another.

And this is meant to engage directly and sympathetically with the PLA since the PLA is characteristically concerned to attack the "conception of incommunicable content the private linguist endorses" (Peacocke, 1992, p. 222). And incommunicable content would of necessity fail of the Discrimination Principle's demand for an account for attributing one content versus another. In this sense, he means to respect the concerns expressed in PI 237 that any explanation (theory) of (cognitive) content must make behaviour intelligible and distinct by reference to intelligible and distinct contents.

Challenges remain however that can be mounted by someone impressed with the intended conclusions of the PLA. The apposite question we might ask is how one might resolve a debate between two people who both seem to possess the concept *plus* but disagree about whether a particular transition falls under it. In what terms can they have this debate? On Peacocke's view, one disputant is *causally* influenced by the form of a transition and the other is not (or is differently influenced).[11] It will not do for them to reason through their dispute since the possession conditions (and indeed what it is for something to be primitively compelling) for *plus* state that one must accept the transition on the basis of its *form* alone and not for other reasons. Indeed it seems on this view there is nothing further to which either of them could appeal in explaining their grasp of *plus*, except that they are compelled to say of this transition that it *seems* right or wrong to them. This seems to run right into PI 258 (above). But now if it is countered that recourse to the determination theory will resolve this impasse, we shall have two further worries. First, if such recourse is through our grasp of the determination theory (or the knowledge we have of what it is for something to be the semantic value of *plus*) then *plus* no longer appears primitively compelling. Second, if one part of me is primitively compelled by the form of the transition, while another part *regulates* such compulsions by its grasp of the determination theory, we seem to have a split personality rather like the one criticised in PI 268. Peacocke has, by his emphasis on marking out concepts by their inferential role, avoided any truck with private language; but it is unclear that he has

---

[11] Peacocke 1992, p. 135.

left us with a formula for *our* grasp of public language sufficiently rich to explain the nature of our reasoning within language. In summary, primitively compelling concepts undermine the idea of the independence of what we understand as is argued in PI 258. Knowledge of how the world has to be is not consistent with a concept being primitively compelling, nor can it be used to regulate thoughts with primitively compelling elements without running into the incoherence argued for in PI 268.

# FODOR

## Theory of concepts

In most cases, our thoughts have the contents they do because of their conceptual composition.[12] Sometimes this is structured and apt for evaluation as true or false, and in that sense suitable for representing facts about the world. This is important if we are to have genuine instances of disagreement about some factual claim—if we have different concepts, we may be making apparently similar but different claims, and thus not disagreeing. It may also be important to successful communication of one and the same fact. However, this need not be the case. My thought that oysters taste better than clams is composed of the concepts of oysters, clams, and taste and yet is not ordinarily thought to be a matter of truth, falsity, or fact (except perhaps on some exotic theories of indexed truth). Any account of concepts will need to ensure that we can communicate our thoughts about the taste of oysters even if the expression of such thoughts do not appear to be statements about matters of fact, or even representations of the world beyond our heads.

Representational Theories of Mind conceive of concepts as mental particulars (things in our minds) with causal powers. Our explanation of our minds follows from conceiving of our thoughts as being composed of concepts interacting causally, with causal consequences such as movement or inference. Given their causal powers, concepts as mental particulars are typically physically realised in the brain. In addition, concepts are symbols with semantic properties relating them to the world. These semantic properties are respected in causal interactions within the mind. In this sense, the mind is a physically realised symbolic system (a.k.a. physical symbol system in the sense used by Newell, 1980), and we can safely use the idea of a semantic relation to refer to the symbolising relation in these systems. So long as the semantic properties of these symbols are set and

---

[12] Some think there is non-conceptual content, particularly in the case of perception.

maintained correctly, then our thoughts, when true, refer to things in the world. Fodor describes the acquisition and maintenance of these semantic properties as elements in the realisation of a Language of Thought (LOT). The idea in the theory of a LOT is that our cognitive contents can be individuated in a way similar to the way we individuate linguistic contents. The common sense thought is that theories should not make the explanation of the relationship between the belief that it is raining and my expression of that belief too occult or tortuous. Indeed, if the relationship is straightforward we shall be able to use our considerable knowledge of the structure of language to analyse the structure of cognitive content and its physical realisers.

Calling his theory a *Language* of Thought is not just a metaphor however. If all the theory claimed was that there are physically realised mental particulars whose causal interactions cause our behaviour, there would be little room for debate. That is simply to give voice to the near consensus belief that chemical (causal) reactions in our brains are responsible for what we say and do. A theory must offer more. Specifically, it must give us principles for distinguishing one mental particular from another, preferably principles that can be employed practically to identify two particulars as more or less alike, even identical within the bounds of the theory. The linguistic distinction between syntax and semantics does some of that work for Fodor. The former can be used to focus on the form of the particular which contributes to a specification of its causal role. The latter can be used to focus on the (intentional) relationship between the particular and its object in the world. Both are important, but the latter is essential to explaining cognitive content.

Fodor's theory of content and thence of concepts is based on the common sense he attributes to several of his relatives, Aunty and Granny, who have a remarkably rich set of pretheoretical ideas. Their basic idea is that we get the concepts for things in the world by our experiences of those things. They think that inferential role theorists such as Peacocke have got things backward by their analytical emphasis on *having* concepts rather than on what concepts *are*. Fodor says

> First you say what it is for something *to be* the concept X—you give the concept's "identity conditions"—and then *having* the concept X is just *having whatever the concept X turns out to be.* (Fodor, 1998, p. 2.)

For Fodor, the analysis of concepts begins with their status as mental particulars (things "in" the head) whose character is whatever is necessary for them to be mental causes and effects. Their causal character explains why ascriptions of cognitive content can ground the psychological explanations we give about others. Fodor proposes his own theory of concepts, one related to his theory of content.[13] Roughly, we acquire concepts A and B by our contact, perceptual and otherwise, with A-things and B-things in the world. We learn *prototypes* for concepts of A and B because we have the sorts of minds which "lock to" the *properties* of being an A-thing and a B-thing (properties which are themselves mind dependent insofar as the properties are individuated by our capacity to lock to them). In this sense Fodor's theory is of a piece with other naturalistic theories of concepts. Thus far, we would only have recognitional (or nominal) concepts of A and B, and this is inadequate for the psychological explanations we give of mental states like judging. So, in addition, we do something "like generalise" from the prototypes to mental *representations* of A and B which are "locked" to the properties of being A and B. That we can produce mental representations of this kind is a product of having minds like ours. Fodor does not say how it is that we can. It could be that prototypes *trigger* innate (native) mental representations, or that there is some causal story. This "atypical" feature of human minds, relative to other things in nature, is, in his view, an excellent subject for psychological research. These mental representations are constituents of mental states, such as "believing that is an apple".

Some inferences can also be explained on the basis of the constituent concepts of mental representations. Consider the following chain of reasoning:

1. apples are fruits
2. this thing is an apple
3. therefore: it is also a fruit.

This is explained on the basis that the mind is causally so arranged to make transitions of the following form, for any mental representations A and B:

1. all As are Bs
2. this thing is an A,
3. therefore: it is also a B.

These mental representations are *symbols* within the computational (causal) mechanisms of our mind—our mental processes. To say of these representations that they are symbols is to say that they have *semantic* properties (meaning or intentional properties) relating to the world (and thus truth); and that they are individuated non-semantically. These semantic properties are instantiated by the process of acquisition described above. Correct *computations* are those transformations that respect and

---

[13] His theory of content has been in development for 25 years. The précis of his theory of concepts I give here is based on Fodor (1998a, 1998b, 2000). The quoted vocabulary is from Fodor (2000).

sustain the semantic properties of the symbols involved. The system of computation "over" representing symbols that are themselves mental particulars with causal powers owing to their syntactic properties is a central feature of representational theories of mind. An important additional feature of Fodor's account is that mental representations have a part/whole *structure* that is respected by mental processes, thus accounting for the way concepts compose. One way to describe Fodor's view of symbols and their properties is as a Language of Thought (LOT), sometimes called *mentalese*.

So, to put it all together, we acquire information about the world as a result of interaction with the world. Because of the minds we have, that information is used to instantiate mental particulars with semantic properties derived *in part* from that information. These mental particulars are the constituents of our mental states. Thinking is computation, where computation is understood as causal relations or processes involving mental particulars. The results of these causal processes respect the semantic properties of the representations that constitute the mental states, so they are in this sense truth-preserving. So our psychological explanations are successful because of the causal and computational laws governing thinking. Notice that there is no talk of identifying the content of a concept by its inferential links to other concepts. In this sense each concept is *atomic*—independent of every other. Inferences respect the semantic properties our minds instantiate in mental representations but are solely the product of the causal relations among such representations within our mental (computational) processes.

## Fodor and (private) language

Interestingly, Fodor's view is not dissimilar in direction from Wittgenstein's early views (see, Summerfield, 1992). Since Wittgenstein's later work, including the PLA, is often understood as a repudiation of his earlier views, there is good reason to expect theoretical conflict. Writing in the early twentieth century, Wittgenstein was very concerned with explanations of logic, mathematics, and *relational* properties. In part his dissatisfaction with his earlier treatment of these very topics, and their relation to language, was the impetus for his later view. It is therefore an interesting question for Fodor how on his view we acquire logical or relational concepts (or prototypes) such as negation (NOT), or plus (+), or BEING-TALLER-THAN as a result of (causal) interaction and generalisation; or what sorts of mental particulars these seemingly purely abstract (or syntactic) concepts are.[14] The most direct point of tension is between

---

[14] Geach (1957) presses challenges of this kind for any associationist or "abstractionist" view like Fodor's.

the LOT thesis and the intended results of the PLA. Fodor takes it, we should note, that a "non-negotiable" constraint on a theory of concepts is that

> Concepts are *public*; they're the sorts of things that lots of people can, and do, *share*. (Fodor, 1998a, p. 28.)

This is one of the premises in Wittgenstein's macro argument above. But if we take Fodor at his word, we will want to ask of his theory what it would be for two people to share the same concept. Obviously, they cannot share the exactly (numerically) identical concept since one cannot have another person's mental particular. Then, on what basis will we want to say they have a concept of the same *type*? We should not want to do so on the basis of the particular's specific causal powers because people may realise computationally correct mental processes and states by various routes. That consideration motivated an earlier move amongst theorists toward functionalism. Nor does it seem like we should wish to do so based on the information from which the mental representations were constructed since we have all of us had varied interactions with the world. We have no choice but to determine the type of concepts by their semantic properties—the representational properties—of the mental representations/symbols. (Semantic properties are referential, not descriptive.) This is precisely one of the benefits of thinking of a LOT as a language. So it looks like two people share the same concept if the concepts have the same semantic properties, i.e., the same content, they refer the same way. But now how should we establish that they do; what would show a common meaning? One recourse would be to public language.[15] That is the intended point of the PLA: we shall have to look to language in the first instance to individuate concepts. However, Fodor should be opposed to this since he is concerned first to identify what a concept *is*, not what linguistic abilities I can manifest if I *have* it. That also seems to commit him to a strong notion of identity, whereas with language we might have a looser notion, say based on common *usage*. Fodor resists the PLA by saying that public language usage is at best a fallible guide to the concepts we have, and therefore what we mean. The concepts we have are individuated by the semantic properties of the mental particulars they are. So, roughly, learning a public language is learning to associate sentences with thoughts, words are reinterpreted

---

[15] Fodor has an interesting aside where he says it may turn out "word meanings just are concepts" (Fodor, 1998a, p. 2). This would be an interesting result since then we would have a basis for saying two people had the same concept, viz. if they used the word the same way. But, because of Fodor's ardent atomism, this would still not give us a purchase on non-word meaning concepts.

(translated) into LOT and that process is fallible.[16] This looks very similar to the idea under attack in PI 265. The moral of that section was that if language has semantic properties at all, means anything, then it will do so with respect to how the world is, *not* derivatively on *intended* associations with our thoughts. Since Fodor does not advert to intended associations, he owes us a non-circular account of such *associations*.

The PLA is said to show that the move from the public language to the LOT is unmotivated since if public language is meaningful, we do not need to postulate a LOT to explain that. In any case, if public language requires a LOT to explain why it is meaningful, what makes a LOT meaningful? This, the argument continues, threatens a regress.[17] Fodor acknowledges the threat. Fodor's rejoinder is that the *semantics* of LOT are different from those of public language, roughly that LOT sentences have meaning in a different way from public language (Fodor, 1975). It is a nice question at this point then to ask in what sense is the LOT a language that relates to the world, rather than, say, a computational system whose symbols are bound within the domain of the system? If it is not a language in the sense that Russian and English are, then it is also nice to ask the nature (or possibility) of an interpretation (translation) between LOT and Russian. The possibility of radical solipsism looms here, for if we cannot take linguistic role as a guide to conceptual identity, it is not clear when or on what basis we could say what someone is thinking, or that we share their thoughts and concepts—a requirement Fodor takes as non-negotiable. Someone says in *our* language that they know what they are thinking about in *their* language (of thought), but they are having difficulty expressing it in *our* language. But we seem now to face the question of the intelligibility of these remarks as we did when confronted with the unintelligible geometer of PI 237. Indeed, on this view, it is not clear what evidential status to give to language. One way to respond is to say that there are only private languages, and shared meaning and language is illusory. That would be to contradict the *de facto* premiss of the PLA, that there is public language based on shared meaning. Denying the premiss is not obviously absurd, but it is counter-intuitive, and in the absence of an explanation of the *appearance* of publicity the pointed question remains as to what for Fodor constitutes two people sharing a concept?

---

[16] That is very rough. Given Fodor's views on mental modularity and his affinity with Chomsky, the actual picture he endorses is one that relates (not necessarily by "translation") mental representations in one module with linguistic representations in the language module. The commonality between those representations, if any, remains an interesting question. See, for instance, Carruthers (2002) and Segal (2001).

[17] See Laurence and Margolis (1997) for a good discussion of LOT regress arguments.

His answer remains that a concept's type is determined by its semantic properties, i.e., its content. We are again owed a theory of content that determines the content of mental representations. Considerations from the PLA remind us that the theory must rely on neither how things seem to a thinker, nor his intentions in using his thoughts. Nor can Fodor's theory rely, *in the first instance*, on the meanings of a thinker's public language, without surrendering the primacy of a LOT.[18] Without a good theory his account founders.[19] In summary, the challenge to Fodor is to retain the plausibility of calling a LOT a language, thus retaining a satisfactory relationship between a thought and its expression. In what sense is LOT a language? It does not seem to get its meanings like public languages do from dictionaries, as in the discussion in PI 265. Nor can it get its meanings by reference to what we find interpretable, or describable in our public language. Without a good account of content, his account imprisons us in inscrutability like the geometer of PI 237. I'll return to this issue below.

## CONTENT EXTERNALISM AND INTERNALISM

The discussion of the PLA and its relation to Peacocke's and Fodor's theories of concepts has revolved around the public character of language. A spectrum has emerged ranging from Wittgenstein and maximum publicity to Fodor and possible ideolectic solipsism, with Peacocke somewhere in the middle. The objections raised thus far in part relate to whether our explanations of psychology will need to advert in the first instance to other people, or to mental properties or states. Before taking that discussion further, I want to touch on another way these tensions get played out in the well-known debate between externalism and internalism in the theory of content. This aspect of the dispute has been discussed in the context of Putnam's famous arguments about elms and beeches in our world and a similar "twin" world. Putnam argues that the meanings of our words are dependent on how other people use them, and consequently that meanings are not intrinsic to the thinker. He is an externalist, a position congenial to Wittgensteinian intuitions. This position has recently been vigorously discussed by Segal (2000) where externalism comes under sustained analysis and attack. This debate is strictly speaking about semantics, not concepts as such, but relates to our discussion as follows. A

---

[18] The theory on offer from Fodor—Asymmetric Dependence—is strained, seeming more like a *description* of the *explanandum* than an *explanation* (Fodor 1998b). All theories that explain concept acquisition through causal interaction in the first instance face a difficult challenge to explain misrepresentation. The use of counterfactuals to solve the problem introduces further well-known and difficult problems. Unfortunately, it is outside my scope to substantiate this claim here.

[19] The presentation of this point owes a great deal to Nicholas Shea.

private language would not depend on anything external, so my state of believing I'm feeling "S" would depend only on where I was in the mental state to which "S" (supposedly) refers.[20] Insofar as the PLA shows the impossibility of a private language, it shows that content must be broad since it must relate to properties of the language I *mean* to speak. The challenge to Fodor was that such a *relation* could not be made out. The challenge to Peacocke was that the *intention* to relate to language this way could not be made out. Both were challenged to give an account of how concept possession could be used to express intentions *within* the formulas of public language. If Segal's arguments against externalism are persuasive, then these challenges to Fodor and Peacocke may seem rather less pressing.

This question has been typically explored within the framework of the famous Twin Earth thought experiments developed by Hilary Putnam (Putnam, 1975). Twin World (or Twin Earth) thought experiments were developed to highlight the difference between the intrinsic and relational views of content. In such experiments, twin subjects are absolute micro-structural duplicates—identical in all respects save being present on different twin worlds. Twin worlds are absolute micro-structural duplicates save some feature specified in the particular experiment. The thought experiments then try to show that the specified difference in the twin worlds has some bearing on the content of the thinker's thoughts. If so, those contents must be relational.

Segal argues, trying to neutralise Putnam (and Burge), that the twin-world thought experiments are not consistent with observations of how individual meanings develop from person to person; and that allowing that individual meanings develop does not undermine psychological explanations. Segal frames the question by asking whether certain psychological properties are intrinsic or relational. The question is framed in terms of properties. Relational properties depend not only how things are with the object in question, but also on something external to the object to which it is related; e.g., for me to be in Massachusetts depends on the existence of Massachusetts. Intrinsic properties have no such dependence; e.g., chemical and micro-structural properties of gold. Relational properties often have intrinsic counterparts, for instance the relational property of being resistant to impact shock is explained in part by possession of intrinsic micro-structural properties. Thus, the question can be rephrased as whether cognitive properties of mental states (contents) are intrinsic or relational? Content which is essentially intrinsic is called narrow and the theory that content is narrow is usually called content internalism.

---

[20] Strictly speaking, this is not true either, see Wright (2001, ch. 8) and Smith et al. (1998, ch. 1).

Essentially relational content is called broad, and the theory in favour of it is usually called content externalism.

## Putnam's elm and beech

The best known version of the Twin Earth thought claims that Putnam does not know the difference between an elm and a beech, but his use of the words "elm" and "beech" refers to elms and beeches respectively. On Twin Earth, in Twinglish (Twin Earth English), "elm" and "beech" are reversed, and thus Twin Putnam refers to beeches when he says "elm" in twinglish, and vice versa. He has a *deferential* understanding of the words (and their associated natural kinds), and means his usage to conform to the prevailing usage as understood by those who know the difference between elms and beeches. He is thus in this instance a "consumer" not a "producer" of language, and the content of his mental states is in part *dependent* on producers' linguistic usage.

## Burge's arthritis

Burge developed his own arguments for broad content following Putnam (Burge, 1979). Here is one of his examples. Alf believes he has arthritis in his thigh, but is told that it is not possible to have arthritis in the thigh since arthritis is an inflammation of the joints. He agrees and modifies his usage accordingly. However, on Twin Earth, where twinglish "arthritis" is used more generally, Twin Alf does use "arthritis" to refer correctly to the pain in his thigh. The case differs from Putnam's since "arthritis" is not a natural kind but a (constructed) theoretical term. This further extends the argument for broad content, by showing that meaning is in part dependent on a linguistic community.

## Against externalism

The argument for externalism depends on the intuition that the consumer uses the same concept as the expert (or producer), i.e., that Putnam intends his use of "elm" and the concept of which it is an expression to conform to that of the expert. There is then a difference between consumer and creator. The expert has a full possession of the concept while the consumer has only partial possession *and* deference to the expert. Therefore the concept and content the consumer uses is *dependent* on the expert's concept. Thus the consumer's content is relational not intrinsic, broad not narrow, external not internal. Segal (2000) argues that the intuition is false because the consumer could have two concepts where the expert only has one. If that is the case, then the content of the consumer's concept need not be dependent on the expert. Segal's first argument is based on the possibility of synonymy between expressions. It seems that Alf could have different thoughts about what he would express by "pain in his joints" and "arthritis" and thus one supposes different concepts. However, the expert could not because he would know that "arthritis" *just means* "inflammation of the joints" and thus are expressions of the *same* concept. The argument does not depend on the possibility of synonymy. The core claim of Segal's argument above is that there could be two words that the misinformed consumer uses to express different concepts, even as those words express a single concept of the expert. In any case, he offers an example of someone who has a partial grasp of a concept without using it deferentially. If the example is good, and we think the example person still has a concept, albeit partially grasped, then it cannot be that the concept is dependent on a relation to the expert, thus it is intrinsic and externalism is false.

## Two factor theories

Matters are not improved if the externalist moves to a theory that posits two factors—internal and external—in concept possession insisting that concepts are fixed by their extension, the external factor. On this view there is a difference in cognitive content between the consumer and the expert's concept but the extension—and thus the identity—of the concept is fixed by the expert's concept. Segal argues that if the cognitive content in which we are interested is that on which psychological explanations are based, then identity or difference of extension is irrelevant because what is cognitively efficacious is the internal factor which is the same. So, Alf and Twin Alf will behave the same way—differently from the expert—on Earth and Twin Earth even though the extensions of their concepts as fixed by their respective experts are different. Thus dependence on the extension fixing character of the expert's concept will not show that the concept used by the consumer is the same as the expert's because it is the cognitive role that is relevant to the concept's being the one it is, not the extension.[21] The matter turns then in part on what the scope of psychological explanation is taken to be.

## EXPLANATION, CONCEPTS AND LANGUAGE

Psychological explanations seek to explain the role of cognition in creatures with minds. One aspect of that is differentiating one cognitive state or process from another, for instance distinguishing believing it will rain, from wishing it will rain, from hoping for snow. One way of doing that

---

[21] Segal doubts whether the extension is fixed by the expert's concept in any case.

is by the attribution of cognitive content associated with each state or process. The theories considered here each attempt to offer a method for productively individuating such contents in a way that permits correlation with behaviour. I have sought to show that the individuation and explanation of cognitive content involving concepts, on some analyses, looks to have a debt to language. The nature of this putative debt is yet to be determined. The discussion of the PLA highlights one way of conceiving the debt that creates significant constraints on what having a concept enables you to do, or on what a concept could be. These constraints extend as well to the terms in which we categorise contents. Are contents to be marked out solely by their referents, or must they be further classified by the cognitive capacities they confer? Specifically, the PLA insists that an analysis of out concepts and our language must not sever the link to the personal (reason involving) and social level. This is essential to understanding human thought and life as principally reason-governed, rather than, say, merely causal. The relation between language and thought touches on areas of psychology, philosophy, linguistics, and cognitive science. The discussion here has been framed principally in philosophical terms, and considerations of space and scope have not permitted more decisive conclusions. My intent as I said was illumination. The status of this debate, and of the associated debates discussed, has consequences for understanding the *meaning* of some psychological research. For example, if Wittgenstein's considerations prove to be *strongly* decisive, then there can be no study of concepts (psychological or otherwise) wholly divorced from the study of language. The character and emphasis of the work will change in ways I suggested at the outset.

Reciprocally, though, the debate is affected by developments in psychology and other fields. The question is with what weight should we conceive the linguistic burden? Even if one is a sceptic about language when conceived as something public, it will not follow that a theory of concepts will have no burden to explain language. Segal, no friend of the publicity of language, has argued, in part with evidence from psychology and linguistics, that the representations with which we think are distinct from those used by our language faculty (Segal, 2001). Therefore, one could be a radical nativist about thinking without being radically nativist about language, or vice versa, or many shades in between. For instance, Burge (1989) thinks we all have ideolects, but that they are socially constituted. More importantly, where one stands on this bears on how atomism about representations is conceived. On the one hand, the opponent of publicity needs to ensure that the representations in thought are not *constitutively* dependent on liaisons to representations in language. One the other hand, they must explain the close connection (correlation) between the representations with which we think and those with which we speak. Methodologically at least, this bears crucially on the evidential relations we allow between language usage and the ascription of concepts. That is, between what we can conclude we think from what we say, or what we *should* be able to say about what we think.

Someone sympathetic to Dummett's priority thesis (described above) may say that the only evidence of *intentionality* we have that is sufficiently rich is *linguistic* evidence. But is that just favouring an epistemic agenda, i.e., favouring an account of how we know of something over what it is independent of us? Not necessarily, since Fodor recommends first that we *know* what a thing is, and then find out how we have it. But, the advocate of the priority thesis insists, how can *knowing* what a thing is not be an epistemic matter? *This* issue does not turn on a question of philosophical realism, on the nature of facts. For Fodor, Peacocke has an epistemic agenda. This dispute is exactly at the root of the conflict Fodor perceives between himself and Peacocke, and any other inferential role theorist. The difference seems to be within realism, between Fodor's self-described "hairy realism" and Peacocke's well-known, presumably well-groomed, realism. One key question to be settled between them is this, "What explanation of the *independence* of meaning-facts does their theory give such that the facts could be known by thinkers?" To put the question another way, what makes if a *fact* independent of me that I am thinking or meaning this rather than that?

## One final consideration

A way of trying to understand the relation between language and concepts is in terms of linguistic and conceptual explanations. Do they *necessarily* constrain each other? It is possible that they do not, in which case theoretical conflict would be illusory. One view is that they are interrelated as above: explain thinking first, then explain language in terms of it. Another way is: explain language first, then thinking in its terms. (There is a third so-called no-priority view also.) One motive for the language-first way—independently of the PLA—is the thought that it is learning language that gives human cognition its distinctive character, its systematicity, its semantics that permit thoughts like, "There are no unicorns", or "No one is here", that are true but have no non-abstract referent.[22] Therefore, notwithstanding language acquisition, focusing on pre-linguistic or non-linguistic modes of thinking will be unexplanatory of distinctively human cognition.

---

[22] How to accommodate the putatively pre-linguistic conceptual thoughts of, say, Helen Keller is a good challenge for this approach.

# REFERENCES

Blackburn S. (1984). The individual strikes back. *Synthese, 28,* 281–301. [Reprinted in Miller & Wright 2002.]

Burge, T. (1979). Individualism and the mental. In P. French, T. Uehling, & H. Wettstein, (Eds.), *Midwest studies in philosophy* (p. 4). Minneapolis: University of Minnesota Press.

Burge, T. (1989). Wherein is language social? In A. George (Ed.), *Reflections on Chomsky.* Oxford: Oxford University Press.

Bowerman, M. (1978). The acquisition of word meaning: an investigation into some current conflicts. In N. Waterson & C. Snow (Eds.) *The development of communication.* Chichester, UK: John Wiley & Sons.

Carey, S. (2001). Whorf versus continuity theorists. In M. Bowerman & S. Levinson (Eds.), *Language acquisition and conceptual development.* Cambridge: Cambridge University Press.

Carruthers, P. (2002), The cognitive functions of language. *Behavioural and Brain Sciences* 25:6.

Diamond, C. (1991). *The realistic spirit.* Cambridge, MA: MIT Press.

Dummett, M. (1991). *Frege and other philosophers.* Oxford: Oxford University Press.

Fodor, J., & Chihara, C.S. (1965) Operationalism and ordinary language: A critique of Wittgenstein. *American Philosophical Quarterly, II,* 281–295.

Fodor, J. (1975). *The language of thought.* Cambridge, MA: MIT Press.

Fodor, J. (1998a). *Concepts: Where cognitive science went wrong.* Oxford: Clarendon Press.

Fodor, J. (1998b). Information and representation. In S. Lawrence & E. Margolis (Eds.), *Concepts: Core readings.* Cambridge, MA: MIT Press.

Fodor, J. (2000). Doing without what's within: Fiona Cowie's critique of nativism. *Mind, 110,* 99–148.

Geach, P. (1957). *Mental acts.* London: Routledge & Kegan Paul.

Harnad, S. (1990). The symbol grounding problem. *Physica D, 42,* 335–346.

Hopkins, J. (unpublished). "Mind as Metaphor: A physicalistic approach to the Problem of Consciousness," unpublished manuscript. Retrieved from: http://www.kcl.ac.uk/kis/schools/hums/philosophy/staff/mindmet.html.

Johnson-Laird, P. (1978). The meaning of modality. *Cognitive Science, 2,* 17–26.

Kripke, S. (1982). *Wittgenstein on following a rule.* Oxford: Blackwell.

Laurence, S., & Margolis, E. (1997). Regress arguments against language of thought. *Analysis, 57,* 60–66.

Malcolm, N. (1959). *Dreaming.* London: Routledge & Kegan Paul.

McCarthy, J., & Hayes, P. (1969). Some philosophical problems from the standpoint of artificial intelligence. In B. Meltzer (Ed.), *Machine Intelligence* 4, Edinburgh University. Available from: http://www-formal.stanford.edu/jmc/.

Miller, A., & Wright, C. (2002). *Rule following and meaning.* Chesham, UK: Acumen.

Newell, A. (1980). Physical symbol systems. *Cognitive Science, 4,* 135–183.

Peacocke, C. (2000). Theories of concepts: A wider task. *European Journal of Philosophy, 8,* 298–321.

Peacocke, C. (1992). *A study of concepts,* Cambridge, MA: MIT Press.

Putnam, H. (1975). The meaning of "Meaning". In K. Gunderson (Ed.), *Language, mind and knowledge.* Minneapolis: University of Minnesota Press.

Samuels, R. (2002). Nativism in cognitive science. *Mind and Language, 17,* 233–265.

Segal, G. (2000). *A thin book about narrow content.* Cambridge, MA: MIT Press.

Segal, G. (2001). On a difference between language and thought. *Linguistics and Philosophy, 124,* 125–129.

Smith, B., Wright, C., & MacDonald, C. (Eds.) (1998). *Knowing our own minds.* Oxford: Oxford University Press.

Summerfield, D. (1992). Thought and language in the Tractatus. In P.A. French, T.E. Uehling, Jr., & H.K. Wettstein (Eds.), *Midwest studies in philosophy 17: The Wittgenstein legacy.* Minneapolis: University of Minnesota Press.

Thornton, T. (1998). *Wittgenstein on language and thought.* Edinburgh: Edinburgh University Press.

Whorf, B.L. (1956). The relation of habitual thought and behavior to language. In J.B. Carroll (Ed.), *Language, thought and reality: Essays by B.L. Whorf.* Cambridge, MA: MIT Press.

Wittgenstein, L. (1953). *Philosophical investigations* (G.E.M. Anscombe, Trans.). Oxford: Blackwell.

Wright, C. (2001). *Rails to infinity.* London: Harvard University Press.

LANGUAGE AND COGNITIVE PROCESSES, 2003, *18* (5/6), 725–757

# Access to knowledge from pictures but not words in a patient with progressive fluent aphasia

Eleanor M. Saffran[†]

*Temple University, Philadelphia, PA, USA*

H. Branch Coslett

*University of Pennsylvania School of Medicine, Philadelphia, PA, USA*

Nadine Martin

*Temple University, Philadelphia, PA, USA*

Consuelo B. Boronat

*Moss Rehabilitation Research Institute, Philadelphia, PA, USA*

We present data from a patient with a progressive fluent aphasia, BA, who exhibited a severe verbal impairment but a relatively preserved access to knowledge from pictures. She exhibited surface dyslexia and dysgraphia and was impaired in the production of the past tense of irregular verbs and the plural form of irregular nouns. She exhibited a mild-moderate impairment in auditory and visual lexical decision tasks that, we argue, was explicable on the basis of a semantic deficit. Knowledge of numbers and body parts was largely preserved even when on tasks involving verbal stimuli. On the basis of this and other evidence, we argue for a distributed, multi-modality system for semantic memory in which information is stored in different brain regions and in different representational formats.

[†] Eleanor Saffran died November 2002.

Requests for reprints should be addressed to Dr H. Branch Coslett, Dept. of Neurology, 3400 Spruce St., Philadelphia, PA 19104, USA. Email: hbc@mail.med.upenn.edu

We thank Dr John R. Hodges for referring this patient to us and Jason F. Smith and Jennifer Ayala for their assistance in various phases of this investigation. Support for this project was provided by NIH grants ROI DC02754 (HBC) and DC00191 (EMS).

http://www.tandf.co.uk/journals/pp/01690965.html     DOI: 10.1080/01690960344000107

Progressive fluent aphasia is a disorder characterised by impairment in naming as well as auditory comprehension and production. The condition is usually associated with prominent atrophy of the infero-lateral portions of the temporal lobe that is typically more prominent on the left (Hodges, Garrard, & Patterson, 1998). Most patients diagnosed with progressive fluent aphasia are impaired not only in word retrieval and comprehension, but perform poorly with pictorial stimuli as well. For example, the picture version of the Pyramids and Palm Trees Test (Howard & Patterson, 1992), which involves matching one of two pictures to a third (for example, a palm or fir tree to a pyramid), is often administered to these patients, and most perform well below the level of normal controls (e.g., Hodges, Bozeat, Lambon Ralph, Patterson, & Spatt, 2000). The poor performance of many of these patients on a variety of tasks with little or no language component such as matching of sounds to pictures or gesture and objects has been taken as evidence that they suffer from a gradual erosion of the knowledge base that supports all types of interactions with the world, that is, semantic memory (Bozeat, Lambon Ralph, Patterson, Garrard, & Hodges, 2000; Hodges, Patterson, Oxbury, & Funnell, 1992). Indeed, the disorder characterised by primary progressive aphasia and loss of knowledge has been termed "semantic dementia" (Snowden, Goulding, & Neary, 1989; Patterson & Hodges, 2000).

In spite of progressive deterioration in language and knowledge of the world, patients with semantic dementia often perform well in a variety of domains. These patients exhibit little impairment on spatial and perceptual tasks (Breedin, Martin, & Saffran, 1994a; Hodges et al., 1992; Snowden, Neary, & Mann, 1996; Srinivas, Breedin, Coslett, & Saffran, 1997), exhibit preserved syntax (Breedin & Saffran, 1999) and often exhibit at least relatively preserved day-to-day memory.

Although most patients with semantic dementia exhibit deficits on comprehension tasks with both words and pictures, several patients who perform substantially better on a variety of language and other cognitive tasks with pictures as compared with words have been reported (Lambon Ralph & Howard, 2000; Lauro-Grotto, Piccini, & Shallice, 1997; McCarthy & Warrington, 1988; Tanabe et al., 1996; Warrington, 1975). McCarthy and Warrington (1988) briefly reported a patient (TOB) who was able to retrieve a great deal of information from pictures, but not from words. For example, he did not know what a "dolphin" was, but provided detailed information when shown a picture of the animal. More recently Lambon Ralph and Howard (2000) reported data from an extensive series of investigations of a patient with a fluent, progressive aphasia (IW), who showed a similar pattern. IW was profoundly anomic and exhibited poor word comprehension with only mildly impaired performance on semantic tasks with pictures. He exhibited a high degree of item consistency between picture naming and spoken and written word definitions. IW repeated words and nonwords well but performed poorly on auditory and visual lexical decision tests. Finally, as emphasised by Lambon Ralph and Howard (2000), a number of Japanese patients have been reported who exhibit prominent deficits in language comprehension and production in the context of relatively preserved understanding of pictures and objects (Nakagawa et al., 1993; Sasanuma & Monoi, 1975; Tanabe et al., 1996). The deficit in these subjects has been termed Gogi, or "word-meaning", aphasia.

There are a number of possible explanations for the striking dissociation between performance with pictures and words. One possible explanation is that these patients exhibit a lexical deficit. On this account, better performance with pictures than words is assumed to reflect the fact that pictures contact normal semantic stores whereas an impairment in language processing results in an inability to contact the normal semantic representations. The precise nature of the putative lexical deficit would, of course, be model dependent. For example, in the framework of an interactive activation model of word processing (e.g., Dell & O'Seaghdha, 1992) this pattern of impairment would be explained by impaired mapping between lexical nodes and semantic representations. The mapping impairment could be due to difficulty maintaining activation spreading between the two levels of representation. This type of deficit, which would be expected to affect both input (comprehension) and output (naming) processing, has been proposed for acquired anomia and Wernicke's aphasia. As such a deficit would disrupt links between semantics and verbal stimuli but not between semantics and non-verbal stimuli, it could explain the performance of patients such as those described above.

A lexical deficit account could also be offered in discrete models of lexical processing (e.g., Levelt, 1989) that postulate separate word form (lexeme) and word meaning (lemma) representations. On this account, a lexical deficit would lie either in the mapping between word form and word meaning or between word meaning and conceptual semantic representations. Conceptual semantic representations would be presumed to be intact.

Alternatively, as suggested by McCarthy and Warrington (1988; see also Lauro-Grotto et al., 1997) and Lambon Ralph and Howard (2000), significantly better performance with pictures as compared with words can be explained on the basis of impaired semantic representations. McCarthy and Warrington (1988), for example, attributed the discrepancy between pictures and words to the fact that these stimuli access different types of semantic information; pictures were assumed to access information stored in a "visual" format whereas words were expected to access verbal knowledge. On this and other accounts that propose that different forms of knowledge are distributed across various subsystems (e.g., visual, auditory, kinesthetic, linguistic, etc.), reflecting the input channel primarily involved in acquiring particular forms of knowledge about objects (e.g., Allport, 1985; Saffran, 2000), discrepant performance with pictures as compared with words would be attributed to varying degrees of disruption of the different forms of knowledge.

In contrast, Lambon Ralph and Howard (2000) argued that better performance with pictures as compared with words can be accommodated by a "unitary", amodal semantic system in which all information is stored in a single representational format. On this account, better performance with pictures as compared with words is attributed to the fact that words bear an arbitrary relationship to the objects they denote, whereas visual representations do not. As a consequence of the fact that there is a principled relationship between the form of an object and knowledge of that object (e.g., its function), pictures are assumed to gain direct access to the semantic system.

A similar argument was made by Caramazza, Hillis, Rapp, and Romani (1990) in their account of semantic organisation, the Organised Unitary Content Hypothesis (OUCH). This account assumes "that the meaning of a term consists of a set of semantic predicates represented in an amodal format. This information may be accessed either from lexical representations in the phonological lexicon or the orthographic lexicon, or from abstract perceptual descriptions of the object. However, the description of an object will also allow 'direct' access to those semantic predicates corresponding to salient perceptual attributes of an object" (Caramazza et al., 1990, p. 183). As an example, they suggest that perceptual information about the tines of a fork can directly access the semantic predicate for tines, which then provides access to the "canonical actions that may be performed with the object" (p. 184). In this model, then, some forms of input may have "privileged access" to particular kinds of information about the object (see DeRenzi & Lucchelli, 1994, and Moss, Tyler, & Jennings, 1997, for similar arguments). On this account, impairment of the amodal, unitary system may disrupt processing of words to a greater degree than pictures.

Here we report data from a patient with progressive fluent aphasia (BA) who exhibited many of the features of semantic dementia. Like several other patients described briefly above, however, BA performed considerably better with pictures of objects as compared with words. Based on a number of lines of evidence described below, we suggest that BA's deficits cannot be attributed entirely to a lexical impairment. Rather, we will argue that the data from BA are best accommodated by a distributed network in which semantic information is coded in different representational formats and supported by multiple cortical regions.

## CASE DESCRIPTION

When first tested in our lab, BA, a university-educated woman in her early sixties, had been experiencing increasing problems with language for 3 years. Her major complaint was an inability to retrieve words, along with increasing difficulty in understanding them. Evaluated at a major medical centre, she was initially diagnosed with Alzheimer's disease, albeit with an atypical presentation. Her husband did further research and concluded that she had semantic dementia, which led to a referral to our laboratory. She had previously been employed as a teacher. At the time of the testing reported here, she continued to work as an accountant.

During the period that we evaluated her (18 months), she was still driving, shopping, and preparing meals for her husband and herself, and travelling across the country to visit members of her family. However, she had great difficulty following conversations and had stopped watching television programmes because she had difficulty understanding what people were saying. On her last visit to the laboratory, in September 2000, BA's speech production had declined significantly; for example, she was having problems finding the right verb and sometimes produced the wrong one (e.g., "cutting" for cooking). Neurologic examination was normal in all other respects.

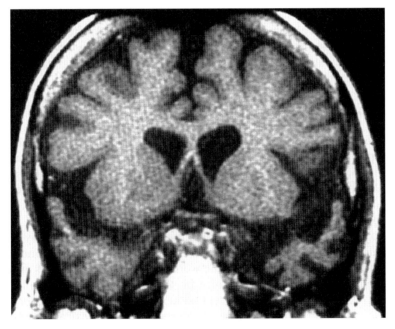

**Figure 1.**    A T2 weighted coronal MRI demonstrating mild generalised atrophy with severe atrophy of the left anterior temporal lobe.

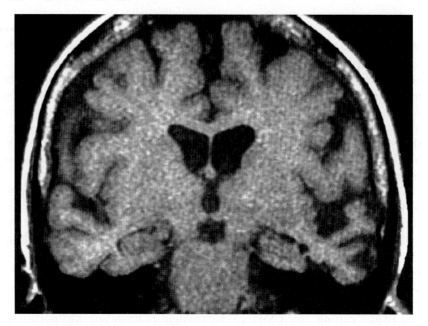

**Figure 2.**   A T2 weighted coronal MRI demonstrating atrophy of the left mid-temporal lobe including the hippocampus.

MRI scan revealed marked atrophy of the temporal lobe that was more pronounced on the left as well as mild generalised atrophy. While most pronounced anteriorly and inferolaterally, the left temporal atrophy was noted to extend to the posterior temporal lobe as well.

## Neuropsychological evaluation

Data on a number of tests, several of which were administered to BA on multiple occasions, are presented in Table 1. It is evident that her performance on language tasks declined over time. BA's performance on the Peabody Picture Vocabulary Test (Dunn & Dunn, 1981) indicates that her ability to retrieve meanings from words was seriously impaired, even at the onset of our investigation. BA also had difficulty with the lexical comprehension subtest of the Philadelphia Comprehension Battery (PCB) in which the distracters come from the same category as the named item (e.g., the alternative choices for the word strawberry were grapes, banana, and watermelon). Her performance on this task declined from an initial level of 75% correct to 50% correct on her last visit to the laboratory. She also showed poorer performance on the cross-category lexical comprehension subtest of the PCB, declining from an initial level of 93% to 75% correct on her last testing session.

TABLE 1
Neuropsychological evaluation

| Test | Date | Score |
|------|------|-------|
| Peabody Picture Vocabulary Test | 2/11/99 | 95/150 ( < 1st%) |
| Shallice–McGill Word Picture Matching | 9/9/99 | |
|     Abstract (nl ≥ 27) | | 16/30 (.53) |
|     Concrete (nl ≥ 21) | | 15/30 (.50) |
|     Emotion (nl ≥ 11) | | 7/15 (.47) |
| PALPA Written Word Comprehension | 28/9/00 | 23/40 (.58) |
|     (chance = .20) | | |
| Philadelphia Comprehension Battery | | |
|     Lexical comp.—within category | 26/7/99 | 12/16 (.75) |
|     (chance = .25) | 20/12/99 | 12/16 (.75) |
| | 29/9/00 | 8/16 (.50) |
|     Lexical comp.—across category | 26/7/99 | 26/28 (.93) |
|     (chance = .25) | 20/12/99 | 25/28 (.89) |
| | 29/9/00 | 21/28 (.75) |
|     Synonymy triplets—nouns | 28/7/99 | 7/15 (.47) |
|     (chance = .33) | 21/12/99 | 6/15 (.40) |
| | 25/7/00 | 9/15 (.60) |
|     Synonymy triplets—verbs | 28/7/99 | 12/15 (.80) |
|     (chance = .33) | 21/12/99 | 10/15 (.67) |
| | 25/7/00 | 9/15 (.60) |
| Grammaticality judgements | 9/9/99 | 71/84 (.85) |
|     (chance = .50) | 28/11/00 | 55/84 (.65) |
|     Sentence comprehension | | |
|     Lexical distracters | 27/7/99 | 60/60 |
|     (chance = .50) | 28/11/00 | 60/60 |
|     Reversible distracters | 27/7/99 | 60/60 |
|     (chance = .50) | 28/11/00 | 59/60 (.98) |
| Visual Object Space Perception Test | 3/11/99 | |
|     Incomplete letters | | 20/20 |
|     Dot counting | | 10/10 |
|     Position discrimination | | 20/20 |
|     Number location | | 10/10 |
|     Cube analysis | | 20/20 |
|     Silhouettes | | 15/30 |
|     Object decision | | 13/20 |
| Warrington Forced Choice Memory Test | 10/9/99 | |
|     Photographs | | 42/50 (.84) |
|     Words | | 30/50 (.60) |

BA had significant difficulty with the Synonymy subtests of the PCB, in which three words are presented and the patient has to select the two that are most similar in meaning (e.g., brook, stream, lake; to rip, to tear, to slice). On these trials, the written stimuli are present until the subject responds; additionally, the words are read aloud by the investigator. Normal subjects respond correctly to 96% of trials with nouns and 97% with verbs. She was also seriously impaired on the Shallice–McGill word-to-picture matching test, showing no differences across the three categories of words (abstract, concrete, emotional).

On the PALPA (Kay, Lesser, & Coltheart, 1992) written word-to-picture comprehension subtest, she scored 58% correct, in most instances selecting semantic distracters (e.g., planet for moon, orange for apple, brush for comb). BA also made a number of errors on the Grammaticality Judgement subtest of the PCB, in all cases missing ungrammatical items; normal performance is 93% correct on this task. Tested again on 29 November 2000, her performance declined considerably. She missed only 3/42 good sentences (93% correct), but accepted 26/42 ungrammatical sentences (38% correct; 65% correct overall). The source of her errors is not entirely clear, but it is possible that they reflect her lexical impairment. For example, the sentence "The man lets his son to help in the store" would be permissible for the verb allow.

In contrast, BA performed very well on the Sentence Comprehension (sentence to picture matching) subtest of the PCB, with both lexical and reversible distracters. This test includes a range of structures, such as actives, passives, locatives and subject and object relatives. She was perfect on the first administration and made only one error on the second administration 16 months later. It may be that the pictures were helpful in identifying the lexical items on this task.

The Philadelphia Name Verification Test involves seeing a picture (taken from the Philadelphia Naming Test) and hearing a word—either the name that corresponds to the picture, a semantically related word (e.g., spine for bone), or a nonword (e.g., suv for sun). The subject must respond yes, if the word matches the picture, or no if it does not. Each picture appears three times, once with the correct word, once with a semantically related word, and once with a nonword; the items are distributed across three sets, with each picture occurring once per set.

BA performed this task on 28 September 2000. She responded correctly to 130/175 words (74% correct), 129/175 of the semantic distracters (74% correct), and 145/175 nonwords (83% correct). A frequency analysis of the errors revealed that the majority occurred on low frequency words. The mean frequency of the items that elicited word errors was 1.29, for semantic errors 1.30, and for nonword errors 1.33.

BA exhibited surface dyslexia and dysgraphia, a pattern of performance that is reported in the majority of patients with semantic dementia (Graham, Patterson, & Hodges, 2000). Nonword reading and writing was relatively preserved. The errors occur largely on words with irregular spellings, although there also appeared to be some difficulty with complex graphemes as well (e.g., -ge, -ise).

BA's performance on the subtests of the Visual Object Space Perception test that assess basic spatial and perceptual functions was very good except for the two tasks that probe object recognition. She performed just below the cut-off on the Silhouette task (15/30; nl > 15/30), a performance that may have been adversely affected by her anomia. For example, she identified the pig as "an animal", a bear as "very big, eats animals, not a cat but related to a cat, very fat", and a seal as a "little animal". In none of these cases was she given credit for her responses.

BA exhibited a mild impairment on the Object Decision task, responding correctly on 13/20 (normal > 14). Most errors entailed accepting non-objects as real. There are several possible interpretations of these findings. One possibility is that BA exhibited a subtle deficit in visual processing that interfered with her ability to match the visual stimulus to a stored representation of the object. Although this possibility cannot be discounted, it is worth noting that there was no clear evidence of a deficit in visual processing on other tasks. Alternatively, as—at least on some accounts—object decision is influenced by semantics, her impairment may be attributable to a semantic impairment.

BA's performance on the Warrington Forced Choice memory test was reasonably good for photographs of unfamiliar men (42/50, at the 50th percentile for her age group) but poor for words (30/50, below the 5th percentile for her age group).

The Corsi Block Span Task (DeRenzi & Nichelli, 1975) was performed to assess her spatial short-term memory. In this task the examiner points to a series of blocks among nine that are arranged randomly on a board. The subject then attempts to point to the same sequence of blocks. Block sequences range from 1 to 9, and five sequences are tested at each length. The test continues through successively longer sequences until the subject makes errors on two items at a particular sequence length. Normal span performance on this task is 5.92. BA performed normally on this task with a span of five items.

## Evidence for differential performance with pictures and words

In this section we present evidence that BA was able to access information from pictures more reliably than from words.

## Pyramids and Palm Trees Test

One demonstration of differential performance with pictures and words comes from serial administrations of the Pyramids and Palm Trees test. The results of several administrations of the Pyramids and Palm Trees test are provided in Table 2. Normal subjects commit 0–3 errors (52–49/52) on each version of the task. It is evident that BA's performance on the word version of the task (on which she was both shown the words and heard them read aloud by the examiner) declined over time; her performance on the picture version was relatively stable over a 13-month interval. Although BA performed considerably better with pictures as compared with words, it is important to note that her performance on the picture version was not normal. Thus, she is impaired with both pictures and words but the deficit is substantially greater for words.

## Responses to Pictures vs. Words from the Philadelphia Naming Test

BA was given the Philadelphia Naming Test (PNT), a 175-item test consisting of black and white line drawings for which control subjects provided the correct word at least 85% of the time (Roach, Schwartz, Martin, Grewal, & Brecher, 1996). She was asked to name the pictures, or failing that, to provide information about the item. She named 45 items correctly (26%) on the first administration (29 July 1999), but only 23 items (13%) 14 months later. Most of the items correctly named were high frequency words (e.g., house, dog, hand, table, etc.). On the first occasion (July 1999), BA was shown the written word corresponding to the 175 pictures of the PNT and was asked to say as much about the item as she could. For many written words, she responded that she used to know what the word referred to, but was no longer able to retrieve that information.

BA's responses from the initial picture and word administrations were rated on a 5-point scale by ten individuals. Each rater was given half of the pictures (either the first or second half) and half of the words (either the second or the first half, so that there was no overlap between the two sets). The raters were instructed to score the item as 5 if the patient named the picture, or if her description was sufficient to identify the item. The mean

TABLE 2
Pyramids and Palm Trees Test

| Date | Pictures (N = 52) | Words (N = 52) |
|------|-------------------|----------------|
| 12/6/99 | 47 | 45 |
| 9/9/99 | 49 | 38 |
| 25/7/00 | 46 | 32 |

rating for the pictures was 3.09 and for the words 1.93. A two-tailed $t$-test performed on the ratings yielded a robust difference, $t = 5.02$, $p < .0001$, indicating that BA performed significantly better in recognising the items from pictures than from words. Examples of the differences in responses to pictures and words are provided in Table 3.

When tested again, 14 months later, her naming responses declined but her descriptions of the line drawings indicated that she continued to recognise most of the items. For candles, she said "they're attractive; they make light"; for chimney, "we have that on top of our house; hot comes out of that"; for towel, "use it to take off the wet"; for boot, "use in the winter if it is snowing"; for fan, "when it is hot, put it on; makes things a bit cooler"; for cannon, "men killing other people"; for ruler, "knowing how big everything is"; for binoculars, "looking at things far away"; for pyramid, "a country, a historic place, south of Europe". Thus, although her access to words had declined (e.g., she substituted "south of Europe" for "northern Africa"), her ability to recognise objects from pictures appeared to be at least largely preserved.

TABLE 3
Differences in responses to pictures and words

---

Candle
Picture: "Many people have this on their tables when they're having dinner because it makes light."
Word: "What you put food inside."

Eskimo
Picture: "Someone who would be up in the north, northern part of the world, and it's very cold. They were in Asia, originally, and they put this around their head" (points to picture).
Word: "I don't remember what that is."

Pyramid
Picture: "I know where that is. In the northern part of Africa. Historical. When people died they were put inside there."
Word: "Something you use. I don't know."

Saddle
Picture: "Ride on a horse with that."
Word: "I don't know."

Slippers
Picture: "This is what I was using in the hospital. I don't really know what it is other than being shoes."
Word: "Something that slips. Food?"

Stethoscope
Picture: "This is what doctors would be using on my heart."
Word: "I don't know."

---

## Other tasks involving pictures

On 11 November 1999, BA was given two tasks, developed in this laboratory, that employ pictures exclusively. The first is the Functional Similarity Test, modelled on a task developed by Warrington and Taylor (1973). The subject is required to choose the two items out of three coloured photographs that have the same function (e.g., button, coin, zipper; air conditioner, fan, TV). BA was correct on 30/36 items, a performance at the mean for normal controls.

A second test, administered on 11 December 1999, examined her ability to complete sequences of pictures (line drawings) that were constrained either spatially or semantically. For example, one spatial sequence involves a boat approaching a bridge, a boat under the bridge, and a choice of a boat moving toward or away from the bridge; one semantic sequence involves a picture of a bare branch, a branch with blossoms, and a choice of a branch of a fir tree or a branch with apples hanging on it. BA was correct on 18/18 (100%) trials with the spatial sequences (normal mean = .91; range = .61–1.00) and 15/18 (.83) on the semantic sequences (below the normal mean of .98; range = .89 to 1.00). It is notable that she had no problem with the most difficult items on the spatial task, which some normal subjects fail.

## Investigations of lexical processing

One potential explanation for BA's worse performance on semantic tasks involving words as compared with pictures is that she suffers from a deficit in access to semantics. This could, of course, arise at multiple levels of processing. We suggest that BA's impairment is unlikely to arise in early auditory or visual processing for several reasons. First, the impairment is of comparable severity for both auditory and written word stimuli, suggesting that the deficit arises after early, modality-specific phonologic and visual processes. Second, several lines of evidence suggest that phonologic processes involved in word recognition and production were largely preserved. For example, BA was able to accurately repeat both words and nonwords and performed perfectly on a number of tasks in which she was asked to judge whether stimulus pairs (both words and nonwords) that differed by a single phoneme were the same or different. Additionally, she performed perfectly on a rhyme judgement task with spoken words.

Impaired access to semantic information from words could arise from a deficit in lexical processing or in the processes by which words are mapped onto meaning. In this section we describe a series of tasks designed to assess the integrity of lexical processes. We note that although lexical decision tests are widely employed in the assessment of language processing, there is no consensus regarding the representations that are assessed with these tasks. Based on the observation that semantic factors such as concreteness influence performance on lexical decision tests (Breedin, Saffran, & Coslett, 1994b; James, 1975; Kroll & Merves, 1986), we believe it likely that the ability to discriminate words from nonwords involves both semantic and phonological processing. Abnormal performance on a lexical decision test may, therefore, not be definitive with respect to the status of BA's lexical processing. Nonetheless, as argued below, a detailed investigation of BA's performance on these tasks may contribute to the understanding of the role of lexical and semantic deficits in her behaviour.

*Auditory lexical decision.*    There are several measures of interest in this task. Hit rates reflect correct recognition of a word as a word. False alarms are instances when a nonword has been falsely accepted as a real word. Overall lexical decision ability is often assessed in a d-prime measure that takes into account rates of hits and false alarms.

Martin and Saffran (2002) examined effects of concreteness on accuracy of lexical decisions in aphasic subjects. They found that concrete words were recognised accurately more often than abstract words and also that there were more false alarms made on nonwords derived from concrete words than from abstract words. Martin and Saffran further noted that this pattern would be predicted by an interactive activation model word processing (with the assumption that word recognition involves both activation of both semantic and phonological representations of a word). They proposed that presentation of a nonword could mistakenly activate a phonologically similar word in the lexicon that, in turn, would activate its semantic representation. Activation from the semantic representation would then feed back activation to stabilise the lexical representation. Feedback activation from concrete word meanings is presumed to be more richly represented than abstract words and thus should be stronger than that from abstract words (e.g., Plaut & Shallice, 1991). Thus, when a lexical representation of a concrete word is mistakenly activated by a similar sounding nonword it would be more highly activated than would abstract word representations that are activated by similar sounding nonwords. Therefore, nonwords derived from concrete words would be more likely to be misperceived as words.

Interactive activation models also suggest an important diagnostic predictor of semantic impairment: a pattern of lexical decision performance in which there is impaired word recognition, but no effect of concreteness (on hit rates or false alarm rates). This prediction holds for other tasks involving input as well such as single and multiple word repetition. Imageability effects on accuracy of word repetition are observed in aphasia, but those effects are also related to the integrity of semantic abilities (i.e., they are more likely to be present when semantic abilities are relatively intact compared with phonological abilities). In BA's performance of word repetition span tasks which will be described later, effects of imageability were dampened. As will be seen below, performance on lexical decision also shows a lack of semantic influence in that concreteness does not affect word recognition (reflected in both hit rate and false alarm rates).

An auditory lexical decision test was administered on several occasions. The test included 180 words and 180 nonwords. Nonword stimuli were created from the word stimuli by altering one or two phonemes in initial, medial and final positions of the word, with the constraint that they were phonotactically legal in English. The words and nonwords ranged from one to four syllables, and the words were varied for concreteness: 90 of the pairs were concrete ( > 5.5; Kroll & Merves, 1986) and 90 were abstract ( < 4.0). Words and nonwords were presented in random order in two different lists. Each set included 45 concrete and 45 abstract words plus 90 nonwords derived from the 90 words used in the other set. BA was instructed to judge whether a spoken stimulus was a word or nonword. Several measures of performance were calculated, including overall sensitivity to lexical status (using d-prime scores), as well as the rates of false alarms and miss errors. The data from BA and eight normal controls are shown in Table 4. Concreteness influenced control performance as reflected in higher hit rates on concrete words than on abstract words, $t(7) = 3.071$, $p = .018$. The mean rate of false alarms did not differ for abstract and concrete words.

BA demonstrated some difficulty in discriminating words from nonwords. Furthermore, her performance deteriorated during the nine month interval between administrations. This is especially evident in the rate of false alarms that increased for nonwords derived from both concrete and abstract words, but especially for the abstract nonwords (from .03 to .15).

TABLE 4
Auditory lexical decision performance as a function of concreteness: Proportion of yes responses and d-prime (d-prime) scores

| | Date of administration | | |
| --- | --- | --- | --- |
| | 3/11/99 | 26/7/00 | Controls |
| Concrete word | .82 | .79 | .984 ± .01 |
| Concrete nonword | .08 | .11 | .12 ± .07 |
| | d-prime = 2.30 | d-prime = 2.02 | d-prime = 3.06 |
| Abstract word | .74 | .78 | .964 ± .03 |
| Abstract nonword | .03 | .15 | .13 ± .11 |
| | d-prime = 2.42 | d-prime = 1.75 | d-prime = 2.97 |

The high rate of false alarms on the second administration of this test is important for two reasons. First, this measure has been variously interpreted as evidence of impairment of phonological representations (Allport, 1984), a deficit in their short-term maintenance (Martin, Breedin, & Damien, 1999) and the mapping between phonological input representations and lexical representations (Martin & Saffran, 2002). Thus, the higher rate of false alarms is evidence of mild, but increasing difficulty in processing input phonological information.

A second important aspect of the false alarm rates has to do with concreteness effects and their implications for the integrity of semantic systems. On the first administration of this test, there was a trend for the rate of false alarms in response to nonwords generated from concrete words to be greater than for nonwords derived from abstract words, $\chi^2(1) = 2.865$, $p = .091$. This pattern was also evident in hit rates for concrete and abstract words, $\chi^2(1) = 1.876$, $p = .171$. On the second administration, there was no difference in hit rates, $\chi^2(1) = 0$, or in the false alarm rates for concrete and abstract words. Also, as already noted, the rates of false alarms increased dramatically for the nonwords derived from abstract words. As noted above, a lack of concreteness effect on hit rates or rates of false alarms is interpreted as diminished semantic input to word recognition in models that incorporate semantic feedback as part of the word recognition process. Thus, this pattern provides further evidence of BA's diminished semantic ability.

BA exhibited a moderate impairment on the auditory lexical decision test. These data are subject to at least two different interpretations. On those models of word processing that incorporate discrete lexical representations (e.g., Caramazza et al., 1990; Coltheart & Rastle, 1994), lexical decision tests are assumed to entail a matching of the visual or auditory input to stored word forms. In models that assume discrete representations of lexical form and lexical meaning (e.g., lexemes and lemmas in Levelt's (1989) word production model), lexical decision could proceed normally when lemmas or the connections with conceptual representations are impaired. Interpretation of these data within discrete models would suggest that BA suffers from a deficit in lexical processing with or without a semantic deficit.

Alternatively, BA's deficit on lexical decision tests could be attributed to a semantic rather than a lexical deficit. As noted above, data from both normal subjects and patients with brain lesions suggest that performance on lexical decision tests is influenced by semantic factors (Azuma & Van Orden, 1997; De Groot, 1989; Pecher, Zeelenberg, & Raaumakers, 1998; Strain, Patterson, & Seidenberg, 1995). Additionally, on both localist connectionist models that incorporate interactions between lexical and semantic representations (e.g., Dell & O'Seaghdha, 1992) and distributed connectionist models (e.g., Plaut, McClelland, Seidenberg, & Patterson, 1996), lexical decision is influenced by semantic factors.

Closer examination of BA's pattern of performance on the lexical decision task provides evidence of impaired semantic input to the lexical decision process. One line of evidence consistent with a weakened semantic input into the lexical decision process comes from the fact that the hit rates on concrete and abstract words are similar. Thus, the usual advantage in processing concrete vs. abstract words that signals a viable semantic contribution to the process is not evident. A second relevant point is that Martin and Saffran (2002) found that false alarm rates tend to be greater in response to nonwords derived from concrete rather than abstract words. This pattern was interpreted within an interactive activation model (Dell & O'Seaghdha, 1992) to reflect a semantic contribution to lexical decision. When a nonword is mapped onto a similar word representation in the lexicon, activation of that word is assumed to spread to semantics and to feedback to the lexicon to maintain activation of the word form in the lexicon. Feedback from semantic representations of concrete words would be stronger than for abstract words, making it more likely that the word form activated by the phonologically similar nonword would be falsely identified as what the subject heard. Thus, the normal pattern is to make more false alarm errors on nonwords derived from concrete words. BA exhibits a diminished concreteness effect. That is, false alarm rates for abstract words are similar to or greater than for concrete words. This pattern, along with the diminished concreteness effect in hit rate data, suggest that semantics contribute less to BA's lexical decision performance than normal.

### Short-term memory

Investigations of short-term memory (STM) have consistently demonstrated that performance on repetition tasks is influenced by lexical and semantic factors. For example, span for familiar words is greater than span for nonwords (Hulme, Maughan, & Brown, 1991). Span is also influenced by word frequency (Watkins & Watkins, 1977), semantic similarity (Shulman, 1971) and category membership (Brooks & Watkins, 1990). Additionally, Potter (1993) has hypothesised a conceptual STM that supports recall of language input that cannot be reproduced verbatim (for example, rapidly presented sentences).

Investigations of word repetition in subjects with brain dysfunction have also demonstrated semantic influences in repetition tasks. Martin and Saffran (1990), for example, reported a patient with transcortial sensory aphasia (ST), a condition characterised by preserved syntax and phonology but impaired access to semantics, whose performance was of relevance in this regard. ST's serial position curve reflected a loss of primacy, a finding typically associated with semantic impairment in aphasia (Martin & Saffran, 1997). This serial position pattern contrasted with aphasic and STM impaired individuals with phonological impairment. The latter group demonstrated a loss of recency and preservation of primacy. Additionally, ST produced errors in which phonemes from one word "migrated" to other positions in the word string. This was attributed to a failure to access semantic information that might serve to bind the phonemes together.

Similar findings have been reported by Patterson and colleagues in patients with semantic dementia. Patterson, Graham, and Hodges (1994) reported three patients with semantic dementia whose performance in serial recall of three- and four-word strings included migration of phonemes within and across words in the string. Subsequently, Knott, Patterson, and Hodges (1997) reported two patients with a similar pattern. As was noted with BA, repetition of one- and two-item lists was intact for all of these patients but performance deteriorated with longer strings; errors included many instances in which phonemes from one word in the string appeared to be inserted into a different "word". Patterson and colleagues argued that semantic representations serve to stabilise or bind phonological elements in STM. On this account, in the absence of semantic support, segments of the phonological representations of words in STM become "unglued" and migrate to other positions of the word string.

### Repetition of word and nonword strings

In order to investigate the possible contribution of lexical and semantic factors to BA's performance, we administered two tasks assessing repetition of words and nonwords. We reasoned that if BA exhibits preserved phonologic processing, she should perform well when repeating nonwords, stimuli for which there is little or no semantic support. If BA suffers from degraded or inaccessible semantic representations, one would expect her to perform poorly on repetition span tasks that require both phonological and semantic support. Critically, she would be expected to produce errors in which phonemes migrate between words.

BA was given a repetition span task comparing immediate serial recall of words and nonwords. The words were high frequency ( > 50 occurrences per million; Kucera & Francis, 1967) names of concrete objects, one or two syllables in length. Nonwords were created from this set by changing two of the phonemes but preserving the phonotactic legality of the phoneme string. Word strings ranged from one to five words in length and nonword strings ranged from one to four items in length. There were 10 words of each length. Word span and nonword span were tested separately.

TABLE 5
Repetition span for words and nonwords: Proportion of words and nonwords and strings recalled as a function of serial position and string length (3/11/99)

| | Position in input string | | | | | Proportion of strings recalled (N = 10) |
|---|---|---|---|---|---|---|
| List Length | 1 | 2 | 3 | 4 | 5 | |
| Real Words | | | | | | |
| 1 | 1.00 | | | | | |
| 2 | 1.00 | 1.00 | | | | 1.00 |
| 3 | 1.00 | 1.00 | 1.00 | | | 1.00 |
| 4 | 1.00 | 1.00 | 1.00 | .70 | | .70 |
| 5 | 1.00 | .90 | 1.00 | .40 | .80 | .30 |

| | Position in input string | | | | Proportion of strings recalled (N = 10) |
|---|---|---|---|---|---|
| List Length | 1 | 2 | 3 | 4 | |
| 1 | 1.00 | | | | 1.00 |
| 2 | .90 | .90 | | | .80 |
| 3 | .90 | .60 | .90 | | .60 |
| 4 | .90 | .60 | .20 | .20 | .00 |

BA was instructed to listen to the string of words or nonwords and immediately repeat the items in serial order. Table 5 shows the proportion of items recalled correctly at each serial position as well as the total number of strings recalled per string length. She is able to repeat single words and nonwords accurately, indicating adequate access and retrieval of phonological representations of words. Errors occur at string lengths of four words and two nonwords. Table 6 shows a summary of her performance and that of normal controls on the nonword repetition task. As the data indicate, BA repeats single non-words perfectly; additionally, she is somewhat better at repeating strings of nonwords than the age-matched controls. These data strongly suggest that she does not have a significant phonological impairment that would seriously limit access to stored lexical-semantic information.

TABLE 6
Repetition of nonword lists: Proportion of nonwords repeated correctly in serial order as a function of string length

| | String length | | | |
|---|---|---|---|---|
| | 1 | 2 | 3 | 4 |
| Normals 60–69 (N = 6) | 0.72 | 0.54 | 0.45 | 0.31 |
| BA | 1.00 | 0.90 | 0.80 | 0.48 |

### Effects of frequency and imageability on repetition of words strings

A word repetition span task comprised of two- and three-syllable words controlled for frequency and imageability was also administered. Four types of word stimuli were created: high frequency/high imageability, high frequency/low imageability, low frequency/high imageability, and low frequency/low imageability. Words drawn from this pool of items appeared only once in a test string. Fifty-four three-item strings and 20 four-item strings were presented.

BA correctly repeated 49 of 54 three-word strings and 3 of the 20 four-word strings. Errors increased in frequency towards the end of the string. For the three-word strings, errors were evenly distributed across the frequency and imageability conditions. Thus, there were no effects of frequency, $\chi^2(1) = .018, p = .895$, or imageability, $\chi^2(1) = .003, p = .955$. In the case of four-word strings, the only correct responses were in the high frequency/high imageability condition. There were no effects of frequency, $\chi^2(1) = 1.569, p = .210$, or imageability, $\chi^2(1) = 1.569, p = .210$.

As is evident from examples provided in Table 7, there was a tendency for parts of a word to intrude into other words, a pattern that has been described previously in patients with semantic dementia (e.g., Patterson et

TABLE 7
Examples of responses on word list repetition

Three-word lists:
| | | | |
|---|---|---|---|
| Target: | vanity | reflex | malice |
| BA: | vanity | /fri-traeks/ | valence |
| Target: | blossom | scissors | zebra |
| BA: | blossom | si ... cease | caesar |
| Target: | building | weapon | bottle |
| BA: | building | wepper | wepole |

Four-word lists:
| | | | | |
|---|---|---|---|---|
| Target: | contents | boredom | reminder | deceit |
| BA: | contents | border | reminder | receipt |
| Target: | party | murder | orchestra | bottle |
| BA: | party | murder | barter | |
| Target: | hammer | nursery | pudding | cigar |
| BA: | hammer | nursery | pusher | cigar |
| Target: | genius | discretion | follow | splendor |
| BA: | genture | did | follow | discretion |
| Target: | blessing | fortune | malice | semester |
| BA: | blessing | fortune | malice | etser |
| Target: | virtue | onslaught | jealousy | conquest |
| BA: | virtue | onslaught | velamy | anslas |

al., 1994). Interestingly, most of the migration errors were perseverative intrusions of phonemes from earlier words into later words.

BA performed as well as controls on a nonword repetition task, suggesting that phonological processes were largely intact. Like other patients with semantic degradation or failure to access semantics, however, she produced frequent errors in which parts of words intrude into other words. These data are consistent with the claim that she suffers from an impairment in semantics.

### Domains of preserved function: numbers and body parts

As briefly discussed in the introduction, a number of investigators have proposed that semantic knowledge is represented in different but interacting brain regions, reflecting the representational format (e.g., visual, olfactory, kinesthetic, prepositional, etc.) in which the information is acquired and represented (Allport, 1985; Saffran & Schwartz, 1994; Warrington & Shallice, 1984). If this is correct, one might expect BA to exhibit at least relative preservation of domains of knowledge that are critically dependent on brain regions such as the parietal lobes that appear to be largely preserved. In this section, we report data demonstrating that two domains of semantic knowledge were at least relatively spared in BA.

*Assessment of numerical abilities.* At the time of the testing reported here, BA was unable to follow conversations on television or in movies yet she continued to work part-time as an accountant, apparently without difficulty. In order to explore this striking dissociation, a series of tasks was administered to assess her knowledge of numbers and of numeric operations. We note that disorders of number processing have long been associated with dysfunction of the parietal lobe (Gerstmann, 1940; Hecaen, Angelergues, & Houillier, 1961; Simon, Mangin, Cohen, Le Bihan, & Dehaene, 2002) a brain region thought to be relatively unaffected in semantic dementia. Additionally, our preliminary and informal observations in other patients with semantic dementia as well as the work of Cappelletti and colleagues (Butterworth, Cappelletti, & Kopelman, 2001; Cappelletti, Kopelman, & Butterworth, 2002) suggest that this semantic domain may be preserved in this disorder.

BA was asked to indicate the meanings of the visually presented words for the numbers 1–20 as well as frequency-matched nouns. The items were presented in two randomised lists; one list included the numbers 1–10 and their frequency-matched words (mean frequency 594 for both; Kucera &

Francis, 1967); a second list included the numbers 11–20 and their frequency-matched words (mean frequency 35 for both).

BA was read each item and was asked to indicate its meaning. (Responses were scored as described in the section on differences between pictures and words.) She responded rapidly and with assurance to the number items, indicating that she thought the definitions were so obvious as to be trivial. BA successfully defined or otherwise indicated her understanding of all 20 numbers. For example, she defined the number 10 by holding up all 10 fingers. She performed significantly less well with words (10/20 correct; Sign test, $p < .01$).

BA's ability to understand and internally manipulate numbers was assessed by presenting a series of auditorily presented addition, subtraction, multiplication, and division problems.

Addition: BA was read 15 two-part addition problems using numbers from 1–20 (e.g., 7 + 5; 17 + 2; 18 + 16). She answered all correctly. She was also read a series of 10 addition problems using numbers from 1–100 (e.g., 76 + 6; 53 + 41; 97 + 31). Again, she answered all correctly.

Subtraction: BA was read 15 subtraction problems using numbers from 1–20 (e.g. 8 – 6; 20 – 4; 19 – 12), and answered all correctly.

Multiplication: BA was read 18 multiplication problems using numbers from 1–20, with up to one two-digit multiplicand (e.g., 8 × 7; 14 × 6; 19 × 5). She answered one problem incorrectly and insisted on solving two on paper (both of which she answered correctly). Counting as incorrect the two she was unwilling to do without paper, she answered 15 of 18 correctly (83.3%).

Division: Twenty-five division problems, which were subdivided into five different categories of problems, were read to BA. The categories were: (a) both numbers from 1–10 (e.g., 9/3); (b) one number from 1–10, one from 11–20 (e.g., 20/4); (c) one number from 1–12, one from 20–50 (e.g., 24/6); (d) one number from 10–40, the other from 50–100 (e.g., 72/36); and (e) one number from 10–25, one from 60–130, with a remainder (e.g., 130/25). BA missed no problems in the first two categories of problems, one in the third, none in the fourth, and one in the fifth. She insisted on having two of the problems in the fifth category written down (one of these she still answered incorrectly, i.e., 85/14). Her overall performance, counting the problems she saw written down as incorrect, was 22 of 25 correct (88%).

Auditory comprehension of numbers and oral number reading: BA was read two, three, and four digit numbers, and was required to multiply them on a hand-held calculator and then read the answers aloud. She was read eleven such problems, which had answers ranging in length from four to eight digits (e.g., 1, 190; 26, 034, 606). She performed all calculations correctly and with no apparent difficulty. In 9 of 11 cases (81.8%) she read and displayed digits correctly (e.g., for 57,447,312, she read, "fifty-seven million, four hundred and forty-seven thousand, three hundred and twelve"). On two trials she gave non-standard responses (i.e., for 142,952 she read, "one hundred and forty-two thousand and nine fifty-two"; for 723,104, she read, "seven twenty-three thousand and one hundred four"). Both of these responses reflect the omission of the word "hundred" in her output (though it appears at another place in the output of each string), and the incorrect inclusion of 'and'.

In summary, BA performed well on a variety of tasks involving numbers, suggesting that her knowledge in this domain is at least relatively preserved. In this sense, she is similar to IH (Butterworth et al., 2001; Cappelletti et al., 2002), a retired banker with semantic dementia who retained many of his numerical abilities despite his severe degradation in other aspects of semantic knowledge.

*Assessment of body knowledge.* We (Buxbaum & Coslett, 2001; Coslett, 1998; Schwoebel, Coslett, & Buxbaum, 2001) and others (Sirigu, Duhamel, & Poncet, 1991) have argued elsewhere that three distinct types of representations underlie our knowledge of the human body. One putative representation, for which we have suggested the term "body image", includes lexical-semantic, propositional information about the human body including the names of body parts, the associations between body parts and artifacts and the function of different body parts. This information is assumed to be linked to the verbal system and accessible to consciousness. A second type of representation, the "body structural description", provides information regarding the shape and contours of the surface of the human body. The local relationships between body parts are assumed to be represented by the body structural description (see Buxbaum & Coslett, 2001). Finally, the third level of representation of body knowledge is the "body schema", a dynamic representation of the body in space that articulates with motor systems in the control of action; the "body schema" is assumed to provide an on-line representation of the body in space that is derived from multiple sensory inputs.

A battery of tests to assess these putative body representations was administered to BA and the results reported elsewhere (Coslett, Saffran, & Schwoebel, 2002). Here we report only the data that speak to the integrity of body semantics (that is, the "body image").

Three tasks addressed BA's access to body knowledge from words. First, she was asked to point to a picture of a named body part. Targets were presented in conjunction with three foils: one was related by function, one by proximity on the body surface, and one bore no clear relationship to the target. For example, the foils for the target *hand* included pictures of a foot, forearm, and nose. There were 24 trials. The task was administered on two occasions approximately one year apart. BA was perfect on both administrations. As body parts tend to be high in frequency and familiarity, we identified 12 body part names and stimuli from the word-to-picture matching task of the PALPA that were matched for these variables. BA performed better with body parts (12/12) as compared with non-body part stimuli (4/8; Fisher's P = .0144).

Second, BA was asked to name 24 pictures of isolated body parts (e.g., the elbow with shoulder and hand cropped). She named 63% and 54% of body parts on different administrations one year apart. As 18 normal subjects correctly name an average of 94%, she was impaired on this task. As previously noted, BA was profoundly anomic, responding correctly on only 14% of the 175 trials of the Philadelphia Naming Test. To assess the contribution of lexical retrieval impairment in her impaired naming of body parts, her performance on the 14 items from the body part naming task for which frequency and familiarity ratings were available was compared with her naming of 28 items from the Philadelphia Naming Test matched to the body part names with respect to these variables. She performed better with body parts as compared with non-body parts on both occasions (12/14 vs. 6/28 and 10/14 vs. 2/28; both Fisher's P < .0001).

As previously noted, BA exhibited surface dyslexia and dysgraphia. One account of surface dyslexia is that it reflects the operation of print to sound correspondence mechanisms in the absence of relevant semantic information (Patterson & Hodges, 1992). On this view, one would expect to observe the regularisation errors (reading of *sew* to rhyme with *few*) that characterise this disorder only when reading words for which semantic information is not available. Thus, if semantic information relevant to the body is preserved, one would not expect to observe surface dyslexic errors in the reading of these words. This prediction was tested by comparing her performance when reading aloud names of body parts and names of items from different semantic categories.

BA was asked to read aloud 25 body part names, including six items containing atypical print to sound correspondences (breast, eye, knee, wrist, shoulder, foot). She read all words correctly. Additionally, she was asked to read aloud six words with irregular correspondences that were matched for frequency and familiarity. She correctly read only two of the irregular words. Despite the small number of items, there was a trend for performance to be better with body part names (Fisher's P = .061).

Body semantics was also assessed with two tasks involving pictorial stimuli. On one task, BA was shown a picture of an item of clothing or jewellery and asked to point to the body part with which the item would be associated. For example, on one trial, there was a picture of a watch as well as pictures of a wrist, ankle, waist, and neck. She performed normally on this task, making one error on the first administration and no errors on the subsequent administration. On another task, BA was shown a picture of a body part and asked to point to the pictured body part that was most similar with respect to function. On one trial, for example, a picture of a knee was presented and potential responses included a picture of the target (elbow), a contiguous body part (thigh) and an unrelated body part (lips). She responded perfectly on two administrations of the task.

BA performed normally on a wide range of tasks assessing body semantics. The tasks involved different input modalities (auditory, visual) and stimulus types (written words, spoken words, pictures). She performed perfectly on two verbal tasks involving body knowledge (word-to-picture matching and oral reading of body part names) and performed significantly better naming body parts than other stimuli matched for frequency and familiarity; in light of her excellent performance on all other measures of body semantics, we suggest that her impaired naming of body parts was attributable to a post-semantic deficit in word production. These data, therefore, argue strongly for the preservation of body knowledge.

## GENERAL DISCUSSION

We have presented data from a patient, BA, with progressive fluent aphasia who, although abnormal on all semantic tasks, performed considerably better on tasks with pictures as compared with words. How can this pattern of performance be explained? One possible account of this deficit is that it reflects, at least in part, a failure to access semantic information from verbal stimuli because of deficits in phonologic or lexical processing. We believe this to be unlikely for several reasons. BA exhibited no clear impairment in phonology; she repeated words and nonwords normally suggesting that she achieved an adequate phonologic representation of auditory input and read non-words aloud reasonably well, a task that is typically assumed to require the ability to derive print-to-sound correspondences and assemble phonemes. Additionally, BA exhibited surface dyslexia and dysgraphia, conditions often attributed to relatively preserved phonologic processing in the context of impaired lexical or semantic representations (Patterson & Hodges, 1992).

Impaired lexical processing also appears to be an unlikely account of BA's performance. Although BA was somewhat impaired in auditory and visual lexical decision tests, performance on these tasks is known to be influenced by semantic factors such as imageability; furthermore, as argued above, the lack of an effect of concreteness on BA's performance on the auditory lexical decision test is consistent with a diminished role of semantics on this task.

In summary then, we suggest that BA's relative preservation of access to knowledge from pictures as compared with words reflects a semantic rather than a pre-semantic impairment. We note that this argument is not without precedent; McCarthy and Warrington (1988) and Lambon Ralph and Howard (2000) offered a similar interpretation of this pattern of performance.

## Implications for the architecture of the semantic system

We believe that the data from BA are consistent with a "distributed" semantic system in which different forms of knowledge are distributed across various subsystems (e.g., visual, auditory, kinesthetic, linguistic, etc.), reflecting the input channel primarily involved in acquiring that knowledge. Thus, shape and colour would be represented in the visual system, information about characteristic sound in the auditory system, knowledge of the manner in which an object is manipulated in the kinesthetic system, information about abstract words solely in the linguistic system, etc. In the normal brain, these forms of information about an object are tightly linked together across subsystems; they can, however, be isolated from one another or degraded in cases of brain damage. Proponents of the multi-modality view include Allport (1985), Warrington and McCarthy (1987), Shallice (1988), and Saffran (2000).

We suggest that BA's impairment is attributable to a deficit to one component of a distributed semantic system, the propositional/encyclopedic store. On this account, BA's impairment on semantic tasks with words is attributed to the fact that verbal stimuli initially contact the damaged propositional/encyclopedic component of the semantic system; pictures or objects, in contrast, are assumed to access structural descriptions that, in turn, contact motor and sensory representations as well as propositional/ encyclopedic information. BA's  impairment with verbal stimuli is attributed to the impairment in the component of semantics initially contacted, the propositional/encyclopedic store.

There is at least one observation that requires additional comment. BA not only provided more information from pictures as compared with words, but she often provided propositional/encyclopedic information in response to pictures that was not evident in the pictures themselves. For example, shown a picture of an Eskimo, she commented that these individuals originally came from Asia; shown a picture of pyramids, she knew their location (northern Africa) as well as their function (people were buried inside them). These comments indicate that she retrieved information from conceptual stores that remained relatively intact, although presumably inaccessible from verbal input. On our account, this is attributable to the fact that in an interactive system, activation of preserved components of the semantic system serves to augment or boost activation of propositional/encyclopedic information (see Borgo & Shallice, 2001 for a similar argument).

BA's mild impairment on tasks involving picture stimuli (e.g., PPT) has at least two potential explanations. First, the deficit could reflect relatively mild damage to other components of the semantic system supporting, for example, kinesthetic, auditory, visual and other types of knowledge. Alternatively, BA's pattern of performance could be attributed to impaired propositional/encyclopedic knowledge. In an interactive system, a deficit in one component of the system may be expected to be associated with reduced activation throughout the system; thus, if propositional/encyclopedic representations are interconnected with other types of semantic representations such that activation in one component increases activation of representations in other components, an impairment of the propositional/encyclopedic component would be expected to be associated with impaired performance on tasks assessing the other components of the system (see Farah & McClelland, 1991, for a computational demonstration).

Support for the distributed semantics account briefly described above comes from the fact that BA exhibits preserved knowledge from at least two semantic domains, numbers and knowledge of the human body. Accounts of semantic organisation that postulate that knowledge is distributed across different brain regions reflecting the manner in which the knowledge was acquired and that this knowledge is encoded in representational formats appropriate to its acquisition provide a natural account of these data. Brain lesions that disrupt specific types of neural processes (e.g., visual, olfactory, sensory-motor, etc.) would be expected to impair semantic representations of objects or concepts for which that processing is critical (McCarthy & Warrington, 1988). As abundant evidence suggests that knowledge of numbers and body semantics is critically dependent on the computational capabilities of the parietal lobe (Coslett et al., 2002; Gerstmann, 1940; LeClec'h, Dehaene, & Cohen, 2000), we suggest that the preservation of these domains of knowledge is attributable to the fact that the parietal lobes (and the mechanisms they subserve) are at least relatively preserved in BA.

We recognise that one potential objection to these data is that the preserved domains are not truly "semantic" but rather encapsulated lawful systems encoding internal relationships. While such an argument may be germane to the domain of number knowledge, we suggest that this is not true of the body knowledge discussed in this context, the "body image". This component of body knowledge is available to verbal interrogation, and provides information regarding the name and function of body parts as well as the types of objects with which body parts are associated. This representation, we suggest, is appropriately characterised as "semantic" under all usages of the term.

One important assumption of our account of BA's performance is that pictures and words initially contact different semantic stores. Support for this assertion comes from several sources. We (Saffran, Coslett, & Keener, in press) asked normal subjects to produce a single word verbal associate in response to pictures and words that varied with respect to manipulability and animacy. We found that pictures elicited more action words (verbs) than words. The largest proportion of action words was elicited by pictures of non-living manipulable objects. Furthermore, associates to words matched standard word associates significantly more often than those elicited by pictures. These data are consistent with the claim that pictures and words initially contact different forms of conceptual information.

Also of interest in this context is the report by Rumiati & Humphreys (1998) that the errors produced by normal subjects under deadline conditions differed as a function of stimulus modality. In this task, subjects were asked to demonstrate how an object would be manipulated. When shown pictures, subjects were most likely to err in the direction of visual similarity (e.g., mistaking a picture of a hammer for a razor and performing a shaving motion). In contrast, with word stimuli, subjects' errors appeared to be semantically based; for example, when shown the word "hammer" subjects were likely to produce the gesture appropriate to a saw. These investigators argued for a direct relationship between visual representations and pathways concerned with action. This finding recalls Gibson's (1979) idea of "affordances"—information with respect to the handling of objects—that could be elicited by viewing objects or their visual depictions.

Finally, in this context the data from Buxbaum & Saffran (2002) are relevant. These investigators studied a group of left hemisphere chronic stroke patients, some of whom were apraxic, with tasks assessing declarative knowledge of artifacts and animals and knowledge of the function and manner of manipulation of artifacts. In the Function condition, subjects were asked to select two of three objects that were similar with respect to function; all three differed in their manner of manipulation. In the Manipulation condition, subjects were asked to select the two objects that were similar in their manner of manipulation; all objects differed in function.

Apraxic subjects were more impaired on the tool than animal items, and more impaired on tool items than the non-apraxics; in contrast, non-apraxics tended to be more impaired on animal than tool items, and were more impaired on the animal items than the apraxics. Correlational analyses revealed that the average apraxia score correlated highly with scores on the manipulation tasks, but not with scores on the functional tasks. The strong relationship between tool knowledge and manipulation knowledge (but not tool knowledge and function knowledge) is consistent with the view that semantic information is distributed across multiple domains and that these domains can be selectively disrupted.

As previously noted, Lambon Ralph and Howard (2000) reported a subject, IH, whose performance was in most respects quite similar to that of BA. On the basis of detailed behavioural investigations as well as an effort to simulate his performance in a connectionist model, these investigators suggested that IH suffered from an impairment in a single, amodal semantic network. These investigators attributed the discrepancy between pictures and words to the fact that there is an arbitrary relationship between a word and its referent whereas a picture provides substantial information regarding an object's function, mode of manipulation and other properties. Thus, on the "assumption of privileged access" (Caramazza et al., 1990), access to knowledge from pictures or objects is facilitated by the knowledge of function conveyed by the physical properties of the object. Like Lambon-Ralph and Howard (2000) in their account of IH, we acknowledge that the data from BA do not decisively adjudicate between the single, amodal semantics account favoured by Lambon Ralph and Howard, the hypothesised semantics architecture described above and, indeed, other hypotheses regarding the nature of semantic representations (e.g., see Humphreys & Forde, 2001; Moss et al., 1997; Saffran & Schwartz, 1994; Tyler & Moss, 2001). We do contend, however, that our account of semantic organisation accommodates all of the data from BA—including the demonstration that some semantic domains may be selectively preserved—for which there appears to be no natural explanation in other theories.

## Does BA have semantic dementia?

BA's pattern of performance was characteristic of semantic dementia in many respects. Like many other subjects with this disorder, she exhibited surface dyslexia (Patterson & Hodges, 1992) and dysgraphia (Graham, Patterson, & Hodges, 2000). Similarly, when asked to produce the past tense or plural form of irregular words she often incorrectly regularised the word; a pattern of performance that has been described in semantic dementia (Patterson, Lambon Ralph, Hodges, & McClelland, 2001). Additionally, her repetition span performance yielded a pattern similar to other subjects with this disorder: preserved primacy and migration of phonemes across words in the input string (Patterson et al., 1994) Finally, BA's understanding of numerical concepts was well preserved, a phenomenon also described in a patient with semantic dementia (Butterworth et al., 2001; Cappelletti et al., 2002).

BA's performance is not typical of semantic dementia, however, in that poor performance is typically observed with both pictures and words (see Hodges et al., 2000). Her performance contrasts sharply, for example, with that of DM, a semantic dementia patient we reported on earlier (Breedin et al., 1994b). DM performed equally poorly on both picture and word versions of the Pyramids and Palm Trees test, and was generally unable to report any conceptual knowledge when confronted with visual representations of objects. As, on our analysis, BA does indeed exhibit evidence of a semantic impairment, we suggest that her data fall within the range of performance that characterises semantic dementia. As noted, Lambon Ralph and Howard (2000) came to the same conclusion in their account of a very similar patient, IH.

Finally, we speculate that the BA's discrepancy between pictures and words may reflect the loci of her pathology (at least as judged by brain atrophy). Data relevant to this hypothesis were provided by Lambon Ralph, McClelland, Patterson, Galton, & Hodges (2001). These investigators found that semantic dementia patients with greater atrophy in the right temporal lobe were more likely to exhibit similar deficits in naming and word-to-picture matching tasks whereas for patients whose atrophy was more pronounced in the left temporal lobe, anomia was likely to be more prominent than impaired word-to-picture matching. Consistent with the findings of Lambon Ralph et al. (2001), BA's atrophy is substantially greater in the left as compared with the right temporal lobe.

Additionally, we note that BA exhibited substantial atrophy of not only the anterior and inferior temporal lobe but also of the left posterior superior temporal gyrus. Although the lack of quantitative data from BA necessitates that comparisons be undertaken with caution, it is noteworthy that, relative to controls, Galton et al. (2001) found that patients with semantic dementia ($N = 18$) did not exhibit significant atrophy in this brain region. On the basis of these data we speculate that BA exhibited greater impairment with words as compared with pictures because the left temporal lobe (including the posterior superior temporal gyrus) is critical for supporting the prepositional/encyclopedic component of the semantic system that may be at least relatively selectively impaired.

# REFERENCES

Allport, A. (1984). Speech production and comprehension: One lexicon or two? In W. Prinz & A.F. Sanders, (Eds.), *Cognitive and motor processes* (pp. 209–228). Berlin: Springer-Verlag.

Allport, D.A. (1985). Distributed memory, modular subsystems and dysphasia. In S.K. Newman & R. Epstein (Eds.), *Current perspectives in dysphasia* (pp. 32–60). Edinburgh: Churchill Livingston.

Azuma, T., & Van Orden, G.C. (1997). Why SAFE is better than FAST: The relatedness of a word's meaning affects lexical decision times. *Journal of Memory and Language, 36*, 484–504.

Borgo, F., & Shallice, T. (2001). When living things and other "sensory quality" categories behave in the same fashion: A novel category specificity effect. *Neurocase, 7*, 201–220.

Bozeat, S., Lambon Ralph, M.A., Patterson, K., Garrard, P., Hodges, J.R. (2000). Non-verbal semantic impairment in semantic dementia. *Neuropsychologia, 38*, 1207–1215.

Breedin, S.D., & Saffran, E.M. (1999). Sentence processing in the face of semantic loss: A case study. *Journal of Experimental Psychology: General, 128*, 547–562.

Breedin, S.D., Martin, N., & Saffran, E.M. (1994a). Category-specific semantic impairments: An infrequent occurrence? *Brain and Language, 47*, 383–386.

Breedin, S.D., Saffran, E.M., & Coslett, H.B. (1994b). Reversal of the concreteness effect in a patient with semantic dementia. *Cognitive Neuropsychology, 11*, 617–660.

Brooks III, J.O., & Watkins, M.J. (1990). Further evidence of the intricacy of memory span. *Journal of Experimental Psychology: Learning, Memory and Cognition, 16*, 1134–1141.

Butterworth, B., Cappelletti, M., & Kopelman, M. (2001). Category specificity in reading and writing: the case of number words. *Nature Neuroscience, 4*, 784–786.

Buxbaum, L., & Coslett, H.B. (2001). Specialized structural descriptions for human body parts: Evidence from autotopagnosia. *Cognitive Neuropsychology, 18*, 289–306.

Buxbaum, L.J., & Saffran, E.M. (2002). Knowledge of object manipulation and object function: Dissociations in apraxic and nonapraxic subjects. *Brain and Language, 82*, 179–199.

Cappelletti, M., Kopelman, M.D., & Butterworth, B. (2002). Why semantic dementia drives you to the dogs (but not to the horses): A theoretical account. *Cognitive Neuropsychology, 19*, 483–503.

Caramazza, A., Hillis, A.E., Rapp, B.C., & Romani, C. (1990). The multiple semantics hypothesis: Multiple confusions? *Cognitive Neuropsychology, 7*, 161–189.

Coltheart, M., & Rastle, K. (1994). Serial processing in reading aloud: Evidence for dual-route models of reading. *Journal of Experimental Psychology: Human Perception and Performance, 20*, 1197–1211.

Coslett, H.B. (1991). Read but not write "idea": Evidence for a third route in oral reading. *Brain and Language, 40*, 425–443.

Coslett, H.B. (1998). Evidence for a disturbance of the body schema in neglect. *Brain and Cognition, 37*, 527–544.

Coslett, H.B., Saffran, E.M., & Schwoebel, J. (2002). Knowledge of the human body: A distinct semantic domain. *Neurology, 59*, 357–363.

De Groot, A.M.B. (1989). Representational aspects of word imageability and word frequency as assessed word word association. *Journal of Experimental Psychology: Learning, Memory and Cognition, 15*, 824–845.

Dell, G.S., & O'Seaghdha, P.G. (1992). Stages in lexical access in language production. *Cognition, 42*, 287–314.

DeRenzi, E., & Lucchelli, F. (1994). Are semantic systems separately represented in the brain? The case of living category impairment. *Cortex, 30*, 3–25.

DeRenzi, E., & Nichelli, P. (1975). Verbal and non-verbal short-term memory impairment following hemispheric damage. *Cortex, 11*, 341–354.

Dunn, L., & Dunn, L. (1981). *Peabody Picture Vocabulary Test—Revised.* Circle Pines, MN: American Guidance Services.

Farah, M.J., & McClelland, J. (1991). A computational model of semantic memory impairment: Modality specificity and emergent category specificity. *Journal of Experimental Psychology: General, 120*, 339–357.

Galton, C.J., Patterson, K., Graham, K.S., Lambon Ralph, M.A., Williams, G., Antoun, N., et al. (2001). Differing patterns of temporal atrophy in Alzheimer's disease and semantic dementia. *Neurology, 57*, 216–225.

Gerstmann, J. (1940). Syndrome of finger agnosia, disorientation for right and left, agraphia and acalculia. *Neurological Psychiatry, 44*, 398–408.

Gibson, J.J. (1979). *The ecological approach to visual perception.* Boston: Houghton-Mifflin.

Graham, N., Patterson, K., & Hodges, J.R. (2000). The impact of semantic memory impairment on spelling: Evidence from semantic dementia. *Neuropsychologia, 38*, 143–163.

Hecaen, H., Angelergues, R., & Houillier, S. (1961). Les varietes cliniques des acalculias au cours des lesions retrorolandiques: Approache statistique de probleme. *Revue Neurologique, 2*, 85–103.

Hodges, J.R., Bozeat, S., Lambon Ralph, M.A., Patterson, K., & Spatt, J. (2000). The role of conceptual knowledge in object use: evidence from semantic dementia. *Brain, 123*, 1913–1925.

Hodges, J.R., Garrard, P., & Patterson, K. (1998). Semantic dementia. In A. Kertesz & D. Munoz (Eds.). *Pick's disease and Pick complex* (pp. 83–104). New York: Wiley-Liss.

Hodges, J.R., Patterson, K., Oxbury, S., & Funnell, E. (1992). Semantic dementia: Progressive fluent aphasia with temporal lobe atrophy. *Brain, 115*, 1783–1806.

Howard, D., & Patterson, K. (1992). Pyramid and Palm Trees Test: A test of semantic access from pictures and words. Bury St. Edmonds, UK: Thames Valley Test Company.

Hulme, C., Maughan, S., & Brown, G. (1991). Memory for familiar and unfamiliar words: Evidence for a long-term memory contribution to short-term span. *Journal of Memory and Language, 30*, 685–701.

Humphreys, G.W., & Forde, E.M.E. (2001). Hierarchies, similarity and interactivity in object recognition: "Category-specific" neuropsychological deficits. *Behavior and Brain Sciences, 24*, 453–509.

James, C.T. (1975). The role of semantic information in lexical decisions. *Journal of Experimental Psychology: Human Perception and Performance, 104*, 130–136.

Kay, J., Lesser, R., & Coltheart, M. (1992). *Psycholinguistic Assessments of Language Processing in Aphasia.* Hove, UK: Lawrence Erlbaum Associates Ltd.

Knott, R., Patterson, K., & Hodges, J.R. (1997). Lexical and semantic binding effects in short-term memory: evidence from semantic dementia. *Cognitive Neuropsychology, 14*(8), 1165–1216.

Kroll, J.F., & Merves, J.S. (1986). Lexical access for concrete and abstract words. *Journal of Experimental Psychology: Learning, Memory, and Cognition, 12*, 92–107.

Kucera, H., & Francis, W.N. (1967). *Computational analysis of present day American English.* Providence, RI: Brown University Press.

Lambon Ralph, M.A., & Howard, D. (2000). Gogi aphasia or semantic dementia? Simulating and assessing poor verbal comprehension in a case of progressive fluent aphasia. *Cognitive Neuropsychology, 17*, 437–465.

Lambon Ralph, M.A., McClelland J.L., Patterson, K., Galton, C.J., & Hodges, J.R. (2001). No right to speak? The relationship between object naming and semantic impairment: Neuropsychological evidence and a computational model. *Journal of Cognitive Neuroscience, 13*, 341–356.

Lauro-Grotto, R., Piccini, C., & Shallice, T. (1997). Modality-specific operations in semantic dementia. *Cortex, 33*, 593–622.

LeClec'h. G., Dehaene, S., & Cohen, L. (2000). Distinct cortical areas for names and numbers independent of language and input modality. *Neuroimage, 12*, 381–391.

Levelt, W.J.M. (1989). *Speaking: From intention to articulation.* Cambridge: MIT Press.

Martin, N., & Saffran, E.M. (1990). Repetition and verbal STM in transcortical sensory aphasia: A case study. *Brain and Language*, *39*, 254–288.

Martin, N., & Saffran, E.M. (1997). Language and auditory-verbal short-term memory impairments: Evidence for common underlying processes. *Cognitive Neuropsychology*, *14*(5), 641–682.

Martin, N., & Saffran, E.M. (2002). The relationship of input and output phonology in single word processing: An evaluation of models and evidence to support them. *Aphasiology*, *16*, 107, 150.

Martin, R., Breedin, S., & Damien, M. (1999). The relation of phoneme discrimination, lexical access and short-term memory: A case study and interactive activation account. *Cognitive Neuropsychology*, *70*, 437–482.

McCarthy, R.A., & Warrington, E.K. (1988). Evidence for modality-specific meaning systems in the brain. *Nature*, *334*, 428–430.

Moss, H.E., Tyler, L.K., & Jennings, F. (1997). When leopards lose their spots: Knowledge of visual properties in category-specific deficits for living things. *Cognitive Neuropsychology*, *14*, 901–950.

Nakagawa, Y., Tanabe, H., Ikeda, M. et al. (1993). Completion phenomenon in transcortical sensory aphasia. *Behavioural Neurology*, *6*, 135–142.

Patterson, K., & Hodges, J.R. (1992). Deterioration of word meaning: Implications for reading. *Neuropsychologia*, *30*, 1025–1040.

Patterson, K., Graham, N., & Hodges, J.R. (1994). The impact on semantic memory loss on phonological representations. *Journal of Cognitive Neuroscience*, *6*(1), 57–59.

Patterson, K., Lambon Ralph, M.A., Hodges, J.R., McClelland, J.L. (2001). Deficits in irregular past-tense verb morphology associated with degraded semantic knowledge. *Neuropsychologia*, *39*, 709–724.

Pecher, D., Zeelenberg, R., & Raaumakers, J.G.W. (1998). Does pizza prime coin? Perceptual priming in lexical decision and pronunciation. *Journal of Memory and Language*, *38*, 401–418.

Plaut, D.C., & Shallice, T. (1991). Effects of word abstractness in a connectionist model of deep dyslexia. *Proceedings of the 13th Annual Meeting of the Cognitive Science Society*, pp. 73–78. Chicago.

Plaut, D.C., McClelland, J.L., Seidenberg, M.S., & Patterson, K. (1996). Understanding normal and impaired word reading: Computational principles in quasi-regular domains. *Psychological Review*, *103*, 56–115.

Potter, M.C. (1993). Very short-term conceptual memory. *Memory and Cognition*, *21*, 156–161.

Roach, A., Schwartz, M.F., Martin, N., Grewal, R.S., & Brecher, A. (1996). The Philadelphia Naming Test: Scoring and rationale. *Clinical Aphasiology*, *24*, 121–133.

Rumiati, R.I., & Humphreys, G.W. (1998). Recognition by action: Dissociating visual and semantic routes to action in normal observers. *Journal of Experimental Psychology: Human Perception and Performance*, *24*, 631–647.

Saffran, E.M. (2000). The organization of semantic memory: In support of a distributed model. *Brain and Language*, *71*, 204–212.

Saffran, E.M., & Schwartz, M.F. (1994). Of cabbages and things: Semantic memory from a neuropsychological perspective—A tutorial review. In C. Umilta & M. Moscovitch (Eds.), *Attention and performance XV: Conscious and nonconscious information processing* (pp. 507–536). Cambridge, MA: MIT Press.

Saffran, E.M., Coslett, H.B., & Keener, M. (2003). Differences in word associations to pictures and words. *Neuropsychologia*, *41*, 1541–1546.

Sasanuma, S., & Monoi, H. (1975). The syndrome of gogi (word meaning) aphasia. Selective impairment of kanji processing. *Neurology*, *25*, 627–632.

Schwoebel, J., Coslett, H.B., & Buxbaum, L.J. (2001). Compensatory coding of body part location in autopagnosia. *Cognitive Neuropsychology, 18*, 363–381.

Shallice, T. (1988). *From neuropsychology to mental structure.* Cambridge: Cambridge University Press.

Shulman, H.G. (1971). Similarity effects in short-term memory. *Psychological Bulletin, 75*, 399–415.

Simon, O., Mangin, J.F., Cohen, L., Le Bihan, D., & Dehaene, S. (2002). Topographical layout of hand, eye, calculation, and language-related areas in the human parietal lobe. *Neuron, 33*, 475–487.

Sirigu, A., Duhamel, J.R., & Poncet, M. (1991). The role of sensorimotor experience in object recognition: A case of multimodal agnosia. *Brain, 114*, 2555–2573.

Snowden, J.S., Goulding, P.J., & Neary D. (1989). Semantic dementia: A form of circumscribed cerebral atrophy. *Behavioral Neurology, 2*, 167–182.

Snowden, J.S., Neary, D., & Mann, D.M.A. (1996). *Fronto-temporal lobar degeneration: fronto-temporal dementia, progressive aphasia, semantic dementia.* New York: Churchill Livingston.

Srinivas, K., Breedin, S.D., Coslett, H.B., & Saffran, E.M. (1997). Intact perceptual priming in a patient with damage to the anterior inferior temporal lobes. *Journal of Cognitive Neuroscience, 9*, 490–511.

Strain, E., Patterson, K., & Seidenberg, M.S. (1995). Semantic effects in single-word naming. *Journal of Experimental Psychology: Learning, Memory and Cognition, 21*, 1140–1154.

Tanabe, H., Nakagawa, Y., Ikeda, M. et al. (1996). Selective loss of semantic memory for words. In K. Ishikawa, J.L. McGaugh, & H. Sakata (Eds.), *Brain processes and memory.* Amsterdam: Elsevier Science.

Tyler, L.K., & Moss, H.E. (2001). Towards a distributed account of conceptual knowledge. *Trends in Cognitive Sciences, 5*, 244–252.

Warrington, E.K. (1975). Selective impairment of semantic memory. *Quarterly Journal of Experimental Psychology, 27*, 635–657.

Warrington, E.K., & McCarthy, R.A. (1987). Categories of knowledge: Further fractionation and an attempted integration. *Brain, 100*, 1273–1296.

Warrington, E.K., & Shallice, T. (1984). Category-specific semantic impairments. *Brain, 107*, 829–853.

Warrington, E.K., & Taylor, A.M. (1973). Contribution of the right parietal lobe to object recognition. *Cortex, 9*, 152–164.

Watkins, O.C., & Taylor, A.M. (1977). Serial recall and the modality effect. *Journal of Experimental Psychology: Human Learning and Memory, 3*, 712–718.

LANGUAGE AND COGNITIVE PROCESSES, 2003, *18* (5/6), 759–787

# Categories for names or names for categories? The interplay between domain-specific conceptual structure and language

Gil Diesendruck

*Bar-Ilan University, Ramat-Gan, Israel*

Various claims have been made in the developmental literature about the relationship between language and categorisation in children. Drawing on the notion of the domain-specificity of cognition, the paper reviews evidence on the effect of language in the classification of and reasoning about categories from different domains. The review looks at the anthropological, infant classification, and preschool categorisation literature. Overall, the analyses suggest that the causal nature and inductive power of animal categories seem to be the least influenced by linguistic and cultural factors, of artifact categories the most, and of human categories somewhere in between these other two kinds. Some gaps on the evidence reviewed are noted and possible theoretical accounts of the emerging pattern are discussed.

And out of the ground the LORD God formed every beast of the field, and every fowl of the air; and brought them unto Adam to see what he would call them: and whatsoever Adam called every living creature, that was the name thereof. And Adam gave names to all cattle, and to the fowl of the air, and to every beast of the field ... (Genesis 2:19–20)

There are at least two interesting ways to interpret the above biblical passage. According to one reading, by giving names to each animal, Adam actually created the categories of animals. On a different, less 'free-will', reading, Adam's names simply mapped onto the divinely established animal categories. Adam, in this reading, did not create the categories.

The relation between language and thought has intrigued students of the human mind for years. Parallel to the two readings suggested above, there

---

Requests for reprints should be addressed to Gil Diesendruck, Department of Psychology, Bar-Ilan University, Ramat-Gan, 52900, Israel. Email: dieseng@mail.biu.ac.il

I thank Susan Gelman and Paul Bloom for thoughtful comments on an earlier draft of this manuscript.

http://www.tandf.co.uk/journals/pp/01690965.html    DOI: 10.1080/01690960344000116

are those who advocate that language exerts a powerful effect on cognition (Bowerman & Levinson, 2001; Leach, 1976; Whorf, 1956), whereas others deny or minimise such an effect (Gennari, Sloman, Malt, & Fitch, 2002; Li & Gleitman, 2002; Pinker, 1994; see also Gentner & Goldin-Meadow, 2003, for representative papers on the two positions). Lately, there has been a revival of interest in the cognitive and language development literature regarding the more specific relation between naming and categorisation. For instance, Gopnik (2001) suggests that, 'the use of a single common name for a variety of objects, for example, may present the child with *prima facie* evidence that there is some common underlying nature to those objects' (pp. 59–60). Waxman (1999) attributed an even stronger role for language, and concluded that, 'infants systematically and naturally extend words, applied to individual objects, to other members of an object category, and these named categories go on to support inference and induction' (pp. 274–275). Finally, Carey (1995) argued that naming not only influences the classification of objects but also the conception of categories in essentialistic terms. In her view, 'essentialism, like taxonomic structure, derives from the logical work done by nouns' (p. 276) (see also Sperber, 1996).

Without exception, the recent proposals about the relation between naming and categorisation have been domain-general (see also Hollich, Hirsh-Pasek, & Golinkoff, 2000; Markman, 1989; Markman & Jaswal, 2003; Sloutsky, Lo, & Fisher, 2001). That is, the implicit assumption is that the effect (or non-effect) of names on the categories children build is independent of the ontological kind to which the to be categorised entity belongs. The effect will be the same whether the entity is an animal, an artifact, or a person.

In recent years, a number of scholars have put forth the idea that from very early on children manifest distinct ways of reasoning about different domains of knowledge (Hirschfeld & Gelman, 1994). The basic idea is that the human mind is equipped not only with a set of mechanisms that apply to all content domains, but also with capacities specialised to handle different types of information. In particular, it has been suggested that children develop distinct mechanisms to process information: about living kinds, a naive biology; about people, a naive psychology; and about inanimate objects, a naive physics. Presumably, in categorisation these mechanisms allow us to discriminate between and identify distinct classes of entities, and define how we are to reason about these entities.

An intriguing proposal is that domain-specific mechanisms are in fact modular ways of reasoning (e.g., Atran, 1990; Carey & Spelke, 1994; Cosmides & Tooby, 1994; Leslie, 1994). That is, the mind employs these mechanisms instinctively and automatically, and not because exogenous factors have 'taught' it to do so (Atran, 2001; Pinker, 1999). Consequently, if a domain is indeed modular, then the specific ways in which we form and conceive of categories in that domain are supposed to be relatively stable and impervious to exogenous factors—the domain should be 'conceptually autonomous'. This raises the possibility that if the above domains differ with regard to their modularity, then they might also differ in the extent to which the classification of and reasoning about entities in them are susceptible to exogenous factors. In particular, the effect of language (e.g., naming) on categorisation might not be the same in the domain of animals, humans, and artifacts.

The present paper will examine the empirical evidence pertinent to this hypothesis. The analysis will focus on two related but separate aspects of categorisation: classification and reasoning. *Classification* has to do with how the environment is broken down into classes of entities. In general, the question here is whether the mind picks out clearcut and exclusive discontinuities in the environment (as in Berlin's, 1992, notion of 'perceptual givens'), or whether instead there are no discontinuities whatsoever in the environment (as in Whorf's, 1956, 'kaleidoscopic flux of impressions' notion) or too many possible discontinuous groupings (as in Dupré's, 1981, 'promiscuous realism' notion). *Reasoning* has to do with how the classes are represented in the human mind. The issue here is whether these representations result from inevitable, universal, and perhaps innate components of our minds (as in Atran's, 1998, appraisal of essentialism as a 'habit of the mind'), or are instead cultural constructions (as in Fodor's, 1998, treatment of essentialism as a 'late and sophisticated achievement'). (See Gelman, Hollander, Star, & Heyman, 2000; Mandler, 2000; Rips, 1989; E. Smith, Patalano, & Jonides, 1998, for similar distinctions.)

The first part of the paper will review briefly evidence about the nature of children's categories in the three domains. The goal here is to substantiate the idea that children do indeed reason differently about animal, human, and artifact kinds. The bulk of the paper will focus on relevant evidence regarding the relationship between language and categorisation. Anthropological studies will be reviewed in order to evaluate the degree of similarities and differences in the way distinct cultures classify and reason about the various domains. Studies with infants will shed light on the nature of prelinguistic categories. The review will close with studies that directly investigated the effect of language on young children's categorisation. Importantly, given that the ultimate goal is to analyse the relationship between language and categorisation, it is imperative that the evidence brought to bear on the nature of children's categories come from non-linguistic tasks, such as classification, induction, and general beliefs. Finding that speakers of different languages have different linguistic means to talk about similar phenomena cannot be taken as evidence that their languages influenced their thoughts (Bloom & Keil, 2001; Brown, 1958).

The analyses may reveal a variety of patterns. For instance, it might turn out that the three domains are impervious to linguistic factors both in terms of classification and reasoning, that the three domains are highly and equally susceptible to linguistic factors on both aspects, or that each domain has a different degree of susceptibility to linguistic factors vis-à-vis each aspect.

## THE DOMAIN-SPECIFIC NATURE OF CHILDREN'S CATEGORIES

The discussion over the domain-specificity of category structure has focused primarily on the distinction between animals and artifacts. This distinction is supported broadly by neuropsychological findings of selective impairment of animate or inanimate knowledge systems (Caramazza & Shelton, 1998), and by the developmentally early differentiation between animates and inanimates (Rakison & Poulin-Dubois, 2001). More specifically, philosophers (Schwartz, 1978) and anthropologists (Atran, 1995), have argued that animals, but not artifacts, are treated by people as having an underlying causal and essential nature that defines their identity. This 'psychological essentialism' (Medin & Ortony, 1989) presumably leads people to believe that categories are a powerful source for induction, are resistant to transformations, have an innate potential, are not defined by their superficial features, and are absolute and real (see Gelman, 2003, for a discussion).[1]

Studies on young children's categorisation reveal that these 'symptoms' of essentialism are more apparent in their reasoning about animals than about artifacts. Children rely on animal category membership for inferring the distribution of novel internal properties (Gelman & Coley, 1990; Gelman & Markman, 1986, 1987), and do so more often for animal than

---

[1] Recently, a debate has arisen as to whether to account for these categorisation phenomena a notion of essentialism is needed, or a notion of causal laws may suffice (cf. Ahn, et al., 2001; Rips, 2001; Strevens, 2000, 2001). The present review does not attempt to decide between these different opinions and its general implications regarding categorisation differences among domains are not substantially affected by this debate. Nonetheless, given that one of the main motives of this review is the domain-specificity view—a view that often and explicitly discusses essentialism—and given that many of the researchers whose studies are reviewed here interpret their conclusions in terms of essentialism, the present analysis is framed around this interpretive construct.

for artifact categories (Gelman, 1988; Gelman & O'Reilly, 1988). More-over, children are more likely to decide on the category membership of an animal based on knowledge of its internal properties, than they are to decide on the category membership of an artifact based on knowledge of its internal, superficial, or functional properties (Diesendruck, Gelman, & Lebowitz, 1998). This domain difference in beliefs regarding deep essential properties is also manifested in children's resistance to category change. In Keil's (1989) studies, for instance, 5-year-olds maintained that superficial transformations to an animal (e.g., dying, wearing a costume) do not change its category membership, but analogous transformations do change artifacts' category membership. In fact, Gelman and Wellman (1991) found that preschoolers seem to believe that an animal's category identity is established by birth. Specifically, 4-year-olds thought that an animal would develop the behaviours and appearance typical of its native kind, even if raised among animals of a different kind.

Finally, studies suggest that children believe that superordinate animal categories reflect 'real' classes in the world whereas superordinate artifact categories are more a matter of arbitrary conventions (Kalish, 1998). Relatedly, Diesendruck and Gelman (1999) found that adults are more likely to treat animals, as compared with artifacts, as having absolute category membership (i.e., an animal is either definitely a member of a category or definitely not a member of a category) independently of their typicality (cf. Kalish, 1995, 2002).

These findings suggest that children believe animal kinds have 'intrinsic' properties that define what they are. What defines the nature of artifact kinds, however, is a matter of some dispute (see Malt & Johnson, 1992, for a discussion). Some argue that children's artifact categories are con-structed on-line, based on simple mechanisms of learning and attention that focus children on the perceptually salient aspects of objects (Smith, 1999; Smith, Jones, & Landau, 1996; see also Barsalou, 1993; Eimas, 1994; Quinn & Eimas, 2000). Others propose that children's concepts are 'theory-like' constructs, that define to children causal relations between object properties, and thus determine which properties might be relevant for category identification (Barrett, Abdi, Murphy, & Gallagher, 1993; Bloom, 2000; Carey, 1985; Gelman & Diesendruck, 1999; Keil, 1989; Kemler Nelson, Russell, Duke, & Jones, 2000).

This debate notwithstanding, for the purpose of the present analysis what is crucial is that on both accounts, children's artifact categories are susceptible to exogenous factors, be they contextual salience or human interaction. Regarding the former, for instance, we found that the relative distinctiveness of functional or physical features of artifacts influenced 5-year-olds' artifact categorisation, but did not affect adults' (Diesendruck, Hammer, & Catz, 2003b; Hammer & Diesendruck, 2002). Regarding the latter, Bloom (1996, 2000) has proposed that children may decide what an artifact is based on intuitions about what it was intended to be by its creator. In fact, Diesendruck, Markson, and Bloom (2003c) found that intentional information led children to both understand that two similarly shaped objects were not of the same kind, and that two dissimilarly shaped but similarly functioning objects were of the same kind (see also Bloom & Markson, 1998; Gelman & Bloom, 2000; Gelman & Ebeling, 1998). Especially under this latter view—with its focus on human intentionality— the way in which people talk about artifacts may have a substantial effect on how children classify and conceive of artifacts.

The third domain of categories to be discussed consists of groupings of people. These involve children's conception of social categories such as race, gender, ethnicity, and social status, and personality traits such as smart, shy, and nice. At this point, it is unclear whether children conceptualise these different kinds of categories in the same way. Nonetheless, these categories are importantly similar insofar as they inform children's social interactions and psychological inferences (Gelman, 1992; Yuill, 1992).

In his pioneering studies on children's racial categories, Hirschfeld (1996) found that preschool children believe that race is more important in determining the identity of a person than is body build or occupation, that racial identity is absolute (i.e., one can be either black or white, but not mixed), and that racial identity is established at birth and thus independent of upbringing environment. Taylor (1996) found a similar pattern to this latter one in children's reasoning about gender categories. Specifically, up to 10 years of age, children responded that a story character's gender-typical behaviours and preferences would be consistent with his/her biological sex, even if raised in an environment with only members of the other sex.

In a series of studies on trait reasoning, Heyman and Gelman (1998, 1999) found that preschool children did not identify traits with certain types of behaviours (e.g., nice people are those who help others) or outcomes (e.g., nice people are those who cause good things to others). Rather, preschoolers determined a person's trait based primarily on the person's motives (e.g., nice people are those who mean to do others good). That is, the underlying cause for trait assignment is internal and non-obvious, much like the cause for assigning animal category membership. Furthermore, analogously to Gelman and Markman's (1986, 1987) findings on animal categories, Heyman and Gelman (2000) found that children inferred novel psychological properties based on the shared trait-category membership of two persons rather than the physical similarity between persons. (See also Gelman, Collman, & Maccoby, 1986, for analogous results regarding gender.) Using a similar methodology, we found that children were more likely to draw inferences based on shared social category membership, while adults were more likely to draw inferences based on shared trait-category membership (Diesendruck, Cropp, & Yamauchi, 2003a).

Taken together, reasoning about human kinds is characterised by a belief that unobservable internal properties cause apparent characteristics, that trait or social category membership are relatively stable, and that human kinds have high inductive—and perhaps innate—potential. These findings hint to the possibility that children's reasoning about human kinds is essentialistic in nature, much as their reasoning about animal kinds, and unlike their reasoning about artifacts (Gelman, 1992; Hirschfeld, 1996; Rothbart & Taylor, 1992). The question to be addressed in the remainder of this review is what is the role of language in the generation of these domain-specific reasoning patterns.

## THE CONCEPTUAL AUTONOMY OF CHILDREN'S CATEGORIES IN DIFFERENT DOMAINS

The present section reviews evidence regarding the extent to which the classification of and reasoning about categories in the different domains vary in terms of their susceptibility to linguistic factors. The review will focus on three sources of data: cross-cultural studies, studies on infant categorisation, and studies on the effect of language on categorisation. Each section will address primarily differences between animal and artifact categories, turning in the end to the less studied domain of human kinds.

Cross-cultural studies will be reviewed in order to evaluate the extent to which both the classification of and reasoning about categories from the different domains are susceptible to cultural and linguistic variations. Findings of cross-cultural consistencies in one or both aspects of categorisation, in a given domain, will support the idea that the domain is conceptually autonomous in that aspect. This evidence is suggestive, however, because, for one, it is impossible to rule out the possibility that unidentified crucial cultural or linguistic factors are similar even across presumably quite distinct sociocultural groups.

Studies on prelinguistic infants will be discussed primarily to evaluate the claim about the varying autonomy of classification in the different domains. The rationale for reviewing these studies is that if infants already show some categorical distinctions in a certain domain before they have acquired the linguistic forms that discriminate between categories, then it is because this aspect of categorisation is autonomous vis-à-vis language.

Finally, the last section will tackle most directly the effect various linguistic factors—mostly naming—have on young children's classification and conception of categories from the different domains.

## Cross-cultural categorisation

*Animal categories.* Anthropological studies on the categorisation of natural environments provide, at first sight, a somewhat mixed picture about the universality of classification and the nature of categories.

On the one hand, a number of studies show that different cultures name, subdivide, or group together different kinds of animals because of the animals' economic, social, or religious importance for each specific culture (Brown, 1985; Bulmer, 1967; Diamond, 1966; Morris, 1984; Randall & Hunn, 1984; Turner, 1987). These findings seem to support Dupré's (1981) notion of promiscuous realism, namely, that there are many possible 'sameness relations' in the environment and that cultures determine which ones get to be represented. The findings further support the argument that categories are defined not by some intrinsic properties, but instead by utilitarian extrinsic properties (Ellen, 1993; Hunn, 1982).

On the other hand, a number of recent investigations reveal similarities across cultures on both aspects of animal categorisation (see Atran, 1990; Berlin, 1992, for reviews). One line of research has focused on the prevalence of category-based induction across cultures. Atran and his colleagues have found that adults from a variety of sociocultural backgrounds (e.g., Itza Mayans, Midwestern college students, Illinois tree maintenance workers) manifest a similar reliance on generic-level animal categories to infer about unknown properties (Atran, 1998; Coley, Medin, & Atran, 1997; López, Atran, Coley, Medin, & Smith, 1997). Atran concludes that the readily identifiable distinctive morphological features of generic species help the categoriser classify living kinds. In Atran's view, moreover, the categoriser believes these features to be causally produced by underlying essential features. It is the attribution of essences to living kinds that allows the categoriser to infer about non-obvious similarities between category members (Atran, Estin, Coley, & Medin, 1997).

In further support of this view, comparative studies find similarities across cultures in the classification of the natural environment. Atran (1995) reports that the zoological taxonomies generated by Itza informants and by rural Michigan residents are both strongly correlated to the scientific taxonomy of their respective local faunas. In fact, when taking into consideration only animals in both local faunas that fall under the same scientific tree, Atran found a significant direct correlation between these two cultures' taxonomies. Similarly, Boster (1987) reported that American students' similarity ratings of South American birds, were strongly related to the classification of these birds by Jivaroans, natives of the environment from which the sample of birds was taken.

As informative as they are about the cultural models of animal classification, studies with adults do not provide decisive evidence regarding the origins of these classification modes. It could be that adults' classification strategies reflect cultural priorities constructed to replace intuitive classification modes. More decisive evidence would come from studies with children from diverse cultural backgrounds. Unfortunately, this type of evidence is scarce.

Stross (1973) reported that most plant categories identified by Tzeltal children were at the generic level, again suggesting its primacy. This evidence is still problematic, however, because it is unclear to what extent the 'primacy' is in the linguistic input the child hears, or in his/her perceptual/conceptual apparatus. Regarding animals, Walker (1999) found an interesting developmental pattern in Yorubans' conceptions of category membership. Namely, she found that mostly adults gave explanations for their categorisation decisions in terms of culture-specific beliefs about animals (e.g., supernatural powers associated with each category). Children rarely did so. Walker concluded that the inclusion of super-natural beliefs into children's conceptions of animals occurs later in development. Finally, Diesendruck (2001) found that children from Brazilian shanty-towns, Brazilian middle-class, and North-American middle-class, were equally likely to be convinced that if two animals share internal properties, then the animals are likely to be of the same kind. In other words, children's beliefs about the essential nature of internal properties for determining animal category membership seemed to be unaffected by the quantity and quality of cultural input children receive about animals.

It seems that the safest conclusion to be drawn from the cross-cultural data on animal categorisation is that the hierarchical level matters (Malt, 1995; Rosch, Mervis, Grey, Johnson, & Boyes-Braem, 1976). In particular, as shown by the work of Atran, Berlin, and their colleagues, we find the greatest cross-cultural consistencies in terms of both the classification and reasoning about animal categories at the generic-species level. At this level, adults and children from diverse cultural backgrounds construe similar animal categories and conceive of these categories in essentialistic terms. As Medin, Atran, and colleagues have argued, the finding that American college students treat certain kinds at the life form level (e.g., tree and bird) as basic-level (Rosch et al., 1976) may be due to their impoverished experience of the natural environment, and thus prove to be the exception rather than the rule about human categorisation tendencies (Medin, Ross, Atran, Burnett, & Blok, 2002). Human categorisers from various cultures who have rich enough exposure to the natural environment, do privilege the generic-specific level in their classification behaviour (Medin, Lynch, Coley, & Atran, 1997; Tanaka & Taylor, 1991). Moreover, even for American college students, the generic-species level is the preferred level for induction (Atran et al.,

1997), suggesting that the salience of other levels of abstraction may be primarily for the purposes of communication (Malt, 1995).

In turn, as revealed by many of the ethnographies mentioned earlier, how people combine generic-level animal categories into superordinate categories, or how they subdivide them into subordinate kinds, seems to vary across cultures and to be more susceptible to culture-specific considerations of utility, functionality, and importance. It is at these levels that language might exert an effect.

*Artifact categories.*   In contrast to the vast amounts of ethnographic data on various cultures' classification of living kinds, there are very few cross-cultural studies on the categorisation of artifact kinds. The reason for this, as Atran (1995) notes, may be trivial: artifacts are by definition cultural constructions, if not individual constructions, and therefore variable across cultures. In fact, not only do different cultures have different artifacts, but also they likely use even the common artifacts in different ways. Some support for this argument comes from Walker's (1999) findings that explanations for artifact categorisation in terms of functional or perceptual-functional properties varied across rural, urban, and elite Yoruba children and adults. Moreover, Malt and her colleagues (Malt, Sloman, Gennari, Shi, & Wang, 1999) found differences in how English, Chinese, and Spanish adults named a variety of containers, despite rating the functional and physical similarity of the containers quite uniformly.

One notable exception in terms of cultural classification of artifacts is an analysis by Brown and colleagues (Brown, Kolar, Torrey, Truong-Quang, & Volkman, 1976). They concluded that the same principles of nomenclature found by Berlin, Breedlove, and Raven (1973) in the taxonomy of living kinds, applied also to artifacts (e.g., vehicles and tools). Wierzbicka (1984) characterises such a similarity as superficial. In her view, artifact taxonomies are fundamentally different from animal taxonomies, insofar as artifact taxonomies (e.g., the inclusion of 'spears' and 'knives' under the superordinate category 'weapon') are not based on a notion of 'kind of thing', but rather on a notion of 'kind of function'. As Atran (1995), she concludes that given that artifact functions are culturally defined, one should not expect to find cross-cultural consistencies regarding artifact 'taxonomies'.

*Human kinds.*   Data from cross-cultural studies on social categorisation reveal that classification systems vary across cultures and even across periods within a single culture (Rothbart & Taylor, 1992). Importantly, it seems that while there are variations with respect to the categories formed, in all cultures, and at all times, there seem to be categories that are essentialised.

As Hirschfeld (1996) discusses, cultural and historical reasons may have led children and adults in the United States to view the category of race in essentialistic terms. Ethnographies reveal, however, that in different cultures different social categories may be essentialised. Work in India shows that brahmin adults believe that a person's caste is inherited from birth parents, rather than acquired from adoptive parents (Mahalingam, 1998, cited in Gelman, 2003; see also Daniel, 1985). Gil-White (2001) found a similar nativist construal of ethnic differences among Mongolian Torguuds. It is interesting to note that in both these cultures, the relevant social categories differ only slightly in terms of physical correlates, and even then these are mostly transient physical properties (see also Boyer, 2001).

In contrast to the above conclusions, Astuti (1995) argued that the Vezo from Madagascar hold a rather non-essentialist view of social group membership, with adults of that culture responding that social identity is determined by the adoptive, rather than the biological, parents. As Gelman (2003) notes, however, children's pattern of responses in Astuti's (1995) study was the opposite. That is, most young participants responded that social identity is determined by birth, thus endorsing a nativist essentialist construal of human kinds.

Further indication that cultures define which social categories get to be essentialised comes from the study by Diesendruck et al. (2003a) mentioned earlier. We found that despite the fact that children were more likely to draw inferences based on social category membership and adults based on personality trait, children and adults agreed in terms of which social categories were most important. Specifically, children and adults' inferences were most strongly influenced by 'ethnicity' (Jew/Arab) and social status (rich/poor), intimating that children may have picked up some cultural message regarding the importance of these categories in Israeli society.

Taken together, the above findings indicate that while the way in which children and adults from different cultures reason about human kinds (i.e., in essentialist terms) is relatively similar, the classification of humans into kinds is susceptible to cultural variations.

*Summary.* The picture coming out of this review of the anthropological literature is that the domains differ on both aspects of categorisation in terms of their conceptual autonomy. The classification of and reasoning about animal categories are the most stable across cultures, particularly at the generic level. It is plausible that cultural—and thus linguistic—forces affect animal categorisation at other hierarchical levels. The literature on cross-cultural artifact categorisation is limited, but there are hints that humans classify and conceive of artifacts quite differently across cultures. Finally, there are cross-cultural similarities in how people reason about human kinds—consistent with it being conceptually autonomous—but the specific human kinds focused on vary across cultures.

## Infant categorisation

*Animal and artifact categories.* Using visual habituation methods, a number of studies have shown that infants as young as 3 months of age discriminate between basic-level animal categories such as cats from dogs (Eimas, 1994; Quinn & Eimas, 1997). These studies show that this capacity in infants is quite robust, and that they can discriminate between these types of categories even when provided with only partial visual information (e.g., faces) about the animals (Quinn & Eimas, 1996). Using a similar methodology, Behl-Chadha (1996) found that 3-month-olds were also capable of discriminating between basic-level artifact categories such as chairs and tables. Moreover, Behl-Chadha found that 3-month-olds discriminated between superordinate living kind and artifact categories, among superordinate living kind categories such as mammals, fish, and birds, but were less proficient in discriminating superordinate artifact categories such as furniture and vehicles.

In contrast to the above findings, studies using a variety of object individuation tasks have found that up to 12 months of age infants seem to have difficulty individuating artifacts based on taxonomic kind (Van de Walle, Carey, & Prevor, 2000; Wilcox & Baillargeon, 1998; Xu & Carey, 1996; Xu, Carey, & Welch, 1999). Findings from object examination tasks also show that, in general, infants younger than 9 months of age fail to categorise objects at the basic level while succeeding at the domain level (Mandler & McDonough, 1993). It is possible that this disparity in the findings from visual habituation studies and these latter studies are due to processing demands or other task-related factors (Mandler, 2000; Pauen, 2002; Xu, 2002). Nonetheless, it seems that from a very early age, infants are capable of discriminating between classes of animals and artifacts.

Akin to the classification-reasoning distinction made in the present review, Mandler (2000) notes that it is important to distinguish between perceptual categorisation—the sort revealed by the studies described above—and conceptual categorisation. The latter type involves what infants think something is, and is revealed primarily by induction tasks. In a series of studies, Mandler and McDonough (1998) have shown that infants as young as 9 months of age draw appropriate inferences based on global categories (e.g., animals versus artifacts), but that even at 20 months they overgeneralise across basic-level categories.

*Human kinds.*   Few studies have systematically investigated whether prelinguistic infants classify humans into distinct categories. Evidently, the sheer possibility of such a classification is limited to human kinds that have some physical correlate. That is, it would be impossible for infants to differentiate physically between human kinds defined by personality traits, such as shy versus outgoing people. Even among social categories, only the minority presumably has permanent physical correlates (e.g., sex), some give the 'false-impression' of having permanent physical correlates (e.g., race), and most have only transient physical correlates (e.g., the dressing codes of religious groups). Thus, not surprisingly, studies on infants have focused on the capacity to discriminate between males and females.

These studies reveal that prior to their first birthday, infants are capable of discriminating between male and female faces (Leinbach & Fagot, 1993; Younger & Fearing, 1999), and associate gender-typical faces to gender-typical voices (Poulin-Dubois, Serbin, Kenyon, & Derbyshire, 1994), and with gender-typical objects (Levy & Haaf, 1994). Nonetheless, other findings show that toddlers may have difficulty identifying their own gender identity (Campbell, Shirley, & Heywood, 2000), and even preschoolers can still be fooled by superficial gender transformations (Liben & Signorella, 1987). In other words, children's construction of gender kinds in particular (see Martin, Ruble, & Szkrybalo, 2002), and human kinds in general (Hirschfeld, 1996) does not seem to be driven solely by perception of distinct natural classes.

*Summary.*   Consistent with the domain-specificity conjecture, from very early on infants discriminate, both perceptually and conceptually, between the global domains of animals and artifacts. Moreover, it seems that prior to their first birthday, infants already distinguish between classes of basic-level animals and artifacts, suggesting that the classification processes in these domains might be independent of language. Of further interest, is how robust these prelinguistic categories are, and how children eventually reason about them. Putting it differently, to what extent, and in what ways, does the acquisition of language affect these categories.

## Language and categorisation

As mentioned earlier, most accounts of the effect of language on categorisation do not differentiate among domains. The claim is that naming, for instance, leads children to group entities into kinds, to search for deep commonalities among entities, to draw inferences about entities, and perhaps even to essentialise kinds (Carey, 1995; Gopnik, 2001; Waxman, 1999; Xu, 2002). The present section analyses to what extent this effect of language applies uniformly to the three domains.

*Animal and artifact categories.* Developmental psychologists have found significant correlations between young children's capacity to exhaustively sort objects into piles and the number of nouns in children's vocabulary (Gopnik and Meltzoff, 1992; Poulin-Dubois, Graham, & Sippola, 1995). As the authors of these studies acknowledged, however, these findings cannot point to the directionality of the effect. To address more directly this issue, Gopnik and Choi (1995) conducted a similar analysis with Korean-speaking children. They found that compared with English-speaking children, Korean-speaking children were delayed regarding their noun vocabulary explosion, and were less successful in an object sorting task. In other words, it appeared that language was driving categorisation abilities.

More conclusive evidence regarding the directionality of the effect, however, comes from experiments that directly investigated the effects of naming on infants' classification patterns. As reported earlier, Xu and Carey (1996) had found that while 10-month-old infants did not differentiate between artifact kinds (e.g., a ball and a toy-duck), 12-month-olds did. Xu (2002) made one significant change to their original procedure, namely, she labelled the objects as they appeared (e.g., 'look, a ball', and then, 'look, a duck'). Xu found that under this condition even 9-month-old infants differentiated between the object kinds, leading her to the conclusion that labelling might play a causal role in object kind individuation.

Waxman and colleagues reached a similar conclusion. Waxman and Markow (1995) found that 12- to 13-month-old infants attended preferably to an exemplar of a novel category (animal and artifact) when their familiarisation to a target category was accompanied by a label than when it was not. In fact, the label effect was particularly strong for categories at the superordinate level. In a subsequent study, Balaban and Waxman (1997) investigated this effect on 9-month-olds' classification of animals. The main finding was that infants exposed to a novel word in the familiarisation trials subsequently showed less attention to a familiar category exemplar—and more to a novel category exemplar—than did infants exposed to a tone in familiarisation. Balaban and Waxman concluded that labels seemed to have facilitated classification.

A question that arises is what exactly the labels did? Were the labels exclusively responsible for the infants' formation of the categories? Or would the infants have formed these very same categories also in the absence of labels? The findings on infants' early classificatory capacities reviewed earlier indicate that the latter might be the case for basic-level categories. In fact, findings from Waxman's studies themselves also seem to support this conclusion. First, the 1-year-olds in Waxman and Markow's (1995) studies indeed seemed to have formed basic-level animal and artifact categories, even in the absence of labels. Second, Balaban and Waxman (1997), using only animals as stimuli, found no difference in the familiarisation trials between 9-month-olds who were exposed to pictures + words and 9-month-olds who were exposed to pictures + tones. Again, but here particularly regarding animals, infants manifested an equivalent capacity to form basic-level categories, whether exposed to labels or not. And finally, it is interesting to note that in two of the three studies reported by Balaban and Waxman (1997), infants in the Word condition did not look at the exemplar of the different category more than expected by chance. The difference between the Word and Tone conditions resulted from the fact that infants in the Tone condition looked at the member of the different category less than expected by chance. In other words, it seems that the label resonated with the infants' representation of the basic-level animal category bringing it to the infants' attention; it did not cause them to create a category they would not have created in the absence of a label. Basic-level animal categories may be prepotent categories ready to be tagged (see also, Waxman, 1999).

In order to assess more directly potential domain differences regarding the effect of naming on basic-level classification, two additional studies would be important. One would be a study using Xu's (2002) procedure, comparing explicitly within living kinds and within artifacts. A second study should be comparable to Balaban and Waxman's (1997) on animals, but using as stimuli basic-level artifact categories. Interestingly, none-theless, Nazzi and Gopnik (2001) found that naming helped 20-month-olds classify *novel* artifacts.

Indeed, cross-linguistic studies indicate that linguistic input may be critical for the classification of artifacts but less so for the classification of natural kinds. After reviewing ethnographic data on the biological classificatory systems of a number of non-Western societies, Berlin et al. (1973) noted that categories at the generic level are usually labelled by primary lexemes (e.g., 'oak', 'rabbit'), whereas categories at the more specific level are usually labelled by secondary lexemes (e.g., 'jack oak', 'cottontail rabbit'). Berlin et al. concluded that 'the linguistic structure of a plant or animal name is usually a good mirror of the taxonomic status of the category which it represents' (p. 241). Generic taxa are the conceptually most salient categories, and therefore they are named with primary lexemes. Their conceptual status is independent of the naming practices.

Regarding artifacts, Lucy and Gaskins (2001) gave Yucatec and English speaking children and adults a number of object classification tasks. Of primary interest was to evaluate the extent to which speakers of these different languages would classify objects based on shape or material. Yucatec differs from English in terms of noun pluralisation and the use of numeral classifiers. Lucy and Gaskins hypothesised that these differences would lead Yucatec speakers to be more reliant on object material and less reliant on object shape in categorisation, than English speakers. Their findings with 9-year-olds and adults confirmed this hypothesis. Imai and Gentner (1997) got compatible results in a study of Japanese and English speaking preschoolers. Japanese—having similar linguistic features to Yucatec—led children to be less reliant on shape. These studies point to the flexibility of the nature of artifact categories, and in particular, their malleability by linguistic factors.

The studies reviewed so far addressed primarily the effect of language in the classification of animals and artifacts into kinds. In turn, evidence regarding the effects of naming on how children reason about animal and artifact categories derives mostly from studies on induction.

In a recent study, Welder and Graham (2001) investigated the effects of labelling on 16- to 21-month-olds' inferences about a novel object's non-obvious property. The objects were made of plastic, metal, and styrofoam, and were covered with various fabrics—in other words, they were artifact-like. The experimenter showed children a novel object and demonstrated a particular non-obvious property it had (e.g., it squeaked when squeezed). The experimenter then showed children a number of test objects of varying degrees of physical similarity to the original one, and recorded children's attempts at performing the original action (e.g., squeezing) on these objects. Importantly, for half of the children the experimenter labelled the original and test objects with the same name, and for the other half she did not. Altogether, Welder and Graham found that children in the Label condition were more likely to attempt the original action than were children in the No-Label condition, at all levels of physical similarity. In other words, the common name seemed to have convinced these young children that two artifacts were of the same kind.

The Gelman and Markman (1986, 1987) studies discussed earlier showed that children are more likely to infer non-obvious similarities between animals based on a common familiar label than based on physical similarity. The straightforward implication from these findings is that children take familiar count nouns as a more reliable cue to the category membership of an animal than its physical appearance. Importantly, this implication is not inconsistent with the idea that children's reasoning about animal categories does not *depend* on the guidance of language or culture. What would be inconsistent with this idea is if in reasoning about animal categories, children would neglect appearance or behavioural cues and be guided by the naming pattern—as did the infants in Welder and Graham's (2001) study. That, however, does not seem to be the case.

Davidson and Gelman (1990) conducted a study along the same lines as Gelman and Markman, but used novel unfamiliar animals or artifacts instead of familiar ones. The crucial items were those in which there was a conflict between the appearance of the novel entity (e.g., it looked different from the target entity) and the label applied to it (e.g., it got the same label as the target). Davidson and Gelman found that especially for animal sets, labelling had little effect on children's inferences of non-obvious properties, which were in turn determined primarily by the physical similarity between items. In other words, children seemed to expect animal categories to cohere, to pick out plausible classes, and were not persuaded that a dissimilar animal would have the same properties as a target animal just because they had the same name. Thus, despite the similarities between the studies by Gelman and colleagues on animals and that of Welder and Graham (2001) on artifacts regarding the basic propensity for induction, there seem to be differences in what reinforces or generates this propensity across domains. Complementing this interpretation, recall that Diesendruck et al. (1998) found that preschoolers' extensions of names were affected by information regarding the referents of names when the referents were animals, but not when they were artifacts. Only in the domain of animals did conceptual beliefs guide children's interpretations of names.

Consistent with the above argument, Gelman and colleagues (Gelman, Coley, Rosengren, Hartman, & Pappas, 1998) found that parents offer mostly implicit cues—via gestures and relational terms—about the relation between category members, but very little explicit input about animal essences. In other words, in conceptualising animals in essentialistic terms, children seem to go beyond the linguistic input they receive from their parents (see also Keil, 1998). Furthermore, Gelman et al. (2000) found that parents were more likely to relate two artifacts, as compared with animals, by saying 'X is a kind of Y'—an expression known to help even 2-year-olds construe an inclusion relation between categories (Diesendruck & Shatz, 1997, 2001).

*Human kinds.*    Social psychologists have for a long time discussed the relationship between language and social stereotypes (e.g., Allport, 1954), and have developed models to investigate this relationship (Hamilton, Gibbons, Stroessner, & Sherman, 1992; Jussim, Nelson, Manis, & Soffin, 1995; Maass & Arcuri, 1992; Semin & Fiedler, 1988). A crucial question, however, is what exactly labels do to social categorisation (Rothbart & Taylor, 1992). Do labels affect how children conceive of certain human kinds, or do labels simply indicate to children onto which human kinds they should apply their conceptual beliefs?

A number of studies show that children's inferences about human kinds change when labels are attached to these kinds. For instance, Heyman & Gelman (2000) found that trait labels lead children to overcome physical dissimilarity in drawing inferences about psychological properties of characters. In a further study, Gelman and Heyman (1999) found that describing a behavioural pattern with a noun (e.g., 'Rose is a carrot-eater') lead children to view the behaviour as more permanent than when it is described with a predicate (e.g., 'Rose eats carrots whenever she can'). Last but not least, Hirschfeld (1996) found that children are more likely to recall a character's race if they have been exposed to that information verbally than if they have been exposed to it visually.

The above findings notwithstanding, it seems that the primary effect of naming is in guiding children towards the relevant human kinds, rather than causing them to essentialise these kinds. First, as has been described earlier, a variety of human kinds seems to be essentialised by different cultures (e.g., Boyer, 2001; Daniel, 1985; Gil-White, 2001), and it is implausible that in all these cultures, similar kinds of linguistic forms convey to children these beliefs. Moreover, there are some experimental indications that the effect of language on children's concepts of human kinds is not in the generation of essentialist beliefs.

First, children in the Predicate condition of Gelman and Heyman's (1999) study were also likely to believe the behavioural pattern was stable, intimating that the label may have accentuated a tendency, not created it. Second, Diesendruck et al. (2003a) found that labelling a psychologically meaningless appearance-based category had a weaker influence on children's inferences than labelling a psychologically meaningful social category. That is, labelling per se did not make a category inferentially meaningful. Third and finally, in a study with Spanish–English bilingual children, Heyman and Diesendruck (2002) found that children's default assumption seems to be to treat personality traits as stable. On a number of different tasks, we described to children behaviours and traits using one of three verbal forms: the Spanish forms 'ser' (which conveys a permanent state of affairs), and 'estar' (which conveys a temporary state of affairs), and the corresponding, ambiguous, English verb form 'to be'. We then asked children to what extent they believed the behaviours and traits were stable. As expected, we found that 'ser' led children to make more stable inferences than 'estar'. Of particular interest in the present context is that the pattern of responses of children in the 'to be' condition was most similar to that in the 'ser' condition. In other words, it was not the case that 'ser' led children to make more stable inferences than a presumed baseline, but that 'estar' led children to make less stable inferences.

*Summary.*   Contrary to Whorf's (1956) and Leach's (1976) claims, there seems to be little evidence that names strongly influence the way in which children classify animals, especially at the basic level. Moreover, and in contraposition to Carey's (1995) claims, there is also scant evidence that naming leads children to develop essentialist beliefs about animal categories.

In contrast, naming does seem to affect both how children classify and reason about artifacts. The general claims mentioned earlier about the role of naming in categorisation might be particularly true of artifacts (Carey, 1995; Gopnik, 2001; Waxman, 1999; Welder & Graham, 2001; Xu, 2002). Names seem to be a powerful indication to children that two seemingly disparate artifacts are actually of the same kind, and the fact that two artifacts share a name provides a very valid reason for children to search for the underlying coherent nature of the artifact kind. In fact, given that children's conceptualisation of artifacts may be strongly tied to their understanding of intentions (Bloom, 1996; Diesendruck et al., 2003c), naming might be one of the best cues for how to categorise artifacts. Intriguingly, this conclusion echoes Locke's contention in his discussion of the role of naming in the conceptualisation of 'mixed modes' (e.g., artifacts):

> For, the connexion between the loose parts of those complex ideas being made by the mind, this union, which has no particular foundation in nature, would cease again, were there not something that did, as it were, hold it together and keep the parts from scattering ... It is the name which is as it were the knot that ties them fast together. (Locke, 1707/1961, pp. 49–50)

Human kinds again seem to present a mixed case. Even though the evidence is scarce, language seems to be more important in defining the classes of entities that constitute a culturally relevant kind than in promoting essentialist reasoning about these kinds.

## General patterns

Three bodies of literature were reviewed in order to evaluate whether the way in which we form and reason about categories in three different domains is conceptually autonomous or susceptible to linguistic and cultural factors. As was pointed out throughout, the 'evidence' reviewed has to be treated as merely suggestive of a pattern. And this is so for a number of reasons. First, there are gaps in the evidence necessary to fully evaluate the domain-specificity conjecture. For instance, we have little knowledge about cross-cultural classification of artifacts, or about infants' classification of human kinds. Second, bridging between findings from the different fields is not always straightforward. For example, the correspondence between the findings from the infant classification literature and the anthropological one requires a closer look at what is meant by basic level. Third, but probably not finally, there are serious methodological issues that need to be addressed in each of the specific fields, such as the effect of stimulus type (e.g., representational toys vs. realistic photographs) in the infant categorisation literature. These qualifications notwithstanding, there seems to be a pattern emerging from these three fields taken together that hints of an answer to the question motivating the review.

The most stable type of category is of generic-species level animals. Studies on preschoolers reveal that children at this age already have conceptually rich beliefs about the nature of these categories. And yet, neither the beliefs, nor the categories themselves, seem to be strongly influenced by language. This was supported by cross-cultural similarities in terms of taxonomic structure and reasoning, by infants' early discrimina- tory abilities, and by the relative impermeability of preschoolers' categories to linguistic factors. There seem to be intuitive, and thus language-independent, mechanisms for classifying and reasoning about generic-level animals. Animal categories at the superordinate (and perhaps subordinate) level, despite being differentiated by infants and being a reliable source for induction, are nonetheless more susceptible to cross-cultural variation, and more influenced by naming.

Artifact categories seem more susceptible to linguistic factors. In fact, the literature on preschoolers' categorisation in itself hints to the idea that the nature of artifact kinds is more strongly dependent on exogenous factors. Moreover, there is presumably great variation across cultures in both the classification and conceptualisation of artifacts, and language seems to influence children's classification of and reasoning about artifacts. One of the puzzling exceptions to this pattern—to be discussed below—is the finding that under certain experimental conditions very young infants discriminate between basic-level artifacts.

Finally, findings with human kinds present a mixed case of susceptibility to exogenous forces. On the one hand, across cultures people seem to reason in similar ways about human kinds, and children's reasoning is only marginally affected by linguistic features. On the other hand, there is variation regarding which human kinds different cultures emphasise, and plausibly infants need external support to identify these kinds.

## Why do domains differ?

The way in which young children think about categories seems to vary across domains. Moreover, the pattern of categorisation summarised above indicates that these domain-specific ways of thinking may vary in how autonomous—or in contrast, influenced by linguistic factors—they are. These variations in the conceptual autonomy of the domains regarding the classification of and reasoning about categories has implications to both the modularity of these domains, and/or to what constitutes a conceptual module.

One possible account for the differences among domains recruits an evolutionary argument (Cosmides & Tooby, 1994). In general, the idea is that cognitive mechanisms used for processing recurrent aspects of the environment in which humans evolved were likely to be selected for, and thus became inherent aspects of our cognitive architecture. The differences across domains result, to some extent, from differences across domains in the stability of the pertinent environmental stimulation. The clearest argument along these lines regards a folk-biological module.

Atran (1990) discusses how the importance of rapidly identifying animals and drawing appropriate inferences about them may have naturally selected minds with the capacity to discriminate between and essentialise folk-biological kinds. In his view, these forces were particularly relevant at the generic-species level because that was the most informative level in human interactions with living kinds. Note that according to this account, the folk-biological module specifies both the reasoning and classificatory mechanisms. That is, intuitive and inductively powerful reasoning biases are tuned to certain perceptual parameters that constitute the entities in the domain.

Hirschfeld (1996) also proposes a modular account in his analysis of racial categories. In his view, people have a 'human kind module' especially devoted to reason essentialistically about the social domain. Importantly, in his view, this reasoning mechanism does not specify a category, and thus cultural or linguistic input is required to define the human kinds onto which essentialism will be applied. More generally, Hirschfeld's proposal raises the possibility that conceptual modules do not define the classificatory mechanisms. Thus children may have well-defined intuitive beliefs about certain categories and yet have difficulty identifying their members (e.g., race), or may be quite capable of discriminating between classes of entities and yet have no definite beliefs for reasoning about those classes (e.g., artifacts).

Consistent with this notion of a dissociation between classification and reasoning is the account that what may be innate are certain reasoning biases, but that the mapping between a bias and a particular domain is determined by cultural or linguistic factors (Pinker, 1999; Sperber, 1996). According to Sperber's 'epidemiology of representations' approach, an innate domain-specific mode of representation (e.g., essentialism) can be deployed not only in the module's innately specified proper domain, but provided with particular cultural input, may be driven to 'adopt' another domain. In his view, language is one of the main factors capable of triggering a module into adopting an additional domain.

Following this argument, it is possible that the reasoning seen in the domain of animals is an instantiation of the mapping between a biology-specific essentialism and its proper domain. Such an 'intuitive' belief, to use Sperber's term, develops automatically through universal perceptual and inferential capacities. These features could thus explain the conceptual autonomy of animal categories. Infants recognise classes of animals, the mind readily attributes causal coherence to these classes, and thus they stabilise as meaningful units of cognition.

In turn, in the domain of artifacts there might be an extension to—an adoption of—that domain by reasoning biases not specific to it, such as essentialism, teleology, or theory of mind (cf. Bloom, 1996; Keil, 1995; Kelemen, 1999). In Sperber's view, such 'reflective' beliefs may require deliberate instruction and involve a more complicated mapping. Arguably then, infants' classificatory proneness in this domain has little to do with a specific conceptual apparatus, and more with some domain-general perceptual discrimination capacity. Given that the mind does not intuitively impute a causal structure onto the discriminated classes of artifacts, it is for language to provide cohesiveness and psychological meaning to them.

Finally, for human kinds there might be a partial adoption by essentialism (Atran, 1990). Gil-White (2001) suggested that the fact that, like animal categories, human kinds constitute endogamous and descent-based groups may prime our biological module into essentialising human kinds. Thus once language helps children identify relevant human kinds, the mind entrusts these kinds with coherence and psychological meaning (see also Boyer, 2001). Evidently, a crucial matter still missing from this general account is a more precise description of the mechanisms that lead to the adoption of domains by various modes of reasoning, and the scope of the adoption.

Last but not least, a third possible proposal speaks not in terms of conceptual distinctions, but rather in terms of perceptual distinctions. Specifically, Gentner and Boroditsky (2001) suggest an individuation continuum that defines the extent of 'cognitive versus linguistic dominance' in the development of concepts. Entities that are high in individuability are perceived as coherent and distinctive units, and thus need little support from language to be individuated. Entities that are low in individuability need more support from language in order to be individuated. It is important to note, however, that the individuation continuum refers to individual entities rather than categories of entities. It is unclear whether the coherence and distinctiveness rank ordering of individual entities applies equally well to categories. One may argue that animal categories have a richer cluster of correlated cues than do human kinds, especially given the variability in terms of physical correlates of the latter kind. However, it seems that it would be difficult to explain the purported pattern of artifact categorisation based on this criterion. Moreover, even if the ranking did apply, the model might still fall short of explaining the differences in how people reason about categories.

In conclusion, the present review provides a different outlook onto important theoretical discussions regarding the domain-specificity of categorisation. In particular, the review illustrates how such a view of the mind might refine our understanding of the interplay between language and thought. Unfortunately—or not—it perhaps opens more questions than it answers.

# REFERENCES

Ahn, W-K., Kalish, C., Gelman, S.A., Medin, D.L., Luhmann, C., Atran, S., et al. (2001). Why essences are essential in the psychology of concepts. *Cognition*, *82*, 59–69.

Allport, G. (1954). *The nature of prejudice*. New York: Addison–Wesley.

Astuti, R. (1995). "The Vezo are not a kind of people": Identity, difference, and "ethnicity" among a fishing people of western Madagascar. *American Ethnologist*, *22*, 464–482.

Atran, S. (1990). *Cognitive foundations of natural history*. Cambridge: Cambridge University Press.

Atran, S. (1995). Classifying nature across cultures. In E.E. Smith & D.N. Osherson (Eds.), *Thinking: An invitation to cognitive science* (pp. 131–174). Cambridge, MA: MIT Press.

Atran, S. (1998). Folk biology and the anthropology of science: Cognitive universals and cultural particulars. *Behavioral and Brain Sciences*, *21*, 547–609.

Atran, S. (2001). The case for modularity: Sin or salvation? *Evolution and Cognition*, *7*, 46–55.

Atran, S., Estin, P., Coley, J.D., & Medin, D.L. (1997). Generic species and basic levels: Essence and appearance in folk biology. *Journal of Ethnobiology*, *17*, 22–45.

Balaban, M.T., & Waxman, S.R. (1997). Do words facilitate object categorization in 9-month-old infants? *Journal of Experimental Child Psychology*, *64*, 3–26.

Barrett, S.E., Abdi, H., Murphy, G.L., & Gallagher, J.M. (1993). Theory-based correlations and their role in children's concepts. *Child Development*, *64*, 1595–1616.

Barsalou, L.W. (1993). Challenging assumptions about concepts. *Cognitive Development*, *8*, 169–180.

Behl-Chadha, G. (1996). Superordinate-like categorical representations in early infancy. *Cognition*, *60*, 104–141.

Berlin, B. (1992). *Ethnobiological classification*. Princeton, NJ: Princeton University Press.

Berlin, B., Breedlove, D., & Raven, P. (1973). General principles of classification and nomenclature in folk biology. *American Anthropologist*, *75*, 214–242.

Bloom, P. (1996). Intention, history, and artifact concepts. *Cognition*, *60*, 1–29.

Bloom, P. (2000). *How children learn the meaning of words*. Cambridge, MA: MIT Press.

Bloom, P., & Keil, F.C. (2001). Thinking through language. *Mind and Language*, *16*, 351–367.

Bloom, P., & Markson, L. (1998). Intention and analogy in children's naming of pictorial representations. *Psychological Science*, *9*, 200–204.

Boster, J. (1987). Agreement between biological classification systems is not dependent on cultural transmission. *American Anthropologist*, *89*, 914–919.

Bowerman, M., & Levinson, S.L. (2001). (Eds.) *Language acquisition and conceptual development*. Cambridge: Cambridge University Press.

Boyer, P. (2001). *Religion explained: The evolutionary origins of religious thought*. New York: Basic Books.

Brown, C.H. (1985). Mode of subsistence and folk biological taxonomy. *Current Anthropology*, *26*, 43–64.

Brown, C., Kolar, J., Torrey, B., Truong-Quang, T., & Volkman, P. (1976). Some general principles of biological and non-biological classification. *American Ethnologist, 3*, 73–85.

Brown, R. (1958). *Words and things.* New York: Free Press.

Bulmer, R. (1967). Why is the cassowary not a bird? A problem of zoological taxonomy among the Karam of New Guinea highlands. *Man, 2*, 5–25.

Campbell, A., Shirley, L., & Heywood, C. (2000). Infants' visual preference for sex-congruent babies, children, toys, and activities: A longitudinal study. *British Journal of Developmental Psychology, 18*, 479–498.

Caramazza, A.C., & Shelton, J.R. (1998). Domain-specific knowledge systems in the brain: The animate–inanimate distinction. *Journal of Cognitive Neuroscience, 10*, 1–34.

Carey, S. (1985). *Conceptual change in childhood.* Cambridge, MA: MIT Press.

Carey, S. (1995). On the origin of causal understanding. In D. Sperber, D. Premack, & A.J. Premack (Eds.), *Causal cognition: A multi-disciplinary debate* (pp. 268–308). Oxford University Press.

Carey, S., & Spelke, E.S. (1994). Domain-specific knowledge and conceptual change. In L.A. Hirschfeld & S.A. Gelman (Eds.), *Mapping the mind: Domain specificity in cognition and culture* (pp. 169–200). Cambridge: Cambridge University Press.

Coley, J.D., Medin, D.L., & Atran, S. (1997). Does rank have its privilege? Inductive inferences within folkbiological taxonomies. *Cognition, 64*, 73–112.

Cosmides, L., & Tooby, J. (1994). Origins of domain specificity: The evolution of functional organization. In L.A. Hirschfeld & S.A. Gelman (Eds.), *Mapping the mind: Domain specificity in cognition and culture* (pp. 85–116). Cambridge: Cambridge University Press.

Daniel, E.V. (1985). *Fluid signs: Being a person the Tamil way.* Los Angeles, CA: University of California Press.

Davidson, N.S., & Gelman, S.A. (1990). Inductions from novel categories: The role of language and conceptual structure. *Cognitive Development, 5*, 151–176.

Diamond, J.M. (1966). Zoological classification system of a primitive people. *Science, 151*, 1102–1104.

Diesendruck, G. (2001). Essentialism in Brazilian children's extensions of animal names. *Developmental Psychology, 37*, 49–60.

Diesendruck, G., Cropp, H., & Yamauchi, M. (2003a). *The role of labels and physical appearance in children's reasoning about human kinds.* Manuscript in preparation.

Diesendruck, G., & Gelman, S.A. (1999). Domain differences in absolute judgments of category membership: Evidence for an essentialist account of categorization. *Psychonomic Bulletin and Review, 6*, 338–346.

Diesendruck, G., Gelman, S.A., & Lebowitz, K. (1998). Conceptual and linguistic biases in children's word learning. *Developmental Psychology, 34*, 823–839.

Diesendruck, G., Hammer, R., & Catz, O. (2003b). Mapping the similarity space of children and adults' artifact categories. *Cognitive Development, 18*, 217–231.

Diesendruck, G., Markson, L., & Bloom, P. (2003c). Children's reliance on creator's intent in extending names for artifacts. *Psychological Science, 14*, 164–168.

Diesendruck, G., & Shatz, M. (1997). The effect of perceptual similarity and linguistic input on children's acquisition of object labels. *Journal of Child Language, 24*, 695–717.

Diesendruck, G., & Shatz, M. (2001). Two-year-olds' recognition of hierarchies: Evidence from their interpretation of the semantic relation between object labels. *Cognitive Development, 16*, 577–594.

Dupré, J. (1981). Natural kinds and biological taxa. *The Philosophical Review, 90*, 66–90.

Eimas, P.D. (1994). Categorization in early infancy and the continuity of development. *Cognition, 50*, 83–93.

Ellen, R. (1993). *The cultural relations of classification.* Cambridge: Cambridge University Press.

Fodor, J.A. (1998). *Concepts: Where cognitive science went wrong.* Oxford: Clarendon Press.

Gelman, S.A. (1988). The development of induction within natural kind and artifact categories. *Cognitive Psychology, 20*, 65–95.

Gelman, S.A. (1992). Children's conception of personality traits. *Human Development, 35*, 280–285.

Gelman, S.A. (2003). *The essential child: Origins of essentialism in everyday thought.* New York: Oxford University Press.

Gelman, S.A., & Bloom, P. (2000). Young children are sensitive to how an object was created when deciding on what to name it. *Cognition, 76*, 91–103.

Gelman, S.A., & Coley, J.D. (1990). The importance of knowing a dodo is a bird: Categories and inferences in two-year-olds. *Developmental Psychology, 26*, 796–804.

Gelman, S.A., Coley, J.D., Rosengren, K.S., Hartman, E., & Pappas, A. (1998). Beyond labeling: The role of maternal input in the acquisition of richly structured categories. *Monographs of the Society for Research in Child Development, 63*, No. 253.

Gelman, S.A., Collman, P., & Maccoby, E.E. (1986). Inferring properties from categories versus inferring categories from properties: The case of gender. *Child Development, 57*, 396–404.

Gelman, S.A., & Diesendruck, G. (1999). What's in a concept? Context, variability, and psychological essentialism. In I.E. Sigel (Ed.), *Development of mental representation* (pp. 87–111). Mahwah, NJ: Lawrence Erlbaum Associates, Inc.

Gelman, S.A., & Ebeling, K.S. (1998). Shape and representational status in children's early naming. *Cognition, 66*, B35–B47.

Gelman, S.A., & Heyman, G.D. (1999). Carrot-eaters and creature-believers: The effects of lexicalization on children's inferences about social categories. *Psychological Science, 10*, 489–493.

Gelman, S.A., Hollander, M., Star, J., & Heyman, G.D. (2000). The role of language in the construction of kinds. *Psychology of Learning and Motivation, 39*, 201–263.

Gelman, S.A., & Markman, E.M. (1986). Categories and induction in young children. *Cognition, 23*, 183–209.

Gelman, S.A., & Markman, E.M. (1987). Young children's induction from natural kinds: The role of categories and appearances. *Child Development, 58*, 1532–1541.

Gelman, S.A., & O'Reilly, A.W. (1988). Children's inductive inferences within superordinate categories: The role of language and category structure. *Child Development, 59*, 876–887.

Gelman, S.A., & Wellman, H.M. (1991). Insides and essences: Early understandings of the non-obvious. *Cognition, 38*, 213–244.

Gennari, S.P., Sloman, S.A., Malt, B.C., & Fitch, W.T. (2002). Motion events in language and cognition. *Cognition, 83*, 49–79.

Gentner, D., & Boroditsky, L. (2001). Individuation, relativity, and early word learning. In M. Bowerman & S.L. Levinson (Eds.), *Language acquisition and conceptual development* (pp. 215–256). Cambridge: Cambridge University Press.

Gentner, D., & Goldin-Meadow, S. (2003). (Eds.), *Language in mind: Advances in the study of language and thought.* Cambridge, MA: MIT Press.

Gil-White, F.J. (2001). Are ethnic groups biological "species" to the human brain? Essentialism in our cognition of some social categories. *Current Anthropology, 42*, 515–554.

Gopnik, A. (2001). Theories, language, and culture: Whorf without wincing. In M. Bowerman & S.L. Levinson (Eds.), *Language acquisition and conceptual development* (pp. 45–69). Cambridge: Cambridge University Press.

Gopnik, A., & Choi, S. (1995). Names, relational words, and cognitive development in English and Korean speakers: nouns are not always learned before verbs. In M. Tomasello & W.E.

Merriman (Eds.), *Beyond names for things: Young children's acquisition of verbs* (pp. 63–80). Hillsdale, NJ: Lawrence Erlbaum Associates, Inc.

Gopnik, A., & Meltzoff, A. (1992). Categorization and naming: Basic-level sorting in eighteen-month-olds and its relation to language. *Child Development, 63*, 1091–1103.

Hamilton, D.L., Gibbons, P.A., Stroessner, S.J., & Sherman, J.W. (1992). Stereotypes and language use. In G.R. Semin & K. Fiedler (Eds.), *Language, interaction, and social cognition* (pp. 102–128). London: Sage.

Hammer, R., & Diesendruck, G. (2002). *The effect of property distinctiveness in children and adults' artifact categorization.* Manuscript in preparation.

Heyman, G.D., & Diesendruck, G. (2002). The Spanish ser/estar distinction in bilingual children's reasoning about human psychological characteristics. *Developmental Psychology, 38*, 407–417.

Heyman, G.D., & Gelman, S.A. (1998). Young children use motive information to make trait inferences. *Developmental Psychology, 34*, 310–321.

Heyman, G.D., & Gelman, S.A. (1999). The use of trait labels in making psychological inferences. *Child Development, 70*, 604–619.

Heyman, G.D., & Gelman, S.A. (2000). Preschool children's use of trait labels to make inductive inferences about people. *Journal of Experimental Child Psychology, 77*, 1–19.

Hirschfeld, L.A. (1996). *Race in the making.* Cambridge, MA: MIT Press.

Hirschfeld, L.A., & Gelman, S.A. (1994). (Eds.), *Mapping the mind: Domain specificity in cognition and culture.* Cambridge: Cambridge University Press.

Hollich, G., Hirsh-Pasek, K., & Golinkoff, R.M. (2000). Breaking the language barrier: An Emergentist Coalition Model of word learning. *Monographs of the Society for Research in Child Development, Serial No. 262, Vol. 65*, No. 3.

Hunn, E.S. (1982). The utilitarian factor in folk biological classification. *American Anthropologist, 84*, 830–847.

Imai, M., & Gentner, D. (1997). A cross-linguistic study of early word learning: University ontology and linguistic influence. *Cognition, 62*, 169–200.

Jussim, L., Nelson, T.E., Manis, M., & Soffin, S. (1995). Prejudice, stereotypes, and labeling effects: Sources of bias in person perception. *Journal of Personality and Social Psychology, 68*, 228–246.

Kalish, C.W. (1995). Essentialism and graded membership in animal and artifact categories. *Memory and Cognition, 23*, 335–353.

Kalish, C.W. (1998). Natural and artifactual kinds: Are children realists or relativists about categories? *Developmental Psychology, 34*, 376–391.

Kalish, C.W. (2002). Essentialist to some degree: Beliefs about the structure of natural kind categories. *Memory and Cognition, 30*, 340–352.

Keil, F.C. (1989). *Concepts, kinds, and cognitive development.* Cambridge, MA: MIT Press.

Keil, F.C. (1995). The growth of causal understanding of natural kinds. In D. Sperber, D. Premack, & A. Premack (Eds.), *Causal cognition: A multi-disciplinary debate* (pp. 234–262). Oxford: Oxford University Press.

Keil, F.C. (1998). Words, moms, and things: Language as a road map to reality. *Monographs of the Society for Research in Child Development, 63*, No. 253, 149–157.

Kelemen, D. (1999). Beliefs about purpose: On the origins of teleological thought. In M. Corballis & S. Lea (Eds.), *The descent of mind* (pp. 278–294). Oxford: Oxford University Press.

Kemler Nelson, D.G., Russell, R., Duke, N., & Jones, K. (2000). Two year olds will name artifacts by their function. *Child Development, 71*, 1271–1288.

Leach, E. (1976). Anthropological aspects of language: Animal categories and verbal abuse. In E.H. Lenneberg (Ed.), *New directions in the study of language* (pp. 23–63). Cambridge, MA: MIT Press.

Leinbach, M.D., & Fagot, B.I. (1993). Categorical habituation to male and female faces: Gender schematic processing in infancy. *Infant Behavior and Development, 16*, 317–332.

Leslie, A.M. (1994). ToMM, ToBY, and Agency: Core architecture and domain specificity. In L.A. Hirschfeld & S.A. Gelman (Eds.), *Mapping the mind: Domain specificity in cognition and culture* (pp. 119–148). Cambridge: Cambridge University Press.

Levy, G.D., & Haaf, R.A. (1994). Detection of gender-related categories by 10-month-old infants. *Infant Behavior and Development, 17*, 457–459.

Li, P., & Gleitman, L. (2002). Turning the tables: Language and spatial reasoning. *Cognition, 83*, 265–294.

Liben, L.S., & Signorella, M.L. (Eds.) (1987), *Children's gender schemata. (New Directions for Child Development, No. 38.)* San Francisco, CA: Jossey-Bass.

Locke J. (1961). *An essay concerning human understanding* (5th Edn, Vol. II). New York: E.P. Dutton (original work published 1707).

López, A., Atran, S., Coley, J.D., Medin, D.L., & Smith, E.E. (1997). The tree of life: Universals of folk-biological taxonomies and inductions. *Cognitive Psychology, 32*, 251–295.

Lucy, J.A., & Gaskins, S. (2001). Grammatical categories and the development of classification preferences: A comparative approach. In M. Bowerman & S.L. Levinson (Eds.), *Language acquisition and conceptual development* (pp. 257–283). Cambridge: Cambridge University Press.

Maass, A., & Arcuri, L. (1992). The role of language in the persistence of stereotypes. In G.R. Semin & K. Fiedler (Eds.), *Language, interaction, and social cognition* (pp. 129–143). London: Sage.

Malt, B.C. (1995). Category coherence in cross-cultural perspective. *Cognitive Psychology, 29*, 85–148.

Malt, B.C., & Johnson, E.C. (1992). Do artifact concepts have cores? *Journal of Memory and Language, 31*, 195–217.

Malt, B.C., Sloman, S.A., Gennari, S.P., Shi, M., & Wang, Y. (1999). Knowing versus naming: Similarity and linguistic categorization of artifacts. *Journal of Memory and Language, 40*, 230–262.

Mandler, J.M. (2000). Perceptual and conceptual processes in infancy. *Journal of Cognition and Development, 1*, 3–36.

Mandler, J.M., & McDonough, L. (1993). Concept formation in infancy. *Cognitive Development, 8*, 291–318.

Mandler, J.M., & McDonough, L. (1998). Studies in inductive inference in infancy. *Cognitive Psychology, 37*, 60–96.

Markman, E.M. (1989). *Categorization and naming in children.* Cambridge, MA: MIT Press.

Markman, E.M., & Jaswal, V. (2003). Abilities and assumptions underlying conceptual development. In D.H. Rakison & L.M. Oakes (Eds.), *Early category and concept development* (pp. 384–402). New York: Oxford University Press.

Martin, C.L., Ruble, D.N., & Szkrybalo, J. (2002). Cognitive theories of early gender development. *Psychological Bulletin, 128*, 903–933.

Medin, D.L., & Ortony, A. (1989). Psychological essentialism. In S. Vosniadou & A. Ortony (Eds.), *Similarity and analogical processing* (pp. 179–195). New York: Cambridge University Press.

Medin, D.L., Lynch, E.B., Coley, J.D., & Atran, S. (1997). Categorization and reasoning among tree experts: Do all roads lead to Rome? *Cognitive Psychology, 32*, 49–96.

Medin, D.L., Ross, N., Atran, S., Burnett, R.C., & Blok, S.V. (2002). Categorization and reasoning in relation to culture and expertise. *Psychology of Learning and Motivation, 41*, 1–41.

Morris, B. (1984). The pragmatics of folk classification. *Journal of Ethnobiology, 4*, 45–60.

Nazzi, T., & Gopnik, A. (2001). Linguistic and cognitive abilities in infancy: When does language become a tool for categorization? *Cognition, 80*, B11–B20.

Pauen, S. (2002). Evidence of knowledge-based category discrimination in infancy. *Child Development, 73*, 1016–1033.

Pinker, S. (1994). *The language instinct.* New York: HarperPerennial.

Pinker, S. (1999). *How the mind works.* New York: Norton.

Poulin-Dubois, D., Graham, S.A., & Sippola, L. (1995). Early lexical development: The contribution of parental labeling and infants' categorization abilities. *Journal of Child Language, 22*, 325–343.

Poulin-Dubois, D., Serbin, L.A., Kenyon, B., & Derbyshire, A. (1994). Infants' intermodal knowledge about gender. *Developmental Psychology, 30*, 436–442.

Quinn, P.C., & Eimas, P.D. (1996). Perceptual cues that permit categorical differentiation of animal species by infants. *Journal of Experimental Child Psychology, 63*, 189–211.

Quinn, P.C., & Eimas, P.D. (1997). A reexamination of the perceptual-to-conceptual shift in mental representations. *Review of General Psychology, 1*, 271–287.

Quinn, P.C., & Eimas, P.D. (2000). The emergence of category representations during infancy: Are separate perceptual and conceptual processes required? *Journal of Cognition and Development, 1*, 55–61.

Rakison, D., & Poulin-Dubois, D. (2001). Developmental origin of the animate–inanimate distinction. *Psychological Bulletin, 127*, 209–228.

Randall, R.A., & Hunn, E.S. (1984). Do life-forms evolve or do uses for life? Some doubts about Brown's universal hypothesis. *American Ethnologist, 11*, 329–349.

Rips, L.J. (1989). Similarity, typicality, and categorization. In S. Vosniadou & A. Ortony (Eds.), *Similarity and analogical reasoning* (pp. 23–59), New York: Cambridge University Press.

Rips, L.J. (2001). Necessity and natural categories. *Psychological Bulletin, 127*, 827–852.

Rosch, E., Mervis, C.B., Gray, W.D., Johnson, D.M., & Boyes-Braem, P. (1976). Basic objects in natural categories. *Cognitive Psychology, 8*, 382–439.

Rothbart, M., & Taylor, M. (1992). Category labels and social reality: Do we view social categories as natural kinds? In G.R. Semin & K. Fiedler (Eds.), *Language, interaction, and social cognition* (pp. 11–36). London: Sage.

Schwartz. S.P. (1978). Putnam on artifacts. *Philosophical Review, 97*, 566–574.

Semin, G.R., & Fiedler, K. (1988). The cognitive functions of linguistic categories in describing persons: Social cognition and language. *Journal of Personality and Social Psychology, 54*, 558–568.

Sloutsky, V.M., Lo, Y., & Fisher, A.V. (2001). How much does a shared name make things similar? Linguistic labels, similarity, and the development of inductive inferences. *Child Development, 72*, 695–1709.

Smith, E.E., Patalano, A.L., & Jonides, J. (1998). Alternative strategies of categorization. *Cognition, 65*, 167–196.

Smith, L.B. (1999). Children's noun learning: How general learning processes make specialized learning mechanisms. In B. MacWhinney (Ed.), *The emergence of language* (pp. 277–303). Mahwah, NJ: Lawrence Erlbaum Associates, Inc.

Smith, L.B., Jones, S.S., & Landau, B. (1996). Naming in young children: A dumb attentional mechanism? *Cognition, 60*, 143–171.

Sperber, D. (1996). *Explaining culture: A naturalistic approach.* Cambridge, MA: Blackwell.

Strevens, M. (2000). The essentialist aspect of naive theories. *Cognition, 74*, 149–175.

Strevens, M. (2001). Only causation matters: Reply to Ahn et al. *Cognition, 82*, 71–76.

Stross, B. (1973). Acquisition of botanical terminology by Tzeltal children. In M.S. Edmonson (Ed.), *Meaning in Mayan languages* (pp. 107–141). Paris: Mouton.

Tanaka, J.W., & Taylor, M.E. (1991). Categorization and expertise: Is the basic level in the eye of the beholder? *Cognitive Psychology*, *23*, 457–482.

Taylor, M. (1996). The development of children's beliefs about social and biological aspects of gender differences. *Child Development*, *67*, 1555–1571.

Turner, N.J. (1987). General plant categories in Thompson and Lillooet, two interior Salish languages of British Columbia. *Journal of Ethnobiology*, *7*, 55–82.

Van de Walle, G.A., Carey, S., & Prevor, M. (2000). Bases for object individuation in infancy: Evidence from manual search. *Journal of Cognition and Development*, *1*, 249–280.

Walker, S.J. (1999). Culture, domain specificity and conceptual change: Natural kind and artifact concepts. *British Journal of Developmental Psychology*, *17*, 203–219.

Waxman, S.R. (1999). The dubbing ceremony revisited: Object naming and categorization in infancy and early childhood. In D.L. Medin & S. Atran (Eds.), *Folkbiology* (pp. 233–284). Cambridge, MA: MIT Press.

Waxman, S.R. & Markow D.B. (1995). Words as invitations to form categories: Evidence from 12- to 13-month-old infants. *Cognitive Psychology*, *29*, 257–302.

Welder, A.N., & Graham, S.A. (2001). The influence of shape similarity and shared labels on infants' inductive inferences about nonobvious object properties. *Child Development*, *72*, 1653–1673.

Whorf, B.L. (1956). *Language, thought, and reality* (Ed. J.B. Carroll). Cambridge, MA: MIT Press.

Wierzbicka, A. (1984). Apples are not a "kind of fruit": The semantics of human categorization. *American Ethnologist*, *11*, 313–328.

Wilcox, T., & Baillargeon, R. (1998). Object individuation in infancy: The use of featural information in reasoning about occlusion events. *Cognitive Psychology*, *37*, 97–155.

Xu, F. (2002). The role of language in acquiring object kind concepts in infancy. *Cognition*, *85*, 223–250.

Xu, F., & Carey, S. (1996). Infants' metaphysics: The case of numerical identity. *Cognitive Psychology*, *30*, 111–153.

Xu, F., Carey, S., & Welch, J. (1999). Infants' ability to use object kind information for object individuation. *Cognition*, *70*, 137–166.

Younger, B.A., & Fearing, D.D. (1999). Parsing items into separate categories: Developmental change in infant categorization. *Child Development*, *70*, 291–303.

Yuill, N. (1992). Children's conception of personality traits. *Human Development*, *35*, 265–279.

# Language and Cognitive Processes
## Subject Index

# Language and Cognitive Processes
## Author Index